KIN

PEARL

Melita Thomas is a co-founder and editor of *Tudor Times*, a website devoted to Tudor and Stewart history. Her articles have appeared in *BBC History Extra* and *Britain* magazine.

THE
KING'S
PEARL

HENRY VIII AND HIS DAUGHTER MARY

MELITA THOMAS

AMBERLEY

For my mother and father.

This edition published 2019

Amberley Publishing
The Hill, Stroud
Gloucestershire, GL5 4EP

www.amberley-books.com

British Library Cataloguing in Publication Data.
A catalogue record for this book is available from the British Library.

ISBN 978 1 4456 9080 3 (paperback)
ISBN 978 1 4456 6126 1 (ebook)

Typeset in 10pt on 13.5pt Sabon.
Typesetting and Origination by Amberley Publishing.
Printed in the UK.

Contents

Background Information

The European World

The backdrop to Mary's life was a complex tangle of alliances and enmities across Europe, but details of alliances and military manoeuvres can make dry reading, so there is a brief outline of the political situation in **Appendix A**.

Calendar

In sixteenth century England, New Year was celebrated on 1 January with the exchange of gifts. The calendar year began on Lady Day (25 March), thus, 24 March 1516 was followed by 25 March 1517. Dates are given using the New Style for years – i.e. beginning on 1 January, while the day dates used are contemporary.

Currency

Money throughout Europe was based on the system devised by Charlemagne in the eighth century. A pound weight of silver was divided into 240 pieces, known as pennies, symbolised with d – 12d made a shilling, symbolised with s; 20s made one pound, or £1. Crowns were commonly quoted – a crown was generally around 5s, making four to the £.

Exchange rates fluctuated depending on the silver content of coins and were announced by proclamation. Other European monetary units were the gold florin from Venice or Florence, worth between 3s and 4s and ducats, more or less equivalent to the crown.

Marriage

Marriages, at all levels of society where there was money or property, were business transactions. Financial arrangements were negotiated prior to the betrothal and recorded in marriage articles. Three types of payment were associated with marriage.

First was the dowry or dote. This was paid by the bride's family and was usually in cash, plate or jewels. It was generally heritable by the woman's children, and often secured by the marriage articles to her younger offspring.

Second was the jointure. This was the land settled on the married couple, jointly, and generally retained by the surviving spouse. For queens, the jointure was a personal estate, which provided an independent income during marriage. It was intended to reflect a return on the dowry, ranging between a five per cent and a twenty per cent return, depending on the bargaining strength of the bride's and groom's parents.

Third was the dower. Although sometimes used interchangeably with jointure, there was a difference. Under common law in England, even if there were no jointure, a widow was entitled to one-third of the income of the deceased husband's estate.

Marriageable age was twelve for girls and fourteen for boys. A betrothal could be made in two ways. Firstly, by *verbi di futuro*, a promise to marry in future, which might be made on behalf of children; it could be set aside by the child on reaching marriageable age. Secondly, by *verbi di praesenti*, which was an agreement to marry immediately, and, if followed by consummation, was a binding marriage. Before consummation, it could be set aside by an ecclesiastical dispensation. Marriage required consent from both parties.

Protestant and Catholic

The term Protestant was not used during the period of this book, coming into use in the late 1540s. The demarcation between conservatives in religion, and evangelicals or reformers, was not clear cut. Many who were evangelicals in the 1520s and 1530s went on to more radical views, but some never left the Catholic Church.

Timeline

Date	Events directly affecting Mary and England	European events
1485	Henry, Earl of Richmond defeats Richard III at Battle of Bosworth and is crowned King of England. Birth of Katharine of Aragon to the Catholic monarchs, Ferdinand and Isabella.	
1489	Treaty of Medina del Campo between England and Spain.	
1491	Birth of Henry to Henry VII and Elizabeth of York.	Charles VIII of France marries Anne, Duchess of Brittany.
1492		Granada falls to Christian Spain. Columbus arrives in the Americas.
1493		Maximilian of Hapsburg becomes King of the Romans. Treaty of Étaples between England and France. Peace of Barcelona – Ferdinand cedes Roussillon and Cerdagne to France.
1494		Charles VIII of France invades the Italian peninsula to claim Naples.

Date	Events directly affecting Mary and England	European events
1495		Holy League against France created – Pope, Emperor, Spain, Venice and Milan. Charles VIII driven out of Italian peninsula.
1497		Double marriage of siblings: Juan and Juana, infantes of Spain marry the Archduchess Marguerite of Austria and Philip, Duke of Burgundy, children of the Emperor Maximilian. Juan dies within months, and Marguerite returns to Flanders.
1498		Charles VIII dies. His widow, Anne of Brittany, marries his successor, Louis XII. Birth of Eleonora of Austria to Juana and Philip.
		Birth of Charles to Juana and Philip.
1501	Marriage of Katharine of Aragon and Arthur, Prince of Wales.	Marriage of Marguerite of Austria to Philibert II of Savoy.
1502	Death of Arthur, Prince of Wales.	
1503	Death of Elizabeth of York. Pope Julius II grants a disputation for Katharine of Aragon to marry her brother-in-law, Henry, now Prince of Wales. Margaret, daughter of Henry VII, marries James IV, King of Scots.	Birth of Ferdinand of Austria to Juana and Philip.
1504	Death of Isabella of Castile.	Ferdinand wins Battle of Garigliano and France cedes Naples to Aragon. Death of Philibert II of Savoy.
1505	Henry repudiates his betrothal to Katharine on attaining marriageable age.	

Date	Events directly affecting Mary and England	European events
1506		Death of Philip of Burgundy. Ferdinand acts as regent for his daughter, Juana in Castile. In the Netherlands, Archduchess Marguerite rules as regent for the infant duke, Charles.
1507	Treaty between Henry VII and Maximilian for Henry's daughter, Mary, to marry Charles.	France annexes Genoa
1508		League of Cambrai formed between Maximilian, now Holy Roman Emperor and Louis XII of France.
1509	Death of Henry VII. Henry becomes King of England and marries Katharine of Aragon.	
1511	Birth and death of Henry, Duke of Cornwall.	
1512		Birth of James V of Scotland. Ferdinand of Aragon takes control of Upper Navarre. Lower Navarre retained by King Henri II of Navarre.
1513	Henry invades France, in alliance with Maximilian. He captures Tournai and Thérouanne. James IV invades England in support of his French ally. Katharine, as regent, raises an army headed by Thomas Howard, 2nd Duke of Norfolk. The Scots army is heavily defeated and James killed. Charles fails to honour his commitment to marry Henry VIII's sister Mary, who marries Louis XII of France instead.	Death of Anne, Duchess of Brittany, to be succeeded, nominally, by her daughter, Claude of France. Pope Julius II dies, succeeded by Leo X.

Date	Events directly affecting Mary and England	European events
1514	Thomas Wolsey becomes Lord Chancellor, Cardinal and Archbishop of York.	Marriage of Claude of France, daughter of Louis XII to her father's heir, François of Angoulême. Death of Louis XII and succession of François.
1515		Battle of Marignano. François takes control of Milan.
1516	Birth of Mary.	Death of Ferdinand of Aragon, succeeded by Charles, now King of Castile and Aragon (in conjunction with his mother, Juana), as well as Duke of Burgundy. Treaty of Noyon – François cedes Naples to Charles, in exchange for annual payment and Charles's agreement to marry one of François' daughters. Treaty of Rouen between France and Scotland. James V of Scotland to marry a French princess.
1517		Treaty of Cambrai between Maximilian, Charles and François. Martin Luther publishes his ninety-five theses, inviting discussion on indulgences and other Church practices he thought corrupt.
1518	Treaty of London – Mary to marry the Dauphin François. Katharine gives birth to her last child – a daughter who dies at birth.	Death of Maria of Aragon, Queen of Portugal. Her widower, Manuel, marries Eleonora of Austria, Charles's sister.
1519	Birth of Henry Fitzroy, son of Henry VIII and Elizabeth Blount.	Death of Maximilian. Charles elected as Emperor Charles V.

Date	Events directly affecting Mary and England	European events
1520	Charles visits Henry and Katharine. Henry and Katharine meet François, Claude and Louise of Savoy at the Field of Cloth of Gold. Follow up meeting between Henry, Katharine, Wolsey for England; Charles, Archduchess Marguerite and de Chièvres for Burgundy/ Spain/Empire.	
1521	Execution of Edward Stafford, 3rd Duke of Buckingham. Treaty of Bruges between Henry and Charles.	Diet of Worms entrenches Luther's opposition to the Church. Charles and François at loggerheads over Navarre. Henri II of Navarre invades Upper Navarre, with French support. Manuel of Portugal dies, to be succeeded by João III who marries Catherine of Austria, Charles's sister. Death of Pope Leo X. Ferdinand of Austria marries Anne of Hungary.
1522	Treaty of Windsor. Charles to marry Mary and he and Henry to invade France.	Pope Adrian VI elected. Duke of Bourbon defects from François to Charles. Marriage of Mary of Austria, Charles's sister, to Louis of Hungary.
1523	After an initially successful campaign in Picardy, Duke of Suffolk forced to retreat. England and France come to terms.	Four-pronged attack on France. Adrian VI dies. Election of Pope Clement VII.

Date	Events directly affecting Mary and England	European events
1524	Mary to marry the widowed François. Negotiations with Scotland for a marriage between Mary and James V.	Death of Claude of France. German Peasants' War breaks out.
1525	Mary appointed to head the Council of the Marches. Although not formally created Princess of Wales, becomes known by that title. Departs for the Marches with a vice-regal household. Henry creates Henry Fitzroy Duke of Richmond and Somerset. Attempts to enforce the Treaty of Windsor fail. Charles does not marry Mary, but enters negotiations to marry Isabella of Portugal. Treaty of The More between England and France, with Mary to marry François or his second son, Henri, Duke of Orléans. Henry begins a relationship with Anne Boleyn.	Battle of Pavia. Charles's viceroy, Lannoy, holds Milan against French attack and takes François prisoner. German Peasants' War ends – commons brutally suppressed.
1526	Negotiations continue for an Anglo-French alliance.	Charles marries Isabella of Portugal. François' sister, Marguerite of Angoulême, marries Henri II of Navarre. Treaty of Madrid between Charles and François. François exchanged for his two sons to be held hostage. The French king is to marry the widowed Eleonora, and the dauphin is to marry her daughter, Maria of Portugal.

Date	Events directly affecting Mary and England	European events
		Battle of Mohács – Louis of Hungary killed, Ottoman Turks advance. Ferdinand of Austria elected as king of part of Hungary.
		League of Cognac formed to try to counter Charles's strength in Italy.
1527	Anglo-French treaties of Westminster and Amiens agreed. Mary to marry François (who denies his betrothal to Eleonora).	Turmoil in Italy as Imperial troops advance. Bourbon's army is refused entry to Rome, breaks through the walls and sacks the city, capturing Pope Clement.
	A secret court is convened in London to investigate the validity of the marriage between Henry and Katharine.	Birth of Philip to Charles and Isabella.
	Clement agrees to an official hearing, sending Cardinal Campeggio to sit with Wolsey.	
1528	Mary's vice-regal household broken up and she returns to permanent residence 'near the king's person.'	
1529	Wolsey disgraced and replaced as Lord Chancellor by Thomas More.	Treaty of Cambrai between Charles and François (the Ladies' peace) negotiated by Marguerite of Austria, Louise of Savoy and Marguerite of Angoulême.
1530	Death of Wolsey.	François marries Eleonora.
1531	Mary sees Katharine for the last time.	
1532	Henry and Anne Boleyn visit France and consummate their relationship.	
1533	Act in Restraint of Appeals forbids appeal to Rome in legal cases.	Henri, Duke of Orléans marries Catherine de' Medici, the Pope's niece.
	Henry and Katharine's marriage annulled in England.	Treaty of Constantinople ends war between Ferdinand and Ottoman Turks in Hungary.
	Elizabeth born.	
	Mary deprived of her title and household.	

Date	Events directly affecting Mary and England	European events
1534	Acts of Succession and Supremacy passed. The first requires all subjects to swear to accept Anne as queen and Elizabeth as heir. The second removes papal authority in England and declares Henry Supreme Head of the Church in England.	Death of Clement and election of Paul III.
1535	Thomas More and Fisher, Bishop of Rochester, executed for refusing to swear the oath of succession.	Charles defeats an Ottoman fleet to capture Tunis. François enters a formal alliance with the Ottomans under Suleiman the Magnificent.
1536	Death of Katharine. Anne miscarries a son. Act suppressing the smaller monasteries in England passed. Anne executed for treason. Mary accepts Henry as Supreme Head of the Church, that her parents' marriage was invalid, and that she is illegitimate. Henry marries Jane Seymour. Reformist Act of Ten Articles passed. Pilgrimage of Grace.	James V marries Madeleine of France. She dies within months. Death of Dauphin François. Death of Francesco II Sforza of Milan reopenes Franco-Imperial hostilities. François invades Savoy.
1537	Birth of Edward and death of Jane Seymour.	Marriage of James V and Marie of Guise.
1538		Treaty of Nice between Charles and François. Battle of Preveza – Ottoman fleet defeats that of the Holy League (Spain, Empire, Venice, Genoa, Papacy).

Date	Events directly affecting Mary and England	European events
1539	Conservative Act of Six Articles passed. Treaty with Cleves for marriage of Henry with Anne of Cleves. Negotiations for Mary to marry Philip of Bavaria. Exeter conspiracy – executions of several of Mary's friends and relatives.	Treaty of Toledo between Charles and François. Death of Empress Isabella.
1540	Henry marries Anne of Cleves – union dissolved within six months. Henry marries Katheryn Howard.	
1541	Execution of Margaret, Countess of Salisbury, Mary's former governess. English court, including Mary, visits York. Katheryn Howard accused of adultery.	
1542	Execution of Katheryn Howard.	Death of James V, leaves week-old-daughter, Mary, as Queen of Scots.
1543	Henry marries Katherine Parr. Treaty of Greenwich agrees marriage between Edward and Mary, Queen of Scots.	Duke Wilhelm of Julich-Cleves-Berg cedes Guelders to Charles in Treaty of Venlo.
1544	Henry and Charles make war on François. England captures Boulogne.	Battle of Ceresole – French victory, but insufficient to retake Milan. Charles and François make a separate peace with Treaty of Crépy. Charles relinquishes the disputed Burgundian lands, and François gives up claim to Naples.

Date	Events directly affecting Mary and England	European events
1545	Mary contributes to translation of Erasmus' Paraphrases on the New Testament.	
1546	Chapuys recalled from English court.	Schmalkaldic War begins between Imperial forces and Lutheran forces of the Schmalkaldic League
1547	Death of Henry VIII.	

Family Tree 1: Mary's English descent from Edward III (simplified)

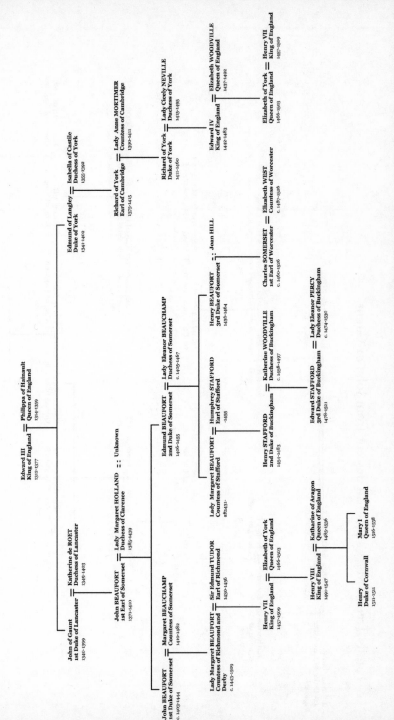

Family Tree 2: Mary's Spanish descent from John of Gaunt.

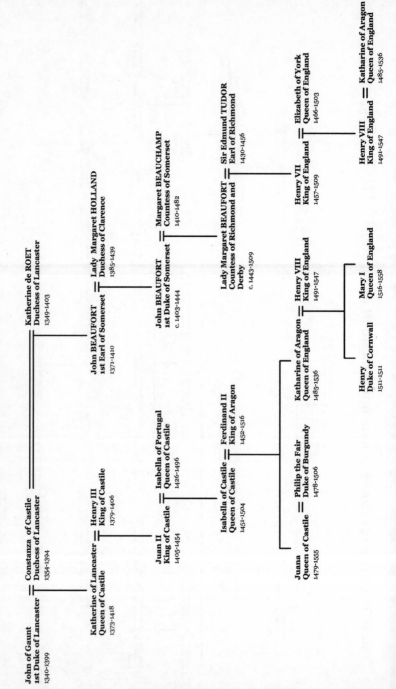

Family Tree 3: Mary's maternal descent (simplified)

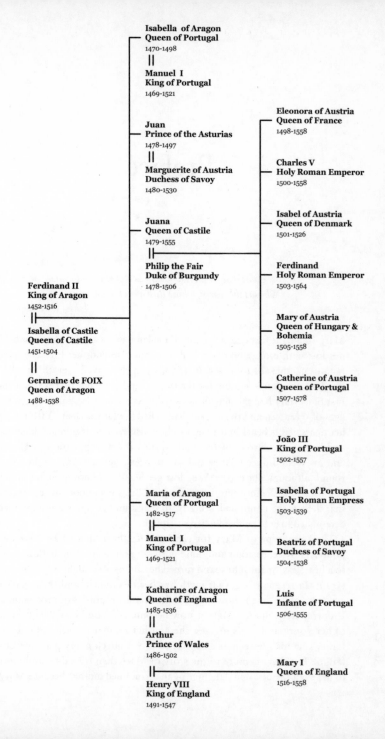

Preface

Whose game was empires, and whose stakes were thrones;
Whose table earth, whose dice were human bones.

Lord Byron

Mary Tudor, the first queen regnant of England, was a gambler. She gambled, not just with money on cards and dice, but also with her life. The most famous gamble she took was in 1553, when she staked everything – life, freedom, religion – in a bid for the throne, and won. But that was not the first time Mary had taken enormous risks. As a young woman between the ages of seventeen and twenty, she had defied her father, Henry VIII: pitting her unassailable belief in her right to be considered his legitimate daughter, and heir to the throne of England, against the determination of Henry, and his second queen, Anne Boleyn, to break her spirit. Mary lost that round (although not before Anne lost her head), submitting to her father, and accepting demotion to bastard status. But she did not entirely accept that defeat; she continued, secretly, to maintain her rights and remained determined to enforce them when she could.

The stereotype of Mary for centuries has been that of an unskilled political novice, hesitant and timid until religious mania and her devotion to a heartless, Spanish husband turned her almost overnight into a bloody tyrant. In recent years, that myth has been examined and the negative accounts of her reign shown to be influenced by centuries of propaganda. Unfortunately, Bloody Mary is now becoming Tragic Mary. The trauma of her youth and the suffering she and her mother experienced at her father's hands are seen as a reason to pity a queen many perceive as a failure. But there is more to the story of Mary than tragedy – and more to her than the devoted daughter of an abandoned mother because Mary, although she is usually associated with her mother Katharine of Aragon, was very much her father's daughter. He too, was a risk-taker. Shaking off the authority of the Church of Rome, although it seems with hindsight to have been an inevitable event, was a huge gamble. The last English king to defy its authority, King John, had nearly lost his crown, and had only been saved by a swift capitulation to the pope. In the 1530s, Henry might have met the same fate.

The relationship between Henry and Mary has never been examined in detail, yet it was complex and multi-layered. Mary was the only person Henry forgave after publicly standing against him. He dispatched the wife, mentors and companions of his youth to exile and death; he executed two wives, one of whom he had loved passionately, and the other a young woman of no more than twenty-one; he sought vicious reprisals against the Pilgrims of Grace, even after they had been granted pardons, but Mary, once sufficiently obedient, was restored to favour and affection.

Henry and Mary's relationship had two strands that sometimes interwove harmoniously, but were often in conflict. First was the bond of father and daughter: Mary's childhood was a sunny period of love and affection between a proud father and an adoring child. This changed into the fraught struggle between stern parent and disobedient daughter that overshadowed her adolescence. Later, Mary was the only one of Henry's children with whom he had an adult relationship. She was thirty-one when he died, while her half-siblings, Elizabeth and Edward, were thirteen and nine respectively, and her other half-brother, Henry Fitzroy, had died at seventeen. As individuals, Mary and Henry had tastes and interests in common – music, gambling, gardening and luxurious clothing being the most obvious, while not forgetting that Henry remained a Catholic, making their day-to-day religious experience, so central to sixteenth century life, the same.

The second relationship between the two was political. In a society that was hierarchical and saw royal blood as almost sacred, Mary had a value that was imparted, not just by her status as Henry's daughter, but also by her kinship with the most powerful monarch in Europe, the Emperor Charles V. Mary's political value fluctuated, at home and abroad, as the three great religious and political upheavals convulsing Europe – the Reformation, the fight for dominance between France and Spain, and the advance of the Ottoman Turks – waxed and waned. From the invasion of Italy in 1494 by Charles VIII of France, to the last campaigns of the Italian Wars in the closing years of Mary's own reign, Spain and France were engaged in war on several fronts, punctuated with short truces. Simultaneously, the Continent faced the threat of the expanding Ottoman Empire. All four of Mary's grandparents were born within thirteen years of the Fall of Constantinople, and while that had brought great intellectual gains to Europe from the scholars of the old

Byzantine Empire, it meant Eastern Europe was in the military front line; major tracts of Poland and Hungary were lost to Christendom in Mary's lifetime. The triumphs or losses of Charles V and his brother, Ferdinand, King of the Romans, or their great enemies, François I of France and Suleiman the Magnificent, materially affected Mary's political standing. To understand the dynamic between Mary and her father, we must be aware of these background forces.

This book explores Mary's life up until the death of her father and how the personal and the political were woven into the tapestry of their relationship.

A Bride for the Dauphin

Part 1
'My Lady Princess'

I

A Bride for the Dauphin

Are you the dauphin of France? If you are, I want to kiss you.

Mary

On Tuesday 19 February 1516, workmen were busy in the grounds of Greenwich Palace, preparing for a baptism. The baby, born the previous day, was the daughter of King Henry VIII of England and his wife of seven years, Katharine of Aragon. The workmen's task was to lay a walkway of gravel and rushes between the palace and the adjacent church of the Observant Franciscan Friars. Arras was hung from rails alongside the walkway to protect the baby and the distinguished guests from draughts. The christening, like most of the celebrations during the first half of Henry's reign, was a family affair as well as a state occasion. Nearly all the participants were either members of the extended royal family, or had served the Tudor dynasty for years. The ladies and gentlemen of the court who were not taking an active part in the ceremony led the procession. They were followed by the king's cousin, Henry Courtenay, Earl of Devon, bearing the basin, assisted by Lord Herbert. Thomas Howard, Earl of Surrey, the king's uncle-by-marriage, held the taper, and another cousin, the Marquis of Dorset, the salt. Lady Dorset carried the chrism. Next came the Lord Steward, George Talbot, Earl of Shrewsbury, and the Lord Chamberlain, Charles Somerset, Earl of Worcester. Shrewsbury had fought for the king's father, Henry VII, at the battles of Bosworth and Stoke, and Somerset was an illegitimate member of the king's Beaufort family. Finally, Elizabeth Howard, Countess of Surrey, appeared, carrying the baby. They were shielded by a canopy borne by Sir Nicholas Vaux, Sir Thomas Boleyn and Sir Thomas Parr and the king's great-uncle, Sir Davy ab Owain.

The first element of the baptism, the singing of Psalm XVI, took place in the porch erected at the church door. The baby was then greeted by her godparents, and named Mary. Her two godmothers were her great-aunt Katherine of York, Countess of Devon, and Agnes Howard, Duchess of Norfolk. King François I of France had been invited to be godfather, but, offended at not having received a letter in Henry's own hand, had rudely refused to send a proxy.[1] In François' stead was Thomas Wolsey, Cardinal-Archbishop of York, Lord Chancellor and Henry's most trusted minister. The three godparents renounced the devil in Mary's name, after which followed the Confession of Faith; the Threefold Blessing; the signing of her head with the cross, accompanied by prayer; the administration of salt and the exorcism of the devil. This done, the procession entered the church.

Inside, the walls were hung with gem-sewn tapestries. The congregation crowded round as the next stage of ritual was carried out – another Confession of Faith, the laying on of hands, a further exorcism and symbolic opening of the ears, a second renunciation of the devil, and anointing with the chrism. In the final part of the ceremony, Mary was held over the silver font and the holy water poured over her head. The same font, from Christ Church, Canterbury, had been used for Henry's own baptism and was transported to and fro by the prior's servants at a cost of £4. On either side of Mary were Thomas Howard, Duke of Norfolk, and Charles Brandon, Duke of Suffolk, the husband of Mary's aunt, Mary, the French queen. Heavily pregnant, the French queen herself was absent, but it is likely that the baby was named with her in mind – both Henry and Katharine being very attached to her. In accordance with custom, confirmation, or 'bishopping', took place immediately. Mary's godmother for this sacrament was Lady Margaret Pole, Countess of Salisbury. Lady Salisbury was a prominent member of the royal family – first cousin to Mary's grandmother, Elizabeth of York, and a close friend of Queen Katharine. The ceremony complete, the participants returned to the palace. Mary was now a member of the Catholic Church, an identity common to every single soul in Europe at the time of her birth – from the lowliest peasant to the Emperor Maximilian himself. It was an identity that was core to the spiritual and political outlook of both her parents, and would be to Mary herself.

It was not customary for the parents of a royal baby to attend the christening. Katharine would have been in bed, not permitted to venture out until her 'churching' – the ritual purification that occurred forty days after childbirth. While she recuperated, the queen sent out notifications of the royal birth. Katharine's period of seclusion was not one of unmitigated happiness. During it, she learnt of the death of her father. Although King Ferdinand of Aragon had died in January, the information had been kept from her, lest the stress bring on a miscarriage. Katharine's track record for childbirth was not good and she was probably nervous about the baby's chance of survival. Mary was not the first of the royal couple's children to be baptised amid elaborate ritual. Five years earlier, a son, Henry, Duke of Cornwall, had been born and presented, with huge fanfare, as the future king, before dying within a few weeks. As well as the little duke, Katharine had suffered at least two miscarriages. With the appearance of Mary, Henry and Katharine hoped their run of bad luck had changed. Mary seemed robust, with only the flaw of her gender to disappoint the king, in an age when there were doubts about women's fitness to rule. This attitude to a female birth was exemplified by the behaviour of the Venetian ambassador, Sebastian Giustinian, who had been rather slack about tendering his congratulations. Had it been a son, he wrote to his master, the Doge, he would have immediately congratulated the king, but there was no hurry for a daughter. When he finally spoke to Henry, he offered the advice that, in this disappointing case, Henry must conform himself to God's will. But Henry was sanguine, responding, 'We are both young; if it was a daughter this time, by the grace of God the sons will follow', before taking his revenge by telling Giustinian that Venice was bound to be betrayed by its French allies.[1]

Henry's courtiers and councillors also hoped that Mary's birth presaged that of sons. While Lord Mountjoy, Governor of Tournai (a French town captured by Henry in 1513) had ordered bonfires and thanksgiving processions to celebrate Mary's birth, he wrote to the king that he was,

> Beseeching our Lord to send you as much rejoicing of my Lady Princess, and make you as glad a father as ever was king, and after this good beginning to send you many fair [sons] to your Grace's comfort and all your true subjects.

Henry was convinced of the need for a male heir. Nothing in English law debarred women from the throne, but the notion of a woman as sovereign had been unpopular since the anarchy of the twelfth century when Matilda, daughter of Henry I, had fought unsuccessfully for her throne, against her cousin Stephen. There was also more recent history to consider. As only the second Tudor king, following the bloody dynastic struggle of the Wars of the Roses, Henry believed only an undisputed male heir could fend off rival claimants, of whom there were many. His nephew, James V, King of Scots, was the closest, but there were other candidates too: the Earl of Devon and the sons of Lady Salisbury – Henry Pole, Lord Montagu; Reginald; Arthur and Geoffrey. More distantly, there was the mighty Duke of Buckingham, descended from two of Edward III's sons.[2]

Henry's own claim to the throne derived from two women: his paternal grandmother, Lady Margaret Beaufort, had been the Lancastrian heir, and his mother, Elizabeth, the senior representative of the house of York. However, there was never any question of them pressing their claims. Lady

Margaret's son took the throne as Henry VII while Elizabeth seemed content for her claim to be embodied in the flesh of her sons, first Henry's older brother, Arthur, then after his death, Henry himself. If a woman did succeed to a European throne, it was widely assumed that her husband would be the effective ruler and Henry did not want England to be incorporated into another man's kingdom by marriage, as Brittany had been subsumed into France.

Katharine may have seen the matter differently. Although she knew it was her duty to have sons (and failure to have children was usually imputed to the woman) Katharine also knew women could be successful sovereigns. Her mother, Queen Isabella of Castile, had been one of the most formidable monarchs in Europe, even expanding her territories through the capture of the last Moorish kingdom in Iberia and the financing of Christopher Columbus' discovery of the New World. Katharine's sister, too, was a sovereign queen, although, in Juana's case, first her father, then her son, were happy to emphasise her fragile mental health as justification for sidelining her.

But, in 1516, with the expectation of more children, Henry was happy enough to have a daughter. Mary would be brought up to promote her father's interests abroad through marriage with a suitable prince. His own sisters had been married to kings of Scotland and France (although not with any appreciable improvement in relations with those countries). Adding to Mary's marriage value was her position not just in the English royal family, but also as part of a wider European network. The children and grandchildren of her maternal aunts, Maria, Queen-Consort of Portugal, and Juana, Queen of Castile, graced nearly every throne in Europe, either as monarchs, consorts or regents. The most important of these relatives were Juana's two sons, Charles, Duke of Burgundy, King of Aragon and Castile (Spain) at the time of Mary's birth, and his brother, Archduke Ferdinand. Charles and Ferdinand's paternal aunt, Marguerite of Austria, who ruled the Netherlands as regent, while only a distant blood relative of Mary's, was Queen Katharine's sister-in-law, having once been married to Katharine's brother, Juan.

The first mention of a possible husband for Mary came in September 1516, although it is unlikely that Henry believed anything would come of it. Her cousin Charles, who was sixteen and unmarried, had entered the Treaty of Noyon with François I of France in hope of gaining an undisputed title to Naples. Under the treaty, Charles was to marry one of François' daughters but the terms horrified Henry and also Charles's paternal grandfather, the Emperor Maximilian. Henry suggested that if Charles were willing to wait for a child to grow up, he should marry Mary. This would be on the understanding that if Henry had no son, Mary would be his heir – both to England and France, which Henry never gave up hope of conquering.

Nothing came of the suggestion in 1516, so far as Mary was concerned, but various treaties were arranged between Henry, Charles and Maximilian.

***

Once she was safely christened, and protected from the wiles of the devil, attention could be turned to Mary's material comfort. Although Mary was her father's heir at birth, Henry had no wish to acknowledge this – she was merely a placeholder until the birth of his son, so, while a son would have had the dignity of his own household, Mary was accommodated within that of her parents. There were, of course, specific duties related to a baby. Mary had four women to rock her cradle: Margery Parker, Anne Bright, Ellen Hutton and Margaret Cousine, who each received an annual salary of 80*s*. Her laundress was Avyse Woode, at a fee of 66*s* 8*d* per annum and there was also a chaplain, Henry Rowle, who doubled up as a clerk. Her wet-nurse was Katherine, wife of Leonard Pole. Mrs Pole was handsomely paid, receiving £20 per annum, while Mary's gentlewoman, Alice Baker, was paid £10. In charge of all was the lady mistress. Two women are named in early accounts as holding the post. In December 1516 Margaret, Lady Bryan, was granted £50 for life as 'Lady Mistress', but the accounts of November 1517 show that Elizabeth Denton, who had been lady mistress to Henry's sisters, held the title, with Lady Bryan to take it on Mrs Denton's demise. Lady Bryan was probably undertaking the job, with Mrs Denton, who was old by Tudor standards, holding the honorary post.[3] Following Lady Bryan in Henry's accounts for 1516, were seven other ladies who may have been appointed to serve Mary. While we cannot be sure these were Mary's attendants, it is likely they were, as among them were Anne Luke who had been Henry's own nurse, and Lady Verney who had been lady mistress to his two sisters, even accompanying his older sister Margaret to Scotland in 1503 to head her household.[4] The seven ladies received annual sums for life ranging from £20 down to £5. Mary may not have had an independent household but Henry was not stinting. At Christmas in 1516, she received the first in a long series of gifts of sumptuous fabrics from her father – 10 yards each of white gold tinsel and white silver tinsel, 12 yards of white satin and 11 yards of white damask for four gowns, three furred with ermine. The cost of maintaining Mary and her attendants in her first year was reckoned to be £1,400. To put that in context, the premier peer, the Duke of Buckingham, had an annual income in the region of £4,000.

Little is heard of Mary in her first two years. While she spent most of her time at Ditton, a moated manor in Buckinghamshire, close to Windsor and reached by the Datchet Ferry, she was also frequently taken to her parents as they moved among the various palaces of the Thames Valley. Between visits, Lady Bryan sent regular messages, updating the fond parents about Mary's health. At New Year 1518, probably spent at Windsor with Henry and Katharine, Mary received an array of presents from her father's courtiers. First on the list was a gold pomander from her aunt, the French queen – not the most interesting present for a toddler but the lucky messenger must have been happy to receive the king's tip of 20s. Continuing the ostentatious present theme was Cardinal Wolsey, who sent a gold cup. Slightly more practical were the Countess of Devon's gold spoon, the Duchess of Norfolk's primer, Lady Mountjoy's two smocks, and Lady Darrell's warden pears. Pears were later one of Mary's favourite dishes, so she probably appreciated being weaned on them. There was also a present of queen apples from a local woman.

Mary uttered her first publicly recorded words on 28 February 1518 when she was just two years old. Henry had received another visit from Venetian ambassador Giustinian. Political discussions completed, Henry sent for Mary to be shown off. Giustinian, the cardinal and the other lords were permitted, after doffing their caps, to kiss her hand – the only part of her they were allowed to touch, for fear of infection. The ambassador observed that more respect was paid to the little girl than to her mother. Henry boasted of her good temper: 'By God, my Lord, this girl never cries,' but immediately, Mary showed another side of her nature. In the room was Fra Dionysius Memo, once an organist at St Mark's, Venice, but now a leading musician at Henry's court, so close to the king and queen that his food allowance came from their personal table. Catching sight of his familiar face, Mary called out, 'Priest', and nothing would satisfy her but that Fra Dionysius should play for her. It is perhaps prophetic that Mary's first recorded words relate to priests and music – two interests that she maintained till her dying day.[5] Shortly after, Henry and Katharine, and perhaps Mary, retired to Woodstock, to avoid an outbreak of infectious disease in the capital. It was during this period that it was whispered Katharine might be pregnant again. When it was confirmed, *Te Deums* of thanksgiving were sung in St Paul's Cathedral. All that was needed was for the child to be a boy, and Henry's cup would have been running over.

As well as spending time with his wife that summer, Henry devoted some hours to working on the first draft of his book – *Assertio Septem Sacramentorum contra M Luther* refuting the criticisms that the Augustinian friar, Martin Luther, had levelled at the Church. Confident that having done God's work in dealing with the pestilent Luther, he would be rewarded with a son, Henry began negotiations for Mary's betrothal to a French prince. The idea had been broached in February, when the Bishop of Paris suggested that if the pregnant Queen Claude bore a son, he should be married to Mary.

Among other benefits of the marriage, thought the bishop, would be the promotion of Christian unity in the face of the Ottoman threat. Nevertheless, so as not to threaten the fragile peace between France, England and the Empire, early negotiations should take place under cover of discussions about Tournai, which François hoped to have returned. On 30 June 1518, Richard Pace, Henry's secretary, wrote to Wolsey that Henry had agreed to the marriage *per verbi di praesenti* even though the children were below marriageable age. A week later, with the news of Katharine's pregnancy now public, Henry informed his other councillors of the negotiations, who confirmed their approval. Articles covering the principles were drawn up and signed at Westminster, and Wolsey was granted a commission to treat with François' representatives over the details.

We catch another glimpse of Mary here. On receiving a letter informing him that one of her servants was sick with a 'hot ague', Henry immediately ordered that she be brought from Ditton to Bisham, where she was to spend a couple of days before moving to The More, to join him and Katharine. She was then to continue to Havering, breaking her journey at Tittenhanger, Hatfield, or Fortescue's Place, depending on the weather, the prevalence of sickness and the distance that was convenient to travel on any particular day.

By late July, the rumours of the betrothal between Mary and the dauphin were spreading. Charles was nervous about the proposed treaty. It was far safer for him for Tournai, on the Franco-Flemish border, to be in the hands of the English, who had no thoughts of encroaching on Flanders, than in those of the French who, he believed, had designs on his territory. So, while agreeing that 'Christian unity' ought to be everyone's primary aim, he asked to send envoys to take part in the negotiations to ensure that nothing was agreed detrimental to his own alliance with England. Wolsey explained the planned alliance between Henry and François was to be based on three principles: Mary's marriage, the return of Tournai and a firm friendship between the two kings. This, said Wolsey, would be the best way to keep François from troubling Charles in Italy.

As well as an alliance with France, Wolsey had a grander vision – a Treaty of Universal Peace encapsulating a mutual defence and non-aggression pact between all the kingdoms of Europe. Although the cardinal was proud, ostentatious and insufferably arrogant, he also seems to have had a genuine belief in peace, compromise and negotiation. He was Henry's most loyal servant and there was real affection between the men, with Wolsey, as the elder, influencing the king – although Henry always knew his own mind and insisted on his own policies, when he felt strongly about anything. If all the rulers of Europe agreed such a pact, then Henry and Wolsey would have the prestige of arbitrating disputes, which, considering the relative size and wealth of England compared with the other kingdoms, would enhance the country's status, at much less cost than military action. Mixed with the laudable desire for peace, was Wolsey's desire to score over Pope Leo X, who was hoping to negotiate a five-year truce across Europe, with a view to a march on Constantinople. In pursuit of this idea, Leo sent a legate, Cardinal Lorenzo Campeggio, to England. Campeggio was received with great splendour, initially at Canterbury, and then by the king and council at Westminster. To agree the Anglo-French treaty, the Sieur de Bonnivet, Admiral of France, and his colleagues, embarked for England at the end of July 1518 – accompanied by thirty gentlemen, fifty archers, wrestlers, musicians and tennis players. As well as negotiating the marriage, they had power to treat for a personal meeting between the kings. By late August, they had landed at Sandwich to be fêted by the mayor. On 23 September 1518 the delegation made a formal entry into London, followed by an entourage of 600 horses, seventy mules and seven baggage wagons. The prospect of a universal peace seemed within reach, and Wolsey plumed himself on being close to achieving what the pope had been unable to manage.[6] The ambassadors were received by Henry at Greenwich. Campeggio was present, as was Giustinian. The Bishop of Paris delivered a long oration, praising peace, and outlining the benefits to be gained by a marriage between Mary and the dauphin. Nicholas West, Bishop of Ely, responded.

Charles was obliged to accept a fait accompli as far as the marriage of Mary and the return of Tournai were concerned. He reiterated his desire for friendship with Henry, and offered a treaty for perpetual peace, rather than Leo's five-year truce. He was not only worried about increased French strength on the Flemish border, but also that peace with England would enable François to pursue an aggressive policy in Naples and Navarre, where Henri II of Navarre was rumoured to be gathering troops. Wolsey wrote in emollient tones, reassuring Charles that Henry would never forget what was due to the ancient alliance between Burgundy and England, so Charles need have no concerns regarding the treaty with the French. On 2 October 1518, the Treaty of London was signed, and Mary's fate was sealed. She was to be married to Dauphin François when he turned fourteen in February 1532. Her dowry was to consist of 330,000 crowns of gold, of which half were to be paid at the time of the marriage, and half on its first anniversary. Her annual jointure, to be paid by François, was to equal that which had been assigned to the wives of Louis XII, but would only be payable if the dowry had been delivered and the dauphin were still alive. In the event of the dauphin's death before succeeding to the throne, Mary's dower would be reduced. Henry was to supply her with a suitable wardrobe and jewels, which she would retain if widowed, with any accumulated personal effects. If she died first, her dote, jewels and effects were to be inherited by her children or, if she had none, by her widower. So much was standard fare in the marriage treaties of princesses. The bitter pill for Henry was the French insistence that Mary be named as Henry's heir in default of sons. Henry agreed to this, only, in Giustinian's opinion, because Katharine was nearly at term, and appeared in good health. Henry was putting all his trust in God that he would have a son. The corollary Treaty of Universal Peace, initially signed by England and France, but open to all other states, had clauses that can be summarised as a mutual defence pact, and an agreement not to harbour each other's rebels. This treaty is generally also referred to as the Treaty of London.

Considering the frequency with which treaties were broken, they were entered with surprising solemnity. On 3 October, Henry, with the Bishop of Paris as proxy for François, and accompanied by some 1,000 knights and gentlemen, rode from the palace of Westminster to St Paul's to swear an oath to observe the treaties. The ceremony was undertaken with great pomp, the ambassadors of Charles and Venice were invited to attend, although they complained the treaties and the oaths were read so quietly that only the parties involved could hear what was agreed. The witnesses were Wolsey and Campeggio.[7] Later that day, the whole court was entertained by Wolsey at his archiepiscopal palace, York Place. The hall was decorated with enormous gold and silver vases, and the food served was equally extravagant. The first part of the evening's entertainment consisted of a performance by twenty-four sumptuously dressed and masked dancers. No doubt the audience, having observed their skill, feigned amazement to see the king and the French queen unmask. The other dancers are a roll call of the companions of Henry's youth. Three of them, Sir Edward Neville, Sir Nicholas Carew and Henry Norris, ended on the scaffold and the Earl of Surrey (later Duke of Norfolk) would only escape death because Henry died first. After the dancing, a vast array of sweets and delicacies was served, and to cater to every taste, Wolsey had provided bowls full of dice and coins for any of the company who liked to gamble. Once the supper tables had been removed, the guests played mumchance (a type of gambling game) then danced until midnight. Henry remained after the other guests had left to gamble heavily with the French ambassadors.

Two days later, on Tuesday 5 October, Mary made her first formal appearance on the international stage when the proxy betrothal took place at Greenwich, in the queen's Great Chamber. Henry's court was dressed in its best finery. The king stood before his throne with Katharine and the French queen to one side of him, Wolsey and Campeggio to the other. In front of Katharine was Mary herself, dressed in cloth-of-gold, wearing a black velvet, jewel-encrusted cap. Proceedings opened with an oration from Cuthbert Tunstall, Master of the Rolls, in praise of matrimony. Mary, her two-year-old legs buckling, was then 'taken in arms' and the cardinals asked Henry and Katharine if they assented to their daughter's marriage. They affirmed their agreement, although Katharine was probably less than thrilled with the prospect of a French alliance that might undermine Anglo-Spanish relations. The proxies for François and Claude also gave their assent. Wolsey placed a ring, small in circumference but boasting a large diamond that he had presented himself, onto Mary's tiny ring finger. It was pushed down by Admiral Bonnivet, acting as proxy for the dauphin. The cardinals blessed the princess, and another round of speechifying ensued, followed by Mass sung by Wolsey himself in the gold-cloth-decorated chapel. Further oath-taking took place with Henry swearing he and Katharine would observe the treaty, and Bonnivet and his colleagues acting for François and Claude. According to an anonymous account sent to Mantua, the precocious princess enlivened the ceremony by saying to Bonnivet, 'Are you the dauphin of France? If you are, I want to kiss you.'

Having worked up an appetite, the court dined. Henry was offered water to wash his hands by his highest-ranking nobles, the dukes of Buckingham, Norfolk and Suffolk, and the Marquis of Dorset, who were permitted to sit at table with the king, flanked on the right by the cardinals and on the left by Bonnivet and the Bishop of Paris. The other ambassadors and lesser stars dined separately. The festivities continued at Greenwich three days later with jousting, followed by dinner. Henry and Katharine sat in the centre of the top table, with the French queen to her brother's left. On Katharine's right sat Wolsey, and then one of the English duchesses, probably Lady Buckingham, as the highest ranking. Campeggio sat next to the French queen. The ambassadors were alternated with ladies down either side of the table. Henry demonstrated his wealth in the approved fashion by the enormous quantities of gold and silver plate displayed – eighty-two vases of gold, ranging in size upward from a foot; four cups, each 2 foot in height, with similarly sized flasks and two large salt cellars. This was merely for display; on the tables there were gold cups for everyone and 'innumerable' silver dishes. The details of the food and wine consumed are staggering – more than 3,000 loaves were eaten and three tuns of wine drunk. A huge array of delicacies was on offer; spices, comfits, saffron, dates, marmalades and fruit are mentioned as well as enormous quantities of beef, mutton, capon, quail, swans, larks, conies, peacocks, 2,500 eggs and 16½ gallons of cream. Among all this culinary magnificence, it is likely that the little princess went to bed with a light supper.

Katharine, in her eighth month of pregnancy, retired early, but the other revellers remained to watch a pageant. The entertainment began with the entrance of a group of drummers, dressed as Turks, and a rider on Pegasus, the winged horse, who introduced a choir of children to sing the merits of the treaty. A curtain was raised to reveal a tableau consisting of an artificial hill, topped with five trees, each of which bore a coat of arms: on the olive were the arms of the Church; on the fir tree, those of the emperor; the third, a rose, bore the English arms; the French arms were supported on a bunch of lilies; and those of Spain were propped up by a pomegranate. On the crest of the hill sat either a lady, according to one account, or a little girl of about three (not Mary herself) cradling a (make-believe) dolphin in her lap – a pun on the title 'dauphin', often written as 'dolphin' in English. Inside the cave, behind a gilded gate, were nine ladies dressed in the fashion of the Indies, embroidered with gold and pearls, and outside were their swains, clothed in red satin. Once Pegasus had extolled the treaty and explained the symbolism, he added that the whole world rejoiced at the new peace. The leader of the Turks objected that *he* did not rejoice at it, and immediately fifteen armed knights entered to fight a tourney with the Turks, whom we can safely assume were roundly defeated! The rescued ladies then danced with their lovers. There were probably fireworks, too; a barrel and a half of 'white-lights' and a powder-beater's wages of 3*d* were noted in the accounts.

Henry liberally rewarded the French delegation. Bonnivet himself, as proxy dauphin, received a robe of cloth of gold, lined with silver, which had been made for Henry himself. He also received silver plate to the value of 3,000 crowns – nearly one percent of the dowry – and three horses. The Bishop of Paris, not needing gold gowns, was given silver plate worth 2,000 crowns and the other two negotiators 1,000 crowns' worth. Presents were also sent to France – plate and garments for François' gentlemen, and for François himself there was a set of horse-harness, decorated with gold filigree and rich embroidery.[8] The news of the treaty soon travelled around Europe. François' Marshal, the Sieur de Lautrec, announced it in Milan on 17 October. It was then posted at all the city gates, to the sound of trumpets.

Meanwhile, plans for Charles to marry François' daughter, Louise, as envisaged by the Treaty of Noyon, had failed on her death in 1517. The original treaty provided for her sister to be her substitute, with any failure by Charles to comply resulting in the ceding of Naples to France. Notwithstanding this penalty clause, the Spanish council refused to entertain the idea of their king marrying a toddler. The most important alliance, in their view, was between Castile and Portugal.[9] Charles was doing his best to maintain this by the marriage of his sister Eleonora to King Manuel, the widower of their aunt Maria, in September 1518, but there was pressure on him to marry one of Manuel's daughters. Henry wrote to Charles that if he joined the new Treaty of London, it would enable him to keep Naples – even if he did not marry a French princess.

As October slipped away, the court awaited Katharine's confinement with bated breath. On 10 November, she went into premature labour and was delivered of a daughter. As if the baby's sex were not disappointment enough, the infant died almost immediately. Giustinian opined that, had the birth and death occurred earlier, Mary's betrothal would not have been solemnised, so repelled were the English by the notion of their country falling into French hands. The grief of Katharine and Henry is unrecorded, but it must have been bitter. Whether or not Katharine realised immediately that her childbearing days were over, there were no further recorded pregnancies. She was only thirty-three, but her mother had borne her last child at thirty-four, as had her prolific sister Maria, Queen of Portugal.

If Henry regretted the betrothal, it was too late to draw back. In December 1518, the English ambassadors were received at Paris to bind the dauphin in a second proxy betrothal, and to receive François' and Claude's oaths in person. Not to be out-done in splendour, François' ceremony equalled the ostentation of Henry's. The ambassadors were received in the great hall of the Louvre. On a raised dais was the royal throne, covered in cloth of gold, with matching footstool, cushions and canopy. The king himself was no less splendid, decked in cloth of silver decorated with embroidered flowers and lined with the feathers of Spanish herons. Rather than a crown, he wore his usual cap. François only had the benefit of one, rather than two, attendant legates, seated to his right and also distinguished with a gold canopy above his chair. While legates might have been thin on the ground, there were four ordinary cardinals, and where Henry had been flanked by three dukes and a marquis, François had the King of Navarre to impart additional prestige. Queen Claude, pregnant again, did not take part in the ceremony, but watched from behind a blind with her mother-in-law. With the French court in position, the English ambassadors were escorted into the hall. There were four chiefs, including the Earl of Worcester and the Bishop of Ely, and twenty other gentlemen. Their clothes were hardly less rich than François' own – sables, black satin, cloth of gold and crimson satin enveloped them. The treaty was read, speeches made and hugs exchanged between François and the English gentlemen. Worn out by all the work, the king went hunting the next day, before attending Mass at Notre Dame on 14 December 1518 to swear to uphold the treaty. Two days later, the Earl of Worcester, a gentleman of some fifty-eight years, acted as proxy for the two-year-old Mary to be 'espoused' by the dauphin.

Following the signing of the Treaty of London by Henry and François, England was eager to have it ratified by Maximilian and Charles. In his letter to Maximilian, Henry piously observed that his reason for entering the treaty was to enable him to thank God for his own smooth succession by undertaking a crusade against the Infidel, a necessary precursor to which was peace in his own dominions. He assured the emperor that the surrender of Tournai would not cause him problems, as France was to send hostages to remain in England for fourteen years.

The future marriage was widely praised. Tunstall's oration was published in 1518, and a presentation hand written copy, now in the Bodleian Library, was given to Wolsey. In France, a short work in praise of the intended match, *Le Livre Oraison Messire Bernadin Rince ... Les Louenges du mariage ... de Le dauphin ... et Marie,* was printed; a copy is now in the Bibliothèque Nationale. Despite any misgivings Katharine may have had, she observed proper etiquette, writing from time to time to Queen Claude to ask after the French royal family, and to assure Claude of Mary's continued good health.

* * *

On 3 January 1519, the political map of Europe underwent a seismic shift when Maximilian died. The race to replace him in the elective office of King of the Romans was on. Once elected the lucky man would be crowned by the pope, making him Holy Roman Emperor. Despite the prestige of the office, there were no revenues attached to it, and the theoretical power the emperor held as secular leader of Christendom was not borne out by reality. The front-runner was Charles – and the prospect of his victory filled François with dismay. If Charles were elected, France would be surrounded by him on all sides – to the south in Spain and Upper Navarre, to the north in the Low Countries, and to the east by the Empire. It would be even worse if Charles and Henry were in alliance, as that would block France to the northwest as well. Both Charles and François were therefore prepared to lay out enormous sums in bribes to the seven electors. The electors were all either ecclesiastics or independent leaders of states within modern-day Germany: the archbishops of Mainz, Trier and Cologne; the King of Bohemia; the Count Palatine of the Rhine; the Duke of Saxony and the Margrave of Brandenburg. Conveniently for Charles, his sister, Mary of Austria, was betrothed to the King of Bohemia (also King of Hungary), and he had been angling for some time to arrange a match between his youngest sister, Catherine of Austria, and the oldest son of the Margrave of Brandenburg. Before that match could be agreed, a speedy marriage was arranged for Charles's (and Mary's) step-grandmother, Germaine de Foix, Dowager Queen of Aragon, to the Margrave of Brandenburg's cousin. This matchmaking was accompanied by heaps of silver (100,000 florins), borrowed from the Fuggers of Augsburg and the promised appointment of the pope's nephew to a lordship in Naples. Charles requested Henry to back him, and François, too, asked for support on what he described as 'this interesting occasion'.

François assured Henry's ambassador, Sir Thomas Boleyn, that four of the electors had already promised him their votes, as they believed he was best placed to lead Europe against the Turk, while Charles believed the same four were actually in his camp. Boleyn thought that François, who was swearing he would spend half his annual revenues to obtain the Imperial crown, was absolutely in earnest on the matter. Boleyn was rather more cynical about François' promise to lead a crusade and be in Constantinople within three years. From Mary's perspective (although she was, of course, too young to have an opinion) the victory of François, while she was betrothed to his son, would make her match more prestigious. Her future husband would not be assured of his own election, but would start as favourite. Henry confirmed to François that he himself would not stand – the requests of the Cardinal of Sion for him to do so were no more than a 'crafty scheme' to 'draw money out of [England] into [Germany]'.[10]

Pope Leo X vacillated between François and Charles, waiting to see who would offer the greatest security to the Papal States. Charles, mindful of the need to keep Henry's goodwill in the election campaign, decided to take part in the Treaty of Universal Peace. He sent his ambassadors to ratify it and they were received with great honour. Henry convened his usual lords and prelates plus an additional seventeen bishops not usually present at court. On 20 March 1519 Henry and Charles's representatives swore to the treaty at Greenwich, after Campeggio, in possession of a new commission from Leo, had celebrated Mass and the company had dined. The queen did not attend – perhaps she was still in poor health or depressed following the loss of the baby the previous November. The company paid her a short visit, during which she 'lavished marks of good will' on the ambassadors. Despite the originally stated objective of the treaty – the pacification of Christendom to enable a crusade – Giustinian reported drily that the French ambassador did not seem very pleased at having a new confederate.

As well as the rivalry for election as emperor, relations were deteriorating between François and Charles over Navarre, and François' suggestion that if he could not be emperor himself, he would support Charles's brother, the Archduke Ferdinand. Charles helped Ferdinand understand where his loyalties lay by increasing his revenues.

Eventually, probably inevitably, Charles was elected. Henry went in solemn procession to St Paul's with Campeggio, Wolsey, Buckingham, Norfolk, Suffolk and the ambassadors of Venice and Scotland to hear a Mass of thanksgiving, followed by dinner at Baynard's Castle. One account says the French ambassador declined the invitation. The new Venetian ambassador, Surian, (Giustinian having been recalled after much importuning) thought the election of Charles made it all the more important for Henry and François to remain allies, although he thought Katharine, as a Spaniard, would not favour this idea, and that Archduchess Marguerite would continue to sow discord between England and France. François put a brave face on the failure of his campaign – finding refuge in the story that the driving force behind it had been his mother.

Campeggio returned to Rome, with the hopes of Henry and Wolsey that the pope would join the treaty. Henry assured Leo that, with Christendom now at peace, he would begin his crusade against the Infidel as soon as he had an heir. Clearly, Mary was still not an acceptable solution to the problem, although we can probably surmise that even if he had had half a dozen strapping sons, Henry would not have set off on crusade.

In August of 1519, flushed with his success at bribing the electors, Charles, now Holy Roman Emperor-elect Charles V, wrote to Henry of his desire to maintain their alliance, while he was also striving to be on good terms with François. He thanked Henry for an invitation to visit and sent compliments to his aunt, Queen Katharine. Meanwhile, in France, François' mother and chief counsellor, Louise of Savoy, was asking questions about Mary having heard worrying, although unfounded, rumours about her health. She promised that Queen Claude would send 'tokens' to Katharine and something to Mary on the dauphin's behalf.

***

Despite Henry's unwillingness to openly acknowledge the unpalatable fact Mary was his heir, that reality, and her future as queen of France, enhanced her status and this was reflected in the size of her entourage. Her overall complement of staff was increased by six gentlemen, paid 7*d* per day, nine valets at 3*d* per day, four grooms of the chamber and twelve grooms of the household each at 40*s* per annum. Lady Bryan was granted another £50 annuity, with an annual tun of Gascon wine. Fond parents, Henry and Katharine kept Mary at court as much as possible once the dangerous summer months, which bred plague, had passed. Mary was with her parents and her aunt Mary, from October to December 1519, largely at Greenwich.

By the end of 1519, Henry was spending huge sums – £10,000 per annum for his personal expenses and £6,000 for building projects at Bridewell Palace in London and New Hall, otherwise known as Beaulieu, in Essex, to include a nursery wing.[11] There was also considerable expenditure on Mary. Among practical household items including beef, buckets and bed linen, there were 'a cloth of estate with two cushions of cloth of gold and red velvet, paned with [a] valance of red silk and gold; a cloth of gold and a velvet chair and thirty pieces of tapestry, 3½ yards deep'. These were all high-status items, particularly the cloth of estate, which would have been hung behind Mary's chair. There are small clues to Mary's daily life in the accounts – payment for cygnets (for the table), fees to Lady Oxford's servant for conveying Mary from Richmond to the abbey at Syon and back, and for culinary treats, particularly strawberries and cherries for which the gardeners at the various palaces received tips. More than £114 was paid to Mary's treasurer, Richard Sydnor, for finding two litter horses for her.

The proposed meeting between Henry and François was discussed throughout 1519. Boleyn was instructed to tell the French king that Henry was so eager to meet, he had sworn an oath not to shave off his beard until they had. Delighted, François promised the same and a date of May 1520 was put forward. A slight diplomatic incident occurred in November, when Louise of Savoy discovered that Henry had shaved. Boleyn assured Louise that it was at Katharine's daily urging, as she always complained when Henry sported a beard. Louise suspected Katharine's request had less to do with her dislike of her husband's hirsute chin and more to do with her dislike of the alliance with France. Disingenuously, since she must have known, Louise asked whether Katharine were not the new emperor's aunt? Boleyn replied that indeed Charles was Katharine's sister's son, but that François need not worry, as Henry preferred *him* to any king living. Louise sweetly remarked that the love between the two kings was 'not in their beards, but in their hearts'.[12]

Henry and François continued their mutual complimenting. Sir Richard Wingfield was sent with personal messages beyond those delivered by Boleyn. He was to offer 'affectuous recommendations' and 'other pleasant devices of the king's grace, the queen, my lady princess, my lord legate [Wolsey], and semblable amiable communications'.

It now became a race between François and Charles to meet Henry first. They both wanted him as an ally – Charles because he owed him large sums of money, and because if English waters became hostile, he would not be able to travel easily between his territories of Spain and the Low Countries. François wanted English support so that when he adventured in Italy, Henry would not appear at his back door. But neither country wanted Henry's friendship to the exclusion of all other considerations – something Henry never truly appreciated.

In late February, Charles informed Henry he was 'desirous of meeting [Henry and Katharine] and enjoying their society'. He would therefore make a brief visit while in transit to Flanders. The details were to be left in the hands of Archduchess Marguerite and her envoy, Jean de la Sauch. It was important, Marguerite instructed, that the English should be under the impression that Charles was close to an alliance with France, and had no need of England.

A date of early June, 1520, was agreed for the meeting with François. The timing was arranged for the benefit of Claude, nearing term on her fifth pregnancy. Henry, as a gallant prince, could hardly object to accommodating a lady, even though he was hoping Charles would be with him throughout May and he would have preferred to wait until mid-June for the French convention. It was agreed that after departing Calais, Henry and Katharine would proceed to Flanders to meet Charles again, this time with Archduchess Marguerite, a reunion which Katharine was said to be anticipating with 'much desire'.[13] Marguerite and Charles's envoys travelled to Greenwich to make the arrangements and were introduced to king and queen. Once all was agreed, Henry turned to Katharine and informed her that her nephew, his 'brother', would visit. She curtseyed low and thanked him, at which he took off his hat and observed that he was eager to meet Charles, so far as his treaty obligations with France permitted. While Katharine's pleasure at the thought of seeing her nephew was no doubt genuine, she was an experienced politician and on good terms with Henry; it no doubt suited him to play up her family feeling as a reason for the meeting, should François be nervous about it. Marguerite's envoys wrote that matters should be expedited as the French were always 'buzzing about the ears' of Henry and Wolsey. Her plan was for enough to be agreed in the first meeting between Henry and Charles for the French meeting to fail, while not concluding anything until the follow-up meeting.

The Anglo-French meeting was full of intricate etiquette. François was searching for the best-looking ladies of his court to be part of the festivities, and hoped that Queen Katharine would bring her most beautiful ladies too: a notorious lecher, François was probably looking for fresh prey. Louise pressed Wingfield again about Katharine's feelings. Wingfield tactfully replied that his queen, being a 'wise and virtuous woman', wished only to please her husband and she was therefore 'entirely affeccioned' not only toward the meeting, but also to the marriage of Mary and the dauphin. Louise asked whether Katharine might be with child. Wingfield replied he had no information on that topic. Louise happily anticipated a time when Henry would have a couple of sons to be 'brothers' to the dauphin. Louise's remarks were tinged with spite – her own daughter-in-law, Claude, was stocking the royal nursery to the detriment of her health, while Katharine was manifestly failing. In fact, Louise added, since François and Claude already had a second son, they might send the dauphin to England to be brought up by Henry and Katharine – no doubt while he contemplated the joy of being king of England as Mary's husband.

Louise was right to fear Katharine's reluctance. According to de la Sauch, the English queen had called her council together to discuss how the meeting with François could be avoided. When Henry entered the room and asked what she was doing, she explained why a French meeting would be undesirable. In this, according to de la Sauch – who may have been guilty of wishful thinking – Henry's chief nobles agreed with her. Alliances with Burgundy and Spain were considered, by the majority of Englishmen, far preferable to alliance with France, for both trade-related reasons, and ancient military history. Far from being angry with his wife, Henry and his council admired her all the more, but, even if the story were true, Henry did not change his policy.[14]

While in France, Wingfield travelled to Blois to see the dauphin, no doubt wondering what manner of child might be his future king. The little boy was undressed so Wingfield could confirm he was sound in wind and limb and well grown for his age. He reported that the two-year-old was 'marvellously disposed to be joyous', manifested by the toddler taking a fancy to one of Wingfield's suite and insisting the man stand up and kneel, over and over again.[15]

By 1 May 1520, Margaret, Countess of Salisbury, had replaced Lady Bryan as Mary's governess. Lady Bryan later claimed to have been governess to all of Henry's children so it is possible she left Mary to join the latest arrival in Henry's family – his illegitimate son, Henry Fitzroy, born in 1519 to his mistress, Bessie Blount. Lady Salisbury was the niece of Edward IV. She had been married early in the reign of Henry VII to his loyal cousin, Sir Richard Pole, and the couple had held senior posts in the household of Henry VII's eldest son, Arthur, Prince of Wales. When Arthur married Katharine of Aragon in 1501, the Poles were part of their household in Ludlow, and Margaret and Katharine became friends. Following Henry VIII's accession in 1509, and his marriage to Arthur's widow, Lady Margaret joined the court. Now widowed, she was permitted to inherit her great-grandmother's earldom of Salisbury, making her one of the greatest magnates in England. Lady Salisbury's outlook was traditional and conservative. Places in her household were sought after for the daughters of the nobility and she spent much of her time in the usual pursuits of great landowners – arranging marriages for her children, endless litigation over landholdings and rigorous religious observance. Two of her sons, Henry, Lord Montagu, and Arthur Pole, were in the king's circle of friends, while a third, Reginald, was educated, both at home and in Europe, at Henry's expense. Lady Salisbury had pulled off a dynastic coup with the wedding of her daughter, Ursula, to Lord Henry Stafford, heir to the Duke of Buckingham. Once duchess, her daughter would rank only after Queen Katharine, the French queen and Mary. Lady Salisbury's rank, impeccable reputation and character, as well as her friendship with Katharine, made her the ideal choice for Mary's governess.

***

The meeting between Henry and François, their wives, and his mother, became known as the Field of Cloth of Gold for its extravagance. The opportunity was taken to reconfirm Mary's betrothal to the dauphin.

While Henry and Katharine were junketing at Ardres, Mary remained at home. There could be no point in subjecting the four-year-old child to a sea crossing, and it might have been risky for Henry to travel with his only legitimate heir. Although no danger was anticipated, if François had proved devious enough to hold Henry hostage, at least Mary would have been available as a figurehead for a continuing Tudor dynasty. On the principle of keeping the mice under the cat's eye, Henry had brought his nearest male relatives to France with him – Buckingham, who might claim to be the Lancastrian heir, and the Earl of Devon, who was the senior Yorkist heir. Lord Montagu did not attend, but since his mother was Mary's governess, perhaps he was considered safe.

The council left behind to manage affairs was headed by the Duke of Norfolk, who wrote on 13 June that the council had attended the princess on the previous Saturday at Richmond, where they found her to be 'right merry, and in prosperous health and state, daily exercising herself in virtuous pastimes'. Given her age, it is hard to imagine her pastimes could be anything but virtuous!

Wolsey wrote from Calais to instruct the council to prepare for a visit from three French gentlemen to Mary. The letters arrived on the 29 June and the visitors in the evening of the same day. There had just been time to prepare the mayor and Corporation of London, who gave them a banquet. The next day, the Frenchmen followed the tourist trail to Henry VII's foundations of the Savoy Hospital and the Lady Chapel at Westminster. They dined with the Abbot of Westminster that day and with the Sheriff of London on the Saturday. On Sunday, they travelled to Richmond by barge with Lord Berners and Lord Darcy.

Mary was on her best behaviour, flanked by lords spiritual and temporal and a full suite of ladies, including Lady Salisbury, the Duchess of Norfolk and her three daughters, Henry's cousin Lady Margaret Herbert, and several others.[15] This was Mary's opportunity to demonstrate her careful training and Lady Salisbury must have had her heart in her mouth – if Mary behaved badly, her governess would be discredited. Fortunately, Mary was not a shy child and, with great aplomb, she welcomed her visitors,

> with most goodly countenance, proper communication, and pleasant pastime in playing at the virginals, [so] that they greatly marvelled and rejoiced the same, her young and tender age considered.

She offered them 'strawberries, wafers and ypocras (a type of wine)'. They obviously made a good meal, as four gallons of wine were consumed. Returning to the city, the gentlemen dined with Norfolk and another sheriff.

Following more sightseeing at the Tower, they sailed home, satisfied with what they had seen, and certainly well fed.

The meeting with François concluded, Henry, Katharine and Wolsey went to their appointment with Charles, Marguerite and their councillor, Chièvres. Chièvres suggested that Henry should break off Mary's betrothal and, instead, betroth her to Charles, who would similarly break off his agreement to marry François' daughter. Not only that, but Charles would attack France on four fronts, not desisting until Henry was invested with his rights as king of France. In return, Henry should promise to facilitate Charles's safe passage to Italy to attack François in Milan. Henry rejected these proposals. He claimed to be shocked that Charles, having sworn oaths to François, should now not only contemplate breaking them but also suggest that other men be oath-breakers. Enjoying, as he always did, the opportunity to lecture, Henry delivered a homily to Chièvres on the duties of honourable men and princes. How, Henry demanded, could Charles expect men would keep faith with him if he behaved so dishonourably? If Charles broke his word to François, what guarantee did Henry have that he would not be served likewise – prophetic words indeed! For good measure, Henry warned Chièvres that an assault on François would lead to repercussions as, in accordance with the Treaty of London, Henry would attack Charles as the aggressor. This firmness on his own part, Henry said, turned Charles's course away from an attack on France. This all sounds extremely high-minded on Henry's part, until we realise the information comes from instructions to Wingfield to impart these choice morsels to the French king. Whether Henry's remonstrances to Charles were of any effect or not, Charles was glad not to be embroiled a war, as Castile had broken out into revolt against foreign rulers and taxation.

On her parents' return, Mary joined them at either Windsor or Woodstock, but was sent back to Richmond in early August as plague was rampant in the Oxfordshire countryside. She returned to them to celebrate Christmas at Greenwich. As the year 1520 ended it seemed likely she would one day be Queen-regnant of England and Queen-consort of France.

2

Empress in Training

My well-beloved future Empress

Charles V

By the time Mary was four years old in February 1520, her formal education had begun. During the Middle Ages, a king's education might consist of reading in Latin and French as well as his own language, history, perhaps some philosophy, law, arithmetic for accounting purposes, and geometry as it related to siege warfare. Academically, not more than this was required. Writing, although learnt, was generally left to scribes as a rather tedious process. Henry was notorious for his disinclination to pick up a pen. The focus was on the practical skills of warfare – strategy, tactics, use of the wide variety of lethal weapons, and leadership. Royal women had less academic training. They did not learn Latin, and their need for a knowledge of history or philosophy was less. Typically they would learn to read in their own language and perhaps French, the diplomatic language of Europe. They learnt accounting and other land management skills, as well as needlework of every sort. Both sexes practised social skills – music, dancing, playing chess and cards, riding to a high degree of proficiency, hunting, hawking, archery and so forth. Religion lay at the heart of everything, but was learnt by example and immersion in society rather than as an academic study. With the coming of the printing press, and the explosion of the Renaissance in Italy, education in royal and noble circles changed out of all recognition in the late fifteenth and early sixteenth centuries, an alteration from which Mary benefited.

Mary's grandmother, Isabella, having brothers, was not expected to inherit the throne and so had received little formal education. On becoming Queen of Castile, and then Queen-consort of Aragon, she found her lack of Latin was a serious bar to effective queenship, and set herself to study it – being taught by one of the first women to hold a university post, Beatriz Galindo, known as 'La Latina'. Isabella was determined her daughters should have all the academic education she had missed and she commissioned a book from the brothers Alessandro and Antonio Geraldini, *De eruditione nobilium puellarum*. As there are no known copies extant, the contents of this work are uncertain but we can infer it advocated an academic curriculum that included Latin. Katharine was probably the first queen consort of England to speak and write in Latin since Eleanor of Aquitaine in the late twelfth century and she and her sisters were considered the best-educated princesses of their time.

As Henry was a younger son there is less information about his education than about that of his elder brother, but he was a proficient linguist, an excellent sportsman, an extremely accomplished musician and a keen theologian. He also had a profound interest in mathematics and astronomy and was fascinated by medicine, often creating and prescribing prophylactics and cures.

Henry and Katharine were not just learned themselves, they appreciated learning in others, and patronised scholars from all over Europe. When Erasmus, the foremost European scholar of the day, wrote to Henry in January 1518, he praised the king for spending a part of each day in study, 'differing entirely' from those princes who took no interest in learning and philosophy. While Erasmus was constantly searching for a patron to pay his expenses, and penned slavish praises to prospects, he did not invent Henry's interest in study. Katharine, too, was praised by Erasmus. He wrote to a friend in July 1518 that the queen was 'not only a miracle of learning, but is not less pious than learned', and the following year that she was 'fond of learning', and had been an 'apt pupil' since childhood.[1] As well as receiving praise from Erasmus, both Henry and Katharine had academic works dedicated to them. The couple surrounded themselves with the best and brightest minds of their generation: Thomas Linacre, who was Henry's physician; Dr Stokesley, Henry's confessor, whom Erasmus praised as a linguist; Sir Thomas More, famous for his *Utopia* and other works; John Fisher, Bishop of Rochester; Cuthbert Tunstall, praised as the most learned man in England and author of an educational work on mathematics; John Colet, founder of St Paul's School; Richard Pace, Henry's secretary; Lord Morley and Lord Berners, who both undertook translations, and Lord Mountjoy, Katharine's chamberlain. In Erasmus' words 'it is a museum more than a court'.

So when the time came to attend to Mary's education, it was into this intellectual world that her parents dipped for advice and practical delivery. Sixty years later, Mary's relative, James VI of Scotland, was to say that he had been taught to speak Latin before he had learnt Scots, and Mary may have had a similar early immersion in both Latin and French. Her first Latin teacher was probably Katharine herself, followed by Dr Richard Fetherstone, Katharine's chaplain. Mary's tutor for French was Giles Duwes. Duwes had been involved in the education of Henry VIII and his siblings and later became Royal Librarian. His wife is mentioned in lists of Mary's attendants. His book *An Introductorie for to learne to rede, to pronounce, and to speake Frenche trewly* was published in 1533, according to Duwes, because Mary had 'commanded' him to record how he had taught her and it opens with a dedication to her. The book is in two parts – the first explaining the rules of grammar and parts of speech and the second devoted to the type of repetition of question and answer still used in language teaching, with French text and English translation. The political landscape had changed by the time of the book's publication, and the second part had a dedication to Henry, Anne Boleyn and their daughter, Elizabeth, which is unlikely to have pleased Mary. However, the contents of the second part are still related to Mary and use her as an example. The subjects range from thank you letters, to conversations about the perpetual peace between England and France (which may date the actual writing of the dialogue to 1526) and even controversial subjects such as the Mass.[2]

Another scholar involved in Mary's early education, although he may not have taught her in person, was Dr Thomas Linacre. Linacre was one of the first Western scholars to learn Ancient Greek. He studied under the humanist Poliziano in Florence, possibly alongside Lorenzo the Magnificent, and read for his degree in medicine at Padua – the most distinguished university for medical studies in Europe. On returning to England, he took a position at Oxford, before becoming tutor to Arthur, Prince of Wales. On Henry's accession, Linacre was appointed as the king's physician and was a founder member of the Royal College of Physicians. He published *Rudimenta Grammatices,* which was based on Latin lessons he designed for Mary. He dedicated the work to the princess, in a full page Latin inscription. In the preface, he wrote that he had been employed by Mary's illustrious father to look after both her physical health and her learning, but that as bodily weakness inhibited him fulfilling all his duties (he died in 1524) he hoped to be of service to her 'noble and instinctive' genius for learning by producing the instruction manual. The first printed copy of the work, by Richard Pynson, dating from 1525, amends the dedication to address Mary as 'Princess of Wales and Cornwall'. Mary became known by that title only in the year following Linacre's death, so it must be Pynson's work.

The second great humanist of international renown co-opted to ensure that Mary had access to every scholastic opportunity, was Juan Luis Vives. After Vives had been hounded out of his native Valencia, when members of his family were executed as 'secret Jews', he studied at the University of

Paris and then took a post at the University of Leuven. While in Brussels, Vives was associated with Katharine's nephews, Charles and Ferdinand. During this period Vives also worked with Erasmus on a commentary on St Augustine's hugely influential *The City of God*, which Erasmus encouraged him to dedicate to Henry VIII. Shortly after, Vives was invited to England, where he secured a post as Reader in Greek, Latin and Rhetoric at Wolsey's new Cardinal College, Oxford. With these familial, social and political connections, it is not surprising that Katharine considered Vives the right man to advise on Mary's education. The relationship was not one of arm's length; the queen met the scholar on many occasions. Whether Vives actually taught Mary himself has been debated, but his recent biographer, Enrique Garcia Hernàn, has shown that in a letter to Wolsey, during Vives' house arrest in early 1528, he wrote that he had taught the princess Latin, and been her 'instructor in wisdom'.[3]

Vives wrote three books that influenced Mary's education. The first, commissioned by Katharine, was a general treatise on the role of women and how they should be educated, with a prefatory letter to the queen, and a dedication to Mary herself. It was completed on 5 April 1523, although not published until the following year. *De Institutione Feminae Christiane* (The Instruction of a Christian Woman) was a work in three parts, dealing with young, unmarried women, then wives, then widows. While to the modern reader the book is extraordinarily misogynistic, based as it is on the assumption that woman's chief virtue was chastity, without which quality no other virtues meant anything, its underlying premise that women could, and should, benefit from formal academic education was groundbreaking. Vives postulated that women were capable of the same intellectual attainment as men, even though the purpose of their education was to fit them to be better wives and mothers. In support of this, he promoted the vision of marriage as for 'indissoluble companionship', rather than purely procreative purposes and observed he knew of no educated woman who was 'bad', by which he meant unchaste. The programme of study he advocated was to include Greek as well as Latin. While Mary became an accomplished Latinist, it is uncertain whether she learnt Greek. There is a reference later to her being well-grounded in it, although the commentator was a visiting diplomat, who only met her once, and it was also mentioned in a funeral oration given in Rome after her death.[4] The curriculum was strong on classical philosophy, but also included modern authors, such as More and Erasmus, both of whom were Vives' correspondents. Unlike most scholars, Vives encouraged the study of the vernacular, as well as Latin, and there are references to Mary understanding, although not speaking, Spanish and Italian. There was also a good deal of Bible study. Often thought of as a Protestant innovation, educated Catholics had been looking afresh at the Bible for nearly fifty years, and Mary read from both the Old and New Testaments every day. Like Erasmus, while Vives remained within the fold of the Catholic Church, he never actively criticised the Reformers and instead concentrated in his writings on the need for Christians to live in love and amity. Amid this heavy academic course, there was little room for entertainment; dolls and romantic stories were rejected, and the pleasures of dancing frowned upon. We can safely assume this latter injunction was ignored; there are numerous records of Mary dancing, all of which praise her considerable skill in the art, and since Katharine is known to have had dolls in her childhood, perhaps she countenanced them for her daughter. Occasional improving tales were permitted – a prime example being the *Tale of Patient Griselda,* a story that later came to be closely associated with Katharine. Vives encouraged women to teach their children to read and write in their own language but it is unlikely that Katharine undertook this role – apart from anything else, Mary was not with her all the time. Vives' book became enormously popular, and Katharine funded an English translation: *The Education of a Christian Woman* by Richard Hyrde. This version advocated a broader range of authors for women to read for pleasure, including mediaeval romances. The translation was not printed until 1540, but it is probable Katharine saw the manuscript version – hopefully she added the lighter reading to Mary's curriculum. Both the original and the translation were widely admired by Protestants as well as Catholics and were important contributors to the leap forward in elite female education in the mid-sixteenth century.

The second work Vives wrote relating to Mary's education was *De Rationi Studiis Puerilis (On a Plan of Study for Children).* Also commissioned by Katharine, and published in 1524, it consisted of two letters, the first specifically prepared for Mary, with the second being for Charles Blount, son of Lord Mountjoy. In this briefer work, Vives listed additional reading, perhaps to fit Mary for the role of queen-regnant, which eventuality was becoming more likely as time passed. Recommended works included Plato's *Dialogues,* Cato's *Distichs,* used as a Latin primer as well as for its moral contents; Horace, Seneca and Lucca and more modern fare of an improving nature – More's *Utopia* and Erasmus' *Education of Christian Princes.* Study was through the method of translation from Latin into English and memorisation of vast quantities of text. As well as private study, Vives recommended Mary have three or four friends to share her schoolroom. There is no information in the records about whether this was arranged – theories that a young Katherine Parr shared Mary's lessons have no basis in evidence, and given their disparity in ages, are inherently unlikely.

Vives wrote a third work, also dedicated to Mary. This was a collection of 213 mottoes and sayings – *Satellitum Sive Symbola.* We can be sure Mary read this with some pleasure as she selected one of the mottoes – *Veritas temporis filia* (truth, the daughter of time) – as her own.

Music was a primary component of Mary's education. Henry was an extremely accomplished performer on a variety of instruments, a composer of some talent, and he also employed numerous musicians. He took a personal interest in his chapel choir, even having informal competitions with Wolsey as to whose men were the best. His choirmaster was the respected William Cornish, whose music is still played today. Mary shared this interest from an early age, learning to play the lute, the rebec (not dissimilar to a lute) and several variants within the harpsichord family.[5] She was considered very talented at both virginals and lute and later descriptions of her emphasise these musical skills as well as her dancing.

She was also proficient enough in arithmetic to check and correct her household accounts. Although there is no record of it, she may well have been taught from Tunstall's mathematical work, *De arte supputandi libri quattuor*, published in 1522, and dedicated to Sir Thomas More.

All this study paid off well. At some time during the period February 1527–8, Mary translated a prayer of St Thomas Aquinas from Latin into English. Her work was inscribed on the leaves of a *Book of Hours of the Virgin*. The Book itself, now in the British Library, was once owned by a member of Henry VII's court. The original owner has not been identified, but there are personal messages in it from Henry VII, Elizabeth of York, Henry VIII and Katharine of Aragon, as well as Mary's translation, suggesting the owner was close to the royal family.[6] The prayer is a complex work, requiring a level of scholarship that would be no mean feat for an adult, let alone an eleven-year-old child. There is no information about how the prayer came to be chosen – whether by Mary, or by her tutor Dr Fetherstone.

Of course, it was not all lessons for the little girl. She was still regularly visiting her parents, crossing the Thames on the Datchet ferry en route to Windsor, Richmond or Greenwich and she was with Henry and Katharine at Greenwich for the New Year of 1521. Presents that year included a gold cross from the cardinal, while her godmothers, the Duchess of Norfolk and Katherine of York, sent candle snuffers and silver flagons respectively. Queen Claude sent a gold pomander and a gentleman named Humphrey Dykers sent three bows, presumably cut to size to fit a child. The Earl of Devon gave a silver flagon and his wife dispatched two smocks. Mrs Pasis of London gave cakes, and a poor woman of Greenwich showed her desire to please a little girl by bringing rosemary bushes covered with spangles. There were also payments to Mrs Brambleton at Windsor for rosewater and 'galifera', and 6s was given to musicians for playing for Mary. A tip was given to the Earl of Kent's servant for bringing rabbits (for the pot rather than as pets), and to unnamed girls for bringing oranges, cakes, nuts, grapes and roses.

Katharine's midwife gave Mary the homely gift of a couple of capons; and her nurse, Margaret, gave her a satin purse.

In late January 1521, a present of perfume and smocks was sent by François and Claude and, at the end of the month, Mary left Ditton for another trip to Greenwich. She took a barge to Richmond on 23 February where, despite her youth, she stood as godmother to Sir William Compton's daughter. The child was named Mary, and 33s 4d were distributed by the lady mistress on the princess's behalf. She also visited her Aunt Mary and her cousins, Henry, Frances and Eleanor Brandon, at the Suffolks' grand home in Southwark. Mary remained with her parents until Easter, which fell late that year, before travelling back to Hanworth, via the Bridgettine convent at Syon where 12d was offered at the altar. After a short stay at Hanworth, she returned to Ditton.

* * *

Throughout the latter half of 1520 and the whole of 1521, Charles and François were preparing for war – seemingly oblivious of the Treaty of London. There were four areas of conflict, Naples, Milan, Navarre and the northeast border between France and the Burgundian and Imperial territories held by Charles, particularly the Duchy of Guelders. Also contrary to the Treaty of London, at least in Henry's view, was François' involvement in Scottish affairs. François maintained he was only trying to persuade the Scots to seek peace with England, but Henry and his ministers were highly suspicious.

As well as these rumblings, religious dissension was growing. In 1517, Martin Luther, an Augustinian friar from Saxony, had publicly criticised the Catholic Church. His original complaint had been over the sale of indulgences but had broadened into an attack on the widespread deficiencies of the Church.[7] Many churchmen were aware of problems and were trying to improve the quality of priestly education and conduct, reduce pluralism and purge the Church of corruption. But these efforts made little headway against entrenched interests and Luther's ideas spread with astonishing rapidity, given wings by the printing press. By 1521, the princes of the Empire were dividing into factions, based on their support for, or dislike of, Luther's preaching, among many other internecine arguments. Their quarrels formed one of Charles's biggest headaches, exacerbated by the difficulty of knowing to which of his vast territories he should attend. While he needed to remain in the German lands to resolve the disputes there, he also needed to advance into Italy to be crowned by the pope and prevent further incursions by France. Simultaneously, his Spanish advisors were beseeching him to return with all speed to settle revolts that were springing up left and right. Now there was the distraction of the tiresome monk, who could not be persuaded to recant, even in the presence of the emperor and the Imperial Diet.

Both François and Charles wanted not so much to be allied to England as to prevent the other receiving English support, which would tip the balance in an otherwise fairly equal contest. Consequently, Charles wanted to overturn Mary's betrothal to the dauphin. He mooted the idea of marrying Mary himself and he and Henry both swore oaths to try to effect the match. Charles wanted his oath only to be binding if the pope granted the necessary dispensation (as first cousins, Mary and Charles were related in the second degree). The English did not want the oath to be dependent on the dispensation, as later events might prevent the pope granting it. The only way around the obstacle was to have a dispensation applied for immediately that would permit the parties to marry in the future, but applying for it would alert the French to the plan. By 1521 Charles, having promoted the idea the previous year, was making difficulties – he wanted Henry to confirm he would discuss an alliance with the Swiss, an attack on France and a defensive league with the pope as part of marriage negotiations, rather than them being treated independently.

Henry would only agree to the defensive league if the pope had already granted the dispensation, professing astonishment that Charles was making so much difficulty. As things stood, he pointed out, England and France were on good terms, Mary was 'honourably bestowed' and Henry had absolutely no need to 'meddle' with the Swiss, make war on France or involve himself in the emperor's wars against rebellious subjects. His only motive for considering the match, he said, was affection for Charles. It was not even as though the marriage were a foregone conclusion, as Charles would only marry Mary if he were still free when the five-year-old princess reached marriageable age. Of course, Henry was considering that Mary was older than Charlotte of France, so Charles would be bound to take Mary rather than wait for the French princess, to whom he was bound by the Treaty of Noyon.

In 1518, when Henry had accepted the French proposition that Mary was his heir in default of a son, he had still been hoping for more children. By 1521, he seemed resigned to the idea of Mary succeeding him. This, he said, made her a more advantageous match for the emperor than Charlotte and ought to attract a reverse dowry. If he subsequently had a son, Henry would pay the same dote of 300,000 crowns as his sister Mary had carried to Louis XII in 1514. Against this sum would have to be set Charles's outstanding loans. For jointure, Henry demanded £14,000 per annum. This was a very handsome income, even for an empress. Any objections to such a munificent sum were to be met with the argument that François had made equivalent promises. So far as an invasion of France was concerned, Henry would be willing to undertake it after the marriage had taken place, although the terms were to be agreed as part of the marriage treaty. At all costs, the utmost secrecy was to be observed.

Henry believed Charles had been willing enough for the match the previous year, without wishing to wait for a papal dispensation – any reluctance now was probably attributable to Charles waiting to hear more from François about what would be offered with Charlotte. Henry gave instructions to Tunstall, his envoy in Spain, that if the emperor's council was seen to be dragging its collective feet, Tunstall was to ask for a private audience with Charles and emphasise the risk that if Mary married the dauphin, and he ruled England in her right, the seas between Charles's Burgundian and Spanish territories would be closed to his shipping. On the other hand, if Mary married Charles, they could close the seas to the French.

To preserve Henry's oath to observe the 1518 treaty with France, discussions with Charles proceeded on the premise that Mary would be available only if François broke the treaty first, by invading Henry's lands – practically speaking, that meant an attack on Calais although, given Henry's oft-repeated fantasy that Scotland was his vassal, he could have used the presence of the Duke of Albany in the northern kingdom as a pretext.[8]

All the while, low-level border incursions were taking place between France and the Empire and seemed likely to break out into serious warfare. The Treaty of London obliged Henry to side with whomever could be shown to be the injured party. This caused Henry to worry he might have to pay for war on three fronts – as well as the European situation, Ireland was restless, and the Scottish border disruptive, despite, or more likely because of, François' intervention. To give Henry his due, he does seem to have made real efforts to prevent war breaking out, either seeing more advantage to himself in peace, or perhaps genuinely believing it to be for the greater good. At any rate, he wanted the kudos of being a mediator between great princes, which enhanced his prestige at little cost. Whether Henry or Wolsey was the prime motivator behind England's foreign policy has been debated but, although the two do not always seem to have agreed on details, overall, they were aligned in their vision.

At this point, Mary had not actually been offered to the emperor, but Henry wanted Charles to agree that, if she were offered within the next few years, he would take her, on the condition of waiting for her to reach maturity. Charles's Chancellor, Gattinara, objected to this, pointing out that Charles would be bound, but as Mary was below age, he could not be sure of her.[9] Tunstall replied that Henry would be equally bound, as if she were promised to Charles, she could not be bestowed elsewhere (blithely overlooking the small matter of her betrothal to the dauphin). Anything less, said Henry, made the whole proposition so far in the future as to be practically worthless. Negotiations became mired in detail as each side sought to bind the other without being bound itself. There was further bargaining over the dote and the spectre of Charles marrying a Portuguese princess was raised by the Imperial side, with the information that King Manuel of Portugal had offered his daughter with a dote of 1 million ducats. Tunstall batted this off with the reply that Mary's chance of inheriting the English crown was worth far more. The requested jointure, too, was disputed, as it far exceeded the customary ten per cent of the dowry that Iberian princesses usually received. Tunstall stuck firmly to the view that the value of Mary's potential inheritance made her worth the price.

In a further round of bartering, the Imperial party declared that Charles could not marry Mary unless he had been released by the pope from his oath to marry Princess Charlotte. Wolsey objected that while in England, Charles had made no such objections, but had been willing immediately to undertake a marriage *de verbi de futuro*. It was Henry himself who had queried whether Charles was bound, having entered the arrangement with Charlotte when he was of age. Wolsey rejected Chièvres' suggestion of another meeting; it would only arouse suspicions in François, and, in his view, with Charles procrastinating, the best course was for Henry to withdraw Tunstall and wait for Charles and François to be at loggerheads, as seemed inevitable. England would then have the upper hand in negotiations. Accordingly, Tunstall returned with the marriage not agreed, and Henry refusing to involve himself in a defensive league with the pope, meeting Charles, or helping him in Spain.

Henry and Wolsey turned their attention to domestic matters. By early May 1521, Edward Stafford, 3rd Duke of Buckingham, had been under secret surveillance for some time, suspected of treasonable activity. Descended from two of Edward III's sons, Buckingham was the only royal duke in England and had a very respectable claim to the throne. Last of the great Marcher lords, he owned enormous estates, living like a prince with a grand household and an army of retainers. He had been present at the Field of Cloth of Gold, and was intimately connected with all the other great nobles: his wife, Eleanor Percy, was sister to the Earl of Northumberland; his daughters were married to the earls of Surrey and Westmorland, and Lord Bergavenny; his son, Henry, was son-in-law to Margaret, Countess of Salisbury; his brother was Earl of Wiltshire, and his sisters were Ladies Hastings and FitzWalter. Despite, or perhaps because of, being at the heart of the nobility, Buckingham did not have a good personal relationship with Henry.[10] He was indicted on a charge of treason and tried on 13 May 1521. According to the indictment, Buckingham had 'compassed' the deposition and death of the king. Evidence was brought that Buckingham had indulged in the dangerous practice of listening to fortune-tellers. Nicholas Hopkins, a Carthusian monk, had told the duke that the king would have no sons, and that one day, Buckingham would 'have all'. That Buckingham was some thirteen years older than Henry does not seem to have given him pause and the duke had agreed that he 'was next in succession to the crown of England', blithely overlooking Mary's rights. On learning of his glorious future, Buckingham could not resist the temptation to hear it repeatedly, and made several visits to Hopkins. Buckingham had also, according to Henry in a letter to François, objected to the treaty with France, and Mary's betrothal to the dauphin. This, with evidence from a disgruntled ex-employee and other reports, confirmed that the duke resented Henry and Wolsey, that he would have been pleased if Henry died, and would have put himself forward as king, in place of Mary.

Presiding over the trial was the Duke of Norfolk. Norfolk and Buckingham had been friends for many years, even though Norfolk was some thirty years older. Norfolk's son, Surrey, was Buckingham's son-in-law. Tears poured down Norfolk's face as, in accordance with his duty, he pronounced sentence. Buckingham was found guilty, and executed on 18 May. While pecuniary motives had probably not been the driving force behind Buckingham's disgrace, the Crown now benefited to the tune of lands worth £6,045 7s 1d annually. The dukedom of Buckingham, the earldoms of Hereford, Stafford and Northampton, the lordship of Brecon and numerous other honours reverted to the Crown, as Henry did not permit Buckingham's son to inherit titles or lands. The family was financially ruined, although, on the advice of his council, the king sent the duchess and the eldest son, Lord Henry Stafford, letters of condolence. Lords Bergavenny and Montagu (Buckingham's son-in-law and the brother of his daughter-in-law respectively) had also been incarcerated in the Tower, but were released upon recognisance.[11]

The duke's execution caused some surprise in Europe. It was no small matter for a king to execute his leading peer. François, ever ready to stir up mischief, sent affectionate letters to Henry, assuring him of his support, and that he would stand by Henry's side. He was sure, however, Henry was so 'wise and well-beloved' of his subjects, that he could not need any help. Henry thanked him for his quite unnecessary concern – he had been aware of Buckingham's being 'ill-disposed' to him for some time. The duke had been detected in treason against the king's person and succession, and against the princess. As for Bergavenny and Montagu, they had been imprisoned only for 'small concealments'. With the benefit of hindsight, it is easy to dismiss as paranoia Henry's fears about Buckingham and the threat he posed to Mary as Henry's heir, or to her marriage with the dauphin. But in the 1520s there were many people, Buckingham and his judge Norfolk included, who well remembered the Wars of the Roses, and might not have had any compunction about another change of dynasty in the event of the king's death. Henry was not the only one concerned about female rule – faced with the prospect of a woman or a Scottish king as the most likely heirs, Buckingham might well have been considered a viable alternative. The immediate effect on Mary of Buckingham's downfall was the removal of Lady Salisbury from her post. The marriage of her daughter, Ursula, to the duke's son, which Henry had approved in 1519, now seemed sinister. There is no record of what reaction, if any, five-year-old Mary had to the disappearance of Lady Salisbury from her daily life.

***

While pursuing a truce with Scotland, Henry and Wolsey were pressing Charles and François to submit to English arbitration. Exactly what Henry and Wolsey were planning has been differently interpreted by historians, or even if the two had the same goals. One school of thought is that far from planning mediation, Henry and Wolsey were preparing a giant double-cross of the French. While exhorting François and Charles to send fully empowered representatives to Calais for mediation, Henry was simultaneously writing to Charles that he hoped the emperor would continue to make war on France, and Wolsey would bring secret instructions to Calais for a closer alliance with Charles. If Wolsey were to go to Calais without the excuse of mediation, François would immediately smell a rat. The other school of thought, vigorously promoted by J. J. Scarisbrick, is that Wolsey, at least, was genuine in his efforts for peace and he was talking to Charles about a separate treaty purely to encourage him to take part in the mediation.

François was adamant that he had been so ill-treated by Charles that he could not, in honour, avoid war. A few days later, Henri II of Navarre took Spanish Upper Navarre with French troops. The English envoys hoped this would satisfy François – evening the score with Charles, who had taken a castle in French Burgundy. But François advanced, sending armies into Luxembourg and Alsace. François sent a long list of his grievances against Charles to Henry. In the main, these consisted of Charles's failure to do homage for Flanders and Artois as Duke of Burgundy; failure to pay the sums due under the Treaty of Noyon; interference with French subjects and shipping, and, at the end of the list, Charles's plans to marry Mary – not, François added, that he believed that Henry would co-operate with such a scheme.

Both Charles and François agreed to accept mediation, but the loss of Upper Navarre gave Charles second thoughts. Instead, he demanded assistance from Henry in accordance with the treaties of 1516 and 1518. A bitter war of words ensued as François and Charles began to arm.

Meanwhile, in Hungary, King Louis (Charles's brother-in-law) was desperate for aid as the Turks prepared to attack Belgrade, Transylvania,

Croatia and Poland. He could not hope for help from Charles while the emperor and François were at loggerheads, but hoped for something from Henry.

Wolsey wrote to the king that he had met and 'felt the minds' of Charles's delegates regarding a marriage to Mary and Henry's other demands, which consisted of an indemnity against the potential loss to Henry of the dower still paid to his sister, Mary, the French queen, and the annual French pension. The delegates were keen for the marriage but protested they would not buy friendship with money, especially as Henry was already bound by treaty to support Charles in the face of French aggression. Consistent with this, Henry began to prepare for military support for the emperor.

Wolsey, with other members of Henry's Privy Council, travelled to Calais to conduct the mediation between the Imperialists and the pope's representatives on one side and the French and Venetians on the other. Wolsey sought a truce, while the French wanted a peace, and Charles probably did not want either, as in Italy his troops were advancing on Milan. It was anticipated the city would fall to Charles, and the French be driven out. Wolsey remained in constant communication with Henry, who sent his approval to matters as they were being conducted – he was particularly pleased that Charles's ambassadors had shown themselves so 'desirous' of the marriage with Mary. He was also glad to have received evidence France had been the aggressor, enabling him to break off Mary's betrothal to the dauphin without breaking his word. From Mary's perspective, whichever of the two protagonists eventually emerged the victor, her future was bright as queen of France, or empress. She would not have been the first English princess to be empress – three of her predecessors had enjoyed that exalted status – Matilda, daughter of Henry I, who was the only previous woman to have been acknowledged as heir to the English throne; Matilda, daughter of Henry II and Eleanor of Aquitaine, and Isabella, daughter of King John.

After several weeks of fruitless talks, Charles requested the cardinal to hasten to Bruges; he was ready to join his army and had only delayed for the negotiations. He was sure a personal meeting would resolve more in a day or two, than weeks of negotiation via ambassadors. Wolsey announced to the French that he would go in person to request Charles to agree to a truce or peace and asked the French to await his return; adding that if Charles were not amenable, Henry would declare his support for François. The French were deeply suspicious, but there was little they could do.

On 16 August 1521, Charles commissioned his aunt Marguerite and her chancellor, Berghes, to treat for a marriage with Mary, to include various terms for war with François and the indemnity Henry required for the loss of his income from France. At this point, another stipulation was introduced by the Imperial Chancellor – Mary was to be sent to the emperor when she reached the age of seven (February 1523), to be brought up at his court. This, Wolsey informed Henry, he had emphatically rejected. If she were sent to Charles before reaching marriageable age, anything might happen – violation, disparagement (i.e. marriage against her will to a person of inferior rank, rather than to Charles) or repudiation and humiliation. Such an idea could only be countenanced if Flanders were to be handed over to Henry as security, with the troops Henry would need to hold it, employed at Charles's expense. Unsurprisingly, this idea found little favour.

Argument continued over Mary's jointure and dower. Charles requested a larger dowry, citing the million ducats (*c.* £250,000) being offered with Isabella of Portugal, but Wolsey believed that the production of the £100,000 England was offering in ready cash would ease the discussions, and suggested that Henry start gathering it.

The French were continuing with their preparations for a further invasion of Navarre. This put the Imperial camp in a quandary; they did not wish to declare open war on France, without English support. If, however, Henry made his declaration in the Imperial favour, the proposed marriage with Mary would come out and not only aggravate Charles's Spanish subjects, who wanted the match with Portugal, but also show him to be breach of the Treaty of Noyon. Charles decided to do no more outwardly than announce he was returning to Spain. A secret treaty, that of Bruges, was agreed on 25 August 1521, in which it was agreed that Charles would visit England en route, while Henry's fleet scoured the Channel for French shipping. A joint declaration of war on France would be made by the Empire, the pope, and Henry, by March 1523, and, in the meantime, Henry would offer Charles 6,000 troops. The treaty would need papal approval and Leo would have to grant the necessary dispensations for Mary and Charles to marry.

Meanwhile, back in Calais, the French delegates were becoming restive and pressing for Wolsey's return. Arriving at the end of August, Wolsey assured the French that both Henry and he were very inclined to the French alliance, to the extent the English people, who favoured Flanders, disliked him. Wolsey also attempted to calm their fears that the requests of a number of English scholars in France to return home boded ill – especially with the rumours of Henry arming a fleet. Wolsey replied that Henry was arming only for the defence of his own realm and the students just wanted to visit their families. While still in Calais, Wolsey received a letter from Henry's secretary, Richard Pace. Henry was intending to go to Easthampstead, where there was no suitable lodging for the princess, and the king wished for Wolsey's advice on the matter. He also wanted some suggestions on who might be appointed as lady governess to replace Lady Salisbury. There were several candidates for the role. Henry himself thought of 'old' Lady Oxford, or else Jane, Lady Calthorpe, with her husband, Sir Philip as chamberlain. Lady de Vere was another possibility. She was suitably mature and discreet, and could be tried 'for a season'. The Calthorpes were chosen and entered the service of the princess at a fee of £40 per annum.

Having disposed of this minor domestic detail, Wolsey turned his attention back to the arbitration. By 3 September he became aware the French were planning to give battle to the emperor within a fortnight. Wolsey was sanguine that if the French won, they would be so exhausted by the battle they would be easy prey for the English, or if they lost, then Henry could enter France as Charles's ally. Henry was delighted with Wolsey's negotiations, only adding that instead of the 6,000 men promised to Charles he would provide an additional 4,000 at Charles's expense and lend him some gunpowder.

Eventually, on 11 October, the single achievement of the Calais conference was agreed. English subjects were to have free traffic in the seas, and fisherman of all nationalities were to be protected when in English waters. The following month, Charles and his allies retook Milan and instituted Francesco Sforza as duke, while far off in Hungary, King Louis, receiving no support from his fellow Christian kings, saw his city of Belgrade fall to the Turks.

***

In December 1521 the balance of European relationships was upset by another event in Mary's extended family when Manuel of Portugal died. With his death, the Castilian Cortes were concerned that Charles's right to the throne would be challenged by the Portuguese claimant, Juana La Beltraneja. To reaffirm the Portuguese alliance was their priority, Charles immediately sent commissions to his ambassador in Lisbon to negotiate possible matches. His envoy was given strict instructions that nothing was to come to the ears of Henry or Wolsey. Manuel had a son, now João III, and daughters, Beatriz and Isabella, already talked of as a wife for Charles. The most immediate result was the marriage of Charles's sister, Catherine of Austria, to João.

Mary was oblivious of the manoeuvring in Europe and her status as one of many negotiating points, spending most of 1521 at Ditton, although she made several visits in the autumn to her parents at Richmond. She spent the Christmas of 1521 and New Year of 1522 at Ditton, under the supervision of Sir Philip and Lady Calthorpe. She received the usual New Year gifts – from her father a silver standing cup, a gold salt from the cardinal and a gold cross from Katherine of York. Rather more practically, Sir Richard Weston gave her twelve pairs of shoes. All the usual feasting and festivities were celebrated, led by John Thoroughgood who, as Lord of Misrule, was paid the fine fee of 40s. There was a boar's head, festooned by a decorator specially brought from Windsor. Three boars 'furious and fell' were purchased at 9s 6d each, either for hunting or consumption. A play was acted, the props for which – clattering staves, marlinspikes, gunpowder and gunners, tambourines and bells – suggest a mock naval battle.

The year 1522 continued much as 1521 had ended – François was aware of rumours of a marriage between Mary and Charles, which Henry's envoy, FitzWilliam, categorically denied, probably unaware himself of the truth of the matter. François accepted the disclaimer, observing there was no better match for Mary than his own son – which, from the point of view of age, was certainly true. Not long afterwards, in late February, François formally confiscated the county of Flanders from Charles, who was, technically, his vassal. He followed this up with a demand to Henry for aid against Charles, who had broken the treaties by aiding François' rebels in Milan.

Charles's ambassador, Lachaulx, and his colleagues visited London in February and March. After an initial briefing with Wolsey about how to handle the French, they were taken to Henry in his private oratory at Greenwich, where the usual compliments were exchanged. They were joined by Boleyn, bringing news from Flanders that the French had invaded part of Marguerite's territory. Henry agreed to send stern letters to François, before adjourning the meeting to take part in a tourney. After dinner, the envoys met Katharine and Mary. The queen asked affectionately after her nephew. Mary, aged six, questioned Lachaulx 'not less sweetly than prudently' about her new betrothed. The 'charms' of the little princess were paraded, and the ambassadors were informed that she was wearing a golden brooch, with the words 'the emperor' picked out in jewels because she had drawn him as her valentine. A few days later, the envoys returned to Greenwich to take leave. After further conversation with the king, Suffolk took them to Katharine and Mary. Katharine again spoke of her affection for Charles and her desire to see him, and followed it up by asking Mary to dance for the company. Mary did not need asking twice. She performed a slow dance and 'twirled so prettily that no woman in the world could do it better', then a galliard. After that, she played on the spinet and

> showed such unbelievable grace and skill and such self-command as a woman of twenty might envy. She is pretty and very tall for age, just turned seven [she was only six, in fact] and a very fine young cousin indeed.

Mary's father was extremely tall, taking after his Yorkist forbears, while her mother was short. In later life, Mary was not considered tall, so she may have just had a growth spurt. In another letter, Lachaulx again praised Mary's musical skill.[12]

In May 1522, in accordance with the Treaty of Bruges, Charles visited England. Unlike his first informal visit two years before, this was a grand state occasion in which Mary played a part. The emperor's visit was the most splendid occasion, in England, of Henry's reign. It was the Anglo-Imperial equivalent of the Field of Cloth of Gold, and marked the high point of the friendship between Mary's maternal kin and her father. The trip was organised down to the most minute detail. The emperor was met at Gravelines on 25 May by his English escort of nobles and Calais officers, led by the Marquis of Dorset, and accompanied to Calais. Once Charles was through the gates, and had heard the Bishop of Exeter's welcome speech, the mayor and Staple of Calais were introduced to him. These dignitaries had been encouraged to bring gifts of seasonal food and wine, wax and spices. In Charles's train were numerous great lords from all over his territories, including the Count of Nassau, the Duke of Cleves, (whose seven-year-old daughter, Anne, would one day be Henry's fourth wife) the Duke of Alba from Spain, the Marquis of Brandenburg and his wife, Germaine de Foix, who was also Charles's and Mary's step-grandmother, and rumoured to have been Charles's mistress. He had his 'grande chapelle' of priests and choir, and his 'petite chapelle', his councils of Castile, Aragon and Flanders, his gentlemen and his household, including cooks, a sommelier, fruiterers and sauciers. Eight trumpeters, a tambourer and several pipers announced his comings and goings and his doctors were on hand to care for his health, while his launderers, barbers and linen-keepers looked after his more personal needs. Initially, his retinue was numbered at 2,044 people with 1,127 horse, but, on reflection, Charles limited the number to a mere thousand. The emperor and his suite crossed the English Channel, arriving at Dover at four o'clock in the afternoon of 27 May. They were met by Wolsey, the Duke of Suffolk and some forty other nobles, prelates and court gentlemen, as well as gentlemen of Kent and Sussex. The honoured guest was conducted to Dover Castle, which had been prepared by the Comptroller of the King's Household. Once the emperor's retinue and baggage had been landed, he was supposed to move from Dover towards Canterbury Castle while Henry was to ride out from Canterbury to meet him, accompanied by another powdering of nobles, headed by the Duke of Norfolk, the Bishop of Durham, seven earls and numerous lesser mortals. The royal party would then turn back towards Canterbury, to be met outside the gates by the mayor and burgesses. A suitably 'discreet and eloquent' personage was to make a speech of welcome. In the event, Charles's baggage took so long to arrive that he remained at Dover and Henry came to him there, arriving on the 28 May. The following day, Henry had the pleasure of showing Charles his great ship, the *Henry Grace à Dieu* and the various other vessels that lay in Dover Roads, preparing for an attack on France, in accordance with the Treaty of Bruges. On the same day, Henry and his council sent Clarencieux King of Arms to France to declare that Henry believed François to have been the aggressor in the conflict with the emperor, and therefore, in accordance with the Treaty of London, he would support Charles. In addition, François had broken the treaty by allowing the Duke of Albany to return to Scotland, and withholding the pension due to England.

On 30 May, the party departed for Canterbury, spending only a day there, rather than the four originally planned. Once inside the city gates, Charles saw the massed ranks of the English clergy on either side of the street as he rode on Henry's right hand (the place of honour) to Christ Church, Canterbury, to be greeted by Archbishop Warham. Offerings were given by both monarchs at the tomb of St Thomas Becket – one of the premier pilgrimage destinations in Europe. That evening, Charles slept in the archbishop's palace, while Henry retired to the monastery of St Augustine. Over the next few days, the two monarchs travelled from Canterbury to Sittingbourne, Rochester and Gravesend, staying at inns en route. At Gravesend, they were met by the 'gorgeously apparelled' barges of the king and other nobles. Charles's suite required thirty barges to convey it to Greenwich. All the remaining craft between Gravesend and Greenwich were anchored along the route, with banners and streamers, and sufficient ordinance to salute the emperor as he passed. They arrived at Greenwich around 6 p.m. on 2 June. Waiting at the palace door were Katharine and Mary. Charles knelt in front of his aunt to ask her blessing. What six-year-old Mary's first impression of her cousin, and betrothed were, we cannot know, but she knew he was her intended husband and she must have looked at him with great curiosity.

While at Greenwich, the emperor was lodged in Henry's own apartments and was entertained royally at Henry's cost. Vast quantities of supplies were ordered, many merchants requiring something to be paid on account, as the royal household was not always prompt in paying its bills. An allowance or 'plat' was made for each individual. This included bread to eat, as well as for trenchers; torches and other lighting materials; red and white wine; fruit, to include apples and pears; a quarter of beef and a couple of sheep; two lambs; twenty-four pullets and an equal number of pigeons; six couple of rabbit or hare; half a veal; quail and partridge or other wildfowl depending on what was available; various other meats; condiments of salt, vinegar, olive oil, verjuice, butter, eggs; spices; sugar; oranges; lemons; olives and capers; wood and coal. For fish days (Wednesdays, Fridays and Saturdays) the meat was replaced with a vast quantity of seafood – sole, salmon, crab, carp, turbot, mullet and more. For Henry's purveyors, the biggest problem was providing enough wine. There were eleven wine merchants in the whole of London, and around thirty taverns that stocked wine. In total, 809 pipes of wine were available. A pipe is usually measured as 1,008 pints, so if Henry's purveyors bought up the whole stock, they would have had 815,472 pints of wine available, equating to about 627,300 modern bottles.

The entertainment continued with a joust held on the 3 June at which Henry and the Earl of Devon led one team, while the Duke of Suffolk and the Marquis of Dorset led the other. Henry's squad wore cloth of gold and silver, with embroidered letters, and Suffolk's men were dressed in russet velvet with gold knots. Charles and Katharine watched from the stands as the two teams first ran at each other singly, and then en masse. Since the chronicle does not mention the winner, we may perhaps infer that Suffolk's team had the victory on this occasion! No mention is made of whether Mary attended. A precedent for her presence throughout is that of her aunt Margaret, later Queen of Scots, who, then aged five, had presented the jousting prizes when Henry had been created Duke of York in 1494. After the joust, the emperor watched the ladies dance, before they were joined by six masked gentlemen in crimson velvet, followed by six more, in long gowns of cloth of gold, among whom were Henry, Suffolk and the Count of Nassau. Not sufficiently exhausted by the jousting, the following day, a tourney was arranged. As Henry was arming, he received a letter from his ambassador in France, Sir Thomas Cheyne, informing him that François denied all of Henry's allegations and saying he had withheld Henry's pension as he had suspected Henry was preparing to use it to make war on him. Henry immediately sent Sir William Compton to let Charles know, and to request his presence. They read the letter over with great excitement, before proceeding to the tourney, in which Charles as well as Henry took part. That evening, another dance was performed by the ladies and gentlemen of the court in front of Henry, Katharine and Charles.

On Friday 6 June, Henry and Charles made a splendid entry into the City of London. The mayor, John Milburn, and his Aldermen had been frantically preparing; finding lodgings in the city for the emperor's suite as well as food and wine was no easy task. A mile outside the city gates, a tent had been set up where the emperor and king rested while the procession formed – and a grand spectacle it must have been. Riding side by side, Henry and Charles were followed by their nobles and households, decked in velvet and cloth of silver. The welcome speech was made by Sir Thomas More. As the procession rode past the prisons of the Marshalsea and the King's Bench, Henry graciously acceded to Charles's request for prisoners to be freed. Tableaux and pageants lined the streets, including one in which Charlemagne gave the sword of Justice to the emperor, and the sword of Triumphant Victory to Henry. Another, which had been arranged by the Italian merchants, showed Edward III and his son, John of Gaunt, Duke of Lancaster, with a structure representing a tree. In the branches were hung some fifty-five images of kings, queens and nobles, with representations of Henry, Katharine and Charles at the top, showing their common descent from the House of Lancaster.

A similar pageant showed them all descended from Alfonso the Wise, King of Castile. There were scenes from King Arthur and the Knights of the Round Table, and representations of the stars and planets. Eventually, they reached St Paul's, where Archbishop Warham met them, and they made offerings at the altar. Charles was lodged in the monastery at Blackfriars, while his retinue was housed in Henry's new palace of Bridewell. A gallery had been constructed between the two, hung with arras. Saturday was devoted to tennis. Sunday, being Whitsunday, the monarchs went in solemn procession, dressed alike in white and silver, to St Paul's, where Wolsey conducted Mass. The emperor's men were disgusted by Wolsey's pride; when he came to the washing of hands, he was waited on by two dukes. After dinner in Bridewell Palace, they went on to Westminster, where Charles was impressed by the size of Westminster Hall. Henry VII's chapel was also part of the tour. On Monday, Henry and Charles were the guests of the Duke of Suffolk at Southwark. No mention is made of whether the queen and the French queen were present, but presumably they were, and perhaps Mary, too. Charles had once been betrothed to the French queen, who was considered one of the most beautiful princesses of her generation – perhaps he speculated on the difference between the attractive twenty-seven year old who could have been his wife, and the six-year-old child to whom he was now betrothed.

Hunting formed the major part of the entertainment over the next few days as the party, except Mary, who remained at Greenwich, moved to Richmond, and thence to Hampton Court where they were entertained by Wolsey. The next stop was Windsor where three or four days of work followed, with the monarchs and their councils discussing detailed terms for the treaties. After all was agreed, Charles took part in a Garter ceremony, wearing his robe and sitting in his own stall. He gave the heralds the impressive tip of 200 crowns. Henry and Charles then took the sacrament and swore to the treaty between them – it must have seemed certain to Henry that by this Treaty of Windsor, one day his daughter would be empress, and perhaps his grandson would be emperor. It was not his ideal – a son of his own would have been preferable, but it was not a consolation prize to be sniffed at. The dowry was finally fixed at 400,000 crowns, against which Charles's and Maximilian's debts to England were to be set. In theory, a further 600,000 crowns would be due if Henry subsequently had a male heir, but Charles agreed it would never be demanded. It was merely for public consumption in Spain, to equate Mary's dowry with that of Isabella of Portugal. Mary was to receive the same jointure as Margaret of York, sister of Edward IV, had received on her marriage to Charles the Bold, Duke of Burgundy, with the exception of the town of Mechelin, which had been granted to Archduchess Marguerite for life. War was to be prosecuted jointly against France before May 1524 – an extension to the original date of 1523. Charles was also to compensate

Henry annually for his loss of the French pension. Despite all this show, the Archduke Ferdinand's ambassador at Charles's court wrote home that not only the food, but the weather, the roads, and the English jousts were atrocious, and that he did not believe for a moment that Charles would marry Mary.[13] His sourness may have been caused by the emperor telling him not to request help for Ferdinand against the Turks, while Katharine had been 'not at all gracious', when he had put the request to her. The war of words with France intensified, with the French sending challenges to the garrison at Calais, and Henry and Charles penning a joint missive to the Duke of Lorraine, who, although a subject of the Empire, was allied with France.

Mary was sent for to bid her betrothed goodbye at Windsor. Ferdinand's ambassador was more positive about her than about anything else he had seen: 'She promises to become a handsome lady, although it is difficult to form an idea of her beauty, as she is still so small.'[14]

From Windsor, Charles headed for Southampton, hunting all the way. At the end of June, thirty English ships departed, with instructions to scour the seas for enemy vessels to safeguard Charles's journey to Spain. The emperor sailed on 6 July, accompanied by the Spanish navy, comprising more than 100 vessels, having borrowed another 150,000 gold crowns from Henry, repayable in a year.

Life for the budding empress continued in its usual routine for the rest of 1522 and 1523. After her father and her betrothed had left, Mary stayed a few days at Windsor with her mother, before returning to Ditton. She was back at Windsor in August, hunting in the park and 5s was paid to John Wylde, son of a local forester, for bringing bread and ale for the princess and her party. As well as hunting, Mary was learning falconry and she received the present of a goshawk from Henry. It was delivered by one of Katharine's footmen, suggesting she and Henry had conferred over the gift. Lord Bergavenny sent Mary a horse although, being only six, she still travelled mainly by litter, carried by two horses. Later in the autumn, she was back at Richmond with Henry and Katharine.

An inventory of Mary's possessions was taken in late 1523. Among the usual household gear, the most interesting items are the tapestries. Tapestry was enormously expensive, the prerogative of the highest ranks. Mary had several dozen pieces of assorted sizes, with scenes from the Old Testament and the New, and from the Greek myths: there were six pieces from the Labours of Hercules, four telling the story of Alexander and four of the Passion of Christ. There were also numerous pieces with the arms of Buckingham; indicating that some of the hoard may have come from his properties. She also had two cloths of estate, one of gold tissue and the other of crimson velvet. There were numerous counterpanes (bedspreads) including one of crimson satin embroidered with lions, falcons and harts and quantities of cushions, valances and testers.

3

Princess of Wales

... as to so great a Princess doth appertain.

Instructions for Mary's household in Wales

The period from July 1522 to early 1525 was one of changing alliances and fraught negotiations as Charles and François continued their war for domination of Italy. Henry, despite his earlier protestations of brotherhood with François, still harboured ambitions to conquer at least some, if not all, of France, emulating his predecessor, Henry V. He could not hope to achieve his dream without Imperial help. But Charles was far more interested in Italy, and regaining the parts of Burgundy lost when Louis XI had refused to recognise Charles's grandmother, Mary of Burgundy, as his vassal for lands held from the French crown. François, on the other hand, wanted to be on good terms with Henry, so he could safely cross the Alps, without an English army appearing as soon as he was out of the way. If François could not be assured of Henry's friendship, he would stir the pot in Scotland to keep Henry occupied in the Anglo-Scottish border. Queen Margaret sought to counter François' actions by promoting a marriage between Mary and her son, the young King James. Meanwhile, Charles was desperate to marry. He was short of cash and needed a regent in Spain while he dealt with the Empire and Italy. This requirement for an adult spouse and the Spanish council's concerns about the Portuguese alliance made Isabella of Portugal, with her 1 million ducat dowry, the ideal candidate. But Charles did not want to push Henry into the French camp, and continued to behave as though he intended to marry Mary, requesting news from Wolsey about his *meaulx aimée future Imperatrix* (well-beloved future empress). As these rivalries played out, Henry, ably assisted by Wolsey, sought to use his one bargaining chip to greatest effect in negotiations with Charles, François and James, and Mary was half-promised to all of them.

In 1523, a multi-pronged attack on France was agreed. Henry was to cross the Channel, while François' vassal, the Duke of Bourbon, who had defected to Charles, attempted the east and a third front was opened in Navarre. The campaigns were a failure. Henry's troops, under the Duke of Suffolk, had some success, but there was insufficient money or manpower in England seriously to threaten the French crown. Henry was forced to withdraw. This freed the French king to send a large force under the Duke of Albany to threaten Spanish Naples, while he himself encamped outside Milan.

In spring 1524, Henry, still hoping for the marriage of Mary and Charles, requested Rome for a dispensation for their union. Shortly after, Louise of Savoy suggested the marriage to the dauphin be resurrected, while Charles should marry one of François' daughters. Charles was not yet ready to break off the alliance with England, and sent another ambassador with specific orders to see Mary. Henry and Katharine refused – Mary was not at Greenwich, but was in the country to avoid the pestilence. They assured him she was in good health, and promised to be tall, while Henry added she now played the spinet better than he did, and was learning to play the lute.

By July 1524, it was rumoured England and France were at peace and Mary would shortly be married to the dauphin, who would be crowned in his father's lifetime, in accordance with the ancient French custom. With the death of Queen Claude in that month, François himself became a prospective bridegroom. Margaret of Scotland wrote to Henry, in September 1524, that the best way to prevent an alliance between France and Scotland would be for twelve-year-old King James to marry Mary. In Margaret's opinion, the commons of Scotland were more inclined to alliance with England than with France. The lords, although favouring France, would abandon that alliance if they could be sure of a marriage between Mary and James. Henry reiterated that Mary was already promised to Charles, and he could do nothing in the matter unless he were discharged of that promise. It is not clear Henry ever had any intention of agreeing a match with Scotland – the overtures seem all to have been on the Scottish side. All his ambassadors would promise was that James would be the preferred choice of husband for the princess if he 'used himself favourably' towards his uncle, and she did not marry the emperor. Charles, hearing the rumours of a match with Scotland, sent instructions to his ambassador, Louis de Praet, to request that Mary be sent immediately to Spain:

> As the said Princess, our future wife and Queen, is fast approaching the age of puberty, she might, after … [a proxy marriage] … come to our kingdom, and live among our subjects, whereby our mutual love and affection would be fostered and greatly increased.[2]

Charles thought this request would force Henry to declare his hand regarding marrying Mary either to Charles himself, or to James. The English response was not only that Mary was too young, but the English people looked upon her as 'the treasure of the kingdom', and the emperor could give no hostages to be sufficient surety for her. The Venetians were certain Henry did not mean Mary to marry outside the realm at all. Their ambassador to the emperor told him that she was used as an owl might be used for bait – to lure the other birds. Charles laughed at the analogy, but did not disagree.[3]

On 24 February 1525, Charles's army, under Viceroy Lannoy, won a resounding victory over the French at the Battle of Pavia, giving him control of Italy and also of François, captured on the field. Henry was overjoyed to hear of his ally's success, and a vision of the crown of France danced before him. There was the slight awkwardness of his flirtations with France and Scotland to be overcome, but Henry and Katharine were both eager to pursue the marriage between Mary and Charles as vigorously as possible. Katharine wrote her own congratulations to Charles on his victory and reminded him of his alliance with Henry:

> As the king, my husband and master, has never failed to be the constant and faithful ally of your Highness – as his words and deeds have sufficiently attested on every occasion – and as from the continuance of such friendship and alliance the best results may be anticipated, I humbly beseech your Highness to persevere in the path of friendship and affection ...
>
> Your good aunt, Katerina.[4]

Mary was again shown off to the emperor's envoys, in the presence of both the king and queen. They addressed her in Latin and she replied in the same language with 'as much facility as if she were twelve years old'.[5] Charles's victory, although impressive, was rather awkward. Despite his long-running disputes with France, he had no idea of getting involved in the impossible task of trying to conquer the country in its entirety. Louise of Savoy was urgent in her requests for a peace settlement and, hampered by an empty treasury, Charles was willing to negotiate, although Marguerite of Austria was instructed to let Henry have men and arms in Flanders at Henry's own cost if he wanted to prosecute the war himself. While Henry was excited about the prospect of at last being declared King of France, he, like Charles, was short of the actual cash needed to fund an army. With no hope of Parliament agreeing to further taxation after the subsidy of 1523, Wolsey hit upon the idea of an 'Amicable Grant'. Unfortunately, many of Henry's subjects were feeling anything but amicable and the collection had to be cancelled amid rioting and widespread discontent.

A direct embassy to Charles, in the shape of Tunstall of Durham, Sir Richard Wingfield and Dr Sampson, departed for Spain. They were to suggest that François be deposed and Henry acknowledged as King of France, although he was willing to accept a reduction in the size of the country in favour of Charles and Bourbon. Henry would like to have Normandy, Gascony, Guienne, Picardy and Brittany returned to England or, at the very least Picardy, plus the annual pension of 100,000 crowns that France owed England. Aware that actually deposing François might prove difficult, Henry was willing to offer 200,000 crowns and personally support an invasion, as well as accompanying Charles to Rome for his coronation as emperor, by which, with his marriage to Mary, Charles would become master of all Europe. Any rumours that Charles brought up about English negotiations with France or Scotland for Mary's marriage were to be met with the answer that Henry had rejected all such overtures. The ambassadors were also to suggest that François could be delivered to Henry to hold as a hostage, in exchange for Mary being sent to Charles, with François to be returned on Mary's marriage. As an alternative, Henry and Mary would travel to France, and Mary would be handed over as soon as Henry had been crowned as King of France. Finally, if all this seemed too difficult, Charles was to be asked what towns he would hand over as surety for Mary, if she were to be delivered immediately. Henry could not take the risk of sending his daughter and heir to a foreign prince when she was below marriageable age without some security, but he needed to push the marriage forward before it slipped from his grasp, now that Charles no longer needed him.

The same set of negotiating points was sent to Marguerite of Austria in Flanders, and included requests for advice from Marguerite on the subject of Mary's clothes. Henry wished her to be dressed in the fashion of her new home, and he would provide 'all manner of cloth of every sort' for Marguerite to 'devise for the making thereof in such manner as shall best please her'.[6] In addition to these negotiation points, the English embassy had an emerald to deliver to Charles, in Mary's name. The present was accompanied by a message:

> Her Grace hath devised this token for a better knowledge to be had, when
> God shall send them gace to be together, whether his Majesty do keep
> himself as continent and chaste as with God's grace she woll, whereby ye
> may say his Majesty may see that her assured love towards the same hath
> already such operation in her that it is also confirmed by jealousy, being
> one of the greatest sins and tokens of hearty love and cordial affection.[7]

This was a coded hint that Henry suspected Charles might be planning to abandon Mary for Isabella of Portugal. Charles asked after the king's health, and heard Katharine's congratulations on his victory at Pavia. He smiled at her message and said, 'he had no fear but lest she should combine with France against him' – a penetrating insight into Katharine's character. He slipped the emerald ring that purported to be from Mary onto his little finger, saying he would wear it for her sake and, asking after her health, commented on 'the manifold seeds of virtue that were in her'.[8] The following day, Charles's government got down to brass tacks. His chancellor, Gattinara, informed the English delegation that Charles had spent well over 1.5 million ducats and was heavily in debt. His absence from Spain, and the various rebellions there, had severely damaged his revenues. His council was unlikely to let him leave until Mary had been sent to Spain so she could be a figurehead regent. To further this, he had written to England to request she be sent immediately, to be brought up in the language and customs of the country. This was important, as Charles himself was perceived as a Burgundian and widely resented for his foreignness. The chancellor also asked that Mary's dote of 400,000 be sent with her, to defray the costs of the joint invasion of France. A further contribution of 200,000 crowns was requested to support Bourbon in Provence. Henry's delegation was stunned at these demands. It was quite out of line with the treaties to send Mary at so young an age to a hot country that might not agree with her health. Moreover, her dowry was to have been paid in instalments, with Charles's debts, including the 150,000 crowns he had borrowed when leaving England in May 1522, to be deducted. What would happen, they asked, if Mary or Charles died before the marriage could be effected? Did they really think that Henry would pay for his own share of the invasion, hand over 400,000 crowns and a further 200,000 crowns for Bourbon? They dismissed the talk of French overtures for peace as a ploy to put Charles and Henry off attacking for another campaigning season. They could not believe, they finally added, that the emperor had countenanced these suggestions.

Charles's ministers confirmed that the requests were genuine. They acknowledged they went far beyond the treaty obligations, but necessity obliged Charles to show his need to his 'trusty friend, the King of England'. The Spanish seem genuinely to have been under the impression that Henry had a limitless supply of funds, but he had been spending money like water since his accession and any reserves built up by Henry VII were long gone. The English responded that Flemish support amounted to very little, and Henry would not be happy to bear all the costs of an invasion. These negotiations expose Henry's difficulties. Even if he had had no sons but several daughters, he would have had a stronger hand – he could have let the eldest daughter go to Spain young, with the knowledge that had she died, one of her sisters could have inherited. Or younger sisters could have been offered to the kings of Scotland and France. As it was, his only negotiating tool was also his heir and had to be protected. Although it would have been difficult for Charles to back out of the betrothal in 1525 if Mary had been sent to Spain, it was a risk Henry could not take while she was below marriageable age.

In June 1525 it all began to unravel. The English envoys were informed Charles's subjects wished him to marry Isabella of Portugal with all speed. Although he would prefer to marry the English princess, he would have to take Isabella if Mary could not be sent to Spain immediately, as he was absolutely compelled to travel to Germany to try to stop the spread of Lutheranism. Henry responded that he would be willing to release Charles from the betrothal if peace were only made with France in a way that would satisfy Henry, who had had no profit from the war as yet and Charles repaid all the monies he owed Henry. Charles was genuinely in a quandary. He never attempted to deny his treaty with Henry, or that he owed Henry large sums and consideration for their alliance, but he was being pressed on all sides for money and stability in government. It is probable that if Mary had been five years older, the match would have been concluded, but a nine-year-old still in England could not help him, compared with twenty-two-year-old Isabella, on his doorstep and rolling in cash. Charles, unlike either of his grandfathers, had some scruples about keeping his word and he hoped to be able to marry Isabella with Henry's blessing. Henry's ambassadors observed that if the betrothal came to nothing, at least Henry 'may have with much thank my lady Princess in your hand, which is a pearl worth the keeping'.[9]

Henry, if he had not already begun to despair of Charles's intentions, now undertook a public act in England, which was presumably designed to provoke Charles, although it is not easy to understand his reasoning. On 18 June, he invested his illegitimate son, Henry Fitzroy, with the dukedoms of Richmond and Somerset and set him up with a grand royal household. Prior to this, six-year-old Fitzroy had lived quietly with his mother, Elizabeth Blount, now Lady Tailboys. The choice of dukedoms was significant. Henry VII had been Earl of Richmond, and the dukedom of Somerset had been in the hands of the Beaufort family, through whom Henry VII had claimed the throne. Henry was signalling he had an alternative heir to Mary, but that was hardly likely to have improved his chances of marrying Mary to Charles. Why would the emperor take her if she were not heir to the English crown? Four other investitures were made, including the promotion of Henry Courtenay, Earl of Devon, to be Marquis of Exeter and Sir Thomas Boleyn to be Viscount Rochford.

It has been claimed Richmond was given higher rank than Mary, but none of the existing royal accounts suggest that. Recipients and donors of grants and gifts are listed by rank, and Mary is always with the queen and the French queen. Richmond comes first among the dukes, placed after the Lord Chancellor, but not as part of the royal family. Mary was always joined with Henry, Katharine and Wolsey in presenting official compliments to foreign rulers, while Richmond was not, so there is no evidence that Henry was trying to introduce him abroad as an official member of the royal family at this time.

* * *

By 6 July 1525, Henry's hopes for the Imperial marriage were dead. He gave a commission to the envoys to rescind the treaties of Windsor and London and agree terms for Charles to repay the monies owed. The level of disappointment Henry felt can hardly be imagined – a year before, he had contemplated conquest of a significant proportion of France, with his daughter to be empress, both great consolation prizes for the personal and dynastic disappointment of having no son. Now he had a jilted daughter, and no prospect of further gains in France. Even the back-up plan of a treaty with Scotland had been whipped away from him as Queen Margaret, exasperated by her brother's lack of support, was renewing ties with France, and confirming the Treaty of Rouen by which James was to marry a French princess.

Before the commission to rescind the treaties had arrived in Spain, Tunstall and his colleagues had a final discussion with the Imperialists who asked for Mary to be sent immediately with half her dowry, or the whole dowry over four months, or at least a loan for 400,000 crowns for the invasion of Provence by Bourbon. The ambassadors replied – they even use the term 'begged' – that the emperor's council should consider what they would do in the same situation.

> [Mary] was only child at this time in whom your Highness put the hope of propagation of any posterity of your body, seeing the queen's grace hath been long without child, and albeit God may send her more children, yet she was past that age in which women most commonly are wont to be fruitful and have children.[10]

Besides, at only nine years old, the movement to another country might be injurious to Mary's health. They went on to add that, as for her upbringing,

> If he should seek a mistress for her to frame her after the manner of Spain, and of whom she might take example of virtue, he should not find in all Christendom a more meet than she now hath, that is to say, the queen's grace her mother, who is comen of this house of Spain, and who, for the affection she beareth the emperor, will nourish her and bring her up as may be hereafter to his most contentation.[11]

They pointed out that if either party died before the marriage were completed, Mary would have lost her dote, without having had her dower secured to her. They even gave an example that should have been close to Charles's heart – his aunt Marguerite, at three years old, had been promised to the dauphin of France and sent to France for her upbringing. When she was eleven, in 1491, the match was broken off, so that her betrothed, now Charles VIII, could marry Anne of Brittany. Marguerite was not returned to her father for another two years, during which she lived in a humiliating limbo in France. Even if both Mary and Charles lived, but Henry died, who would look after Mary's rights?

Charles wrote to Ferdinand on 31 July that he was still awaiting English permission for his marriage to Isabella, and had therefore postponed his trip to Italy. Shortly afterwards, to expedite matters by a personal appeal, Charles himself wrote to Henry, explaining his need to marry swiftly.

> If, therefore, I should be obliged to marry (Isabella), I beg you not to take it in bad part, or suffer it to be the cause of our mutual love and affection being lessened ... [12]

In Italy, the pope was frantic. He had supported Charles in his desire to curb French influence in Italy, but, with François now in captivity, it was apparent to Pope Clement that Charles had too much power.[13] He begged Henry to intervene by making peace with François, who should withdraw his Italian claims and work with Henry to expel Charles. Henry would then, tempted Clement, have all Italy at his feet and be able to bestow it as he wished, as its protector and defender. As a plan, this seems to defy all likelihood of fulfilment.

As it became apparent there was little hope of Charles marrying Mary, Henry sought a rapprochement with France – he needed to salvage something from the debacle. Henry called the emperor ungrateful in victory and, in return for restoration of his French pension, plus additional sums payable in his own lifetime and that of his successor, agreed to enter a defensive league with France, to include Scotland. The English informed the French that they believed Mary would be free within six months, and François was to be urged not to rush into a marriage with Charles's sister, Eleanora, the widowed Queen of Portugal, which was being mooted as the price of the French king's release. Henry gave instructions to his ambassadors to dissuade all the parties from a marriage between François and Eleanora – the Imperialists with the argument that it would encourage François to aim at being made emperor, the French that it would be detrimental to their position in Italy, and Louise that it would undermine her own position of authority. If Charles was determined to marry Isabella, then Henry wanted Mary to marry François instead. Rather aggravatingly for Henry's ambassadors in Mechelin, Marguerite of Austria blamed Henry's refusal to send Mary and her dote to Spain immediately for the breaking off of the marriage. Wingfield huffily replied that Henry had not refused to do anything the treaties bound him to. He had been under no obligation to send Mary to Spain at so young an age.

***

By the spring of 1525, Henry had concluded that he and Katharine would have no more children. He thus had two possible heirs – his legitimate daughter, Mary, and his illegitimate son, Henry Fitzroy. While in the early Middle Ages, illegitimacy had not been an insuperable bar to inheritance, by the sixteenth century it was highly unlikely that an illegitimate child would be accepted as sovereign. On the other hand, a daughter would be unlikely to command the respect and support that a son would. Given that there were examples of capable queens and women rulers across Europe, it was not impossible for Mary to be queen, and Henry could have approached the problem by training her as he would have done a son, marrying her early to someone he could keep under his eye, and hoping for a grandson. There were precedents in Europe of women acting as regents for their sons, rather than claiming the crown for themselves, although not in England. Henry hedged his bets. He promoted Fitzroy to royal duchies, but he also gave Mary additional standing, sending her as his representative to preside over the council for the Marches of Wales.

The Marches of Wales were a hazy geographical area stretching along the Anglo-Welsh border where Crown control was weak. The region suffered endemic low-level warfare, characterised by theft, kidnappings, raids and feuds as the penal laws enacted by successive English kings against the Welsh led to misery, and the Marcher lords attacked each other. During the 1470s, Edward IV had set up a council to be based in the Marches to increase Crown authority. Nominally headed by his son, later Edward V, it was known as the Prince's Council. A similar arrangement was made in the 1490s for Henry VII's eldest son, Arthur, Prince of Wales, who spent much of his time in the Marches. On Arthur's untimely death, the council continued its work. Henry, although created Prince of Wales in 1503, was not sent to Ludlow, and, so far as is known, had no involvement with the affairs of the Marches prior to becoming king in 1509.

By the sixteenth century, many of the Marcher lordships had fallen into Crown hands via inheritance – the de Bohun lands to Henry V, and the Mortimer holdings around Ludlow and Wigmore to Edward IV. The execution of Buckingham brought in a great swathe around Chepstow and the Black Mountains – perhaps contributing to Henry's desire to be rid of him. That the Marches were still troublesome during the early years of Henry's reign is reflected in the numerous commissions set up to enquire into rebellions, insurrections and Lollard heresies. By 1525, another solution was sought and in July the Prince's Council was reconstituted as the Princess's Council, with Mary as its head. The council and commissioners were to hold courts of oyer and terminer, administer justice and keep the peace. At nine years old, Mary did not, of course, have any power, but the position enormously enhanced her status. There has been much discussion over whether Mary was officially Princess of Wales. The English title, Prince of Wales, has been held by the eldest son of the king of England since 1301, when Edward I bestowed it on his son, later Edward II. There is a difference between being 'created' Prince of Wales, a declaration by the sovereign confirmed by Letters Patent, and 'investiture', which is a formal ceremony. Henry's elder brother, Arthur, had been both created and invested as Prince of Wales. Henry himself had been created by Letters Patent but was not invested. Years later, Mary's half-brother was referred to as Prince of Wales, but he was neither created nor invested as prince before Henry's death.

Although there was no precedent for creating a woman Princess of Wales, there is nothing to prevent the sovereign bestowing any title by Letters Patent, on either a man or a woman. Edward III had promoted Margaret, Countess of Norfolk, *suo jure*, to duchess, and there would soon be the example of Henry creating Anne Boleyn Marquis of Pembroke. However, Henry neither created Mary as Princess of Wales by Letters Patent, nor invest her with the title.

According to J. L. MacIntosh in *From Heads of Household to Heads of State* Mary was informally referred to by the title because of the institution of the Princess's Council, and because the state with which she was attended implied that she was the king's heir but that there is no official documentation referring to Mary as Princess of Wales. Nevertheless, I would argue Mary's status was more than informal. From mid-1525, government documents do refer to her as Princess of Wales. For example, the grant of the office of Chamberlain of South Wales and the Counties of Carmarthen and Cardigan to Sir Giles Grevile, dated 14 August 1525, refers to him as having been 'in the service of Mary, Princess of Wales'.[14] Similarly, the grant of office to Walter Devereux, Lord Ferrers of Chartley, in 25 May 1526, appointed him to be 'steward in the household of Mary, Princess of Wales and Chamberlain of South Wales, Carmarthen and Cardigan'. There is also a patent of March 1529, granting £10 per annum to Margery Parker, 'servant to the Princess of Wales'. So, while Henry did not issue formal Letters Patent, the title was used in documents and grants, Mary was referred to as Princess of Wales and, by inference, was his heir. Similarly, a despatch from the Imperial ambassador in Rome, the Duke of Sessa, dated 25 August 1525, called her Princess of Wales.[15] Charles, too, used the term in his letters. It was clearly public knowledge that Mary was being sent to the Marches in an official capacity, as Lorenzo Orio, the Venetian envoy, wrote home in early August that,

> On Saturday last, the princess went to her principality of Wales, with a suitable and honourable estcourt, and she will reside there until the time of her marriage. She is a rare person and singularly accomplished, most particularly in music, playing on every instrument, especially on the lute and harpsichord.[16]

Henry did not wish to commit himself to either Mary or to Richmond, but perhaps intended to let events play out and see which option attracted widest support.

As well as the Princess's Council, there was also her household. The two overlapped, but were not identical. In the original appointments, John Vesey, Bishop of Exeter, was appointed as President of the Council, while the Marquis of Dorset was named as Grand Master of the Princess's Household. J. L. MacIntosh argues convincingly that Mary was granted revenues from specific lands to maintain her household. Valuers were sent to assess,

> the lordship of Yale, the king's possessions and hereditaunces whatsoever they bene in the countrys palentyne of Chester, Wales and the Marches of the same and also Bronfielde Yale and Chirckland or elsewhere nowe assigned to the princesse.

Bromfield, Yale and Chirkland had been within Buckingham's lordship – the duke's death was materially, of great benefit to Mary.[17]

Ordinances were drawn up for the governance of Mary herself. The most probable author was Wolsey, but Henry, when he was interested, had an eye for detail, and it is reasonable to assume that in this matter he paid close attention. Whether Katharine's opinions were requested is another question; given the praise bestowed on her in February about the fitness of her example for bringing Mary up, and the fact that king and queen were still on good terms, at least on day-to-day matters, it is likely she was involved. The instructions exemplify the concerns Henry and Katharine had for the welfare of their daughter. Great store was set on the necessity of fresh air and exercise for health. Mary was to walk in 'gardens, sweet and wholesome places'; anything 'noisome or displeasant' was to be kept from her. She was to dance and practise her music as well as to attend to her Latin and French, although not to the extent of weariness, and everything about her was to be 'pure, swete, clene and holesome, and as to so great a princes doeth appertaine'. Her meals were to be served to the accompaniment of 'comfortable, joyous and merry communication, in all honour and vertuous maner'.[18] Mary's female attendants were Margaret, Countess of Salisbury, reinstated as lady governess; Katherine, Countess of Devon, and twelve other ladies. Dr Wootton was dean of the chapel, Dr Fetherstone was schoolmaster and there were two chaplains, and an apothecary. Chester Herald was to take official communications, supported by the pursuivant, Wallingford, and there was a cofferer, a clerk of the closet and various others, amounting in all to some 304 individuals, at a combined annual salary bill of £741 13s 9d.

It does not seem likely that all the appointees were expected to go to Wales: the Marquis of Dorset and the Countess of Devon probably had honorary positions, rather than real roles to play. The ladies who actually accompanied Mary were Lady Salisbury; Lady Katherine Grey, Dorset's daughter, and thus Mary's second cousin; Katherine Montagu, who was probably Lady Salisbury's fourteen-year-old granddaughter; Constance and Elizabeth Pole, probably the wife and daughter of Geoffrey Pole, Lady Salisbury's youngest son. Elizabeth Pole was a child, probably younger than Mary. There was Anne Knyvett, who was probably the daughter of Sir Thomas Knyvett and Muriel Howard. Sir Thomas had been a great favourite with both Henry and Katharine before his loss at sea in 1512, during a battle with the French. As niece of the Duke of Norfolk, Anne Knyvett would certainly be entitled to a place in the princess's household, although she must have been at least four years older than Mary. Next were Mary Dannet, who was to marry Dorset's half-brother, George Medley; Cecily Dabridgecourt (who remained in Mary's service until she died a couple of months before Mary herself) and Anne Rede, probably the niece of Archbishop Warham, who married Giles Greville, Comptroller of Mary's household, and remained in Mary's service when she was queen. There was also Mrs Mary Wycter whose identity cannot even be guessed at and Mrs Petir, about whom nothing is known. There was Mrs Anne Dannet – possibly Anne Elmbridge, the wife of Sir John Dannet. Presumably the two Dannet ladies are linked but it is not clear how. There was also Mrs Anne Darrell, again, there is no certainty about her identity but Katharine had a Lady Darrell in her entourage, and later had a maid-of-honour, Elizabeth Darrell, so there may have been a family connection there. There are two other women in the list, Mrs Parker and Mrs Geynes who were both to be dressed in black damask rather than the black velvet of the other ladies. The most likely candidate for Mrs Parker is the Margery Parker who was appointed as one of Mary's rockers in 1516, but another possibility is one of the daughters of Lord Morley – Jane, Margaret or Katherine. Jane Parker later married George Boleyn, but was always considered to have been a supporter of Katharine and Mary – if she had spent time with the young princess, that may have settled her loyalties. The second sister, Margaret, married Sir John Shelton, Anne Boleyn's cousin, but received gifts from Mary later, suggesting an old friendship.[19]

David Loades suggests in his biography, *Mary Tudor,* that despite Juan Luis Vives' recommendations that girls should have schoolfellows with whom to share lessons, Mary had no childhood companions and was essentially a lonely child.[20] However, if these identifications of her attendants are correct, then she did have young companions, and that is certainly more likely – most royal children did. Henry himself had been brought up with Sir William FitzWilliam, Henry Courtenay and Edward Neville.

The accounts for Mary's old household were made up from 1 October 1524, to 11 August 1525, implying that the new household was formally constituted on 12 August 1525. In a mark of increased rank, the household was to wear Mary's own livery, of green and blue, rather than the standard Tudor green and white. The senior servants received a total of 348¼ yards of blue and green damask. The cloth for the majority of the servants, in the same colours, came to 525 yards, at 4s a yard, with others, including the servants of the ladies and gentlewoman, dressed in cloth of 3s 4d the yard – thus were the distinctions of rank preserved. Sir Philip and Lady Calthorpe shared 12 yards of black velvet for gowns (the loose outer garment worn by men and women). It is not clear how the roles of Lady Salisbury and Lady Calthorpe, who had previously held the position of lady governess, were differentiated.

On 18 August, a large order was given for all the necessary equipment for Mary's new household. It covered everything from the 'true yard of iron, sealed by the standard' for weighing and measuring, to a large washing stool. The Keeper of the Great Wardrobe, Sir Andrew Windsor, received orders to provide appropriate furnishings for the princess's chapel. This included three altars, two pairs of vestments for the high altar, and four pairs for the other two altars, four Mass books, eight corporasses (communion cloths) with their cases, four cushions, two of cloth of gold and two of crimson velvet. He was also to provide a quantity of bedding. Mary had her own riding horse, as well as a litter. A warrant was sent by Bishop Vesey to Sir Andrew Windsor for money to be advanced to James Vaughan, Master of the Horse, to buy palfreys. There was also a warrant for cloth of gold for unspecified purposes. Some additional items were receipted on 17 October 1525 as coming from the Bishop of Coventry and Lichfield (the former President of the Council). They included ordinary household articles such as a pestle and mortar and a bread grater, as well as a rather more sinister item – a chest containing irons for prisoners. The bishop also passed over books and muniments related to land parcels in the Marches.

Ludlow, the official seat of the council was in disrepair, so arrangements were made for works to be done before Mary's arrival. Master Sydnor, who was treasurer of the chamber, was also the princess's surveyor general. He commissioned works from Walter Rogers of Ludlow and his sub-contractors – carpenters, tilers, plumbers and masons – including soldering the lead in the roof above the princess's chamber, necessary in an area where rain is frequent! The work cost £45 17s and 9d, including 10d for a 'potation' for the workmen, which is likely to have endeared their princess to them. There is no direct evidence of Mary living at Ludlow, although the repairs mentioned above, and further works in April 1526, together with the information that in 1531, half of her chapel plate was there, suggest she did.

It is not easy to ascertain Mary's precise whereabouts over the next few years, especially as letters are often not dated with the year and internal evidence sometimes contradicts the order within letter collections. One of the few sources that can be used to give accurate dates is the journal of Prior William Monk, of Worcester Abbey, who noted down the regular visits of Mary to the abbey. In particular, it is unclear when she last saw Katharine, before heading west. There is a letter, usually calendared to July 1525, although it is undated, from Katharine, at Woburn, in which the queen assured her daughter that her own health was 'meetly good', although she was sad because she had not seen Henry or Mary for some time. She was glad to hear Mary was better from some unspecified ailment and to know that Mary would now be taught Latin by Master Fetherstone but she asked that once the schoolmaster had read Mary's work it might be sent on to Katharine, ' ... for it shall be a great comfort to me to see that you keep your Latin and fair writing and all'.[21] Katharine asked to be remembered to Lady Salisbury.

According to a letter from the Bishop of Exeter to Wolsey, Mary was at Woburn during the time of preparation. Exeter recorded his concern that no suitable doctor or apothecary had yet been appointed. One possible candidate had declined, fearing a lack of experience. The problem was solved by the appointment of Doctor Butts. In his letter, Bishop Vesey, either from genuine gratitude or to ingratiate himself with Wolsey, mentioned he had written to the queen's almoner to inform him of how generous Wolsey had been to the princess 'so that Her Majesty and the king may know of it'. If the dating of Katharine's above-mentioned letter is correct, she must have departed Woburn before her daughter's arrival. Mary and her household left Woburn on 15 August for Reading Abbey. They then travelled west, heading for Thornbury Castle in Gloucestershire, possibly via Kingswood Abbey, at Wotton-under-Edge and arriving before 1 September. Exeter wrote to Wolsey,

> Upon my report of your most honourable letters of commendation with daily blessings to the princess' Grace, and manifold labours sustained in expedition of her affairs, she thanked your Grace, saying that you show yourself with continuance unto her a very kind spiritual father, desiring of Almighty God ability partly to deserve the same ...

with other 'loving well-set' words that were a credit to the princess's age, or even that of someone far older. We can perhaps imagine nine-year-old Mary sitting under her cloth of state, Lady Salisbury prompting her as she made formal answers to the letters the bishop read aloud.

Thornbury Castle, once the jewel in the vast lands of the Duke of Buckingham, had been in course of renovation at the time of the duke's execution, the south side completed with 'curious works' and stately lodgings, mainly built of ashlar stone. The east range was the original building and of 'homely' fashion, while the north and west wings were still under construction. The whole was surrounded by gardens and orchards. Lady Salisbury may have sighed at the sight of the magnificent castle – had matters gone otherwise, her daughter, Ursula, would have been mistress of it. As it was, Ursula was merely 'Lady Stafford' and her husband was constantly watched.

Mary and her suite left Thornbury for Gloucester on 12 September 1525 and the detail of her visit to the city was captured in the minute book of the council. It was a day of great moment for the town. The retinue approached the city from the south, to be met at Quoddisley's Green, outside the city wall, by a welcoming committee of the mayor, John Rawlens, the aldermen, and the two sheriffs, William Matthew and Henry French. These dignitaries were dressed in scarlet and were followed by around 100 burgesses of the town, waiting in formation for Mary's approach. When the princess arrived, the dignitaries bowed, without dismounting. They showed her one of the town maces, symbol of their charter rights. After she had admired it, the procession formed up to enter the gates two by two. The town sergeants were at the head, followed by the knights, squires and gentlemen of the locality, then the mayor. Following the mayor, side-by-side with the sergeant-at-arms, was Mary. Behind came all her ladies and gentlemen, then her liveried household servants and officers, followed by the stewards and burgesses of the town. The procession trooped to the town cross where they were met by the clergy in their copes, with ceremonial crosses. Mary, still mounted, kissed the offered cross. Continuing in the same order, they rode along St Edward's Lane to the Benedictine abbey of St Peter, now one of the best examples of mediaeval architecture in England. In the porch were the abbot, swathed in his cope, and his monks. The mayor and aldermen led the way into the abbey, which was a place of pilgrimage for those who wished to venerate the memory of Edward II. Edward, a truly hopeless king, had been murdered after being deposed by his wife, Isabella of France, and her lover, Sir Roger Mortimer; all three of the protagonists in this story being Mary's ancestors. King Edward's son, Edward III, had built a shrine to his father, and there had been attempts to have him canonised. Unsurprisingly, given the record of his reign, this had not come to fruition. The record does not say whether Mary saw the extraordinarily beautiful tomb of Edward II. At the high altar, Mary kissed the cross and offered a purse of gold. After these exertions, she retired to her lodging for the night – probably in the abbot's quarters. On the following day, her servants received her gifts from the city – two fat oxen and twenty fat wethers – 'of the best that might be gotten'. Mary's reception at Gloucester probably reflects the ceremonial that attended her on every step of the journey. Before long, she would have grown used to it, making the loss of it later hard to bear.

In November 1525, Mary's court was at Tewkesbury, preparing for the Christmas season ahead. The Bishop of Exeter was expecting 'a great repair of strangers' for the festivities, and wanted Wolsey's opinion on the purchase or loan from the king of a silver alms dish, shaped like a ship, becoming to Mary's 'high estate'. He was also hoping for spice plates to be sent, and additional musicians – trumpeters and rebecs. He requested further instructions on whether the feast should be celebrated with a lord of misrule and the customary festivities, plays and interludes. Another thorny question was that of gifts – what should Mary's official presents to her parents and to Wolsey consist of?

After Christmas, Mary moved to Tickenhill, high on a hill above the route from Ludlow to the Severn crossing at Bewdley. The manor was probably built by Edward IV and part of the house still remains, behind an elegant Queen Anne façade. Dendrochronology has dated the attic timbers to the 1460s, and it is believed that the original chapel is the room currently used as a drawing room. Outside, the land drops to the east, giving a superb view of the town and river below. In the garden is an enormous oak tree; unfortunately, no dendrochronology has been undertaken on it, but from its size it is certainly possible that the tree was there during Mary's period of residence.[22]

Early in the New Year of 1526, Mary left Tickenhill for Worcester, staying either at the priory itself, or the nearby manor of Battenhall. She remained there at least between St Wulfstan's Day (19 January in the English Church) and Candlemas on 2 February. For the first of these feasts, Prior William More celebrated Mass at the high altar of the abbey and the princess offered 3s 4d in gold. For Candlemas, Mary gave two gold crowns for tapers, and Lady Salisbury gave one. Easter of 1526, which fell on 1 April, was also celebrated at Worcester, with Mary offering a crown of 4s 4d value. As she knelt in the abbey church, did Mary wonder about her predecessor in the Marches, her uncle Arthur, once married to her mother, but now resting in his beautiful chantry, not far from the altar? Or did she take the lessons of King John, one of England's most hated kings, whose bones are also spending eternity in Worcester?

By mid-April 1526, Mary was at Hartlebury Castle, the property of the Bishop of Worcester, but on 3 May, Exeter wrote of his concerns about plague in the area.[23] Lady Salisbury and the council thought it best that none of the councillors who were engaged in listening to the 'suitors thronging the court', should be allowed into Mary's presence for fear of infection. He was worried that if sickness entered Hartlebury, there would be nowhere safe for the princess to go – Tickenhill was infected, and we can infer her other usual residences were also considered dangerous. Perhaps in response to the outbreak of infectious disease, Mary's council received instructions to report on her health monthly, consulting with Mary herself and with Lady Salisbury, as necessary. In August, she was in Worcester and attended the Assumption Day Mass in the abbey on 15 August, offering 3s 4d again. From Worcester, Mary returned to the southeast to see her parents. Henry intended to meet her en route. He himself (probably with Katharine, although she is not mentioned specifically) had been at Lady Salisbury's castle at Warblington and at Winchester, where he had had 'great cheer'. He was angry, however, that while at Warblington, he had received a letter from the Duke of Suffolk, warning of deaths from plague at Woodstock. FitzWilliam was obliged to write to Suffolk that the king 'marvelled' that Suffolk had not thought fit to leave Woodstock and inform the king immediately, as he was now not sure where he should go to avoid contagion and 'had lost the opportunity of seeing his daughter'.

There are the first hints of Henry's dissatisfaction with Wolsey creeping into correspondence in the late summer of 1526. Following FitzWilliam's letter, Dr Knight wrote to Wolsey that when he (Knight) had suggested Henry might want to change his travel arrangements to be closer to Wolsey, the king had replied that 'he did not see great cause why he should alter his progress', as his intention was to see Mary. Matters were rearranged so that Henry and Mary met at Langley in Oxfordshire. Dr Sampson wrote to Wolsey that:

> My lady Princess came hither on Saturday; surely, sir, of her age, as goodly a child as ever I have seen and of as good gesture and countenance ... Her Grace was not only well accompanied with a goodly number, but also with diverse persons of gravity ... I saw not the court, sir, better furnished with sage personages many days than now.[24]

Together, Henry and Mary travelled on to Bicester, Buckingham and Ampthill, departing Ampthill on 1 October with Mary returning to Hartlebury. She wrote a letter of thanks to Wolsey, referring to her 'supreme delight' in being able to spend a month with her parents and regretting that she had not had the opportunity of seeing him.[25] The formal letter to Wolsey is the only one that exists giving any insight into Mary's feelings about her life in the Marches. It suggests she missed her parents but, that aside, her time there is likely to have been happy. Lady Salisbury cared deeply for her, and she was the centre of attention both in her own home and among the many who 'repaired' to her household. Her studies progressed well, and the regular life was good for her health.

Although Mary was not yet eleven, she was already subject to the relentless requests for favours and preferments that were a feature of the Tudor court. Ralph Brereton wrote to his brother, William, a groom in the privy chamber, that if William wanted to be granted various offices, he needed to get his warrant signed by the king quickly, as Sir Ralph Egerton, Treasurer of the Princess's Household, was travelling to London with her. Ralph knew Egerton wanted the offices in question and William was advised to make suit to the Lady Princess as well as to the Bishop of Exeter and the rest of her council. Ralph Brereton added that Mary had given a warrant to her secretary, John Russell, for a buck from Shotwick Park in Cheshire.

> Perceives that the lady Princess has, by the king's placard, authority to kill or give deer at her pleasure in any forest or park *within the room that is appointed to her*; and so, if her warrants are not served, displeasure will ensue.[26]

The word 'room' equates to the modern idea of role or office, supporting the idea that she was perceived as Princess of Wales.

4

Queen, Dauphine or Duchess?

... his daughter, the pearl of the world ...
Dr Clerk, English ambassador to France

While Mary was busy in the Marches, studying diligently, practising her music and exercising regularly, the see-saw of diplomacy between France and the Empire continued. By early 1526, Charles had forced François to sign the Treaty of Madrid. Under its terms, François was freed on condition that he marry Charles's sister, Eleonora, and hand over his two oldest sons, the dauphin and the Duke of Orléans, as hostages. In February, the exchange was completed by two boats, one containing the king and the other the boys, crossing the river at Fontarabia. The craft met in the middle to allow the father to embrace his sons – François would not see them again for five long years. The pope and the other Italian states were now nervous about the ascendancy of Charles, who was using every means possible to raise money from the defeated territories to pay his armies. Even the Duke of Milan was having second thoughts about his former ally, and by July 1526, Milan, Venice and Clement VII were concluding the League of Cognac, which would ally with France to drive out the Imperialists. Henry declined to join, but was named as the League's protector.

Money was short. Wolsey began a crackdown on expenses, drawing up the Eltham Ordinances, to save money in the king's household as well as ensure it ran in more seemly fashion, purged of 'rascals and vagabonds'. Dogs, too, were banished, other than 'a few spaniels for the ladies', as were ferrets. It is delightful to imagine the Duke of Norfolk keeping a pet ferret! Financial problems were exacerbated when the emperor failed to repay Henry the vast sums of money he owed. Charles's advisors divided the debts into three categories – first, money he admitted he had borrowed personally; second, money borrowed by his predecessors, which required 'further proofs'; and third, the monies that Henry felt he ought to receive for the lost effort in gathering an army and preparing to invade France in pursuit of the treaties between the countries. Henry's new ambassador, Edward Lee, pressed for payment but met the usual stonewalling tactics of those who either cannot or will not pay their debts – the money was not really owed, it would be sent in due course, they must check with their master, and so on. Lee was particularly annoyed that some four years before, Charles had raised money from the Castilian Cortes on the understanding that it was to repay Henry but had not used it for that purpose. On this being denied, the exasperated Lee waved the printed Act in the chancellor's face 'so I run in an endless circle from one to another, without any answer, which nothing soundeth to the emperor's honour'.[1] Lee was hampered because Charles, although he understood Latin to a point, did not speak it, while Lee spoke very little French (Charles's first language).

Nobody was now willing to take the post of ambassador to England – perhaps the nominees feared being harangued by Henry on the topic of the broken engagement and the embarrassing debts. At last, Don Inigo de Mendoza was appointed. He would be given bills of exchange for 150,000 crowns, which Lee pressed the chancellor to confirm could be exchanged for ready money. The chancellor merely said he believed Henry would be satisfied. The Archduchess Marguerite would arrange payment of the other debts, and the indemnity for war preparations would be paid by François. Lee's frank reply that he could not imagine François paying Charles's debts was met with no more than a shrug. Dissatisfied, Lee told Wolsey to be firm with Mendoza, as it was widely believed that François would renege on the Treaty of Madrid, in which case Charles would want Henry's help again. This is exactly what happened. Once home, François refused to ratify the treaty, saying he needed to consult with his council, and he showed no signs of forwarding the match with Eleonora, while fortifying Burgundy, which he was supposed to return to Charles. Clement VII was busy sending missives to all sides and pleading for peace in Christendom so that action could be taken against the Turks.

In early November, Henry pressed François to perform the agreed marriage with Mary, despite the Treaty of Madrid. Dr Clerk assured François, who was irritable and felt unable to make a final decision, that Henry would be better able to mediate with the emperor for the release of François' sons if he knew what sum the French king was willing to pay. François was reluctant to state a figure. Clerk pointed out that surely he must trust Henry 'for he was ready to give unto him in marriage his daughter, the pearl of the world and the jewel that his highness esteemed more than anything on earth'.[2] François' response was that before he had gone to Italy, he had been more minded to marry Mary than any other woman in the world. On Clerk replying it was in his own hands, as Henry's offers with her were so good, and the princess herself so beautiful and virtuous that he could not understand the problem, François snapped. He was so well aware of the princess's beauty, virtue, education, parentage and all of her other attributes, and how good it would be for him to marry her, the French king fumed, that he did not need Clerk to embroider the subject. He was just as keen to marry Mary as he could be to marry anyone, but he was also promised to Eleonora.

Clerk discussed the marriage with Louise of Savoy. French policy, not surprisingly, was directed toward the freedom of the princes. Louise told Clerk that their intention was to demand Eleonora, in fulfilment of the Treaty of Madrid, but that when Charles refused, as they anticipated, François would declare himself free, and marry Mary. Apart from anything else, Mary's age and virtues were so much in her favour as to make her 'pleasant and delectable' to François, while the thirty-year-old Eleonora was far less appealing, despite being the emperor's sister. One hopes Louise was not alluding to the sexual taste for very young girls that François later displayed.

Besides, Louise continued, Charles showed little affection for his sisters; he had failed to restore Isabella's husband, Christian of Denmark, to his throne, and given scant help to Louis of Hungary, husband of his sister Mary. She asked Clerk what Henry advised to end the interminable wars. Clerk, not wanting to insult Eleonora or Charles, confined himself to saying that because Mary was so young, she could be brought up to be as 'loving, lowly and humble' to Louise as to her own parents – a hint that a mature woman who had been a queen would be unlikely to tolerate Louise's influence. Louise, tears in her eyes, doubtless of the crocodile variety, assured Clerk that she herself would be as loving and humble to Mary as queen of France as she was to her son the king, and that Mary would be as 'esteemed, worshipped and honoured' as any queen of France had ever been.

Clerk doubted that François would be able to avoid marrying Eleonora if he wanted his sons back. Where else could Charles marry Eleonora so advantageously? Louise, while not admitting this more-or-less self-evident truth, changed tack slightly and offered one of the princes for Mary, if his father were unavailable. Instead of renewing the betrothal to the dauphin, whom the Treaty of Madrid reserved for Maria of Portugal, she suggested the second son, Henri of Orléans, since England would need its own king, while the dauphin would have to remain in France. Besides, Henri had not just been named after his godfather, Henry VIII, but also resembled him in looks and mannerisms. Considering the pictures of the two men, this idea is remarkably far-fetched! For this reason, if Orléans were sent to England while young, he would be acceptable to the English as their king. Clerk displayed no enthusiasm for this idea, objecting that the dauphin might die, so Henri would then have to stay in France. He pointed out that if François did not marry Mary, he might see her married in a manner that would not please him at all. François, harassed, responded that if it would recover his children, he would marry the emperor's mule, never mind his sister.

Clerk wrote that 'they (the French) do savour and smell how fain and prone ye be to join and conclude this matrimony with France' and that François therefore believed Henry wanted to frustrate any compromise between François and Charles, delaying the return of the French princes, rather than mediate between them. Henry's proposals to France were more than generous. He offered a perpetual peace, and to give up his claims in France other than the County of Guisnes, which he was to receive in return for an annual payment (the word 'tribute' was very specifically excluded) of money and salt. Mary was to be married to François, with a suitable dower and jewels and was named Henry's heir if he had no legitimate sons. If it transpired that she did not inherit, a dote equivalent to the amount promised to Charles would be paid, and sureties given for its delivery. If the marriage proved childless, the treaty would fall and the countries would be restored to the *status quo ante*. If François accepted, he and Henry could combine against Charles to have the French princes freed.

Henry was making a last attempt to arrange for his grandchildren to have a greater place on the world stage than he had done, but it must have been a sad day for him. For his grandson to be emperor would be a great achievement, even if England became part of the Empire, but for England to be ruled by France would be almost his worst nightmare, only marginally better than surrendering his country to Scotland – France was at least the most prestigious country in Europe and French queens took precedence over others. The very generosity of the offer suggests that Henry was desperate to have Mary married, before he set in motion any public questioning of his own marriage, and that he may already have been formulating a plan to father a male heir, other than with Katharine so that Mary would not carry the English crown to France.

François, on hearing that Henry would grant him Mary on 'easy terms', seemed almost genuine in his gratitude, exclaiming that if the match really took place he would reject Eleonora out of hand. Louise assured the English ambassadors that Mary's 'manifold virtues' were such that François was very anxious to marry her. Nevertheless, all Clerk and his colleague, the Bishop of Worcester could be sure of was that François would do whatever was needful to get his sons back. Charles's success in Italy being less than he had hoped, it might be that he would relax his terms. Clerk was certain that, in the end, François would pay a large ransom, pardon Bourbon, and marry Eleonora. Worcester concurred. He added that Eleonora was already talking of herself as Queen of France, and that he had been told that François had, in fact, spent considerable time with the widowed queen during his captivity, spoke well of her, and was rather more personally eager for the match than he had allowed the English to believe.

On 9 January 1527, the papal nuncio in France, whom Wolsey had pressed to encourage the match, wrote that he believed François was determined to carry it out, especially as the pope thought it would be conducive to peace in Italy. François decided to send the Bishop of Tarbes, who had been ambassador to Spain during François' captivity, the President of the Parlement of Toulouse, M. le Viste, and the Viscount of Turenne to London to negotiate detailed terms. Their first mission would be to wait upon Mary and arrange to have her picture painted. Clerk wrote that François and his mother were far more effusive in their protestations of friendship toward Henry and Wolsey than they had ever been before. As well as the envoys, François sent Mary a letter, in which he told her that he desired her honour, health and prosperity as much as his own. It is probable she did not like the idea of marrying François; she had met her previous betrothed, Charles, and the whole of her later life suggests that she had formed some attachment to him – or at least as much as a little girl can form in a few days for an older, seemingly kind, relative. Additionally, there can be little doubt that Mary would have had instilled from birth the usual anti-French views of both the English and Spanish of the sixteenth century. She might have asked her aunt Mary, who had known François well during her short period as Queen of France in 1514, what the king was like – perhaps being reassured with stories of his charm. While these fruitless negotiations dragged on, Mary was spending her last winter in the Marches, probably at Tickenhill, which she left in early February for Worcester, before she was summoned back to court to meet the French envoys. She arrived at Windsor on 20 February, then went to Richmond in March, where she was attended by Lady Bergavenny.[3] Whatever Mary, now eleven, was anticipating might be her future, she could never have imagined the chaos and misery that were about to descend on her, her parents and her country for the next ten years, all of which took place against the backdrop of the conflict in Italy.

Imperial forces were rampaging across Italy. Charles's Viceroy of Naples, Charles de Lannoy, was asking hard terms of the pope to withdraw from the Papal States, Spanish troops had returned to Milan, while the French and Venetians were hoping to prevent Bourbon's unpaid German landsknechts from entering Tuscany, having seen the devastation they were wreaking in Lombardy. Henry and Wolsey still sought to broker peace but both François and Charles were becoming suspicious that, in reality, the English intended to keep them at loggerheads to promote their own interests. Henry wanted the Duke of Bourbon to be reconciled to François and given Eleonora as a wife, freeing François to marry Mary, but a marriage between Bourbon and Eleonora was extremely unlikely –

Charles would never give Eleonora to Bourbon unless he were Duke of Milan, while the Milanese absolutely would not accept Bourbon as duke, and nor would François or Lannoy. The viceroy marched toward Rome, ostensibly to protect the pope from the French, although the pontiff was equally terrified of him. The viceroy sent terms to Clement: the pope must pay 150,000 ducats for the viceroy's troops and support the emperor against any Italian making an attempt on Imperial territory. Charles would enter Italy to be crowned emperor, and would put down the Lutherans at Clement's bidding. The towns of Piacenza, Parma and Civita Vecchia were to be handed over as security and Henry was to be the arbitor of the treaty. Clement was inclined to accept the terms, but was dissuaded by Henry's envoy, Sir John Russell, and the Venetians, who thought the Imperialists would be forced to fall back for lack of funds. Clement, having received financial aid from Henry, felt obliged to listen to him. This proved to be a terrible mistake: for Clement, for Rome, and for the unity of Christendom.

On 10 February 1527, Clement wrote a gushing letter to Henry, thanking him for the 30,000 crowns he had received, which had put new heart into his efforts to resist the Imperialists. He was also pressing his nuncio in France to advance the marriage between François and Mary, warning François that if it did not take place, the pope would be obliged to come to terms with Charles. He was awaiting the news of the marriage's completion 'with great anxiety' as 'the peace of Christendom depend(ed) on it'.[4] François hastened to reassure Clement, sending more money and promises that he had, or would, marry Mary. At the same time, Ghinucci, the Italian Bishop of Worcester who was Henry's envoy to Spain, gave it as his considered opinion that François had no intention of marrying Mary, while Clerk wrote from France that François would conclude the match on immediate delivery of Mary and an offensive league for the recovery of the princes. François' sister, Marguerite of Angoulême, now Queen of Navarre, told Clerk that François, having praised Navarre as a husband, boasted that he would be an even better spouse to Mary, whose virtues he highly commended. The positives in such a match, Clerk thought, included François' willingness to listen to female advice, although the king's rather cavalier treatment of the late Queen Claude would not be an advertisement for François as a faithful spouse.

On 1 March, Clerk reported to Wolsey that François was still negotiating with Charles, but simultaneously assuring Clerk of his devotion to Henry and his eagerness to marry Mary. The scent of François protesting too much wafts from the page even after 500 years. Nevertheless, recently-arrived French envoys presented themselves to Wolsey. The initial meeting did not achieve anything, but the next day, they again attended the cardinal at Westminster. Wolsey was at the receiving end of a long oration in Latin by the Bishop of Tarbes, flattering him and thanking him for promoting peace between Henry and François, and for offering the princess in marriage. Wolsey graciously accepted the compliments, modestly lying that he did not feel he deserved them, but observing that after meeting François at Ardres he had felt such a respect for his 'nobleness and virtues', and his likeness to his own master in person and habit, that no intervening circumstances (a war between the countries) had altered his feelings. However, the ambassadors were wrong to say that Mary had been offered in marriage by him. He was certainly not in a position to offer such a noble lady. She was a princess of such virtues that she must be asked for, not offered. Nor could her father consider bestowing her on anyone with whom he was not certain of perpetual peace. For that reason, the peace agreed in the last treaty, for the duration of the two kings' lives, must be reinforced with a treaty of perpetual peace.

The French ambassadors were stunned. Surely the current treaty was adequate? This was a wholly new demand. Not at all, replied Wolsey, he had already made this requirement clear to François, and the request had been confirmed by acceptance of the cession of Boulogne and Ardres to Henry, a 50,000 crown pension and 15,000 crowns' worth of salt to be paid by France each year. Indeed not, the ambassadors returned. François had already declined the permanent pension as dishonourable. François could not buy a wife so expensively, when the treaty would be of great profit to both parties. But Wolsey insisted. How could Henry abandon his league with the emperor unless he were assured of perpetual peace, a pension and the salt? Besides, was François actually free to marry? He had referred to Eleonora as his wife in letters and gone through a ceremony of betrothal with her. The French quickly reassured him. The Treaty of Madrid had been made under duress, and Eleonora had not been delivered up when François sent his sons to Spain as hostages. Charles's failure to keep his end of the bargain freed François to walk away.

Wolsey professed that he would be satisfied with this, if the pope confirmed that François was free. However, without a treaty of perpetual peace, the money and the salt, nothing could be done. Especially, he added, as Charles was trying to persuade Henry not to ally with François, by sending one of the French princes to Henry as a hostage, handing over some border towns, and paying the pension himself. François ought to be aware that if the marriage to Mary did not go ahead, the pope would despair and throw in his lot with the emperor to drive the French from Italy. The ambassadors said that no reliance could be placed on Charles's word. They agreed the marriage was important and they had all the necessary powers to agree it. Wolsey continued to reiterate that without Henry's demands being met, the matter could not be concluded. Nevertheless, he would tell Henry of their meeting and see them again in a few days.

Wolsey was right that even though Charles had not married Mary himself, he was determined she should not marry François, but the emperor's way of dealing with the threat was to push the match with Eleonora. His councillors told Ghinucci and Lee that Henry ought not to give up his claims to France. The emperor would be able to offer him Normandy, Guienne and Gascony. Lee retorted that Charles had already broken his agreement to invade France and ensure Henry was crowned as king of the whole country. The Imperial chancellor changed tack, to emphasise the long-standing alliance between England and Burgundy, which had subsisted with the goal of 'despoiling' France. The English needed Flemish friendship. In typical English fashion, the English maintained that the Flemish had only become wealthy through trade with England and that Flanders needed England more than England needed Flanders.

Back in England, Wolsey feigned anger with the French ambassadors, particularly when they claimed that Mary's earlier betrothal to the dauphin had had far more moderate terms. He waved that aside – the agreement had been made when the children were under age, merely to promote peace between the countries, and had not been intended as a long-term agreement. He added that he had had enormous trouble persuading Henry to the idea of the marriage at all, and if they did not co-operate, the matter would fall apart. The French insisted that there was no possibility, then or ever, of François agreeing to terms that required his country to pay an implied tribute to Henry by means of salt. The argument continued in a circle, Wolsey claiming that François had already approved the demands, and that he could not understand why the ambassadors had no instructions to agree the detail, with Tarbes and his colleagues affirming that François had never, and would never, agree. Eventually, Wolsey declared it was obvious they were just wasting time while negotiations continued for Eleonora. If that were François' real intent, then he would be happy to help promote it, if only they would be honest.

To counter Wolsey's high-handedness, Henry unleashed a charm offensive on the ambassadors. They were taken to Greenwich to be met by the king, flanked by Norfolk, Suffolk, Exeter, Shrewsbury and the bishops of London and Ely. Henry oozed bonhomie, said he was delighted the French sought his 'little daughter' who 'did not deserve such an honour', and that he loved François so much he would be glad to bestow her on him, even if he were no more than a private gentleman. The same matters were trotted out – there could be no marriage without a treaty of perpetual peace, a pension and a salt payment. The ambassadors rejected this, saying they could only talk about perpetual peace after the marriage, and that the treaty for life was enough. Not so, thought Henry. Although he and François were fast friends, their successors might feel differently. And besides, what about Eleonora? The ambassadors became hot under the collar. They had already assured Wolsey that François was not bound to Eleonora. He had given his word on the subject and it would be dishonourable to question it. Henry answered that his council had advised that he could not risk sending his daughter to a marriage that might be annulled. The ambassadors were ready to give up. There was no point in discussing the matter further – they could only ask François again to confirm his freedom. Seeing they had pushed far enough, Henry and Wolsey retreated slightly, and Wolsey invited them to a further round of talks while Henry took Turenne aside to comfort him with the thought that complex matters such as these always took time. Turenne, unimpressed, warned Henry not to ask anything dishonourable of François.

On 8 March 1527, further talks were held at York Place. Pending communication from François on the topic of Eleonora, discussion on the other terms continued. The French informed the cardinal they would not discuss the matter of a universal peace without the involvement of their allies, the papal and Venetian ambassadors, or treat with the emperor until the marriage with Mary had been arranged. Wolsey disagreed. François, he said, had told Clerk that he would talk of the peace first. His ambassadors could only shrug and say that that was not in accordance with their instructions. What if Charles wanted the marriage of Eleonora as the price of a universal peace? Perhaps, said Wolsey, Eleonora could be given to Bourbon? This angered the ambassadors. Bourbon had nothing to do with the matter and François would not involve him. The following day, the ambassadors brought their instructions for a perpetual peace to show to Wolsey, together with the papal and Venetian ambassadors who had similar powers. Following this, Wolsey became slightly more emollient, saying the terms of the marriage contract would be easy – there were precedents to work from, and, as Henry had no male heirs, the most 'sumptuous' would be chosen as a template.

Tarbes was insistent that Mary would have to go straight to France, but Wolsey resisted on account of her age. Surely, Tarbes asked, all the virtues and graces that Wolsey had described Mary as possessing more than compensated for her youth? The French believed Henry was only withholding agreement to Mary being immediately dispatched to enable him to wriggle out of the agreement, but this is probably unfair. It was common knowledge that Mary's great-grandmother, Lady Margaret Beaufort, believed her own early marriage and childbirth had been detrimental to her health and fertility, and had insisted the marriage of Henry's sister Margaret be delayed until she was nearly fourteen. Henry's concern for his daughter's health was genuine. That it might make it easier for the marriage to be annulled was probably not a factor now, as he was, in parallel to these discussions, but unknown to almost everyone, seeking to have his own marriage annulled. It was vital that Mary be safely disposed of before the matter became public knowledge.

Lord Rochford invited Tarbes and Turenne to attend court at Greenwich. After dinner, they were invited into the queen's chamber, where Henry was awaiting them with Katharine. After some polite nothings, Katharine asked if they intended to agree a universal peace. Tarbes said that that was dependent on achieving their first objective but, unsure whether Katharine was privy to the matter, did not specify what that was. It is evident Katharine had been informed, and was playing a part in the negotiation in accordance with a pre-agreed plan. Whether Katharine agreed with the plan is another question. It is highly improbable she wanted Mary to marry François, as it would damage the alliance with Spain of which she was the representative, and at a human level, she is unlikely to have wanted her daughter to marry a notorious lecher, rumoured to have syphilis. Nevertheless, her role was to be queen of England so, at this juncture, Henry told her, smiling, that Tarbes was talking of the marriage of Mary to François. If Henry *was* springing it on her, Katharine behaved impeccably, accepting their requests for her to favour the marriage. However, she said, the treaty of universal peace was more important than the affairs of just two kings, and ought to come first. The French countered this by saying that once Henry was François' father-in-law, he would be able to influence him to ensure a peace that pleased all parties. Katharine responded that to contract the marriage first might make the emperor suspicious of François' motives and less inclined to treat for the universal peace. She was assured by the ambassadors that the two kings together would be powerful enough to dictate terms. Then the ambassadors were treated to a tour of Henry's furniture and armour, designed to impress them with his military capability.

Further discussions were held with Wolsey, covering the same ground – the pension, the salt and the eligibility of François to marry, with the additional information that Henry needed a positive financial benefit from the treaty to persuade Parliament to ratify it. The French were highly suspicious of this, not believing that the English Parliament had any standing in approving treaties or the succession to the crown.

A few days later, the French received further instructions and a new envoy, M. D'Ouarty. In the next round of negotiation, Wolsey became increasingly angry. He claimed he was only pursuing the matter because of his affection for François, the rest of the council was against the offensive league against the emperor, the demands were so small he had never thought François could have a problem with them, and king and Parliament could never agree a perpetual peace and withdrawal of English claims to France without compensation. As it was, people hated him, Wolsey, for promoting the idea. Did François want to see him murdered in his bed? (The true answer to this was probably a resounding 'yes'!)

The ambassadors then proffered the salt during the lifetime of Henry and Katharine, which would make France a tributary. Wolsey paid as much attention to this as he would have done to the 'gift of a pair of gloves'.[5] He abused them for misunderstanding their instructions, as he said François had already agreed all the points with Clerk, and Parliament would not agree the treaty without taking away all occasion for future war, which could only be done if England were suitably recompensed. That ended the interview, with it being agreed that D'Ouarty would visit Henry.

D'Ouarty trundled off to Greenwich for an audience. Henry read the letters and said he could not see why 15,000 crowns' worth of salt was a problem – he often lost that much money gambling. As for the pension, François could not expect him to give up his claims to France and his only daughter for no return. Mary's standing as Henry's heir was not important, the ambassadors assured him. If he had had a dozen daughters, François would want to marry one to show his commitment to his friend. Henry exercised his charm – he put his arm around D'Ouarty and told him that, unlike Charles, *he* would never forget his affection for the French king. Wolsey would be instructed to be reasonable, if they were. He then took D'Ouarty to Katharine to deliver his messages from Louise and the Queen of Navarre.

A further wearying round of proposal and counter-proposal took place. The dauphin was suggested as the bridegroom or, in a completely new departure, the Duke of Richmond for a French princess. The French wanted the marriage agreed first, the English the peace; the French to have Mary immediately, the English when she was marriageable; the French to pay only the usual dower, the English for a long-term pension. The idea of marriage to François' second son, Orléans, was again mooted. With this, the pension and salt would be paid, the kings would sign a peace treaty, and, if peaceful means to recover the French princes failed within a given period, they would jointly make war on the emperor. Any truce between the pope and the viceroy would be bad for the French position, and their only remedy would be the marriage with Mary. Wolsey called the Venetian and papal ambassadors into the negotiations, and said Henry would be willing to join the League of Cognac, provided they all agreed not to treat with the emperor without Henry's knowledge. Henry was becoming increasingly angry about Charles's failure to pay his debts. One point on which Henry would not yield, was that Mary could not go to France until both Katharine and Louise agreed that she was physically mature enough to consummate the marriage, and nor would he give hostages in the meantime. In that case, the French replied, they had no guarantee that if Henry died before the marriage occurred, they would have Mary. If that happened, what did England think would become of the 50,000 crown pension and the salt? Reasonably, Wolsey replied that, in that case, of course, the bargain would be null. He repeated that if François wanted to marry Eleonora, then they should start making arrangements for Mary to marry Orléans.

While the marriage of François and Mary was widely expected, Henry and Wolsey were aware of the increasing pressure on François to marry Eleonora. Dr Clerk again asked whether François was contracted to the Eleonora.

François, using his favourite expression 'on the faith of a gentleman', assured Clerk that if he had not been certain he was completely free to marry he would not have sent commissioners to ask for Mary. As for Eleonora, on the advice of his council, he had written to her, but he was not bound to her in any way.

On 25 March 1527 the French ambassadors dined with the lord mayor, and the following day went to Hampton Court, where Mary had arrived some ten days before. Wolsey asked for the French response to the latest proposals, but all they would say was that François' instructions must be sought. They doubted he would be happy with them, as Mary was not to be delivered immediately.

The ambassadors dined with Wolsey and the council, before being taken to meet Henry and Katharine in the queen's chamber. Katharine and Wolsey chatted to Tarbes, while Henry talked to Turenne and le Viste about Lutheranism and shared some of the insights from his own book, impressing them with his learning. Katharine then withdrew, while Henry continued conversing with them all for some time, before Wolsey took them to another meeting, with Norfolk, Suffolk, Rochford and FitzWilliam. But still nothing was decided – Wolsey emphasised the need for the universal peace, while the marriage and the offensive league were the concerns of the French.

Tarbes and his colleagues received further instructions. François wanted to marry Mary himself, rather than wait for Orléans to be old enough in 1533, as the worst case for consummation for Mary and François would be in February 1528, when she turned twelve, or a little later if she were not sufficiently mature. If Mary could not be handed over, the offensive league should start on 1 June 1527, and last until she was given to the French.

Wolsey changed tack, advising that the French should offer a ransom of 2 million crowns for the princes, and if Charles still insisted on the marriage of Eleonora, they should accept it, in return for the boys, with no ransom in lieu of dowry. This would be better than risking the rupture of peace. No offensive league could begin until Charles had shown himself to be unreasonable.

The French, beyond exasperated, replied if François had wanted to marry Eleonora, he could have done it already, without English involvement, but Henry and Wolsey's arguments against it had persuaded François it would be better to marry Mary. They demanded the prompt delivery of the princess, an immediate offensive treaty and the renunciation of the English claims on France – but Wolsey still refused to agree that Mary should go straight to France. The cardinal may have thought he had pushed them far enough, presumably in a bid to test their sincerity. He was, of course, privy to the conversations that Lee had been reporting from Madrid – that François was not planning to marry in England at all.

Wolsey sent an update to Clerk, who visited François. The French king suggested a meeting at Calais, with Mary being handed over there. Clerk assured François that Henry would do as much as possible, but could not risk that his only child 'should miscarry [of what] fruit came by her'.[6] François responded that it was absolutely necessary for Mary to be handed over. He did not dwell on the consummation aspect but instead sent Clerk to Louise to discuss Mary's health and capacity for consummation, as this was a matter 'more fitted for ladies'. Louise took a very light view of the matter. She herself, she said, had been married at eleven-and-a-half, and had come to no harm. She thought Mary was twelve (in fact, she was just eleven) and might therefore be delivered in six or seven months without any danger. The best plan, Louise continued, was for Mary to be brought to Calais, for the wedding to take place, and François to 'abedde himself' with her for less than an hour, after which, the marriage now indissoluble, Mary could be taken back to England until she was 'more able'. She assured Clerk that François, being a man of 'honour and discretion' would 'use no violence', especially as Mary's father and mother would be nearby. Clerk, bound by Louise to write her opinions to Wolsey, did so, but 'thought it very strange'. Just as Henry and Wolsey played 'good cop and bad cop', so did François and Louise. At his next audience with Clerk, François said that he, too, thought Louise's suggestion 'very strange'. It was especially odd, said François, as women in France did not come so soon to the marriage-bed and the law in the matter was clear.

The French ambassadors requested permission to visit Mary at Richmond, but Katharine refused, saying Mary was ill. This may have been genuine, of course, but the Spanish envoy thought it was an excuse, perhaps because Katharine disliked the marriage, but more likely in concert with Henry as part of the negotiating tactics.

As April advanced, the marriage appeared to be inching closer. There were three treaties, one for the marriage itself, one for a peace treaty between England and France, and one for an offensive treaty against aggressors, each dependent on the others. François was to offer Charles 2 million crowns and the return of the Flemish town of Hesdin, to confirm Charles in his sovereignty of Flanders for life and to pay Bourbon's revenues. Even if the marriage did not take place, if Charles refused the conditions, Henry would be bound to enter the offensive league. If Mary married Orléans and acceded to the throne, the perpetual peace was to be observed. Finally, if Charles insisted on François marrying Eleonora, the kings would reconsider.

Lee wrote to Henry of his most recent interview with Charles. He had begged Charles on bended knee to cease making war on the pope and, in return, Henry would let him have as many men as he could for the war against the Turk. Charles replied that Henry knew he was peace loving, as evidenced by his leniency towards François, but when the pope was trying to take Naples and Milan from him, what was he to do? Surely Henry did not expect him to tolerate such treatment?

A few days later, Lee wrote a letter to Wolsey that confirmed their worst suspicions. He had seen a letter from the Imperial envoy in France, Perot, which described a conversation Perot had had with François, in which the king had said,

> The king of England would have me to take his daughter, and to give him (Boulogne). Nay, nay! The Cardinal wrote to me, desiring and most instantly beseeching me that, for a continuance of new amity between the king of England and me, I should send my orators into England, and give them mandatum to common and conclude there, and, to colour the thing, that I should ask the daughter of England. But I had much liever that the emperor would send a gentleman hither, that we may common our matters among ourselves; for I would not have it concluded at the king of England's hands.

'I well perceive,' wrote Lee, 'that they (the Imperialists) would in any wise the marriage should go forward between my lady Eleanor and the French king; ... When we commoned of a wife for the Duke of Richmond, he [Perot] said "that in no wise we may [have] the daughter of my lady Eleanor, because of the treaty of Madrid"; and he named the daughters of Denmark.'[7]

On 17 April, in another interview with Charles, Henry's ambassadors again tried to present Henry in the role of mediator, but Charles was losing interest in English mediation. He would not discuss possible ransom amounts, saying he was only interested in peace, and experience had led him to put no faith in the French king. He also exclaimed that since Clement was trying to take his lands away from him, he would refuse his authority and call for a General Council to be convened – a General Council being the favourite threat against the pope, to which princes resorted from time to time. Although there was some ambiguity about their power, it was generally considered that the authority of a General Council was greater than that of a pope. As to a universal peace, Charles doubted that, despite Henry and Wolsey's hopes, François would do what Henry desired. Moving on to Mary's marriage, Charles hinted that François would no more keep his word to Henry, than he had to Charles.

Henry's envoys then said Henry might begin to feel 'ill-used' if, attempting to mediate between Charles and François, any resulting treaty was made in Spain rather than England. To show Henry's goodwill toward Charles, he was willing to forgo the marriage between Mary and François, if Charles could put forward a suitable kinsman. Henry also offered the Duke of Richmond for one of Charles's female relatives. The young duke was described as 'near of [Henry's] blood and of excellent qualities, and already furnished to keep the state of a great prince, and yet may be easily by the king's means exalted to higher things'. This probably meant kingship in Ireland, but might have meant the replacement of Mary as heir to England.

Charles merely pointed out that Henry had insinuated himself into the negotiations between him and François, rather than being asked to mediate. He neither refused nor accepted the offer for Richmond, but said he would try to think of some suitable lady. He dismissed the envoys to speak to his advisors, who claimed to regret that Charles had not married Mary instead of Isabella as the empress's huge dowry had now been spent, while the Portuguese had not delivered the promised military aid. As for Mary marrying François, Henry should put that out of his mind. The French king would undoubtedly marry Eleonora. All that was wanting was the ceremony and the consummation, which had only been delayed by the Imperial side.

Henry and Mary should bide their time, the councillors added – who knew but that the empress might die, leaving a vacancy for the English princess? Lee countered by broaching a marriage for Richmond with one of the emperor's nieces. Of course, this was all diplomatic talk and spin. Henry had two chips in his game of royal matrimony, both flawed – Mary because of her gender, and Richmond because of his illegitimacy. It was incumbent on him to get the best deal he could.

***

On St George's Day 1527, the French ambassadors went to see Mary at Greenwich. After dinner, Henry led them into a hall in which Mary, Katharine and the French queen were present, with a large company of ladies and gentlemen. The proud father told the ambassadors to speak to his daughter in Latin, French and Italian, and she was well able to respond in all three languages. She also wrote in French for them, before performing on the spinet. The ambassadors agreed the young lady was very accomplished for her age, which was eleven years and two months. Contrary to the previous description of her as tall, Turenne thought that although she was very pretty, she was so 'thin, spare, and small', that she could not possibly be married for another three years. From the opposing descriptions of her, we can perhaps infer that none of them is terribly accurate – those who wanted her to be considered ready for marriage described her as tall and robust, while those who wished to delay matters spoke of her as small.

By the Treaty of Westminster, concluded on 30 April 1527, Mary was to marry either François or his second son, Henri of Orléans, at Henry's option, as it was unseemly for a gentleman to be able to reject the lady. On Saturday 4 May, the French ambassadors returned to Greenwich, accompanied by Rochford and the Bishop of Ely. Henry received them formally, seated on his throne, flanked by knights of the Garter. Wolsey was there, as were the papal and Venetian ambassadors. Henry politely stood to embrace them and Tarbes made a formal speech, in Latin, saying that François wished to preserve their friendship and marry the princess. The Bishop of London made the formal answer, and Henry observed that he was glad that matters were coming on so well. The following day, after Mass, Henry solemnly signed the treaty. Tarbes and Turenne dined with the king while Wolsey and the rest of the lords dined with M. de Vaulx and le Viste. Earlier that day there had been a tourney, and it was now followed by a masque, or 'triumph' in which Mary took part – probably the first time she took part in an adult entertainment. First there was the dinner. The king, the queen, Mary the French queen, and all the nobility and honoured French guests were in attendance in the Great Hall, as were the ambassadors of Venice and Milan. As they ate, they listened to the minstrels in a gallery supported by two great triumphal arches decorated with the arms of Henry and Katharine, and Henry's motto, *Dieu et Mon Droit*. The meal was a sumptuous feast, with a huge range of fish and flesh served, from conger eel and tench to crane, heron, peacock and pheasant. Mary's own cook, Master Hugh Piggott, was paid for creating a marzipan tower, with two chessboards with their pieces garnished in gold. The other subtlety was a dungeon and manor, surrounded by swans and cygnets swimming in the sugary moat.

The company then went into the new Revel House, where staged seating allowed everyone a view. Henry sat alone on a high platform, his wife and sister at his feet. The walls were lined with canvas, while the ceiling was covered with linen and gold cloth. A backdrop, costing £8, was made of purple velvet 'richly powdered' with motifs of knights riding upon mountains with ladies throwing darts at them. Surrounding the knights and ladies were clouds, and the whole was 'flourished' in between the motifs with Venetian silver thread, gold damask thread and gold broom. Lions, dragons and greyhounds – probably representing the king's beasts – held torches. Enormous quantities of silver plate were brought from strongboxes in the Tower of London and Baynard's Castle to glitter in the torchlight, and a further eighty basins coated in silver paint were distributed around the set. St George, of course, was represented, in a coat that took two days to make. The masque, called the *Pageant of the Father of Heaven*, was set among the Olympian gods and involved the arbitration of a dispute as to which was better – Riches or Love. Unable to conclude by argument, a battle ensued. Following this, a grotto was revealed, from which eight beautiful ladies, led by Mary, emerged, dressed in cloth of tissue and red tinsel, with their sleeves hanging almost to the ground, their hair gathered into jewelled nets, surmounted by velvet caps. Made by John Skutt, the queen's tailor, each gown cost 10s for making and was trimmed with a yard-and-a-half of red ribbon, provided by Mrs Phellype. Mary, whose gown was covered with jewels, led the damsels onto the dance floor, walking hand-in-hand with Lady Exeter. After a figure dance, eight young men joined them for more dancing. Eight more men, dressed in black and masked, entered, among them the king.

They were all wearing black velvet slippers, as Henry had recently hurt his foot, and could only wear a soft shoe. There was more dancing; then Henry took Mary's cap off. Either accidentally or deliberately, her hair was freed from the net, and a profusion of fair tresses fell over her shoulders, to the admiration of the company. Her hair is described as silver; she may have still had the white-blonde hair of childhood. Later, her hair darkened to a more reddish hue. Following the pageant, Mary danced with M. de Turenne, while Henry danced with Lord Rochford's younger daughter, Mistress Boleyn.

On 7 May 1527, Wolsey informed Tarbes and the others that he had received news from Charles that François could not possibly marry Mary as he was promised to Eleonora, and the only reason the agreement between them had not been consummated while the king was a captive in Spain was because Charles had delayed matters. François was merely trying to dupe Henry. As proof, Wolsey had been given copies by the Imperial ambassadors of letters from François to Charles, Empress Isabella, and Eleonora, referring to her as his wife. In the same dispatch, Charles was, apparently, asking for advice from Wolsey, giving his ambassadors powers to treat for peace, and, rather tastelessly, informing the English that the pregnant Isabella was so weak, her doctors did not expect her to survive childbirth, in which case, Charles would be eager to marry Mary. We can only hope that Isabella did not hear that her probable death was to be welcomed! In a further indication of how keen Charles was to prevent Mary marrying François, he was willing to accept the Duke of Richmond for Eleonora's daughter with a dowry of up to 400,000 ducats. Charles was hoping to promote the universal peace so he could help his brother fend off the Turks, an aim that required the unity of all Christians – he had already been offered money and men by his loyal subjects in Spain.

Wolsey recounted this to the French, adding that Charles had received a chilly reply: England was well aware that, in fact, the Spanish Cortes had refused to help the emperor against the Turks, but that Henry and François would help if Charles accepted reasonable terms and that Henry was sorry to hear of the poor state of health of the Empress, but thought it dishonourable for overtures of marriage to another lady to be made while she was still alive. In addition, Henry did not like the idea of marrying his daughter to someone who had previously refused her – he would rather marry her to a simple gentleman. Richmond was far too young to be thought of for marriage, although when the time came he would be able to make an honourable match. As for the letters purporting to be from François about his marriage to Eleonora, the English took them to be bad forgeries, and nothing like the king's own writing. They even produced samples for comparison. The cardinal continued by suggesting the terms that Henry and François ought to request from Charles – it was quite a shopping list, in which the chief points were that the French princes were to be ransomed for 1 million ducats, of which 500,000 should be handed over immediately, out of which Charles should repay his debts to Henry. Charles would retain sovereignty of Flanders and Artois for life; Sforza should be restored to Milan, paying 50,000 crowns annually to Charles, who would pay the annual sum to France agreed after the battle of Marignano for Naples; Henry wanted Tournai and Théouranne returned with the unpaid indemnity he should have received under the Treaty of London.

In a spirit of reasonableness, Henry agreed that the return of the princes was paramount, and he would take only half the money he was owed from the first tranche of ransom, and the rest annually. His claims to Castile, Tournai and Thérouanne and the indemnity would be put on hold. Considering François was supposed to be eager for the return of his sons, the French greeted these suggestions with a distinct lack of enthusiasm. The French could not pay 1 million ducats immediately, and if they could, such a sum would only tempt Charles into more warfare. Not at all, replied Wolsey, as the sum in Charles's hands would be considerably diminished by the payment of the debt to Henry. If Charles did run amok with the money, Henry would support François. The exhausted ambassadors returned home on 8 May, accompanied by letters from Henry expressing his satisfaction at their conduct, and assuring François that he would act on the treaty.

In early May, it was reported that the pope had agreed terms with the Viceroy of Naples and entered a league with the emperor. Erasmus wrote of his disgust – how long, he asked, could the pope keep allying, now with one prince, now with another, till all hope of peace was lost? Anticipating that the Imperial troops would now withdraw, and for lack of money, Clement disbanded his army. Bourbon advanced towards Rome, his disorderly German troops leading Russell to write that 'never were Infidels more cruel than the Imperialists'. Bourbon requested permission to pass through Rome, en route to Naples, promising he would pay for provisions. He was refused entry, and the following day his troops broke through the walls, unleashing on the Holy City one of the most appalling acts of barbarity in the history of Europe. For twelve days, the Imperial troops sacked Rome – men, women and children were indiscriminately slaughtered. Houses were blown up, churches desecrated, priests murdered and nuns raped. Clement escaped into the fortress of Castel Sant'Angelo but both he and the viceroy were powerless to stop the carnage. It was reckoned that nearly half the population were killed, either by the looting soldiers, or the subsequent epidemics.

The Sack of Rome profoundly shook Christendom and the subsequent actions of Clement must be understood in this light. While Charles 'deplored' what he described as 'the unfortunate incident at Rome against the pope and his palace', the result was that he was now effectively in control of Italy – and the pope.[8]

Part 2
The Cursed Bastard

5

The King's Secret Matter

... done by him for pure conscience's sake.

Scarpinello, Milanese Ambassador

The turmoil in Rome had international repercussions and so too did an event that took place in London on 17 May 1527, just before news of the Sack reached the capital. A secret court was convened at York Place, presided over by Wolsey and Archbishop Warham of Canterbury, to investigate the validity of Henry and Katharine's marriage. The marriage between Mary's parents had been a political match but, for the first five years, Henry had been devoted to his wife, comforting her through at least two miscarriages, and the death of their eight-week old son in 1511. Henry had consulted Katharine on all political matters, and left her as regent in 1513, a role she fulfilled with admirable success. In 1514, a second betrayal of Henry by her father, Ferdinand, and the rise of Thomas Wolsey, diluted Katharine's political power. Katharine was jealous of Wolsey's influence, and had little respect for his ostentatious lifestyle. Nevertheless, the marriage remained strong, cemented by the birth of Mary, as Henry hoped for more children. Despite the queen's final miscarriage in November 1518, during 1519 Henry was still presuming their marriage would last for life. He commissioned Pietro Torregiani, the Florentine sculptor who had created the fabulous tomb of Henry VII and Elizabeth of York, to carve a similar masterpiece for Katharine and him. Typical of Henry's desire to always be the best, it was to be a quarter as large again as his parents' tomb. But by 1520, Katharine was losing her physical appeal. François rudely referred to her as 'old' and 'ugly', while Henry was in his prime.

Notwithstanding fevered speculation, there is only actual evidence of two extra-marital relationships on Henry's part. The first with Elizabeth Blount, which resulted in the birth of Henry Fitzroy in 1519, and the second with Mary Boleyn, daughter of Sir Thomas Boleyn. So far as the latter relationship is concerned, there is no evidence of its extent or duration. We only know that Henry slept with Mary Boleyn because of later events. But at some time in about 1525 or 1526, Henry became enamoured of Mary Boleyn's sister, Anne.

Anne had been maid-of-honour to Katharine's sister-in-law, Marguerite of Austria, and then to Queen Claude, and possibly to Marguerite of Angoulême. Anne returned from France at the end of 1521, to settle a dispute about the earldom of Ormond by marriage to her cousin, James Butler. The marriage did not take place, and Anne became Katharine's maid-of-honour. She and Henry Percy, the son of the Earl of Northumberland, fell in love and planned to marry, but the match was broken off by Wolsey. It has been speculated that Wolsey was acting on Henry's orders, and also that this action seeded a hatred in Anne for the cardinal and a desire for vengeance she would never forget. Anne's refusal to conduct an affair with the king simply increased his ardour – whether or not that was Anne's intention, or was just the natural result of Henry, who was used to having anything or anyone he wanted, being denied. In parallel to Henry's pursuit of Anne, and his fading desire for Katharine, was his urge to have a male heir and his anger at Charles for jilting Mary. These different pressures came to a head for Henry in 1526 and when he read his Bible, a passage in Leviticus stood out: 'If a man take his brother's wife, it is an unclene thinge, he hath uncovered his brother's secrettes, they shalbe childlesse therfore.'[1] For Henry, God was speaking – his marriage to Katharine was cursed and he must escape from its sinful toils.

Despite the official line on marriage being indissoluble, the practice of popes finding that a marriage was invalid, and granting an annulment for fundamentally political reasons, was not uncommon among royalty and the higher echelons of nobility who could pay for the privilege. Henry's own sister, Margaret, Dowager Queen of Scots, was granted an annulment in 1527 – much to his disgust, as he made a great fuss over the sanctity of marriage. Louis XII had been allowed to put aside his wife Jeanne of France, despite her vociferous protests, to marry the widowed Anne of Brittany and retain French control of her duchy. Henry was not unreasonable in expecting that the pope would similarly help him, especially as his argument canonically had some merit, although it was not watertight. Leaving aside that Henry and Katharine were not childless, as Henry found some support for a translation as 'without sons', there is an opposing passage in Deuteronomy, requiring a man to marry his dead brother's wife, if the deceased had been childless. It was therefore arguable whether the marriage between Henry and Katharine was forbidden by divine law, or positively enjoined by it.

Over the centuries most, but not all, theologians had agreed that such a marriage could take place, but required a papal dispensation to remove the 'affinity' between the woman and her husband's brother, created by sexual relations in the first marriage. If the first marriage had not been consummated, a different dispensation was required, one relating to 'public honesty'. When Arthur died, there was doubt about whether his marriage to Katharine had been consummated. Pope Julius II granted a dispensation in 1503 on the assumption that sexual relations had taken place, but it was amplified by a papal brief that said the marriage had 'perhaps' been consummated. Henry's basic argument was that it was beyond the pope's powers to dispense affinity between Katharine and him, because of the prohibition in Leviticus. Katharine's counter-argument was that, because her marriage to Arthur had not been consummated, no affinity existed. Henry would have been better advised to pursue the argument (raised by Wolsey, but not taken up) that the wrong dispensation had been given. This would have been an easier matter for Clement to swallow – a mistake as to facts rendering a dispensation invalid would have been far more acceptable than the argument that Pope Julius had acted outside his powers.

Henry faced four obstacles, any one of which might have been overcome individually, but which together dragged the whole annulment suit into a quagmire of argument, counter-argument, bribery, politics, pleading and prevarication for seven years. His first and greatest problem was Katharine herself. Katharine's life since she was four years old had been built on the foundation that it was her God-given destiny to be queen of England, and to bear an heir to the English crown. To this end, she had left her home for a foreign land at the age of fifteen, been married to a stranger and widowed within months, subjected to humiliating dependence on her parsimonious father-in-law, betrothed to Henry but not married when he reached maturity and lived in a depressing limbo for seven years. When she and Henry had finally married, their personal happiness had seemed to make all that had gone before a price worth paying. Then came the tragic trail of deaths, stillbirths and miscarriages, out of which Mary had sprung to be Katharine's vindication. Since she had had no son, for Katharine, Mary was to be the fulfilment of the Anglo-Spanish alliance. At all costs, she must prevent the throne passing to the child of another woman – whether a French princess, or her own maid-of-honour. Added to this may have been the belief that during a time of religious turmoil, Katharine could best maintain the faith by upholding the authority of the papacy (however little she respected Pope Clement personally). Finally, there was personal pain. Katharine struggled to accept that her once-devoted husband no longer loved her, a truth made more bitter by jealousy of Anne. For Katharine, the idea that her marriage was invalid was completely wrong, from start to finish, and she prepared herself to fight with every weapon she had, beginning with her oft-repeated oath that her marriage to Arthur was unconsummated. While this has been questioned, her utter adherence to it, her oaths on the sacrament and in the confessional, and what is known of her character, make it likely to have been true. Royal wives who had been subjected to annulments in the past had had little choice but to conform, but Katharine was clever and determined – she knew that by making the case a political one, she would have the support of the emperor and not be shuffled off to a nunnery as other discarded wives had been.

This gave Henry his second problem – the reaction of Charles. While Charles had been willing to risk the alliance with England by refusing to wait for Mary to be marriageable, he hoped to maintain friendly relations through his aunt's position as queen. If she were repudiated, Henry might well form an alliance with France, which, as we have seen, Charles was eager to prevent. So far as possible, he would block Henry's annulment, although he would never go to the lengths that some of his advisors wanted – an invasion of England, and early pressure on the pope to excommunicate Henry and deprive him of his crown.

The third problem was the pope. Clement VII, from the Florentine Medici family, had received support from Henry for his candidacy in 1524, and was well disposed towards the king, but he was by nature indecisive and vacillating, a situation exacerbated by the exigencies of the constant warfare in the Italian states and, most of all, by the horrors that had befallen Rome during the Sack. His whole policy, in so far as he can be said to have had a policy, was directed towards protecting Rome from a second invasion. To do this, although he would have welcomed freedom from Imperial shackles, he would take no risks and would bow to Imperial pressure, while making feeble attempts to accommodate Henry's wishes.

Clement wanted to placate Henry because of the turmoil in the Church at large, which was Henry's final obstacle. Since Luther's protestations in 1517, the floodgates had been opened. Heresy, as the Church saw it, was springing up everywhere. By the late 1520s, large parts of the Empire and the Scandinavian countries were leaning towards Lutheranism. For Clement to accept Henry's premise that Pope Julius had acted outside his authority in granting the dispensation for Henry and Katharine to marry would be to give fuel to the Reformers.

In May 1527, however, Henry probably assumed the pope would grant the annulment, once he had gone through the appropriate legal manoeuvres, and so he insisted on the court being convened. Wolsey and Warham presided. Having protested his loyalty to the king, Wolsey demanded an answer to the charge that, in contravention of God's law, Henry had been living for eighteen years in apparent matrimony with Katharine, widow of his brother, Prince Arthur.

The matter was adjourned to 20 May when Henry's proctor, Dr Bell, entered an admission of the facts and accepted there was a case to answer, a few days later producing a copy of the 1503 dispensation. On 31 May, objections to the dispensation were entered: that Arthur and Katharine had been married; that they had co-habited and Arthur had 'carnally known' his wife; that the pope did not have the power to grant a dispensation in this case, and finally that Henry had repudiated the match when he reached his fourteenth birthday. Unfortunately for Henry, international events intervened. On 2 June Wolsey wrote that Clement's being subject to Imperial control, would 'hinder the affairs of the king, which hitherto have been going on so well'.[2]

While the secret court was deliberating in London, Henry's envoys, Clerk, now Bishop of Bath, Lord Rochford (Anne Boleyn's father) and Sir Anthony Browne, were in France to take the signing of the treaty oath from François. The Duke of Lorraine and his brothers conducted them to the Louvre where François waited with Louise; Princess Renée, sister of the late Queen Claude; the King and Queen of Navarre, and their daughter, Jeanne d'Albret. There was a grand official reception, with speeches, bowing and doffing of caps. The next day, Whitsunday, François travelled in procession to Notre Dame, and, having listened to another Latin oration about the virtues of peace, as he sat in his traverse, hung and carpeted with purple velvet and fleurs-de-lis, he swore the oath at the high altar, with his hand on the Mass book. That done, all returned to the Louvre for dinner, the English envoys noting the solemnity with which François was served. On the following Thursday, an elegant masque was held, showing France and England embracing.

Henry commissioned Wolsey on 18 June to meet François to continue the marriage negotiations and also to ascertain what support the French king might offer regarding the annulment. Four days later, Henry broached the matter with Katharine. Why he elected to tell her before the court had reached a conclusion is a mystery. He may still have been fond enough of her not to wish to deceive her; perhaps, since he now genuinely believed their marriage was unlawful, he thought he would convince her with his arguments. Katharine, notably pious, would not deliberately live in a state of sin once it had been pointed out to her. But he was too late. Katharine had already been warned of what was afoot. If he thought the matter could be amicably arranged, Henry was soon aware of his mistake. Although having the rumours confirmed by Henry led her to break down in tears, Katharine had already prepared her arguments. She absolutely refuted the suggestion that their marriage was invalid, and set out to fight.

En route to France, Wolsey wrote to Henry that he and Warham had discussed how badly Katharine had taken the news, and Henry's reassurance to her that he only wished to discover the truth, following the question being raised by the Bishop of Tarbes. This is the first record of the claim that the validity of Henry and Katharine's marriage had been raised by Tarbes during the negotiations for Mary's marriage. It seems unlikely that Henry would have invented the claim entirely, yet it is hardly feasible that Henry and Wolsey could have acted swiftly enough to convene a court on 17 May when Tarbes was only in London from 26 February to 8 May. On the other hand, given the hard negotiating tactics the records reveal, with all sorts of claims, counter-claims and accusations of pre-contracts and consanguinity being dragged up, it is not impossible that Tarbes raised the question as a negotiating ploy, on which Henry seized – or perhaps Tarbes had heard rumours of Henry's thinking and brought it up. It may be that Warham himself believed this to be Henry's motive as he agreed with Wolsey that however little Katharine liked it, the truth and the law must prevail.

The third element of Wolsey's mission was to try to convene a quorum of cardinals at Avignon, under his direction of course, to deputise for Clement, unable to act freely because of the Imperial control of Rome. If this had taken place, Wolsey and the cardinals could have annulled Henry's marriage and presented Clement with a fait accompli. But Henry and Wolsey's careful plan came to nothing. On 18 July, Dr Knight wrote to Wolsey that Henry had given a passport to Katharine's steward, Francisco Filipez to travel to Spain. Having discovered that Felipez' excuse was manufactured, and that he was about some business of Katharine's, the king wanted him 'molested' in France and prevented from travelling, but Filipez outwitted his pursuers, reached Spain, and informed Charles of the plan to have his aunt's marriage annulled.

***

Mary knew nothing of this and, in late July, was at court with her parents. Dr Sampson wrote to Wolsey that they were all in good health. The 'secret matter' was proceeding well. Henry seemed far more cheerful with Katharine, who was now less suspicious. The 'merry visage' had returned and the royal couple had departed together for Beaulieu, with Henry waiting for his wife, even though he was ready to leave before her. We can infer that Mary returned to Hartlebury, as a letter from Lady Salisbury to Dame Anne Rede was dated from there on 20 August 1527.

Wolsey wrote to Henry that it was essential for the pope to approve a sentence of annulment in case Katharine declined to accept Wolsey's jurisdiction. Alternatively, acceptance by the College of Cardinals of his sentence might be enough. As for the first, unless the pope were delivered from the emperor's clutches, it would be unlikely to happen.

Charles had received his ambassador, Mendoza's, latest dispatch, as well as Filipez's personal messages from the queen by 13 July. He replied on the 29th, enclosing a letter for Henry, which he had enciphered himself, despite the trouble this had cost him. The gist of Charles's letter was that he could not believe that Henry really meant to undertake an act that would 'astonish the whole world'. He and Katharine had lived together so honourably for so many years, Katharine was such a virtuous queen and wife, and Mary so 'gentile' that he could not contemplate that Henry would wish his daughter or her mother to be so dishonoured. Further, the matter could cause a disputed succession, with the claims of Mary and James of Scotland being promoted by factions, leading to everlasting feuds in England.

Mendoza was to make three points: that Charles hoped Henry would take his advice in good part, as he was thinking of the best interests of both Henry and himself; that Henry would end such a scandalous proceeding for the honour of God; and that he should keep all mention of it secret. Charles himself would maintain discretion to preserve the honour of Henry, Katharine and Mary and for the benefit of the whole kingdom of England. Mendoza was also to deliver a letter to Katharine, informing her of the contents of his message to Henry and console her in her present affliction.[3] Simultaneously, Charles sent dispatches to the viceroy in Italy, for him to obtain a letter from Clement in the mildest terms, exhorting Henry and his ministers to desist from pursuing the matter. Clement was to wield the stick by either stripping Wolsey of his legatine powers or, at the very least, forbidding the cardinal and the English ecclesiastics from involving themselves in the matter, ordering that it must be brought before the whole College of Cardinals. He also wanted Clement to reject Wolsey's scheme for deputising.

Wolsey, unaware that Charles already knew what was mooted, wrote to Lee in Madrid that a rumour had sprung up in England that Henry was contemplating a divorce. Nothing could be further from the truth – an investigation was being made into the validity of the marriage to satisfy the Bishop of Tarbes, who had questioned it. Katharine had got hold of the wrong end of the stick, but had been quite reassured now. If Charles mentioned it, Lee was to assure him the investigations were to confirm the marriage, rather than undermine it.

When Wolsey finally arrived at the French court, he found François laid up with a swollen leg. He told the king he had come to agree the final points of the treaty with regard to the marriage of Mary, the delivery of François' sons, and the rescue of the pope. François treated Wolsey with great honour. He was so pleased that Henry and he were now 'knit and married in [their] hearts' that he thought they should be joined by neck and leg also – a hint that the Orders of St Michel and the Garter should be exchanged. Wolsey planned to discuss the 'secret matter' in 'so cloudy and dark a sort that he shall not know your utter determination', meaning either Wolsey did not intend François to realise that Henry had set such store by an annulment, or that the king's ultimate purpose (to marry Anne Boleyn, if indeed he had decided to do so by that point) should be kept hidden so that François might think another matrimonial alliance, this time with Henry himself, might become available.

Wolsey asked, in his capacity as Mary's godfather, and thus responsible for her welfare, how the marriage between Mary and François could possibly take place when everyone's priority must be the release of the dauphin and Orléans? François admitted the best course was for him take Eleonora and for Mary to marry Orléans. Wolsey suggested that a convention of François, Louise, Charles and himself should take place, to iron out the details. Having agreed this with François and Louise, Wolsey wrote to Lee and Ghinucci; they were to inform Charles that he, Wolsey, was in France to treat of the marriage between François and Mary but, if Charles would be more reasonable, England would give up the marriage and promote the one between the French king and Eleonora. Henry had obviously decided his priority was now the annulment, rather than Mary's marriage, and wanted to please both fellow-monarchs to smooth the way.

On 11 August, Wolsey wrote to Henry that he had still not mentioned the secret matter to François, and the French king was showing himself to be very friendly. Wolsey said he knew Archduchess Marguerite in Flanders had found out about it, so it was inevitable that Charles would have heard of it by now. (Wolsey was still unaware that Charles had already written to Henry.) Wolsey thought the emperor would do everything he could to stop it, so it was now a race to get to Clement: Wolsey to persuade him to allow the cardinals to convene at Avignon, and Charles to prevent him either granting an annulment himself or allowing Wolsey or Warham to do so. To curry favour with Clement, it was agreed that the English, French and Venetians would provide 30,000 men under the leadership of François' general, Lautrec, to try to wrest the pope and Rome from the emperor's clutches. But militarily, matters were moving Charles's way. Andrea Doria, the Genovese condottiero, was recruited to the Imperial side. A more surprising development was the defection to Charles of the Duke of Urbino, supreme commander of the League of Cognac.

Knight wrote to Wolsey from England that Henry was making an additional proposal for incorporation in the Treaty of Amiens, as the final agreement for Mary to marry Orléans was called. This was that Mary should marry Orléans, François should marry Eleonora, and Richmond should marry Eleonora's daughter, Maria of Portugal, while Milan, which François was being forced to cede, should be bestowed on Richmond and Maria. In the fond English hearts of Henry and Knight, the Milanese would prefer this to the reintroduction of Francesco Sforza. Knight added that Henry approved the plan of bringing François, Louise, Wolsey and Charles together, although he was concerned that the emperor bore Wolsey 'inward hate, malice and grudge'. Henry also accepted Wolsey's advice that the annulment needed either papal consent or that of the cardinals. Ultimately, this was the wrong decision. If Wolsey had pronounced judgement, with Warham, Clement would probably have accepted it – or at least kicked any appeal by Katharine into the long grass.

The Treaty of Madrid was finally agreed between François and Charles, the key points of which were that the princes would be ransomed, François and the dauphin would marry Eleonora and Maria of Portugal respectively, while François would renounce most of his Italian claims and cease supporting the Duke of Guelders or Robert de la Marcke against Charles. Milan was to be renounced by both, and François was to withdraw the army under Lautrec.

***

On the surface, life in the royal family continued as before. Henry was still ordering furnishings embroidered with Tudor roses and Katharine's badge of the pomegranate, and both Mary's parents were still eager to see her. She returned to court some time before 10 November 1527, as on that date she took part in a pageant. François' hints about an exchange of chivalric orders had been accepted and Henry had been presented with the accoutrements of the French Order of St Michel. To celebrate, after the dinner at which Mary dined at the same table as Henry, Katharine and Wolsey, there was dancing, Mary partnering the Grand Master of France. This was followed by the masque. Mary led a troupe of eight ladies, all wearing cauls of damask gold over their hair, and dresses adapted from those used for the masque in May – even Henry could economise occasionally. The purport of the play was the overcoming of Heresy, represented as Luther and his wife, and Heresy's companions, False Interpretation and Corrupt Scripture. On the winning side (we can presume) were Ecclesia, Religion and Verity. Other characters were the dauphin, the Duke of Orléans, and the ladies Peace, Quietness and Tranquillity. The cardinal and the Apostles were also represented. The Garter was sent to François, and Louise told Wolsey that now that she had seen her son and Henry 'under one clothing' she hoped they would continue to be at one in their hearts.

Meanwhile, Mary's council was still conducting business in the Marches. Exeter wrote to Wolsey that the learned men of the council would attend better if they lodged within her court, suggesting that he anticipated Mary would soon return to the Marches.

On 5 December 1527, Wolsey furnished Gregory Casale, an Italian who had been in Henry's service for some time, with detailed instructions on how to negotiate with Clement for the annulment. As the pope was in captivity,

Casale was sent 10,000 ducats to bribe the guards to gain access to Clement. Once in the pope's presence, he was to show his letters of credence from Henry, including one with a paragraph written in Henry's own hand, and he was to inform the pope that Henry and Wolsey were doing everything possible for the pontiff's release. As soon as Clement was convinced his hopes for freedom lay in Henry and Wolsey's hands, he was to be told of the king's scruples about his marriage, the desire of the whole nation for Henry to have a male heir, and the conviction of 'the more thoughtful' that his failure to have a son so far was the result of the invalid marriage. If he had no son, the country would be plunged into faction and war, which the pope, as Father of Christendom, should try to prevent. The situation clarified, Casale was then to remind Clement that, in the face of the trials and tribulations the Church was currently suffering, no champion had been so stout a defender as Henry. Even if a less virtuous man than the king had had scruples, Clement ought to listen to them and give redress; in the case of such a paragon as Henry, he should act immediately.

Action was to consist of granting a brief for Wolsey to hear the arguments and to pronounce sentence on the validity of the marriage. An additional dispensation was also requested: to allow Henry, if his marriage to Katharine were to prove illegal, to marry a woman with whom he was connected in the second degree of consanguinity – that is, a sibling or daughter of someone with whom Henry had had carnal relations. The dispensation should also provide for marriage to a woman who had previously been contracted to marry another man, provided that the first union had not been consummated. This would permit Henry to marry Anne Boleyn, despite having had a sexual relationship with her sister Mary, and Anne having been pre-contracted.[5] That Henry had the same degree of affinity to Anne as he claimed he had to Katharine, was of no concern to him, suggesting either breathtaking hypocrisy or an entirely literal reading of the Bible, which is silent on marriage to the sister of a former mistress.

If Clement were to do as requested, Henry would spare no effort to have him released, and had already sent money to the King of France for military aid. There was a long list of arguments for Casale to make if Clement had already been liberated, or if he objected to granting Henry's request. Wolsey was nothing if not thorough. Shortly afterwards, news arrived that the pope had escaped from San Angelo and was at Orvieto. When Casale found him there in late December, he was 'miserable and alone'. Casale tried to hearten him and persuade him to resist Imperial demands by saying that Lautrec was advancing. Clement, although glad to hear it, was not resolute enough to defy Charles until Lautrec's arrival. Casale thought that if Lautrec did succeed in freeing him, Clement would grant Henry's demands, but not otherwise.

Mary was at Greenwich for New Year 1528 with Henry and Katharine. The new French ambassadors, du Bellay, Bishop of Bayonne, and de Brosse, gave news of Lautrec's advance. Henry was thrilled to hear of the pope's escape and expressed himself warmly towards François and Louise, speaking for nearly an hour, unusually long for the impatient king. Then the envoys attended Mass with him, before being conducted to the queen's chambers, where, after polite greetings to Katharine, they bowed to Mary and gave her letters from François and Louise. They were impressed by her behaviour, saying she thanked them most honourably, and 'could not have conducted herself with better grace'.[6]

Out of the emperor's immediate grasp, Clement was willing to help Henry. The dispensation for a second marriage, if the first were deemed invalid, was granted, and a commission for Wolsey sent. A subsequent request for an additional commissioner was also allowed. He told Casale in early January that he had consulted with two cardinals, and Henry should proceed on the basis of the commission granted to Wolsey or rely on Wolsey's legatine power. Wolsey should review the case and, if he determined that the marriage was invalid, pronounce sentence. If Katharine appealed, Clement would be bound to hear the appeal, but it would be harder for her to challenge a sentence, once given. If the matter were to come before a court whose validity Katharine challenged before sentence, then Clement would have no alternative but to call the case to Rome for determination. Henry rejected this advice – he wanted the matter unequivocally decided, with no room for appeal. Pressed to send a second legate, Clement nominated Cardinal Campeggio. This choice was designed to please Henry. As has been previously mentioned, Campeggio had visited England on several occasions and held the bishopric of Salisbury.

On 27 January, Charles gave a stern answer to Clarencieux Herald, who had been sent to Madrid to declare Henry's grievances against the emperor and make an official declaration of war. Among those grievances was Charles's non-payment of the penalty of 500,000 crowns for his failure to observe the Treaty of Windsor and marry Mary. Charles denied the obligation on several grounds: first, that penalties related to marriage were invalid in both civil and canon law; second, that Henry had breached the treaty first by negotiating with James of Scotland for a marriage with Mary, and third, by refusing to deliver Mary when requested. Charles took the war into the enemy's camp, saying that he himself had the greater cause for war if the rumours abroad that Henry intended to divorce Katharine were true. Charles added he did not believe the story, which had incensed the Spanish nobles, as he had copies of the dispensation that proved it to be so ample that it could only be impugned by questioning the pope's authority to grant it.

Stories had now crept into the papal ears that Henry's desire for divorce was less grounded in the prickings of his tender conscience and more in his wish to marry a gentlewoman 'of not so excellent qualities as she is here esteemed'. Wolsey hastened to reassure Clement that Henry's motives were pure; he loved and esteemed the queen and intended to treat her honourably and with all the respect due to her as his sister-in-law, although he was sure their marriage was invalid. As for the gentlewoman in question, she was a paragon of virtue. Wolsey was right that the two matters were not initially linked in Henry's mind, but everyone else assumed they were, particularly Katharine and Mary. As Henry's infatuation with Anne deepened, the annulment, and his marriage to her, became indissolubly entwined.

***

On 3 February 1528, Mary's council discharged some of her household officers, on the understanding they could be recalled if necessary. Despite these economies, the costs of the household were high and, six weeks later, Henry gave orders that the remainder of Mary's household be discharged. Henry Colier, her Master of the Jewel House, was sent to the Marches to fetch her jewels and plate, and her chapel items were collected from Ludlow by William Cholmeley. Why was Mary's household disbanded? Henry wanted his marriage annulled, but he was not, at this stage, desirous of branding Mary illegitimate, before he had a male heir. Although Mary had now reached marriageable age, it seems unlikely her household would have been dissolved in contemplation of a marriage to François or Orléans until it looked more likely to happen. Perhaps it was no more than a cost-cutting exercise, and not considered permanent by anyone – on the death of her chamberlain, Sir Giles Greville, in March 1528, Sir George Throckmorton asked Wolsey for the office. The reason given at the time was that 'for her own better education, and for the consolation of the king and queen, it has been ordered that the princess should reside near the king's person'.[7]

Henry and Katharine may have wanted Mary close to them because of concerns over her health. That spring, she caught smallpox, as did several maids in Queen Katharine's household. Smallpox was not so virulent in the 1520s as it later became, but it was a dangerous sickness, and could leave the sufferer badly scarred. Even hostile descriptions do not mention Mary being scarred so perhaps, since she was still young, she was only lightly touched. By 4 August, she was reported to be better again, and in the company of her parents. A letter from a member of Lady Salisbury's council mentioning that Lady Salisbury was unable to request a resolution of dispute to the king in person, as her attendance on the princess kept her away from the court, suggests Mary had left the court by the end of August. She may have been sent to the country to make a full recovery from her illness or, more probably, to keep her from seeing and hearing the public court case that was now anticipated, Campeggio having at last arrived to convene a hearing.

We do not know who told Mary about the annulment, nor what information she was given. Although at twelve she was considered marriageable, it is unlikely she was treated as an adult, and what she heard was probably carefully controlled by her mother and Lady Salisbury. It seems unlikely Henry would have broached the subject. The emotional response of Katharine when he informed her he was seeking an annulment had left him bruised; he would not have wanted to be confronted by his daughter's tears. Initially, Mary was perhaps given Henry's original version – that the Bishop of Tarbes had questioned the legality of her parents' marriage and that Henry, initially taking steps to have it validated, came to believe that it was contrary to the law of God. Henry insisted, and in 1528 Katharine still purported to believe him, that his scruples were genuine prickings of conscience, while Katharine's conscience was equally clear that their marriage was valid. Mary was thus taught, at a very impressionable age, not just by her mother but also by her father, that the dictates of conscience must be followed, regardless of how unpalatable the outcome might be. We should not, therefore, be surprised that Mary internalised this lesson and strove all her life to act according to her own conscience. We may think that both Henry and Katharine's principles were in remarkable accord with their desires, but it is unlikely that a girl of Mary's age would have been so cynical.

When Mary became aware of Anne Boleyn's relationship with her father is also a mystery. Anne was still officially Katharine's maid of honour, and Mary would have been used to seeing her about the court. It is certainly possible she knew Anne was her father's mistress without connecting her with the annulment case, as Henry was very eager to keep the two ideas separate. Eventually, of course, there could be no hiding from the fact that Henry wanted the annulment to replace Mary's mother, a royal princess, with a mere knight's daughter, and to replace Mary herself with an unborn son, with all the personal and political pain that that entailed for her.

Campeggio pleaded with Katharine not to contest the annulment. Henry was willing to offer the most generous terms to her – she could retain her state, and her rank, as well as the guardianship of Mary. Henry was even willing to have the succession assured to Mary in default of a male heir; nothing would be lost to her except her 'use of the king's person' which, Wolsey had assured him, had already been lost to her for many years. But Katharine would not budge.

Simultaneously, the suggestion was made to Henry that Clement would grant another means for him to be satisfied as to the succession – he would give a dispensation for Mary to marry Richmond. If people were questioning the pope's competence to dispense with the marriage of a man to his sister-in-law, heaven knows what would have been made of half-siblings marrying. Campeggio does not seem to have had the slightest concern about its morality as a solution, but he was very sure it would not meet Henry's objectives.

Campeggio urged on Wolsey the danger of upsetting the emperor. The cardinal, proving as politically prescient as ever, replied that the emperor would not involve himself in another war. He had done nothing for his two sisters, driven out of their kingdoms, so would be highly unlikely to do anything for his aunt and cousin.[7] Wolsey also told Campeggio, six years before it happened, that if the pope did not co-operate, the authority of Rome would be finished in England.

The French were hesitant about committing to any further marriage discussions, fearing Mary would lose her rights to the succession in favour of the son Henry was sure he would have by a second marriage. The plan, thought du Bellay, was to give her a good marriage, but to avoid her having any claim to the succession.

The New Year of 1529 was spent at Greenwich. We can detect Mary's presence from the information that Henry paid her players £4 for a performance. A further £40 was given to her clerk, John Bury, to distribute among those who attended her at court, while 'my Lady Princess's household' at Ludlow received 22s, suggesting a skeleton staff remained.

As the prospect of Mary marrying the French king diminished, Henry's Scottish envoy, Dr Magnus, wrote that he believed the Scots were open to a marriage between James and Mary. Although James was supposed to marry one of François' daughters, matters were not progressing and he was talking of treating with the emperor for a wife. Nevertheless, an English match might be welcome. On 13 February 1529, James of Scotland, now nearly seventeen, claimed he had not previously answered overtures regarding Mary, as he believed her betrothed to the Duke of Orléans. However, no bride could please him more, and he was planning to write 'familiarly' to his uncle about it. Magnus, probably influenced by Queen Margaret's wishful thinking, seemed quite sure no other match would be made for the Scottish king without taking Henry's advice.

At the end of May 1529, two years after the secret hearing at York Place, the trial of King Henry and Queen Katharine's marriage finally began at Blackfriars. The court opened with both Katharine and Henry appearing in person. The Dean of the Chapel, Henry's representative, stated that Henry had felt a scruple about his marriage from the beginning. Katharine rejected the court as partial, and claimed it was rather late in the day for Henry to be worrying about the validity of their marriage. Henry replied that he had suppressed his scruples out of his great love for her, and that he only wished the marriage *could* be declared valid (although he was sure that it was not). He continued that it was perfectly safe for the matter to be heard in England – Katharine had had counsel and advice, whereas in Rome, where she wished the matter to be heard, the pope was under the sway of the emperor. It was at this point that the queen left her seat, knelt before her husband and begged him to consider the honour both of themselves and Mary, and drop the matter. Henry, appalled at this embarrassing and emotive action, tried to raise her, but she remained kneeling. She asked him for permission to write directly to the pope, to defend her honour and her conscience. Henry, the eyes of the court upon him, and perhaps moved by the spectacle of his kneeling wife, granted consent. Rather than returning to her seat as expected, Katharine swept out of the court, never to return. As reported by the French, if Henry's judges had been women, Katharine would easily have won. They shouted encouragement to her at her entrance and exit. She requested their prayers and 'used other Spanish tricks'.[8] The case continued without the queen, but no sentence was passed. Campeggio adjourned the case, *sine die,* and Wolsey did not have sufficient confidence in his own power to continue without him. There is no record of thirteen-year-old Mary's whereabouts during the trial. Was she waiting impatiently to hear the outcome of the deliberations? How did she react to hearing about her mother's famous defiance of king and cardinals? We can only speculate.

In August 1529, a new resident Imperial ambassador came to London. Eustace Chapuys was a 45-year-old lawyer from Savoy, with a long career in Imperial service. It is to Chapuys's detailed reports that we owe much of our knowledge of the English court between 1529 and 1546. Chapuys became a determined partisan of Katharine and Mary, as well as a staunch defender of Catholicism in the face of the Lutheranism he believed Anne Boleyn and her family to be championing. While it was his job to report events in England as accurately as he could to his master, and he employed a wide range of informants and spies, we must bear in mind that he may unconsciously have interpreted events or conversations in the light most consistent with his own views, or to influence Charles to his own recommended course of action. This does not mean his evidence should be dismissed, but it is important to remember there may be alternative interpretations – as well as the possibility he was deliberately fed information Henry wanted him to have.

In October 1529, Wolsey's failure to obtain the annulment was punished when he was found guilty of obtaining legatine bulls from Clement VII, against the 1393 Statute of Praemunire, which forbade subjection to a power outside the realm. This was harsh, considering Henry had exerted considerable pressure on successive popes to grant the bulls. Wolsey was formally pardoned, but his enemies, who were legion and headed by Anne Boleyn, were determined that Henry should be given no chance to soften towards his former chief minister, and ensured he was excluded from Henry's presence. Wolsey was replaced as Lord Chancellor by Sir Thomas More, who was a popular choice, also pleasing Katharine's faction as he was believed to support her. The dukes of Norfolk and Suffolk were considered by the French and Imperial ambassadors as having the most sway with the king, although du Bellay observed that Henry was not so easy to manage as they supposed.

It was around this time that another potential solution to the annulment impasse was set in motion. Thomas Cranmer, a Fellow of Cambridge University, suggested to his old friend Stephen Gardiner, once a member of Wolsey's household but now the king's secretary, that the doctors of theology at the universities of Europe should be canvassed for their opinion on the legality of the royal marriage. Accordingly, messengers were sent far and wide to garner academic opinion. Cranmer, who had reformist tendencies, became chaplain to the Boleyn family. While this initiative was in hand, Henry sent Rochford on yet another mission to the pope. When in Rome, Rochford assured Tarbes that should Anne come to be queen, with François' assistance, she would always favour the French.

During the autumn and early winter of 1529, Mary was at Windsor while Katharine was at Greenwich. The queen was unhappy at being apart from her daughter, but Mary's location was a decision for Henry. Chapuys wrote a report to Charles, relaying the latest news. First was the rumour that Mary was to marry the Duke of Norfolk's son, Henry Howard, Earl of Surrey. Apparently it was originally Anne's idea, to put Mary in the control of her family (Surrey was her cousin). Chapuys weighed the pros and cons of the idea and suggested he would promote it, his thinking being that Norfolk's attachment to his niece Anne was not so great that he would not prefer to forward his son's and daughter-in-law's interests. Chapuys thought Katharine might be an obstacle to the match – she was not on especially good terms with Norfolk, and such a marriage would be far below Mary in status. Next, Chapuys assured Charles that Henry had been pleased to hear the emperor believed his motives for seeking an annulment were genuine scruples of conscience, while the public imputed Henry's actions to enmity toward the emperor, and to love for Anne Boleyn. Charles was also given the news that many people said Henry had an 'even greater affinity' with Anne than with Katharine. Since the affinity via Mary Boleyn was the same, we can only assume that Chapuys was referring to the rumour that Henry had slept with Anne's mother, Lady Elizabeth Boleyn – a charge Henry later denied, almost certainly truthfully.

For Christmas 1529, Mary was probably with both Henry and Katharine at Greenwich. Henry left the queen there after Epiphany (6 January) while Mary had moved to Eltham by February, at which time Katharine was given orders to go to Windsor. Mother and daughter were together again at Richmond for a few days in May, and Chapuys received permission to visit them. Henry and Katharine were still usually in the same house, and in public, behaved with great propriety. At the end of June 1530, they were at Hampton Court. The Milanese ambassador, Scarpinello, reported that,

> They pay each other reciprocally the greatest possible attention, or compliments in the Spanish fashion, with the utmost tranquillity of spirit, as if there had never been any dispute whatever between them … At any rate this most virtuous queen maintains most strenuously that all her king and lord does is done by him for pure conscience's sake, and not from any wanton appetite.[9]

Whatever Katharine really thought, it was easier for her pride to swallow that explanation rather than the idea Henry wished to abandon her for another woman. Mary is highly likely to have accepted this explanation, which would perhaps have softened the pain, and assured her that her father did not wish to repudiate her mother or herself from any base motive. The public behaviour of Henry toward Katharine may also have lulled Mary into believing all would turn out well. Although intelligent and educated, she was only thirteen and unlikely to have understood the complexity of adult emotions. According to Scarpinello, she continued to occupy herself with 'her very becoming studies, at her usual residence', probably Eltham or Richmond.

In July 1530, any hopes Henry entertained that François would marry Mary were dashed when the French king finally married Eleonora, and had his sons restored, consequent on the Treaty of Cambrai. The treaty had been brokered by Marguerite of Austria, with Marguerite's erstwhile sister-in-law, Louise of Savoy, and Louise's daughter Marguerite of Angoulême, Queen of Navarre. It was probably welcome news to Mary, unlikely to have wanted to marry a man of a similar age to her father, with a reputation for philandering, and disliked politically, if not personally, by her mother.

Aside from the annulment, for Mary, life continued as usual. She was still a princess and continued to pursue her customary pastimes. In August, Henry paid her new chamberlain, John, Lord Hussey, £66 13s 4d in total for saddles and harnesses for Mary and six of her gentlewomen, as well as for winter coats for three of her footmen. According to Hall's Chronicle, in the autumn of 1530, Henry, although he 'made no manner of mirth or pastime as he was wont to do, dined and resorted to the queen as he was accustomed and much loved and cherished their daughter, the Lady (sic) Mary'. But Henry was nearing the end of his tether. On 7 October 1530, he wrote to Clement, castigating him, not without reason, for indecision and inconsistency. He explained the majority of universities across Europe had declared that no pope could dispense God's law, and for Henry to be kept in a situation that the pope knew to be wrong would cause Henry to offend

God. Henry would only impugn the pope's authority if he was forced to do so, but his patience was wearing thin. Ghinucci was still urging that Clement remit the case to England, but Clement was also receiving equally passionate messages from Katharine, begging for the case to remain in Rome.

In about November 1530, a new friend came into Mary's life, who would be one of her closest companions until her death. This was Lady Margaret Douglas, daughter of Mary's aunt, Margaret, Queen of Scots, by her second husband, Archibald Douglas, Earl of Angus. The marriage of Queen Margaret and Angus had been annulled in 1527, and James V (Margaret's son by her first husband) had banished Angus from Scotland. Angus had become an important part of Henry's Scottish policy, and his daughter, whom he had brought with him without her mother or half-brother's consent, now came to the English court and was placed in Mary's retinue. Margaret was four months older than Mary and they soon became close. Henry, too, became very attached to his niece.

At the same time, Wolsey was rewarded for his twenty years of faithful service by being arrested for treason. Fortunately for the ageing cardinal, he died en route to London, and was thus spared the misery of a trial and certain execution.

In early December, Scarpinello reported that Mary was 'growing in wisdom and stature'. As usual, she joined her parents for Christmas at Greenwich and Henry gave her £20 with which to 'disport' herself, while Lady Margaret received £6 13s.4d.

* * *

In January 1531, Katharine lost a political ally when her sister-in-law, Archduchess Marguerite of Austria, regent of the Netherlands, died. The new regent was Mary's cousin, another Mary, Dowager Queen of Hungary, who had been widowed by the Battle of Mohács in 1526.

Henry began a slow, but sustained, attack on the English Church, building arguments supporting the supremacy of the king of England in his own country. His council recited a long string of precedents to Chapuys, showing that England ought not to be subject to papal authority. Chapuys sidestepped the question of the pope's authority, but said if his own master had possessed such a daughter as Mary, he would not dream of remarrying, even though he had many realms to govern. Even better, by selecting a husband for Mary, Henry could be assured of choosing a successor he approved of. Norfolk's only reaction was to be 'cold' and inform Chapuys that Henry fully intended to remarry.

In February 1531, the first open attack on papal authority was made when the Convocation of Clergy, under Archbishop Warham, was fined

£100,000 for the crime of praemunire. Convocation asked that the crime be either defined more clearly, as they were not sure how to avoid it, or that the fine be considered sufficient to cover any unfortunate future lapses. Henry rejected the latter notion indignantly. An open-ended, ill-defined offence that he could hold over the heads of the clergy suited him very well. Thoroughly cowed, Convocation also accepted Henry as Protector and Supreme Head of the Church in England. They were permitted to add the saving clause 'so far as the law of Christ allows', but not their preferred formula of 'so far as the law of the Church allows'.

Mary arrived in Richmond on 7 March 1531 to stay with her mother for five or six days and was still there two weeks later, to the queen's 'great satisfaction'. By the beginning of April, Mary had fallen ill. Chapuys wrote on 11 April that for the previous eight days she had had a pain in her stomach so great that she could not eat, although he hoped she would soon be better. Historians have assumed that Mary, who had just passed her fifteenth birthday, had menstrual problems, based on the report from Scarpinello that her doctors had diagnosed her as having *mal de madre*, usually translated as hysteria. Hysteria, now a pejorative term that has been used to denigrate Mary (and countless other women) for 500 years, was believed to be a medical condition. The symptoms were ill-defined but could include faintness, shortness of breath, irritability, anxiety and loss of appetite. The cause, mediaeval doctors thought, was the uterus wandering around the body, blocking passages and obstructing breathing. Alternatively, the symptoms might result from an accumulation of female fluids, equivalent to male semen. It was a handy diagnosis – any non-specific illness must be related to the woman's womb and it has been repeated for centuries in Mary's case, always with an implication of female inadequacy. Given that we now know that 'hysteria' is not a gynaecological condition, we can perhaps look at Mary's symptoms afresh. Whatever ailed Mary then, and throughout her life, was certainly not a 'wandering womb' or an excess of female semen, because such disorders do not exist. We should also be careful of concluding that because Mary later suffered from phantom pregnancies, she had menstrual problems from her adolescence. Phantom pregnancies were, of course, unusual, but other women in the Tudor era suffered them – Lady Lisle suffered one in the late 1530s, despite already being the mother of seven children, and Dr Lipscomb postulates in her *1536: The Year that Changed Henry VIII* that Anne Boleyn also had one.

Mary's illnesses may have been gynaecological, or they may have had another cause and been attributed to 'hysteria' – although her doctor's reports to Henry do not indicate that diagnosis. It comes only from Venetian sources. Chapuys, who was certainly closer to Katharine and Mary than Scarpinello, reported that Dr Bartelot, who attended her, had told him the disorder was severe indigestion. It is very plausible that stress could have induced gastric trouble – a condition that certainly does exist. Whatever the underlying cause, Mary became subject to bouts of debilitating illness, often making her too ill to write. Symptoms described over the years include headaches, stomach-aches, sickness, palpitations of the heart and faintness. These symptoms might also suggest migraine, especially as Mary had poor eyesight. On this first occasion of severe illness, perhaps to cheer her up, or to allow her to pray for recovery, Henry gave Mary £10 to distribute in alms as she thought fit, while the doctor was paid £20.

Henry still dined with Katharine on festival days and in early May 1531, they were together at Greenwich. Henry opened the conversation on a positive note, praising Charles's efforts against the Turk, but went on to criticise Katharine for not ensuring that her physician was constantly with Mary, who was still ill. The following day, Katharine requested permission to visit Mary, to which Henry replied that she could visit, and stay there, if she pleased. The queen did not fall into the trap – she could not be seen to leave her husband, even for her daughter, and remained at Henry's side. Mary wrote to Henry, saying that the best medicine would be for her to see both her parents again, and requesting leave to come to Greenwich. Henry refused. Chapuys believed this was to please Anne, who, on hearing Mary praised by her father, had spoken very unkindly about her – jealous of Henry's continuing affection for his daughter, and perhaps worried that this affection would keep him tied to Mary and to her mother. From this time, Henry saw less of his daughter.

For the annulment case to be heard in Rome, Henry and Katharine would both have to be called. The king was adamant that to accept a summons would be inconsistent with his sovereignty, and since the pope was dominated by the emperor, Henry would not receive a fair hearing. Accordingly, some thirty of his ministers and councillors were sent to Katharine to ask again for her consent to a hearing in neutral territory. Katharine swiftly demolished every argument against her. She affirmed that her marriage to Arthur had not been consummated; that she had no reason to expect favourable treatment at Rome, as, in fact, Clement had shown himself very eager to please Henry if he could, and that while she agreed she had been very well treated in England, she did not accept that she had been given good counsellors – Warham would say nothing but that 'the wrath of princes was death', the Bishop of Durham that he would not meddle, and Fisher of Rochester that she should keep her courage up – none of which was of the slightest use. Besides, Henry had not originally objected to the matter being heard in Rome. Wiltshire (Anne's father, promoted from his title of Rochford) said nobody had envisaged Henry being summoned to appear. Katharine replied that that was not her doing – if the law required it, then that was all there was to it. After more useless argument, the men retired, unable to change her mind. Henry was not surprised to hear of her firmness. He had expected it, both from her courage and her 'fantasy'. But another remedy would have to be found.[10]

The nobility of England was torn. Norfolk and Suffolk wished the whole question of a divorce had never been raised. Norfolk, especially, favoured the old alliance with Burgundy and Spain, rather than friendship with France. Born in 1474, the ingrained hostility toward France was hard for him to overcome and for a man who strongly objected to Wolsey, and later Cromwell, on account of their birth, it seemed as if the world had been turned upside down for a princess such as Katharine to be set aside for a gentleman's daughter, even if she were his own niece. But he was a faithful servant of the king and was angry Henry had been called to appear in Rome. He regretted the marriage with Katharine had ever taken place, he told Chapuys, except that it had produced such a 'pearl' as Mary, one of the most 'beautiful and virtuous ladies in the world'. He told Chapuys he had visited the princess twice recently to present his duty, and Henry, too, had visited her and had had 'great cheer' with her. But Mary had been ill again. According to Scarpinello, she had been at Richmond with what he termed a 'respectable court', but so sick that her doctors, attributing, he said, the cause to her uterus, let blood. Now recovered, he described her as 'tall and wise beyond her years'.[11]

In July, Katharine went to Windsor. While she was there, she wrote a letter in favour of one of her servants to the Duke of Milan. It was sent to Henry at Guildford for counter-signature, which he did in his own hand, referring to her as his consort, showing that even at this late date, he was observing propriety and being careful not to anticipate the papal sentence. Shortly afterwards, both Henry and Mary arrived at Windsor. Anne was also there. Finally, the ménage à trois became too much and one day Henry and Anne failed to return from hunting. Receiving no messages for six days, when it had been customary for them to exchange letters every three days, Katharine wrote, asking after his welfare. A severe message was returned, forbidding her from writing to him again. On this occasion, she disobeyed and was treated to a long letter which savaged her for obstinacy, for causing Henry to be cited at Rome, for obeying the emperor rather than him, and for persisting in her lie that her marriage to Arthur had never been consummated. In the face of Henry's aggressive missive, Katharine tried to remain cheerful and enjoy the fact that Mary was still with her. They amused themselves by hunting and visiting the other royal properties in the vicinity.

Katharine received orders to leave Windsor before Henry returned. She was given a choice of three houses to which she could move, while Mary was to go to Richmond. Chapuys opined that this separation was to force Katharine to withdraw her appeal for the annulment hearing to be in Rome and accept a hearing in England. Neither Katharine nor Mary could have known they would never meet again, so they probably parted with no more than their usual sadness, anticipating that in due course they would be together – certainly at Christmas, if not before. Katharine was not, at this point, sent anywhere unpleasant, but went to The More, near Rickmansworth, a former palace of Wolsey's.[12] Her household, although curtailed, was still regal.

***

Mary's prospective bridegroom, Orléans, was now being promised to the pope's niece, Catherine de' Medici. Chapuys reported the English council expressed pleasure at this news, partly to gain favour with the pope, but also to remove any obstacle to the divorce that might have arisen from a betrothal between Mary and Orléans. They thought François would be more inclined to help Henry if his potential daughter-in-law were not being dishonoured.

Whatever Henry's anger against her mother, he did not, in September 1531, have any intention of taking it out on his daughter. Sir Andrew Windsor, Master of the Wardrobe, received a warrant for an enormous amount of finery for the princess. It included a fabulously expensive cloth-of-silver gown, to be lined with plain silver cloth, and a purple velvet gown, to be lined with purple cloth. The inclusion of purple is significant as, although the sumptuary laws did not apply to women, only men of royal rank were allowed to wear it. There was a third gown of black tinsel, lined with black, a fourth of crimson satin to be lined with cloth of gold tissue and a fifth of black velvet, lined with ermine. Each gown was made of a sumptuous 11½ yards of material. There was a nightgown (not a bedroom garment, but an informal evening dress) of black velvet, lined with coney (rabbit) fur as well. There were three kirtles (the decorated underskirt) and matching sleeves for the gowns, each of 7 yards of material, in cloth of gold, cloth of silver, and black tinsel. There was satin for lining hoods and sleeves as well as partletts of black velvet and satin, lined with sarcenet (a fine, soft fabric, usually silk) and a dozen everyday partletts of lawn. A partlett was the short jacket-type garment that can be seen worn around the shoulders in paintings of the period, covering the bust. There was linen for smocks and nightrails (for sleeping in); ribbons for garters and points (the little ties that held clothes together), sixteen pairs of shoes and hose, two dozen pairs of Spanish gloves, three French hoods with black velvet, crimson satin and white satin for the biliment (the part of the headdress that sat on the crown of the head, often edged with jewels). There were thread and needles, and the astounding quantity of 10,000 pins. Twenty ells of low-quality cloth were provided for 'certain necessaries'. It is generally thought that Tudor women did not wear drawers, so the cloth may have been for sanitary purposes. Included in the warrant was payment for the making up and furring of all of the clothes.

This was a lavish gift, even by royal standards. Henry could be extravagantly generous; he loved his daughter and was still treating her as his legitimate child, and possible heir. Perhaps also he was showing that his behaviour was impeccable, compared with Katharine's shocking disobedience, and he may have been indicating to Mary where her duty lay. It was probably a most welcome gift to Mary, who displayed her father's love of fine clothes all her life. Clothes were not just about personal ornament; they were also a strong indicator of status. This is exemplified by the difference between Mary's clothes and the wardrobe ordered for her cousin, Lady Margaret. It too was lavish, but nowhere near the scale of the clothes given to Mary – consisting of a gown of tinsel, and two black gowns, one velvet, furred with ermine and one damask. She received only twelve pairs of gloves and half the amount of ribbon. Mary was not just dressed in finery herself, her servants were also treated generously. Her servant Simon Burton was granted 10 yards of black camlet for a gown, to be lined with black velvet and furred with budge (lamb's wool). He was to have to black doublets, one of velvet, one of damask, lined, and a black jacket.

Henry tried yet again to persuade Katharine to accept a court in England. On 16 October 1531 he sent Lee, now Archbishop-elect of York; the Earl of Sussex; FitzWilliam and Dr Sampson to plead with her that the matter would be better dealt with in England in front of the bishops, rather than at Rome, where, for fear of the emperor, Henry would not receive a fair hearing. Better yet, they should agree the matter amicably, rather than through the full rigour of the law. Katharine replied that when Henry had first broached the matter, she had suggested that very solution – the bishops to be summoned and put on oath, but he had rejected it, wanting the case to proceed according to justice for the sake of both of them, and for the princess. Now that Katharine knew that, far from being moved to his desire for annulment by a scruple of conscience, he was pursuing it in the grip of passion, she would not be so ill-advised as to accept a judgement in a court where everyone was so dependent on the king that they would swear black was white. Henry had started the matter, and given her leave to appeal to Rome, and she would continue to pursue justice.

At this point, the councillors fell on their knees and begged her to reconsider – for the good of the realm, of her daughter, and herself. Not to be outdone in drama, for which Katharine always had a flair, she too sank to her knees, asking them to turn the king from his scandalous course and return to her. If he truly had scruples, he should let the pope consider the matter. As to Clement's impartiality, she did not believe Charles, a virtuous prince, would put pressure on him. In saying that, Katharine was either disingenuous, or so sure, perhaps, of the merits of her own case that she did not believe any external pressure on Clement would be necessary.

Surrounded as they were by Katharine's attendants, used to thinking of her as queen for more than twenty years, and perhaps moved by her emotional appeal, the gentlemen shuffled off, adding that Henry would give her the choice of staying where she was, retiring to another house, or going to an abbey. Katharine, gilding the lily, said she would go wherever her husband commanded her, even to the fire. It is generally claimed that Katharine was banished from court after she was told to leave Windsor, but this is not strictly accurate. She and Henry both dined at the Serjeants-at-law feast at Ely House on 13 November 1531. The king and queen were entertained in separate rooms, and there is no record of whether they came face to face, but we can infer that Katharine was still conducting her public role, at least in part. So long as Henry hoped for a papal sentence in his favour, it behoved him to treat Katharine as his queen, formally, at any rate.

Whether or not Katharine saw Henry, she did not see Mary, who left Richmond in early November for a castle owned by the Bishop of Winchester, possibly at Anne Boleyn's suggestion, to get her out of the way, but more likely, thought Chapuys, for change of air. Her destination was probably Farnham Castle, where her uncle, Prince Arthur, had spent his early years, and an elegant palace had been built by Bishop Fox outside the walls of the mediaeval castle in the early 1500s.

***

Although Clement had refused Henry permission to try the case again in England, in late December 1531 a delay in proceedings was granted, obviating the need for the pope to take steps regarding Henry's failure to appear as summoned. In the letter reporting this, from Katharine's proctor at Rome, Dr Ortiz, to the empress, Ortiz added that Katharine had been banished from court and he wished that Katharine and Mary were out of England. All of Dr Ortiz's correspondence is imbued with an exaggerated sense of foreboding, and is frequently wildly inaccurate, so should be taken with a pinch of salt. In this particular missive he said Anne Boleyn had had a miscarriage. Although not impossible, this is unlikely as Henry and Anne were probably not sleeping together.[13]

The year 1532 opened with the usual New Year gifts. First in the list, but with the space for the present left blank, was Katharine. This was the first New Year that she did not receive a present from Henry since 1510. Second on the list, as she was second in rank, was the French queen, who received two gilt pots of 82 oz and a gilt cup with a cover of 19 oz. Mary, although third in rank, received a larger present than her aunt or anyone else – two gilt pots of 102 oz, three covered gilt bowls of 104 oz and a gilt layer (a type of platter) of 12 oz. The various ecclesiastics and nobles, including Richmond, received plate, as did Mary's schoolmaster, not named, but probably still Dr Fetherstone. Lady Salisbury, Lady Margaret Douglas, Lady Rochford (Jane, wife of George Boleyn) a lady named as Mary Rochford, (presumably the widowed Mary Boleyn) and Lady Oughtred, whose sister, Jane Seymour, would later be Henry's third wife, were also given plate.

Chapuys noted that Henry did not give gifts to Katharine's or Mary's ladies that year, an indication their rank was being subtly lowered. This is not entirely true, Lady Salisbury and Lady Margaret Douglas were both part of Mary's establishment, although not in the same category as ordinary ladies-in-waiting. As usual, Mary received £20 in cash to 'pass the time', with Margaret Douglas receiving £6 13s 4d. Katharine's gift to Henry of a gold cup was returned, together with a prohibition on sending him any more gifts. Disappointingly, we cannot tell what Henry received from either Mary or Richmond as there are blanks in the manuscript. His sister gave him a pair of writing tables and a gold whistle, while Mary's tutor gave the king a book.

The Lady Anne, as the accounts term her, was not given the standard gift of plate, but, according to Chapuys again, was presented with a room hung with cloth of gold and silver, and embroidered crimson satin. In return, Anne gave the king richly ornamented darts – probably in an allusion to Cupid, although a vision of Henry flinging darts at a black and yellow wheel while supping a pint of ale is engaging! Lady Calthorpe, Mary's former governess, gave Henry a box with flowers of needlework, probably her own doing, and six Suffolk cheeses. Other ladies gave various items of needlework, including Mary Rochford, who gave the man who had once been her lover, but who was now enamoured of her sister, a shirt with a black collar.

Parliament opened again, with Bishop Tunstall of Durham, and Bishop Fisher of Rochester, who were Katharine's legal counsel, not summoned, lest they object to forthcoming anti-papal legislation, but in a sign that Henry was still prepared to accept dissent based on a genuine scruple of conscience, he granted his cousin, Reginald Pole, a licence to leave the country and study abroad, and even continued to pay Pole's pension. Pole had been offered the archbishopric of York, if he conformed to the king's view of the divorce, but had felt unable to do so. Cranmer later reported to Wiltshire on Pole's arguments in favour of the marriage, among which was that the people already believed Henry to have a suitable heir in Mary, and any uncertainty in the succession could bring back the bad old days of Lancaster and York.

Henry's strategy was now to delay matters in Rome, as it was apparent that the case was unlikely to move in his favour. So long as no sentence was given, he would not be openly defying the pope by continuing to appear to seek resolution while he began the process of dismantling papal authority in England. Charles and Katharine were urging a speedy settlement so Henry could be forced to take his wife back – they still hoped and believed Henry would obey a direct command. To facilitate this, Dr Ortiz, convinced that Katharine and Mary would be in personal danger if Anne bore Henry a son, was desperate for a papal brief, excommunicating Henry if he did not abandon Anne and return to Katharine. Clement, whose indecision was almost pathological, toned Ortiz's draft down to a mere exhortation for Henry to return to his wife, accompanied with complimentary words about Henry hitherto having been the Church's most zealous defender. He appealed to Henry not to cause a scandal that would give comfort to heretics.

In late March of 1532, one of the last acknowledgments of Henry's life with Katharine and Mary came with a warrant to the Keeper of the Great Wardrobe to release various items for the Chapel Royal for Palm Sunday – this included a yard of purple velvet for the king's palm, and a yard of crimson velvet for garnishing the queen's and the princess's palm. This hints at the possibility that rather than the last time Mary saw her mother being August 1531, it might have been six months later. There is no evidence as to the whereabouts of Katharine or Mary for Easter itself, which fell on 31 March, although Mary addressed a letter to Katharine from Richmond on 15 March. The most likely explanation is that the material for Mary and Katharine's palms was sent to them, or that their palms were presented at Greenwich, where Henry probably was, without their presence. Mary was at Richmond during April, recovering from another bout of illness that required Henry to send a physician, but she was well enough in late April to receive visitors, among whom was Lady Lisle, wife of her great-uncle, Viscount Lisle.

Two more possible husbands for Mary were talked of during 1531–1532. The first was Wilhelm, son of the Duke of Cleves. Cleves was part of the Schmalkaldic League, which included the Duke of Saxony, the Landgrave of Hesse, and others who were all heads of Imperial states that had accepted the Confession of Augsburg, the definition of the Lutheran faith. The League hoped for support from Henry and François against the emperor. The second was the Voivode of Transylvania, John Zápolya, who ruled part of Hungary. There would have been a certain logic to this, as the Voivode was a thorn in the side of Ferdinand, King of the Romans, who ruled the rest of Hungary. One suitor, at any rate, was now unavailable. Norfolk had arranged Surrey's marriage to the daughter of the Earl of Oxford, Frances de Vere. If Anne had originally promoted the idea of a match with Mary, she had thought better of it and Norfolk was prepared to arrange a marriage he thought poor, rather than be suspected of promoting his son's prospect over his niece's.

Despite Mary's household having been disbanded, the council in Wales was still referred to as the Princess's Council in a letter of 3 May to Thomas

Cromwell, a former servant of Wolsey's whose influence with Henry was increasing daily. Some of Mary's equipment was still at Ludlow, too – there is an item in the 1532 accounts for William Chester, who fetched a bridle from Ludlow in early May. The bill for this and another for oats for her stable were paid by the Princess's Council.

In late June 1532, Norfolk called on Chapuys and they discussed a number of matters – the emperor's recent illness, the Diet of Nuremburg, and the proposed marriages of the King of Denmark's daughters, one of whom, it was suggested, might marry James of Scotland. Norfolk was certain that James still wanted Mary, but, as they were cousins, the marriage would not be allowed. On being asked his opinion about Wilhelm of Cleves, Norfolk replied that the father was mad, and the son might turn out to be mad too. Nevertheless, it was a match to be preferred to one with Scotland. Whomever Mary might marry, he would be a man of high birth, as she was still heiress to the kingdom, and although Norfolk was sure Henry would remarry, he might not have sons, in which case, Mary would remain the preferred heir. Norfolk would ensure that anyone who said she was illegitimate would have his head cut off.

On 22 August 1532, William Warham, the aged Archbishop of Canterbury, breathed his last. He had been archbishop for more than thirty years, and had married and crowned Henry and Katharine. Assigned as counsel for Katharine in 1527, he had proved little better than useless; although lukewarm about the divorce, he was disinclined to go against Henry. He had presided over the Convocation of Clergy that had accepted Henry as 'Supreme Head of the Church in England, so far as the law of Christ allows', but Henry could not quite bring himself to cast off Rome during Warham's lifetime.

With the archbishop gone, it was time for a more vigorous approach. First was the need to gain French support and by the late summer of 1532, Henry was planning another visit to Calais to meet with François. This time he was to be accompanied by Anne, rather than Katharine. According to Chapuys, bets were being laid that Henry intended to marry François' daughter, Madeleine, to prevent her marrying James. Nevertheless, the ambassador dismissed the idea, not believing that François would allow Madeleine to marry Henry before an unarguable sentence of annulment had been passed by Rome, and also aware Anne had told people that that which she had long anticipated (her marriage) would take place during the trip. A couple of weeks later, Anne was invested as Lady Marquis of Pembroke, giving her rank after the dukes of Richmond, Norfolk and Suffolk, and the marquises of Dorset and Exeter. She also received lands worth £1,000 per annum. The new title would enable her to meet the ladies of the French court as a woman of rank – the only problem being that no French ladies planned to attend.[14]

Shortly before his departure for Calais, Henry met Mary by accident 'in the fields'. Henry was at Greenwich and it is possible Mary was there too, although etiquette would have prevented her coming into her father's presence unless summoned. A more likely location for her is Eltham, about 4 miles away. According to Chapuys, the king was pleased to see his daughter and asked after her health, promising to see more of her in future. Chapuys thought Henry would have said more, but he was being overheard by two of Anne's servants. Chapuys was sure Anne was determined to keep Mary well away from the court, as she did not wish to see her or hear about her. Henry did not see more of his daughter, but he sent her £10. The Venetian envoy gave a rather different report, saying Henry had spent three hours with her, and that the two of them had gone on a large-scale hunt, with 100 buck being killed.[15]

The meeting at Calais went ahead, but achieved little. On Henry's return, according to a report to the Venetian Signory, Mary accompanied him to the Tower of London on 15 December to see progress on alterations there. Chapuys mentioned that Henry had taken Anne and various courtiers to view the works on 9 December, and invited the French ambassador to see them as well, but does not mention Mary's presence. If the Venetian account is correct, then that takes Mary's last contact with Henry, before the birth of Elizabeth, to the end of 1532. It is certainly consistent with his affection for Mary, and Anne's dislike of Henry spending time with his daughter, that he might have seen her at the Tower alone.[16]

6

The Bastard's Servant

I know of no other princess in England than myself.

Mary

Although 1533 opened as usual materially for Mary, with New Year gifts of plate from the king for herself and Lady Salisbury, it became one of the bitterest years of Mary's life. She lost her status, her place as her father's only daughter, and became aware that she was unlikely ever to see her mother again.

It was probably on 25 January 1533 that Henry married Anne Boleyn, who was in the early stages of pregnancy, showing that their relationship had at last been consummated, although the marriage was kept secret and Henry continued prevaricating with Rome.

Katharine was beside herself when she heard that Henry's excuses for answering his summons to Rome were being tolerated. She had been pleading for sentence to be given for three-and-a-half years and was desperate for resolution. She was angry with Clement, who seemed determined to make her 'die of grief'. She remained stubbornly certain that once the pope pronounced sentence in her favour, Henry would obey. However, if he did not, she at least would feel vindicated and Mary's rights to the succession would be assured, while failure to obey the papal sentence might cause Clement to put the kingdom under an interdict. When this had occurred in the reign of King John, leaving the people of England cut off from the Church, rebellion had ensued. But Katharine was losing touch with the reality of the political situation, both at court and in the country. While only a vanishingly small number of people had imbibed the doctrinal changes mooted by the Reformers, a far larger number resented the power of the pope and of the Church generally. A huge uprising to maintain the pope's authority was unlikely, especially as it was being chipped away, little by little, rather than attacked wholesale. The principal fear the Commons expressed at the idea of throwing off papal authority was that if the kingdom were declared schismatic, the English wool trade would suffer, while those in favour of leaving the pope's authority thought Henry would be followed by numerous others who would be desperate to trade with England. Again, while Anne was unpopular and Katharine and Mary much-loved, rebelling against a lawful king was a step that not many would be willing to take.

One reason for the secrecy over Henry's marriage to Anne was the need not to provoke Clement before a new archbishop of Canterbury had been installed. Henry wanted Thomas Cranmer and wrote requesting Clement to confirm his choice. Chapuys made sure Clement was informed that Cranmer had Lutheran leanings, with a view to the bulls confirming his office being delayed, or hedged about with limitations. But Clement, eager to please Henry where he could, sent the usual bulls, and Cranmer was enthroned as archbishop on 30 March 1533.

Henry was at last ready to act. His councillors and advisors had concluded that, the universities having, on balance, declared the marriage to be illegal if Katharine's marriage to Arthur had been consummated, and that consummation could be proved by presumption and by a supporting document Henry had produced suggesting that Henry VII and Ferdinand of Aragon had believed it consummated, then the matter could be decided by the archbishop. Confident and determined, Henry sent a delegation to Katharine, including the dukes of Norfolk and Suffolk and the Marquis of Exeter. They asked her one last time to accept the verdict of an English court. By doing so, she would earn not only the king's gratitude, but that of the whole nation, for avoiding war. Katharine remained immoveable. They then informed her of Henry's marriage to Anne and told her she was forbidden from trying to return to him, or to use the title of queen. If she contented herself with her former rank of Princess Dowager of Wales, she would have all of her previous dower, and anything else she might need. Otherwise, she would be obliged to retire to a small house and live on the income Henry would assign her. Katharine defiantly replied she would continue to use the title of Queen, and she hoped the king could spare the expense of her doctor, apothecary, chaplain and two women. If not, she would go out and beg for her bread.

Chapuys was overcome with anger and disgust at Henry's actions and, in a letter rather undermining his role as ambassador, called on Charles to invade. He was convinced that, other than Norfolk and two or three others, the country would rise up to support Katharine and Mary, and that the emperor had a duty to prevent the spread of Lutheranism. He was also afraid that once Anne was firmly in power she would injure Katharine, and

Mary too. She had been heard to boast that she would have Mary for her servant or marry her to some 'varlet', which would ruin the princess's chance of the succession. By the end of his letter, Chapuys seemed to think he might have gone too far, so he asked pardon for speaking out, asserting it was from compassion for the queen and princess.

From early April 1533, following the passing of the Act in Restraint of Appeals, it became a crime for anyone in England to appeal to a foreign jurisdiction against a sentence given in England. The Act was retrospective and returned any case already appealed, such as Katharine's, to English jurisdiction. Cranmer, as the chief ecclesiastic in the realm, was free to pronounce sentence on the validity of Henry and Katharine's marriage, and any appeal against it by Katharine, or anyone else, would be an offence.

On 9 April, Chapuys had an audience with Henry, at which he remonstrated about the recent Act and the story that Henry had married Anne. Henry told him that he needed an heir, to which Chapuys replied Mary was his heir, and the princess, whom he described as 'endowed with all imaginable goodness and virtue', was now of an age to marry and bear children. To this he added, tactlessly, that as Henry had received the principal title to his kingdom through his mother, he should not mind restoring it to a female. Henry took this with surprising equanimity, replying that he was wiser than his daughter, and in any event, he wanted his own children. Greatly daring, Chapuys pointed out there was no certainty the king would have more children, at which Henry drew himself up and repeatedly asked Chapuys if he were not a man like any other man? Besides, Chapuys did not know all his secrets, a comment which led the ambassador, correctly, to infer that Anne was pregnant.

It was Chapuys's opinion that Henry himself was by nature kind and generous, but Anne had 'so perverted him' that he seemed like a different man. She would not rest until she had destroyed Katharine as she had Wolsey, whom she had not hated half so much.[1] Katharine, he said, was not concerned for her own safety or future, but she was worried about Mary's. While she was to call herself princess dowager, no change had yet been made to Mary's title or status – Henry needed to wait until Anne had a child, lest she miscarry and he be left with no heir if Mary had been formally demoted.

On Easter Sunday, Anne appeared in public as queen for the first time, attending Mass in the Queen's Closet at Greenwich. Orders were given for her to be prayed for as queen throughout the kingdom from that date. This was not Henry's only order. In a command that must have nearly broken his daughter's heart, he forbade Mary either to write or send verbal messages to her mother. Mary and Katharine were used to exchanging messages every week or ten days. Mary begged her father to allow her to have a special messenger who would only exchange information about their health, or who would show any letters sent between them to Henry, but he would not relent. The only pressure he could put on Katharine was through her longing to see or hear from Mary.

On the same day that Mary received this prohibition, she was given the news that her father had married Anne Boleyn. Her immediate reaction was to be 'a little sad', but pulling herself together, she made no comment, only resolving to write immediately to her father. She was pressed by the messengers for a verbal reply, but declined to comment, other than to give them the letter to deliver. The letter itself is unknown to history, but Chapuys said Henry was pleased with it and praised his daughter's prudence. From this, we can perhaps infer Mary said nothing of substance, but assured him of her obedience to his commands. Mary's own position remained the same – she was the king's daughter, Princess of the Realm, perhaps Princess of Wales, and his only heir. But Thomas Cromwell, who after the fall of his old master, Cardinal Wolsey, was rapidly becoming the king's chief advisor, was already thinking about the future. In one of his 'to-do' lists, dating from the time between Anne's marriage and her coronation, he noted that a bill of succession would be required.

Despite Chapuys's continual urging of Charles to invade England on Katharine and Mary's behalf, the emperor had no inclination to do so. He wrote to Ferdinand that although Henry's marriage to Anne, and his treatment of her as queen, was injurious to their aunt and cousin, the best course was to continue to ask for justice in Rome. He also ordered his ambassador in France to urge the French king, if he were not willing to publicly denounce the marriage to Anne, at least not to accept it, and not to interfere with justice being done by the pope.

Cranmer convened an ecclesiastical court in Dunstable and on 23 May 1533 he pronounced Henry and Katharine's marriage invalid from the start. The king's marriage to Anne Boleyn was therefore legal. No ruling on Mary's legitimacy was made. It was widely accepted in ecclesiastic law, although not a cast-iron certainty, that the children of a marriage later found to be invalid were legitimate if the parents had acted in good faith so Mary was entitled, even if she accepted Cranmer's ruling, to consider herself legitimate. For Henry, it was not necessary for Mary to be declared illegitimate. He confidently expected Anne to be carrying a son, which would have solved his problems – even the most die-hard supporters of Katharine and Mary would probably have preferred Henry to have a male heir. In that case, Mary would have been displaced automatically, and, if still legitimate, could continue her useful role on the international marriage market.

***

Mary was now in the unenviable position of being a weapon in the war between her parents. Katharine was told that not only would she and her servants be punished if she refused to obey Henry's orders, but she would be forbidden from seeing Mary and that Mary too might be punished. Katharine continued to resist, repeating that until the case had been decided against her in Rome, she would maintain her position. As for Mary, Katharine refused to bow to the emotional blackmail. She would be sorry indeed if Mary were mistreated but, as Mary was Henry's daughter, he must do as he pleased. Not even for her daughter would Katharine damn her own soul, and that of her husband, by accepting that their marriage was invalid.

Mary continued in her accustomed manner. She addressed a letter to Cromwell from Otford, the palace of the archbishops of Canterbury, where she had been living for some time. It was a routine letter, requesting that the father of one of her servants be excused from appearing at court to be knighted, as he was nearly eighty and lived in Cheshire.

Anne was crowned as Queen of England on 1 June 1533. Later that month, Chapuys was summoned to meet the king's council. After praising him, not very truthfully, for his attempts to keep the peace between Charles and England, they assured him that although Henry had now married Anne, and could not permit Katharine to retain the title of queen or to enjoy the queen's revenues, yet, since they acknowledged her to be a virtuous lady of high birth, she would be treated humanely. Chapuys replied that the archbishop's sentence could in no way prejudice Katharine's rights. He also thought she should retain the title of queen, as Henry himself had acknowledged her as his wife for so long, and their daughter was born in wedlock. Titles, he added, were important to women. The Duchess of Suffolk had retained the title of Queen of France, and Henry himself liked to use the title King of France, at which François took no offence.

During the early summer, Mary was again ill; although no symptoms are recorded, perhaps distress at the news of Anne's coronation triggered a reaction. Mary was granted permission for Katharine's doctor and apothecary to treat her and the order against writing to Katharine was relaxed. Perhaps Henry was now so confident that he would shortly have a son, he felt Katharine and Mary's correspondence could be no threat. Recovered, Mary left Otford on 27 June for Beaulieu in Essex. The inhabitants of the villages en route turned out to welcome her, to the displeasure of Anne, who wanted them punished. That same month, June 1533, Mary's aunt, the French queen, died. Mary had known her well, and had spent a good deal of time with her in childhood, so this loss of another familiar and sympathetic face probably added to her sorrows.

In July, Clement gave an interim ruling, requiring Henry to send Anne away and take Katharine back as his wife by 30 September or face excommunication. Katharine was pleased but she had now come to the conclusion Henry would not obey without pressure from Charles. This ruling may have led to Henry taking the first steps to diminish Mary's state. Although she had not been stripped of her title, Cromwell was already referring to her in his notes as 'Lady Mary'. In one of them he reminded himself to send a message to her cofferer, William Cholmeley, to furnish him with information as to all of her household staff. A warrant was sent to her chamberlain, Lord Hussey, to hand her jewels over to Frances Aylmer, one of her ladies, to take them to Cromwell as Master of the King's Jewels.

Lady Salisbury set herself out to make Hussey's task as difficult as possible. She claimed there was no inventory of the jewels, and it was as much as Hussey could do to get her to produce the items and inventory them herself in front of him, but she refused to hand them over to Frances Aylmer without an express warrant from the king. Hussey wrote that he had never seen the jewels when Mary was not wearing them and requested further instructions as he could not override Lady Salisbury – she outranked him as a countess, a member of the royal family, and Mary's lady governess. A royal command soon arrived, followed in late August by one for plate, both that of the king's that Mary might hold, and her own. Mary's Clerk of the Jewels showed that she did not have any belonging to the king – at least, there was none noted in the inventory he had agreed with his predecessor on coming into office. He did not mention any that might have been given to Mary after that date. As for Mary's own items of plate, Lady Salisbury claimed they were all necessary when Mary was ill. Not only were Mary's plate and jewels being demanded, despite Lady Salisbury's efforts to put off the evil moment, but Cromwell also made a note for Lord Hussey to send in any 'nursery stuff' that might still be among Mary's possessions. Given the general level of spending of Henry and Anne, this was a petty move, designed to undermine Mary's position, rather than based in any necessity. Rumours were spreading abroad about the treatment of Katharine and Mary. In response, Henry sent messages to Charles telling him not to doubt that both women were very suitably treated.

In August 1533, Anne 'took her chamber' at Greenwich in preparation for the birth of her first child. Chapuys reported that, the physicians having promised a son, Henry was determined to celebrate his arrival with splendid jousts. Henry had also arranged for Anne to receive a superbly rich bed, in the royal collection from the ransom of a French nobleman in the past. Despite this, Henry and Anne had quarrelled – Henry's eye had wandered and Anne had rebuked him. It was generally the rule that couples should abstain from sex during pregnancy, but perhaps Anne had hoped Henry loved her enough to remain celibate. Henry told her she must close her eyes to it as 'more worthy' persons had done before, and that he could humble her further than he had exalted her. Nevertheless, Chapuys did not think the matter was more than a lovers' tiff.

The original drafts of letters in Anne's name, heralding the birth of a prince, were hurriedly amended when, on 7 September, she gave birth to a daughter. Dispelling rumours that the child was to be called Mary, to completely obliterate her half-sister, she was christened Elizabeth, after both her grandmothers, in a ceremony very similar to that which had attended Mary's baptism, seventeen years before. Many of the players were the same. Her godparents were Archbishop Cranmer, the Dowager Duchess of Norfolk, who was Mary's godmother, and the Dowager Marchioness of Dorset. The godmother for the bishopping was the Marchioness of Exeter, Gertrude Blount. Lady Exeter was gritting her teeth – she was known as a warm supporter of Katharine's and was there more or less under protest. However, claims that her presence was insisted on out of spite are probably unfair. Lord Exeter was Henry's nearest adult male relative in England, and his wife was performing the same duty as his mother had done for Mary. Elizabeth's title as 'Princess' was proclaimed with trumpets and the king's heralds announced that Mary was no longer to be referred to by that title. Shortly after, the members of Mary's household were deprived of their gold embroidered livery coats bearing her arms. Instead, they were to wear only the king's arms. This instantly demoted Mary from Princess of the Realm with a position and title of her own, independently of Henry, to just a daughter of the king. Chapuys spoke to the council, saying that while he saw no harm in Elizabeth being called 'princess', it ought to be very clear that this was in no way meant to imply that Mary had forfeited her rights to the succession. He reminded Norfolk that the duke had said he believed Mary to be legitimate, regardless of the validity of her parents' marriage, but Norfolk, having been reprimanded by Anne for being too intimate with the ambassador, was not to be drawn on the subject. Lady Exeter told Chapuys that Henry had sent messages throughout the country urging the people to give thanks to God that the kingdom now had a lawful heir – the implication being that Mary was to be disinherited.

Mary, whom Chapuys refers to as 'wise and gracious', made no public comment on Elizabeth's birth but wrote a comforting letter to Katharine. While Mary's letter no longer exists, Katharine's reply is preserved, giving a deep insight into their relationship.[2] Katharine assured Mary that while God was testing her, so long as she obeyed His laws, all would be well in the end – in heaven if not on earth. For practical matters, Mary was to obey Henry in everything that was not an offence against God or her conscience. She was not to discuss the annulment or to get involved in wrangling about it; she was to be vigilant and keep her keys herself, and was to be careful not to think of marriage at present. This advice suggests that Katharine feared treasonable writings or a forged acceptance of the annulment might be insinuated into Mary's papers. Nor was Mary to decide on her 'manner of life' – either in respect of marriage, or taking vows as a nun. Katharine remembered Lady Salisbury in her letter, and assured them both that they would never come to the kingdom of heaven but by troubles. Mary was to solace herself with her virginals or lute – although Katharine had obviously heard that her daughter's material circumstances were about to change, as she added the words 'if you have any'. She sent two books as well, for Mary's further comfort – *De Vita Christi,* and the *Epistles of St Jerome to Eustochium and Paula.* The first was a devotional work by Ludolph of Saxony, popular since the fourteenth century. Mary's own copy, probably not the one Katharine gave her, but a later gift, is at Lambeth Palace. The *Epistle of Jerome* gives a fascinating insight into what Katharine wanted Mary to understand and consider. Written to Eustochium, who had taken vows of chastity, like many texts, it praised virginity, while not condemning honourable marriage. It urged her to avoid temptation and be extremely careful not to drink too much wine. Katharine was obviously afraid that Mary, lonely and unhappy, might, under the influence of alcohol, be drawn into a love affair or even a forced marriage. Any lack of chastity or marriage to a low-born man would ruin her chance of succession.[3]

It was not long before Katharine's fears that Mary would be put under pressure to accept her change in status proved to be true. In mid-September, while Mary was still at Beaulieu, Lord Hussey was summoned to Greenwich and ordered by the council to inform Mary and her household that her 'high estate' of the 'name and dignity' of princess was to be diminished. When he broached the matter with Mary, the seventeen-year-old was highly indignant. This is the first direct evidence we have about Mary's attitude to the annulment. There is no prior information about anything she did or said in relation to it. We know her views were the same as Katharine's because of her actions from this time forward, but Henry might not have contemplated the possibility of disobedience – after all, a daughter's first duty was to obey her father. It may have been on this assumption that the order was given to Hussey verbally, without anything to back it up. But if Henry had believed that Mary would quietly acquiesce, he was mistaken. Imperiously, she told Hussey she could not believe she was anything other than Henry's lawful daughter, and that, without a direct command from the king, she could not accept any alteration in her status. Her servants, doubtless led by Lady Salisbury, backed her up. They would, of course, obey orders from the king, but not a verbal instruction from Hussey. He wrote to the council on 20 September, asking them to 'weigh' the matter further. The council responded via Sir William Paulet, Comptroller of the King's Household, who dispatched a letter to Beaulieu with orders for the princess to move to

Hertford Castle. Lord Hussey brought the letter to Mary. She immediately sat down to write an answer directly to her father. In it, she said she was surprised to see the order addressed to her as 'Lady' Mary, omitting the title of princess. This, she said, had made her 'marvel'. She was sure that Henry could not be privy to it. She took herself as his true-born daughter, born in holy matrimony, and had no doubt he thought the same. She could not, in good conscience, think otherwise, but was, of course, prepared to obey him in other matters.

Henry was not pleased with this response. Shortly afterwards, the earls of Oxford, Sussex and Essex and Dr Sampson arrived at Beaulieu. Their charge was to announce first, that Henry was surprised to hear both from Hussey and from Mary herself, that she had so far forgotten her 'filial obedience' that she had 'arrogantly' attempted to usurp the title of princess. In order to stop the spread of her 'pernicious' example, they were to point out to her the 'folly and danger' of her conduct and to give her the king's orders as to how she was to conduct herself fom now on, with regard to her title and household. She deserved severe punishment, but, if she behaved herself in future, Henry might forgive her. The delegation's message was probably a terrible shock for Mary. Although there is no evidence that she had seen or heard from Henry since late 1532, all her life she had been his beloved daughter. For him to send such a message via intermediaries must have been deeply hurtful. It is easy, with hindsight, to dismiss Mary's response as tactical – designed to confirm her status, but it is very possible that she was hoping against hope that Henry did not really mean to declare her illegitimate. Status was a vital component of self-worth in the sixteenth century and a change in status for a girl who had been brought up to envisage herself as an empress or a queen, even if only a consort, to that of a bastard, similar to Richmond, who was the fruit of an illicit affair, must have been hard to comprehend. There would also have been all the pain of personal jealousy – her father had a new baby, and this incident perhaps confirmed her worst fears that he no longer loved her.

Mary refused to hear the commissioners privately, lest they later put words in her mouth. Despite all their pleadings, she would not yield and by the end of the meeting they were all in tears – perhaps not surprisingly as the men had known her since babyhood, and may well have disliked browbeating a girl of seventeen. It cannot have been easy for Henry, either. He certainly had given every indication of loving his daughter, but he was also a king and if he could not enforce obedience from his own child it would ultimately reflect badly on his kingship. He had little choice but to be harsh. There is no evidence that Henry ever discussed the annulment or her change in status personally with Mary. Henry disliked doing unpleasant things himself and punishments were always meted out by others. The conversation he had with Katharine in 1527, when he told her was seeking an annulment, is the only recorded instance of him facing up to difficult personal conversations. The pain and distress he caused his wife and her tearful reaction were perhaps enough to put him off for life – his other wives were dispatched from afar. He also struggled to maintain his anger against an individual in person – Anne and her supporters had been desperate to prevent Henry seeing Wolsey, lest he be overcome with affection for his old friend, and later, he was prevented from seeing Katheryn Howard. Katherine Parr circumvented a plot against her by seeing the king before her enemies could pounce. It was this facet of Henry's personality that lay behind the concerted attempts by Anne and her friends to keep Henry away from Mary.

As noted, Henry had not necessarily wanted Mary to be branded a bastard – had Elizabeth been a boy, the problem would have gone away, and Mary could have been displaced without losing all her status. Similarly, if no living child had resulted from the pregnancy, he would still have had an heir who had not been declared illegitimate. But he was now faced with disaster – two daughters. To preserve everything he had done, and enforce Elizabeth's status, Mary had to be sacrificed. The timing may relate not just to Elizabeth's birth, but also to Clement's bull requiring Henry to return to Katharine by 30 September. Meanwhile Chapuys was urging Charles to follow up the papal ruling with more realistic threats to enforce it, and recommended that the emperor should 'get into [his] power' Reginald Pole, now studying in Padua. Chapuys said many thought Pole to have a legitimate claim to the throne and that both Katharine and Mary would favour a marriage between Pole and the princess.[3]

* * *

On 1 October 1533 Mary's household accounts began again with the description of her as 'the serene Lady Mary, daughter of the king'. At the top of the list of her attendants was Lady Salisbury, who was allowed nine attendants of her own, including two gentlewomen. Mary's other female attendants were her cousin Lady Margaret Douglas, Lady Maltravers, Lady Hussey, Frances Aylmer, who was still probably looking after such jewels as Mary had left; Mrs Butts, the wife of Mary's former physician, Dr Butts, who now served Henry; Mrs Peter de Bruxia; Mrs Giles Duwes, wife of her French tutor; and Mary Browne. Dr Fetherstone was still her schoolmaster, and Beatrice ap Rice her launderer. This household, containing 162 persons, although hardly that of a pauper, was somewhat curtailed and Chapuys reported on the reduction in indignant tones.

Mary wrote another letter, informing Henry she would be obedient to his commands, but could not derogate from the titles and prerogatives that 'God, nature and her parents' had given her. As she was the daughter of a king and queen, she had the right to be called princess, and she would do nothing either expressly or tacitly to cast doubt on either her own legitimacy or her mother's marriage. She would follow Katharine's example to 'commend everything to God' and be patient.

Of course, it was in Mary's long-term interest to maintain her position. Katharine would have told her of the triumphant reign of Mary's grandmother, Isabella, which, combined with a taste of power during her days as de facto Princess of Wales, would have made Mary just as likely as anyone else to have had ambitions to be monarch. There was nothing of the shrinking violet about Isabella or Katharine and Mary took after them. Aged seventeen, she was prepared to fight for her rights, against Henry and his council, just as Isabella had fought an army. Chapuys speculated on Henry's reasons for demoting Mary – he considered it might be 'the malignity of the Lady (Anne)', or that Henry wished to obtain a grant from Parliament, usually given on the birth of an heir. Perhaps harshness to Mary was a ploy to persuade Katharine, which Chapuys thought unlikely to be successful. Another possibility might be that Mary was being degraded so she could be restored to the succession after any sons, to please Charles, in exchange for the emperor accepting the king's marriage to Anne. It might just have been Henry's own 'evil star', causing him to increase God's wrath. Chapuys expressed concern that Mary might be forced into a convent or married against her will – reflecting the need for the advice in Katharine's letter, mentioned above.

By mid-October, Mary had had to accept her removal from Beaulieu, which was given to Anne's brother George, Lord Rochford. She herself went to Hertford Castle – by no means so attractive a home as Beaulieu. In Cromwell's 'to-do' list for the forthcoming Parliamentary session, he noted that any of Mary's possessions that were 'not meet for the princess (Elizabeth)' were to be brought to the Jewel House.

In early November, further action was taken against Mary. Now, she was not just deprived of her title, but also of her attendants, and required to live in the same household as Elizabeth. Appalled, she wrote to Chapuys for advice. He recommended that she protest against such an idea as prejudicial to her position, but that if she were forced into it, she must repeat daily that this was not evidence of her acquiescence. Cromwell claimed to be too busy to hear Chapuys's complaints so the ambassador wrote, pointing out that a subordinate [position] in Elizabeth's household would be degrading and contrary to the promises made to Charles that Katharine and Mary would be well treated. He added that 'friends could become enemies' very quickly. Cromwell's reply was evasive. It was a council matter and he could not discuss it without the king's consent, however, he could assure Chapuys that Henry would act reasonably. He knew very well that friends could turn, and, in a splendid non sequitur, told Chapuys that he had often warned Henry of the instability of King François. The council were all keen to preserve the amity of the emperor; he, Cromwell, always urged the good treatment of Mary and her mother.

Despite Chapuys's protests, on 16 December, the council sent the Duke of Norfolk, the Earl of Oxford and the king's Almoner to Mary to inform her that she was to go the 'court and service' of the Princess Elizabeth at Hatfield. Mary replied that she knew of no other princess in England than herself. Norfolk cut off debate with the statement that he had not come to dispute, but to carry out the king's orders. Mary, accepting the inevitable, said she was quite prepared to obey her father in the matter of a move to Hatfield, but asked for half-an-hour to prepare. This granted, she took the opportunity to write a letter of protest, based on a draft that Chapuys had given her. The protest was to protect her rights should she be forced into a convent or tricked into marriage.

Returning to Norfolk, Mary requested that her servants might have a year's wages, and asked whom she might bring to wait upon her. The response was that she did not need a large retinue, as there would be plenty of people already at Hatfield. Only two waiting women could go with her. At this, Lady Salisbury exclaimed that she would travel with Mary and furnish a suitable retinue out of her own purse. Norfolk rejected this idea out of hand – Lady Salisbury would not be going.

Mary, who had been used to having a vast household, all dressed in her livery and treating her as heir to the throne, was now to be treated as of minor status in the retinue of a baby. The humiliation in a status-conscious society was immense and it may have been almost impossible for Mary to accept that her previously loving father truly meant to treat her so badly. Norfolk reported back that, on arrival at Hatfield, when he asked Mary if she would not go and pay her respects to the princess, Mary again responded that she knew of no princess other than herself. As for 'Madame Pembroke's daughter', since Henry had acknowledged the child as his own, she would call her sister, as she called Richmond 'brother'. This was a nice little jibe – Richmond was illegitimate in anyone's eyes, including those of Norfolk, who was now his father-in-law, the young duke having recently married Lady Mary Howard. Departing, Norfolk asked Mary for any message to be conveyed to the king. The defiant girl responded only that his daughter, the princess, begged his blessing. The duke refused to carry such a message, so Mary told him not to bother, and retired to cry alone. Henry was angry when he heard of her defiance – believing that Norfolk had been too soft with Mary, he swore he would humble her stubborn pride.

The placing of illegitimate royal children in the households of their half-siblings was commonplace and usually worked to the advantage of both. The illegitimate off-spring could be provided for, and the legitimate ones were generally assured of their loyalty with no rivalry for position. By placing his 'illegitimate' daughter, Mary, with his 'legitimate' daughter, Elizabeth, Henry was following an acceptable precedent. But for Mary, the inversion of roles was unbearable. As well as the loss of status, Mary was now parted, not just from her parents, but from the governess who had been with her for eight years. Mary was, of course, seventeen, considered adult in the sixteenth century, and it is true that many children left their homes at a much younger age. But for Mary, going among enemies, it was a bitter blow. Chapuys interpreted the dismissal of her governess as a sign that Mary was to be isolated so she could be quietly dispatched – either to a nunnery, a degrading marriage, or more permanently. To add to Mary's misery, Lady Margaret Douglas was given an honorary position in Elizabeth's household, but sent to wait on Anne – increasing Anne's prestige, and separating the cousins. Following the break-up of Mary's household, more than £700 worth of her plate was returned to the mint for melting down. Nearly one thousand pounds'-worth of Katharine's followed it and twelve hundred pounds'-worth belonging to the Duke of Richmond. Richmond, having been promoted as a possible rival to Mary for the succession, now needed to be downgraded lest he compete with Elizabeth.

Chapuys had received no reply to his earlier remonstrances about Mary's treatment but now received a notification from Henry, via Norfolk and Cromwell, that the king wished to receive Chapuys's questions in writing – not to delay answering, but so that he could take advice. Chapuys replied that the meat of his argument was that Henry had no power to declare Mary illegitimate or deprive her of her title. The response from the councillors was that that might be the case in Charles's dominions, but matters were quite different in England. The ambassador reiterated that Mary's legitimacy was a matter of ecclesiastic, not English, law. Norfolk and Cromwell had nothing to say to this, so they told Chapuys they would discuss his point with Henry. They repeated to Chapuys that Henry would not do anything to indicate that the decision by Cranmer was not final and binding. After further discussions, in which Henry proved immoveable, Chapuys told the emperor that he would not remonstrate further with the king about Mary's treatment – it only irritated him and made him more 'fierce and obstinate'. He had heard that Henry intended Parliament to pass an Act declaring Mary illegitimate and barring her from the succession, which he interpreted as Anne's doing, saying that Henry dared not displease her. Chapuys was very sure the people of England were outraged at Henry's behaviour and suggested that Charles invade and claim the crown himself, based on his descent from John of Gaunt – an outcome that Chapuys was certain would be greeted with joy. At the very least, Charles ought to ban trade with Flanders, which would so materially damage the English economy that Henry would be forced to rethink. But invading England was no part of Charles's plans. He already had problems in Flanders where the regent, Mary of Hungary, was in poor health. Cromwell was told of a rumour that if she died, the emperor would try to obtain either Katharine or Mary to take her place but the English envoy, Hacket, had told the Flemish that the ladies were treated honourably at home, and that neither could leave the country without Henry's permission. As for the pope and the emperor, if they realised what harm Henry could do them, then the pope would probably prefer to 'wipe his arse with his briefs' against Henry's marriage, rather than publish them.

The French too, were unsure what action to take. Chapuys reported a conversation with the French ambassador, who thought that, since Henry had made up his mind about the marriage, the best course would be for Charles (and by implication, François) to press for Mary's legitimacy, as born in good faith, and her place in the succession to be assured. If Mary were then married to a strong husband, Elizabeth would have few supporters beyond adherents of her Boleyn family.

***

The Christmas of 1533 was dismal for Mary – even the two ladies she had been permitted to take to Hatfield had been dismissed, and her personal entourage reduced to a single chamber woman. For New Year 1534, for the first time, she did not receive a present from her still-enraged father. She was not entirely forgotten. The Scottish ambassador requested a match between her and King James – even if she were illegitimate, he would still take her because she was so virtuous. But Henry was having none of it. The marriage of Mary to his next male heir would be too great a threat to his, and Elizabeth's, position.

Mary was still acting as the mistress of a household was expected to do, in promoting the welfare of her former servants. Sir Brian Tuke, the king's secretary, wrote to Lord Lisle, now governor of Calais, asking him to find a post for Richard Baker, who had been Mary's gentleman usher. Mary had asked Tuke to find a good position for him. This suggests Mary was still free to communicate with the court, and that, although Henry was angry with her, his courtiers did not dismiss her requests as negligible.

On 17 January, Henry went to Hatfield, without Anne. His purpose was two-fold: to visit Elizabeth, and to speak to Mary personally, to persuade her to obey his commands. According to Chapuys, after he had left, Anne became concerned that in Mary's presence, Henry would weaken and take his daughter back into favour. She therefore sent Cromwell after Henry, to request (or command!) that he refrain from Mary's presence. Orders were sent ahead for Mary to keep to her chamber. Rather than Henry speaking to her himself, Cromwell, Norfolk and the captain of the guard went to her room to order her once again to renounce her title. She refused. She had already answered, and it was useless to press her further. Nothing could make her change her mind, she declared – not ill-treatment, nor rudeness, nor even the possibility of death.

She gave them a message to her father, asking to come into his presence so she could kiss his hand. Henry refused, but desperate to make some appeal or to see the father she loved, Mary went up onto the roof of the house to watch his departure. He caught sight of her, and she sank to her knees, holding out her hands in supplication. Henry bowed and touched his hat to her, after which all of his retinue also saluted her. Henry must have been almost as torn as Mary. A disobedient child could not be indulged, but his fatherly instincts were strong, and it probably pained him not to see the daughter he had once doted on.

Anne was angry when she heard of Mary's defiance, and complained to Henry that the girl was not kept strictly enough. She did not believe that Mary could have been so stubborn or given such prudent answers without someone to prompt her. Henry assumed that Mary's obstinacy was founded on trust that Charles would protect her. To an extent, both Anne and Henry were right. Chapuys was certainly stiffening Mary's resolve, and probably assuring her of Charles's support for her, but the ultimate decision to resist the pressure on her was Mary's own.

Following the visit to Hatfield, Henry informed the French ambassador that he had refused to see Mary because of her obstinacy, which he blamed on her Spanish blood. The French ambassador responded that Mary had been very well brought up, at which Henry came close to tears and praised his daughter. Anne continued to feel this affection as a threat to her position and that of Elizabeth – a servant of the Earl of Northumberland's told Chapuys that Northumberland knew for certain that Anne intended to poison Mary. This is a curious statement. While Anne probably did speak intemperately on this, as on other matters, it seems odd that Northumberland, who had once hoped to marry Anne, should believe and repeat such a story. Chapuys may not have known of their history but he wrote that the story was credible because of Northumberland's 'great credit and familiarity' with Anne. Chapuys certainly took the threat seriously, sending a warning to Mary to be on her guard. He also brought the Scottish ambassador to put forward the idea that there would be no peace with Scotland until James's right to succeed Mary had been agreed – presumably the idea being that Henry would ensure Mary's safety rather than risk James inheriting.

On 8 February 1534 Katharine wrote to Charles. Angry and disappointed that the pope had not yet firmly declared his judgement, she castigated

Charles for not having put more pressure on Clement. She wrote that she and Mary were treated 'like the most miserable creatures in the world', subject to 'daily surprises and insults'. Nevertheless, she would continue to defend her rights, as failure to do so would imperil her soul. She hoped Mary would do the same.[4] Later that month, Chapuys persuaded Norfolk, who continued to favour an Imperial over a French alliance, to arrange an audience with Henry. During the meeting, Chapuys requested permission to appear in Parliament, where a Bill of Succession was being debated, to speak for Katharine and Mary. In a long discussion, Chapuys pointed out that Mary was legitimate, regardless of the state of her parents' marriage and Henry had continued to treat her so until the birth of Elizabeth. Henry responded that, even if that were the case, Mary deserved to be disinherited for her disobedience. Chapuys certainly would not be permitted to go to Parliament – it was quite contrary to all custom to allow foreigners to appear. In any event, neither the pope nor any other prince had any right to interfere within his kingdom. According to its laws, his heir was Elizabeth, or any subsequent children he might have – and he was in good hopes of more. Legitimacy was a matter for his lay judges. Chapuys relinquished the request to visit Parliament, which he had known would never be permitted, in the hope that a follow-up request for Mary to be allowed to live with her mother or, at any rate, in a separate household from Elizabeth, would be granted. He suggested that if anything happened to Mary, even a death from natural causes, Henry would be blamed, as Henry II had been blamed for the death of Thomas Becket. It can hardly have been music to Henry's ears to have the Imperial ambassador imply that he would connive at the secret murder of his own daughter, yet he restrained himself, merely responding that his daughter was very suitably accommodated where she was.

So worried was Chapuys about the treatment of Mary, that he even floated the idea that she should accept being demoted from the title of 'Princess' if she could live with her mother. On the other hand, he argued against himself, if she renounced her rights, she might lose the support of those who did not understand her reasons. Also, if a reconciliation were effected, she might be in greater danger from an Anne who purported to be her friend than her open enemy. Anne had sent orders to her aunt, Lady Shelton, who was now in the position of lady governess to Mary, that Mary was not to use the title of Princess, and that, if she did, she was to be struck 'as the cursed bastard that she [was]'.[5] She was also to be forced to eat at the communal table, rather than in her own chamber. The purpose of this was probably a combination of making her take a place at the table showing her of lower rank than Elizabeth, and dispelling rumours of poison.

Mary was suffering practical difficulties – she may still have been growing, as she found herself to be short of clothes. She sent a messenger to Henry to ask for either money or clothes, but the courier was not to accept anything written that did not use the title of princess. While previous accounts indicate that Mary was left without any servants of her own other than her chamber woman, this implies that she had at least one male servant. He was also to ask for permission for her to attend Mass in the parish church. A warrant for clothes was issued in March, but the second request was refused – probably so that she could not attract local support. As Mary had been cheered as princess by the local inhabitants when she was seen walking along a gallery, orders came that she was to be kept more strictly. Norfolk and Rochford complained that Lady Shelton was not treating her severely enough. Lady Shelton replied that, even if she had been no more than the bastard of a gentleman, Mary would deserve to be treated kindly for her 'goodness and virtues'. This speaks well of both Mary and Lady Shelton. Clearly Mary was not taking out her anger and frustration on Anne's aunt who was only obeying orders. There was other sympathy in Elizabeth's household for Mary's plight. One of the gentlemen was dismissed for having undertaken some service for Mary – perhaps it was he who had been sent to ask Henry for clothes.[6]

In late February, or early March, Anne herself came to Hatfield. She sent a message to Mary, saying that if the girl would attend her and honour her as queen, Anne would intercede for her with Henry. Mary sent back a message that she knew of no other queen in England but her mother, but that if Lady Anne would speak kindly of her to her father, she would be very grateful. Anne sent further messages, evolving from pleas to threats as Mary refused to move. Eventually, she gave up in disgust – saying she would humble the pride of Mary's 'unbridled' Spanish blood.

Parliament deliberated the Succession Bill and a further Bill making Henry Supreme Head of the Church in England. Chapuys wrote that Henry had deliberately excluded bishops or lords whom he thought would oppose him, including Fisher of Rochester. Chapuys was sure there were many nobles and gentry who, if Charles gave so much as a hint of military support, would rise up against Henry, but, as things stood, Henry would get his way by bribes, threats and promises. There was little objection in Parliament to the Bill of Succession, other than from some cities, which had given sureties at the time of the marriage treaty between Henry and Katharine, concerned that their merchants would be badly treated in Charles's territories. The Bill for exchanging Katharine's jointure lands as queen, with dower lands due to her as Arthur's widow, appeared extremely generous, as the annual values were considerably higher. Talk was cheap – Henry knew that Katharine would refuse to accept any income as princess dowager. There were some who were willing to accept Katharine's displacement, who were less sanguine about the overthrow of the pope's power. Even Norfolk was reluctant to accept it, saying to the French ambassador that neither he, nor his friends, would tolerate it. He rapidly lost favour at court, although no concrete action was taken against him.

On 16 March, the French ambassador in England, Castillon, wrote to François that he had discussed with Henry that the pope, if left to himself, would judge in Henry's favour, and a marriage between Mary and Alessandro de Medici, now Duke of Florence, would resolve the matter. It would be an honourable marriage for her, as she would be Duchess of Florence, and it would not affect the rights of Henry's children by his second marriage. Henry rejected the notion. He was very angry with Mary for her disobedience and intended to punish her. He was so bitter against her, in fact, that Castillon described him as hating her. Instead, he proposed either of his nieces, Lady Margaret Douglas or Lady Frances Brandon – he would give them rich dowries.

Less than a week after this conversation, the 1534 Act of Succession became law. It required all the king's subjects to swear an oath accepting that his marriage to Anne was valid and that the succession would vest in his children by her. In addition, it denied the authority of the pope, referred to as the Bishop of Rome, in England, although implementation of this clause was to be held over until St John's Day (24 June). The Act did not declare Mary to be illegitimate – it did not mention her at all. Thus, on the basis of the doctrine that children born of a union entered into in good faith, are legitimate, Mary, although displaced from her position as Henry's immediate heir, had a valid claim still to be a lawful successor in the event of Elizabeth's death. Levine, in his detailed article on this point, concludes it was a deliberate decision on the part of the drafters of the Bill, probably led by Cromwell, to leave Mary's legitimacy intact, although Mary may not have appreciated this legal subtlety.[7]

Meanwhile, in Rome, the Consistory of Cardinals finally pronounced Henry and Katharine's marriage valid. The ground given was not that Arthur and Katharine's marriage was unconsummated, a matter which they felt was not susceptible of proof that could rebut the legal presumption of consummation, but that Henry, despite being in possession of all the facts, had waited eighteen years before questioning it. The sentence needed papal ratification, and it was also Clement's role to pronounce sentence on any failure of Henry to restore Katharine – deprivation of his kingdom and permission for any Christian king to take it from him. Clement, still reluctant to push the English king to extremes, did not immediately act. Nevertheless, Henry greeted the news by instructing sermons vilifying the pope and implementing those elements of the Act of Succession that had been put on hold. He also wrote to François, declaiming the sins of Clement and Charles, and requesting his 'good brother' to 'withdraw' from the pope and stand by him.

Charles had received the cardinals' sentence with pleasure, in principle, but was puzzled as to what action he should take. He had always claimed he would uphold any sentence of excommunication and interdict against England (which would absolve him from all treaties, and also bar trading with England) but he had never wished to push the matter to depriving Henry of the crown. Chapuys urged Charles to act while public opinion was still strongly in favour of Katharine and Mary. He feared that delay would be fatal as the 'new sect', Lutheranism, was increasing daily. He suggested a trade embargo for a few months would force Henry's hand, but Charles had enough problems without alienating his Burgundian homeland with trade restrictions.

Mary was not officially informed of the cardinals' sentence but Chapuys found means to send her a message, bidding her remain steadfast in her opposition. She replied the news made her happier than being given a 'million of gold'. How Chapuys communicated with her is a mystery, but in the letter in which he reported this to Charles, he mentioned that the French ambassadors had visited Elizabeth. They had not been permitted to see Mary, but it is possible that one of the retinue took a message from Chapuys and passed it on.

Petty insults against Mary continued. In mid-March Norfolk visited her and, to prove his loyalty after the suspicions aroused by his statement of support for the papacy, took away her remaining jewellery, telling her that she was not a princess, and her pomp and pride must be reduced. Part of this punishment was owing to Mary's refusal to travel behind Elizabeth in a move to a new location. She would go where commanded but would not openly be seen to accept an inferior position. Mary took her objections to travelling behind Elizabeth to the limit, and on 26 March was manhandled into a litter with Lady Shelton, behind her half-sister, protesting all the while, and maintaining her rights. Chapuys was shocked she had gone so far and thought that a verbal protestation, followed by submission to filial obedience should have been enough.[8] After she had left, her servants and her rooms were searched and a report sent to Cromwell. The record is so mutilated by fire that it is impossible to distinguish whether anything was found, other than a bag of purple velvet with letters in it – there is nothing to indicate whether the letters were harmless or might have been considered treasonable. Given Katharine's previous warning to Mary to keep her keys herself, she had probably been too careful to leave anything of an incriminating nature to be found.

***

On 30 March 1534, king and Parliament issued a proclamation affirming that Henry and Katharine's marriage was null, and his marriage to Anne was valid. Furthermore, calling anyone other than Anne and Elizabeth 'queen' or 'princess', would be high treason, and anyone who 'murmured' against the Act of Succession, or concealed knowledge of any crime under it, would have their goods confiscated and be subject to imprisonment. Katharine was to be called Princess Dowager of Wales, and was to be 'well-obeyed and used, according to her honour and noble parentage'. Despite the years of wrangling over the annulment and the complete breakdown of their marriage, Henry always maintained, in public, at least, respect for Katharine as a princess of royal blood. Cromwell made a note to himself to have the Acts of Succession read in front of Katharine and Mary, and their answers taken. It was reported in Rome, obviously incorrectly as to details, that Mary had been deprived by Parliament of the principality of Wales, from which we can again infer that she was widely perceived to have had that position. The report also said it had been conferred on Elizabeth – which was not exactly true, as Elizabeth was not created Princess of Wales by Letters Patent either, nor was the terminology ever used of her in state papers, but it did reflect Elizabeth's status as heir to the kingdom.[9]

In April, it was reported that Mary was being offered as a bribe to James V, along with lands and money previously taken from Scotland, in lieu of his proposed marriage to Madeleine of France. In return, Mary and James were to give up all title to England. This rumour was quickly scotched by an announcement from the council that, although illegitimate, Mary was too close in blood to the king for such an idea to be countenanced. Chapuys reacted by continuing to woo the Scottish ambassador from the French alliance to a warmer relationship with the Empire, through a match with one of the many Imperial ladies. He also pushed the Scottish ambassador to inform Henry that if Mary were not the legitimate heir, then James was. Chapuys hoped that with the prospect of a Scottish invasion in support of such a claim after his death, Henry would be motivated to keep Mary safe.

Chapuys was either free to correspond with Mary and Katharine or, more likely, had covert means of dispatching items to them. He sent Mary books of consolation and assured Charles that Mary was very much comforted by them. He also warned her to refuse any overtures of marriage from the Marquis of Saluzzo, a puppet of François'. Mary promised not to marry without the consent of her mother, and the emperor. While it must have been a great relief to Mary to feel that she had support, and it is easy to feel sympathetic to Chapuys who seems to have let his emotions run ahead of his diplomatic position, yet he was encouraging Mary to disobey her father in favour of a foreign monarch – not an action most of Henry's subjects would have approved, no matter how badly they thought Mary had been treated.

***

On 18 April, Elizabeth was taken to visit her parents at Eltham, probably leaving Mary behind at Hatfield. Sir William Kingston wrote to Lord Lisle that Elizabeth was 'as much in the king's favour as goodly child should be'. If Mary heard this, and surely one of the household would have made the effort to share the information, it would have been a painful reminder of happier days when she and her parents had been together as a loving family unit. In Elizabeth's absence, Sir William Paulet and Anne's father, Wiltshire, tried to persuade Mary to accept the oath of succession. As a choice of messengers, Wiltshire was hardly likely to be convincing and Mary refused. The next day, Henry and Anne returned with Elizabeth to Hatfield. Mary was ordered to keep to her chamber, and her chambermaid, who had initially refused to swear to the Act of Succession, was locked in her room and, to Mary's distress, bullied into acceptance. Mary herself was informed by Lady Shelton that Henry no longer cared whether she renounced her title or not, as she had been confirmed by statute as a bastard. In the king's place, Lady Shelton declared, she would kick her out of the house for disobedience, and the king had said Mary would lose her head for it. Mary, frightened by this overt threat, asked to see her former doctor privately – he was still in the household, officially attending Elizabeth. This was refused, so the quick-thinking Mary spoke to him publicly. She told him it was so long since she had practised her Latin that she could barely string two words together. He suggested she say a few words, so she immediately told him about the threat that she would be forced to conform to the Act or be executed. Mary had obviously not lost her competence in Latin – she could think and speak fluently in it without notes or books. The physician was shocked, but he merely told her she was right to think her skills had deteriorated – her words made no sense. He then secretly arranged for a message to be sent to Chapuys.

The king's councillors spread through the country, to take oaths to the succession. In addition, the monasteries were required to swear to the king's supremacy, and to pray for Henry, Anne and their daughter, and for the Archbishop of Canterbury. The pope was to be considered no greater than any other bishop. There were few objections, although the monks of the London Charterhouse were among those refusing. Two of their number were taken to the Tower in early May.

Henry and James agreed a treaty on 11 May in which the English king accepted the marriage of James and François' daughter. His earlier objections were based on the desire to prevent a closer union between France and Scotland but he had little ground for interference, and no desire to alienate François who was still his chief friend in Europe. It was probably also desirable to remove the possibility of James marrying Mary, who thus lost another suitor.

7

Resistance

She is my death and I am hers.

Anne Boleyn

Chapuys continued to urge Charles to take forceful action against Henry, before Mary and Katharine's supporters were reconciled by time to the removal of papal authority. He reported that Henry was still desperate for Mary to acquiesce in her demotion and had asked Lady Shelton whether Mary were persisting in her obstinacy. Hearing that she was, Henry became certain she was being encouraged by secret communication from Katharine. Lady Shelton thought the only possible messenger was Mary's chamber woman. In this she was correct. The maid had been smuggling letters in and out. She was dismissed, as was Mary's confessor, to be replaced by one whom Chapuys characterised as 'Lutheran'.

Henry, either seeing that threats were useless, or genuinely eager to be reconciled with his daughter, sent messages assuring her that if she would only accept his marriage to Anne, she would retain a royal title and dignity. Mary's response was that she could not be tempted by such promises to believe her parents had lived in adultery, or that she was illegitimate. According to Chapuys, Mary had little faith in Henry's promises, believing the use of the carrot, rather than the stick, was just to remove any suspicions that she would be poisoned. If she were, she was certain she would go straight to heaven, and be free of earthly troubles. The only thing that upset her now was thinking of her mother's troubles. How much of this rather melodramatic announcement was Mary's own words, and how much was Chapuys's interpretation is impossible to tell. Did Mary really think her father would connive at her being poisoned?

Henry tried another tack to persuade Mary, and Katharine, to obedience. Chapuys was summoned to Westminster at 7 o'clock one morning in May 1534, to be greeted by the full panoply of the English government – Norfolk, Suffolk, Exeter, Wiltshire, the archbishops of Canterbury and York, the bishops of London, Durham and Ely, Cromwell, the Lord Chancellor Audley and many others, including the principal judges and Drs Sampson and Fox. Business opened with Fox making a long Latin speech in which he first conveyed Henry's compliments on Chapuys's conduct of his office of ambassador, and then explained that Henry had been legally separated from his 'detestable and abominable' first marriage, had lawfully married his present wife and had issue by her. Parliament had therefore declared the child of this marriage, Elizabeth, his heir. This decision had been supported by the voluntary oaths of his subjects – the only ones to refuse having been Katharine and Mary. Neither Henry, nor his chief advisors, had been able to induce them to swear and, therefore, Henry would be compelled to use the full rigour of the law against them, unless Chapuys could persuade them.

Chapuys responded with a criticism of the statute, saying it could not apply retrospectively to Mary's legitimacy, and further, the validity of the marriage rested with the Holy See, not the English Parliament. Even if it were within Parliament's competence, since neither Mary nor Katharine had been allowed to make representations either in person or through him as their proxy, the statute could not be valid. The very fact that people were being asked swear the oath made it obvious that the statute was not sufficient of itself, he said, before adding that it was not Katharine and Mary who were obstinate, as the marriage had been pronounced good by the Consistory of Cardinals. Even if he himself were convinced by the council's arguments, he certainly had no influence over the ladies, and if he had, he would not use it, with no instructions from Charles to do so. He would be very happy to send whatever message the king liked to Charles, since he was certain that in the face of Katharine and Mary's general humility and obedience, Henry must want to treat them well and not bring upon himself the opprobrium of foreign princes by treating them badly. If Henry were really desirous of peace, continued Chapuys, he would respect the fact that Charles thought of Katharine as a mother, and Mary as his sister or daughter and was bound to protect their rights, as well as maintain the authority of the Church. The bishops of Durham and London made further points, which Chapuys also rebutted.

Eventually, Norfolk, tired of listening to the arguments, announced there was no merit in discussing the marriage, or questioning the validity of the statutes. The thing was done and Mary and Katharine must conform. Chapuys replied this was nothing more than maintaining law by force, rather than reason. Katharine and Mary, he added, had no thoughts of disturbing the peace, and Katharine had often exhorted the emperor that no war should be fought upon her account – a claim not entirely consistent with some of his letters. The meeting closed with the councillors telling Chapuys that they would convey Henry's intentions to him, after which Chapuys took Cromwell aside and told him that, in order to maintain peace, Henry should treat the ladies more gently. Cromwell promised to see to it, but Chapuys thought him too frightened of Anne's wrath to do so. Cromwell did agree that Spaniards living in England would be exempt from the oath. If Chapuys really did harangue Henry's council in the manner he reported to his master, he was a brave man – it was not unknown for diplomatic immunity to be ignored.[1]

Henry was considering another summit with François in the summer of 1534 but he was in two minds about the visit; he was nervous that if he left the kingdom without taking measures for Anne and Elizabeth's safety, the emperor might invade in support of the papal sentence. To mitigate the risk, he asked François to provide vessels to patrol the Channel and to agree to retaliatory action if Charles did attack.

On 7 June 1534, Mary signed a Latin declaration, protesting against being declared illegitimate and being deprived of her title of Princess of Wales. She wrote that she would not marry, enter a convent or take any step at the will of her father, without her mother's free consent. The paper had been pre-prepared by Chapuys and given to Katharine in the previous autumn to pass on to Mary. Mary had added another sentence in her own hand, confirming that it was her own assertion, made in full knowledge and after mature deliberation, signed and sealed by her.[2] The document was smuggled out to Chapuys, who had it notarised, and sent on to Brussels. How Mary was now communicating with Chapuys after the dismissal of her maid has never been discovered – even he did not know how she had employed 'her angel and incomparable wit' to smuggle the declaration past her guards. Since a number of her former servants were still in the household, even if they were now serving Elizabeth, she must have found one who was sympathetic to her and willing to run a significant risk to help her. While Mary was being treated shabbily, Richmond, who must have been willing to swear the oath, had been appointed to represent Henry in the sovereign's place as the annual Garter ceremony.

Chapuys heard that Anne was swearing that when Henry crossed to France, she would use her power as regent to have Mary put to death, either by starvation or some other means. Rochford warned his sister such an act would incur Henry's wrath, but Anne claimed she did not care – she would see it done, even if she were to be burnt for it. How seriously we should take Anne's threats, if she did indeed make them, is debatable. It is hard to imagine she would have had Mary starved to death, but it is not inconceivable that, if she could, she would have had her tried and executed, according to law, for failure to swear the oath of succession. As long as Anne did not have a son, she knew that Elizabeth would be unlikely to be preferred to Mary in the event of Henry's death. She certainly would have meant Mary to be intimidated. Rochford's warning that harming Mary would anger Henry suggests the king still loved Anne, but not, perhaps, to the exclusion of all other feelings. Although it was now eighteen months since Henry had seen his elder daughter, other than the brief bow he made to her in the courtyard at Hatfield, not all paternal feeling was dead – quite apart from the political repercussions that might follow if Anne caused Mary's death.

Pressure was being exerted on two other people whose reputations, both national and international, caused the government to deem their agreement to the Act of Succession vital to its success. The former Lord Chancellor, Sir Thomas More, and Bishop Fisher of Rochester had both agreed that they would accept Queen Anne's children as heirs to the crown, but they would not accept the Act in its entirety, although they gave no reasons for not doing so. Cranmer thought this compromise ought to be accepted – it would take the wind out of the sails of Katharine and Mary and their supporters and, since much had been made of More and Fisher's integrity, it would be a propaganda coup and perhaps lead others to conform. Henry would not accept the compromise lest it set a precedent for picking and choosing. Rochester, described as so weak that he could hardly bear the clothes on his back, reaffirmed his willingness to accept the new succession, and would even promise not to 'meddle' further on behalf of Katharine, although he could not swear the whole oath. Still Henry refused.

That July the pope finally confirmed the cardinals' ruling in favour of the validity of Henry and Katharine's marriage. This was probably the spur to another attempt made to persuade Mary to renounce her title. Wiltshire was sent and made it plain that, if she would obey Henry, he would treat her generously, but if not, she would be further punished. Once again, the attempt was fruitless. The involvement of Wiltshire was bound to aggravate Mary and make her less likely to accept the oath; perhaps, deep down, Anne did not want Mary to submit but would have preferred her to be punished for failure to sign and thus be removed from Elizabeth's path. Henry, frustrated, sent word that Mary was to be kept in her room when he went to visit Elizabeth at Eltham.

In early August, Anne, Lady Hussey, formerly one of Mary's attendants, was interrogated in the Tower by three councillors. Lady Hussey was asked how often she had visited Mary since the latter had been deprived of her title. She replied that she had only visited on one occasion since being dismissed from her post in December 1533 – the Whitsun just past. Nor had Mary sent for her at any time. The visit had occurred because she was accompanying

Hussey to Parliament and took the opportunity to visit her old mistress. She was then asked if she knew that, according to the laws of the realm, Mary was no longer to be considered princess, and, if she did know, why had she twice referred to her by that title, once to say that the princess wanted a drink, and once to say she had gone for a walk? Lady Hussey assured the men it was a slip of the tongue; she had been used to addressing Mary by that title, and had forgotten to correct it. She denied having heard anyone call Mary 'princess' since it was forbidden or proclaiming the marriage of Katharine and Henry to be valid since it had been adjudged invalid, nor had she heard anyone argue that Mary was legitimate because her parents' marriage was made in good faith. She admitted that she and Mary had exchanged 'tokens' – small presents sent as a sign of friendship – and had asked after each other's health. She had previously thought the king's first marriage to be legal, but now that it had been judged otherwise by Parliament, she had accepted that it was not. She finally protested that she was very sorry to have offended the king, and promised not to do so again. She remained in the Tower to reflect on her misdemeanours.[3]

Charles and Chapuys were still coming up with schemes for Mary's marriage. Chapuys was pushing the Scots ambassador for a marriage to James, while Charles was suggesting that a marriage to the Duke of Angoulême (François' third son) would be the best outcome – giving both François and Charles reason to force Henry to reinstate Mary as his heir. Charles's instructions to his ambassador in France were to sound François gently on the idea – if no agreement transpired, he did not want François telling Henry of the suggestion.

Henry was being faced by rebellion in Ireland, which he suspected the emperor was encouraging. One of Chapuys's contacts told him Cromwell thought that Charles would never declare war because of the importance of trade to Flanders and Spain, and that the best way to restore amity between Charles and Henry would be the deaths of Katharine and Mary. Chapuys immediately replied that that would give Charles an even greater incentive to intervene. He was worried that Parliament, due to reassemble in November, would be asked to pass the death penalty on the women, in accordance with the Act of Succession.

Mary wrote to Chapuys three times, asking his advice on what to do when Elizabeth's household moved from Eltham. If she protested at taking the inferior position, she might be carried by force as before. Chapuys advised her to protest, but not to let herself be manhandled. Perhaps also wanting to avoid an embarrassing display of force, Henry's Comptroller, Sir William Paulet, agreed that Mary could ride, rather than go in a litter, so, although she was forced to walk out of the house after Elizabeth, once mounted she rode on swiftly, to arrive at the barge an hour ahead of the rest of the party.

Entering it, she took the place of honour. There was no possibility she would be forcibly removed in public, so Elizabeth's entourage had to accept the situation. Chapuys disguised himself and watched from the river bank as the barge passed Greenwich.

The constant need to protect her position, and the stress these acts of defiance caused, may have been the root cause of the bout of illness Mary suffered in late August, manifesting as pains in her head and stomach. According to Chapuys, she had been slightly ill when obliged to leave Eltham, and moving had exacerbated it. Lady Shelton had had her diagnosed and treated by a Mr Michael, presumably the household physician. The pill he gave her made her sicker than ever, so, afraid he would be accused of poisoning her, he declined to treat her again without a colleague, especially as Lady Shelton would not allow Chapuys's messenger to see her. Henry sent Dr Butts to treat her. Butts sent for Katharine's physician and apothecary, no doubt to assuage any suspicions of foul play. They were only to speak English and were not to see Mary except in the presence of others. Butts diagnosed the same illness as had troubled Mary in the spring of 1532.

In September 1534, Chapuys reported that Henry doubted that Anne was pregnant. She had had 'a goodly belly' in late April, and her pregnancy was also mentioned in June as a reason for the proposed meeting with French being all male. She should, therefore, have been at term by the end of September, but there is no record of a delivery or a miscarriage. Lipscomb in *1536: The Year that Changed Henry VIII*, postulates a phantom pregnancy. Perhaps in disappointment, Henry had been renewing his suit to a very beautiful young lady. The woman in question, whom no one has identified, sent Mary a message saying she should be of good cheer for matters would improve for her. As soon as she could, the mystery woman would show herself to be Mary's true servant. Chapuys noted that much of Anne's boldness had diminished in the face of this rival, but she and her sister-in-law, Jane, Lady Rochford, had hatched a plan for the woman to be sent away. The scheme backfired. Henry was furious, banishing Lady Rochford instead and telling Anne she should be grateful for all he had done for her – if he had to begin again, he would not do as much. But Chapuys thought Charles ought not to set too much store by this – Anne knew well how to manage the king.

Mary was sufficiently recovered by late September to write to Sir Nicholas Carew, a gentleman of Henry's Privy Chamber, and an old friend of the king's. Mary had known him for many years, and he was her loyal supporter. This immediately aroused suspicion, and Lady Shelton was asked by Henry to find out who had taken the letter, and what the response had been. Mary told Lady Shelton the letter had been taken by her servant, Randall Dodd, and a response had been received from Carew's wife, Elizabeth. Lady Carew was the daughter of Lady Bryan – formerly Mary's governess, now Elizabeth's.

Lady Carew had sent an open letter, urging Mary 'for the Passion of Christ' to obey her father, or she would be utterly undone. Lady Bryan confirmed the truth of the statement. Nevertheless, Henry was right to be suspicious. Lords Hussey and Darcy had both told Chapuys that an invasion by Charles would command much popular support and Carew was no friend to Anne Boleyn, despite his wife being Anne's cousin. The mention of Dodd, who had been in Mary's household since 1525, suggests she was not as isolated as Chapuys claimed.

Henry wrote a stiff letter to Charles, insisting the rumours that he treated Katharine and Mary badly were quite untrue. Katharine had been assigned an excellent portion as dowager princess, despite having behaved very badly towards Henry. As for his daughter, he did not need any instruction on how to treat her. If Chapuys had reported matters properly, Charles could not be in any doubt of how honourably Henry had behaved.

In Rome, Clement VII finally died, probably to his own great relief. He was succeeded by Paul III, who said, first, that he would call a General Council, and second, that he would look on the King of England as a dear son. Casale, still acting for Henry in Rome, seemed to think reconciliation might be possible, as the French had promoted Paul's election.

Anne was becoming nervous about her place in Henry's affections, and needed to increase the pressure on Mary to conform, which she did through encouraging the household around Mary to treat her rudely and aggravate her. Chapuys, on being informed of this, went to Cromwell to remonstrate, although he purported to have more important business, and only mentioned Mary in passing. He reminded Cromwell that the minister had spoken very highly of Mary and asked him to promote peace and concord by making sure that Mary did not have to renounce her title or let Elizabeth take precedence. Mary's actions could not affect Henry's will, but to succumb to losing her title and being forced to cede precedence to her half-sister might seriously damage her health. Chapuys was sure that Henry could not want such an outcome, either personally, or for the sake of his reputation. Cromwell assured Chapuys he would continue to do what he could for Mary. He had only spoken to her once, he said, presumably referring to the meeting at Hatfield in January 1534, but had seen 'great gifts of grace and nature' in her.[4] He had also received orders from Henry that she was to be well treated, and that Chapuys was to let him know if he found she were not – Chapuys had been given permission to send a servant once a week to check on Mary's health. Cromwell added he did not think there would be any further problems with Mary's treatment, as he knew the king to have a strong paternal affection for his daughter. Although Mary had, perhaps, been treated sternly by her father, this was because she had refused to recognise his second marriage – at heart, his affection for her was as strong as ever.

Only recently, when members of the council, seeking to curry favour with Henry and Anne, had made disparaging remarks about Mary, the king had reacted so angrily that no-one, not even Anne, would dare criticise her again.

Cromwell added that, although no-one else knew it, he was confident that Henry was far more attached to Mary than he was to the baby Elizabeth, and would soon give evidence of it. While it is not necessarily surprising that Henry might feel more attached to a daughter he had seen grow up and had spent time with, rather than a year-old-baby he had only seen a handful of times, the idea that he would soon unmistakably show his affection was more likely to have been a sop to Chapuys to pass on to Charles than grounded in any actual plans Henry had. Chapuys certainly thought Cromwell wished to promote good relations with the emperor, to reduce his interference in Ireland. To this end, Cromwell always spoke respectfully of Katharine and Mary, and apologised for not being able to use their old titles, explaining that he was obliged to obey the law.

Despite taking Cromwell's assurances about the king's affection for Mary with a pinch of salt, Chapuys soon saw some truth in them, as on 22 October, while at The More with Elizabeth, Henry allowed Mary to be visited by the ladies and gentlemen of the court, to Anne's great irritation. Chapuys was torn between hoping that Henry's feelings for Mary were genuine, and encouraged by his new mistress, and fearing they were a ploy to divert suspicion should anything happen to her. The next day, Mary and Elizabeth were to transfer to Richmond and Mary was allowed to travel in a velvet litter, like Elizabeth's, instead of the leather one she had previously been demoted to. Mary, Chapuys thought, was being rewarded for following his advice about not making too much of the matter of precedence, and declaring that she was happy to obey her father in the matter. Despite her words, to avoid travelling behind Elizabeth, and also because she had arranged a ruse by which Chapuys might see her, Mary elected to leave her litter, and travel by barge once they reached the river. She had sent word to Chapuys, and nearing a pre-arranged spot, requested the bargemen to row her close to the bank. She had the canopy of the barge drawn back, and stood up, allowing Chapuys to see her. Her appearance, he wrote, was happy and cheerful – she seemed in good health and not too thin. While the half-sisters were at Richmond, Anne came to visit Elizabeth, accompanied by Norfolk, Suffolk and various court ladies, but Mary refused to come out of her chamber.

Chapuys was full of schemes for Charles to improve Mary's lot. First, he reiterated the idea that the emperor should promote a marriage between Mary and the Duke of Angoulême. There was also the possibility of a marriage with King James – or, best of all, Chapuys hinted, an invasion to be led by Reginald Pole, on the understanding he would marry Mary.

Mary aged about 9, by Lucas Horenbout; note the 'Emperor' brooch. (© Alamy Stock Photo)

Above: Mary's birthplace: Greenwich Palace. From *Medieval London* by William Benham (Public domain)

Below left: Katharine of Aragon, Mary's mother, showing her as a mature woman, about 1520, by an unknown artist. (© Rippon Cathedral)

Below right: Henry VIII, in about 1520. (© Alamy Stock Photo)

Eltham Great Hall, the nursery palace for Henry and his siblings, Mary and Elizabeth. (© Melita Thomas)

Eltham Great Hall, interior, a typical great hall. Mary would have presided here from the dais when living in the Marches, but been relegated to a lower table at Hatfield. (© Melita Thomas)

Emperor Charles V, about the time Mary met him. (© Victoria & Albert Museum, London)

Cardinal Wolsey, Mary's godfather. (From the Life of Cardinal Wolsey by George Cavendish, 1827)

Possibly Margaret, Countess of Salisbury, cousin of Mary's grandmother, Elizabeth of York; friend of Katharine, and Mary's Lady Governess. (© Alamy Stock Photo)

Right: Letter from Katharine to Mary, as she was leaving for the Marches, 1525. (© British Library Board)

Below: Thornbury Castle, once the Duke of Buckingham's property, where Mary lived at times during 1525–1528. (© Melita Thomas)

Left: Gloucester Cathedral. Mary was ceremonially greeted at the Abbey in 1525. (© Melita Thomas)

Below: Roof timbers at Tickenhill, dating from 1460s. Mary lived here, as did her predecessors in the Marches, Edward and Arthur. (© Melita Thomas)

Nave of Worcester Cathedral, frequently visited by Mary (© Melita Thomas)

Great Hall at Hartlebury Castle, another of Mary's homes during 1525–1528. (© Melita Thomas)

Ludlow Castle, official seat of the Council for Wales and the Marches. (© Melita Thomas)

Tewkesbury Cathedral, another abbey visited by Mary. (© Melita Thomas)

Book of Hours, with Mary's translation of a prayer by Thomas Aquinas, and a personal message to a friend in her own handwriting. (© British Library Board)

James V of Scotland, there were negotiations for a marriage between Mary and her cousin. (© Amberley Archive)

Anne Boleyn, by an unknown artist. (© Ripon Cathedral)

Farnham Palace, Mary came here for a 'change of air' in 1531. (© Melita Thomas)

Otford Palace, the palace of the Archbishops of Canterbury. Mary lived there during 1532– 1533. (© Melita Thomas)

Guildford Castle, one of the royal houses where Mary had apartments. (© Melita Thomas)

Hatfield House, the Great Hall. Mary was sent here after Elizabeth's birth, as the junior member of the household. (© Melita Thomas)

Left: Holbein portrait of John Fisher, Bishop of Rochester, executed in 1535 for refusing to accept Henry as Supreme Head of the Church in England. Mary feared she would suffer the same fate. (Wikimedia Commons)

Below: Tomb of Katharine of Aragon, in Peterborough Cathedral. (© Melita Thomas)

Above left: Thomas Cromwell, Henry's chief minister; he helped bring about the reconciliation between Henry and Mary in 1536. (© Alamy Stock Photo)

Above right: Jane Seymour, third wife of Henry VIII, she and Mary were friends. Mary was chief mourner at Jane's funeral. (© Ripon Cathedral)

Right: Dom Luis of Portugal, Mary's cousin, and a potential husband during the 1530s and 1540s. (Creative Commons)

A drawing, perhaps of Mary, by Hans Holbein, from the late 1530s. (© Elizabeth Norton/Amberley Archives)

Grimesthorpe Castle, Lincolnshire, the home of the Duke and Duchess of Suffolk. The court visited en route to York. (© Melita Thomas)

Right: Wilhelm, Duke of Cleves, a brother of Anne of Cleves; he was a suitor for Mary in the 1530s. (Creative Commons)

Below: The Whitehall Portrait, painted in 1544, showing the Henry, the late Jane Seymour, Edward, Mary and Elizabeth. The background figures are probably Will Somers and Jane the Fool, Henry and Mary's jesters. (© Alamy Stock Photo)

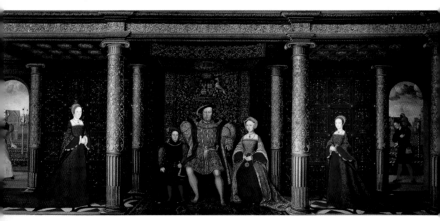

Left: Henry in later life, represented in the Great Gate at Trinity College, Cambridge. (© Elizabeth Norton/Amberley Archives)

Below: Mary Tudor on a lead plaquette. (Courtesy the Metropolitan Museum of Art)

Chapuys was convinced such an undertaking would be supported by lords Bergavenny, Hussey, Dacre and others.

Whatever hopes James V might have had for inheriting the crown of England with Mary, he was too practical to think that the matter would be easily accomplished. He therefore wrote to Charles, thanking him for the offer, but pointing out that as the emperor did not have Mary in his control, and that to accomplish the match would be too difficult, he would prefer the emperor to arrange a marriage for him with one of his nieces of Denmark.

The Admiral of France, Philippe de Chabot, Seigneur de Brion, came to London to discuss fulfilment of the 1518 treaty betrothing Mary to the dauphin. The French were of the opinion that even if Henry's marriage to Katharine had been invalid, Mary was legitimate and the legal heir to the crown. The English council insisted that she was not, and offered Elizabeth as a bride instead. Anne was furious – clearly Mary was considered Henry's legitimate heir outside the kingdom, and probably largely within it. Until Anne had a son, or Mary publicly renounced her claims, Elizabeth's prospects were bleak. The admiral dined with the king, but, on being asked whether he would like to meet Queen Anne, replied only that he would do so if it would please Henry. Henry's official response to François was that the suggestion of a marriage between Mary and the dauphin, and the princess Marguerite of France with the emperor's son, were being made by Charles to break up the alliance between France and England. If, however, François could obtain a declaration that the sentence given by the pope against Henry was void, among other demands, Henry would consider relinquishing his title of king of France and discuss a marriage between Angoulême and Elizabeth.

Reflecting Anne's anger over foreign support for Mary, the slight alleviation in her treatment soon relapsed into further bullying from Lady Shelton, to renounce her title of princess. She again fell ill, her condition exacerbated by unkindness and the imprisonment of an unnamed lady whom Norfolk suspected of passing information to Chapuys. The duke had got wind of Mary's river trip past Chapuys's house and wanted to know how it had been arranged. Henry, on hearing of his daughter's illness, sent his physician to her, saying that he would not have anything happen to her for all the world. The physician (presumably Dr Butts) reported Mary's illness was aggravated by harsh treatment, and advised that she be sent to live with Katharine, both to improve her health, and to reduce suspicion of foul play if she died. Henry, 'heaved a great sigh', and refused. It was unfortunate Mary was so obstinate that he could not treat her as kindly as he would like to. Although he acknowledged it would be good for her to be with Katharine, he was certain that, if she were, she would never be brought to obey him.[4] It had become a battle of wills – Henry could not be seen to accept her disobedience. It undermined his authority as king and Supreme Head of the Church too seriously.

When the expenses of Elizabeth's household for the period from 31 December 1533 to 24 December 1534 were made up, there was an entry relating to Mary's diet. When in her own house, she had been accustomed to eat meat as soon as she was ready in the morning. Lady Salisbury and Lord Hussey had given orders that, unless it were a fast day, she should dine between 9 and 10am. Once in Elizabeth's household, Lady Bryan found this to be inconvenient, dinner could not reasonably be provided before 11am. Mary had therefore been given a larger breakfast, to preserve her health. This, with occasional suppers served to her in her own room had increased the household's expenses from the budget by £26 13s 4d. These details indicate that the bullying of Mary was psychological, rather than any physical ill-treatment, although a lack of her accustomed physical exercise was probably taking its toll.

***

The New Year of 1535 began as gloomily for Mary as the old year had ended. In January, she was told the oath of succession would be administered both to her and to her mother. Failure to swear it, or persistence in calling herself 'princess' or her mother 'queen', would result in being sent to the Tower. Aware that More and Fisher were incarcerated there for failure to swear, Mary was terrified, and again fell ill, leading Chapuys once more to urge Cromwell to arrange for Mary to be with her mother for the sake of her health. The king's physicians were unwilling to treat Mary without Katharine's physician present, lest they be blamed if she did not recover. Whether or not disposing of Mary by unnatural means was ever really considered by Anne or Henry, everyone was chary of being put in a risky situation. Charles was not above a spot of intrigue and asked Chapuys whether it might be possible for Mary to be smuggled out of England. To have had Mary in his hand would have opened a world of opportunities for Charles.

Admiral de Brion was becoming restive with Henry's refusal to give a straight answer to an English marriage for either the dauphin or Angoulême. The French would accept Elizabeth instead of Mary for the dauphin, if Henry could guarantee that Mary no longer had any rights to the succession. Henry's problem was that Mary herself would not accept that position, so it would always be open to her to challenge Elizabeth later. Henry told the admiral he would resolve the matter in the personal meeting with François he hoped would be organised soon, but de Brion was not satisfied. As a mark of diplomatic chilliness, the ambassador refused to appreciate the hospitality offered; even being shown the Tower of London and the ordnance failed to amuse him. He was also offended by Anne, who had burst into laughter in the middle of a conversation with him. The insulted de Brion asked if she were laughing at him. Anne replied that she was laughing because Henry, who had excused himself on the pretext of fetching the admiral's secretary, had been waylaid by a young lady and forgotten his errand.

With nothing concluded, the admiral departed. He was vexed, according to Chapuys, because he had been unable to see Mary. He was eager to meet her, both because he had heard high praise of her from Henry and the rest of the court, and because she was the cousin of his queen, Eleonora.

In the last week of January, François confirmed he was willing to agree a marriage between Elizabeth and Angoulême, provided she was acknowledged as Henry's heir and some means was found of preventing 'Lady Mary' from claiming the crown. Henry reassured the new envoy, Gontier, that Parliament had proclaimed Elizabeth's legitimacy, and everyone took Mary for 'the bastard she [was]'. Henry would acknowledge no heir other than Elizabeth, and since Mary was in his hands, there was no chance of her becoming queen or claiming any rights. To make doubly sure, François should put pressure on the pope to accept the annulment of Henry and Katharine's marriage. Henry would even be willing to give up his claim to France to smooth the passage to an agreement.

Gontier thought all this was marvellous, and added that if Henry gave up the 50,000 crown pension and the claim for salt, then everything in the garden would be rosy. Henry became huffy at this point; he was already giving up so much that his people would not be pleased. Since he was offering his heir to a younger son, he should rather be demanding more, than giving away what was already owed. Nor did Henry want any resulting treaty expanded to include Charles, which he told the French would be unnecessary because, he said, Charles had already offered to accept his marriage to Anne, and Elizabeth as his heir, with Mary inheriting in case of Elizabeth dying.

In a second interview with Gontier, Henry spoke for three hours, complaining of being ill-used by Charles, and hinting that he thought François and Charles were negotiating behind his back. He was particularly irritated that François was negotiating simultaneously for a match between the dauphin and Charles's daughter, the Infanta Maria. François would be far better off throwing off the shackles of Rome, the king insisted, and in the meantime, when was François going to repay the money Henry had sent with the express intention of funding a campaign to prevent Archduke Ferdinand being elected as King of the Romans and heir to Charles? Henry allowed himself to be placated by Gontier, and told him to work out with Cromwell the details for a marriage between Angoulême and Elizabeth.

A few days later, Gontier and his colleague, Morette, were again summoned to Westminster to discuss the details of the proposed Anglo-French summit. Henry was happy that the Queen of Navarre would attend, and the ambassador assured him Queen Eleonora would also be there, despite her affection for her siblings, Charles, and Mary of Hungary. Later that day, Gontier saw Anne, to deliver letters from the admiral. Anne chided him for the delay, saying it had caused her husband to doubt that the marriage with Elizabeth would take place. If the admiral did not assuage the king's fears, she herself would be 'ruined and lost'. She felt herself to be in more trouble and grief than before her marriage. She could not say more as her husband and his lords were watching her, nor could she write.[6] So long as Mary resisted pressure, Anne's position was insecure. No foreign ruler would prefer a marriage with Elizabeth, whom everyone outside England (and most of those within) deemed illegitimate. There was little hope that Elizabeth would succeed while Mary was alive and prepared to defend her rights. Mary must be brought to accept the annulment – or be removed.

Chapuys indulged in a little verbal fencing with Cromwell over the possibility of a betrothal between the dauphin and the Infanta Maria, decrying it as inappropriate on account of the disparity of age. It would be much better, said Chapuys, for the dauphin to marry Mary. Cromwell countered that with a suggestion that the best match of all would be between Charles's son Philip and Elizabeth, at which Chapuys laughed. The upshot of the conversation was an invitation to attend Henry the next day to explain the rumour that Charles had taken it upon himself to offer Mary to Angoulême. Chapuys hastened to say, untruthfully, that the suggestion had come from France, and the emperor, although he would approve such an alliance, had no power to effect it. Henry and Chapuys discussed ins and outs of possible combinations of forces in Europe – Henry thought the offer of Milan as dowry to Infanta Maria and a French husband foolish, as it would give the French the opportunity to attack Naples again. The king pointed out that if he and François were to combine to attack Flanders, that would cause grievous harm to Charles, but would serve him right. Charles was showing no consideration for Henry – sowing dissent in Ireland and offering wives to James of Scotland. Chapuys denied both the latter charges, and he and Henry agreed that a treaty between Charles and Henry would be much the best outcome, and in Chapuys's view, easily achieved. When Henry asked how, Chapuys replied it was self-evident what the problem was. But, if the matter were too raw, time would soften the issue, and perhaps provide remedies. Henry responded that new obstacles might intervene – probably, he was still hoping for a son from Anne.

The following Sunday, Chapuys was again summoned, to hear Mass with Henry and to meet the council. He attended the council first. The councillors were there in force, all claiming to be delighted to see him. Wiltshire, the best French speaker, told Chapuys he had been summoned because Mary was dangerously ill, and they wanted him to select two physicians to attend her, along with the king's, who had refused to take sole responsibility. Katharine's physician had apparently declined to attend as well. Henry claimed to be as grieved by his daughter's sickness as any father could be. Chapuys praised Henry's affection for his daughter, but could not resist pointing out that had he been listened to the year before when he had said that the stress Mary was under would make her ill, then she probably would not be in such a case. He refused to take any responsibility for choosing doctors. Henry and the council must have a far better idea of who was suitable than he could and Charles might object to him interfering, lest it imply a lack of trust in Henry. Henry sent back a message that if Chapuys would do nothing about choosing doctors, he should at least undertake to send someone to watch over the treatment so he could be assured that everything possible was being done.

Henry then saw Chapuys in person and gave him the news that his physicians thought Mary would not survive. This made Chapuys nervous – he did not think Henry was unduly troubled by Mary being ill, and he was fairly sure that there was nothing wrong with her that liberty and the relief of stress would not cure, especially as the doctor had said the same to Norfolk. Was Henry softening him up for the eventuality of Mary dying? He was disgusted to hear that some of the councillors thought that Mary's death would remove any source of contention between Henry and the emperor.

Fortunately, news soon came that Mary was considerably recovered. Chapuys referred to it as her 'usual illness', and added that she had not yet eaten or drunk much, reinforcing the possibility that Mary's troubles were digestive, rather than gynaecological. In response to Charles's earlier question about the possibility of Mary escaping, Chapuys reported that although she might be willing to try it, the strictness of the guard about her would render it both difficult and dangerous.

In mid-February, Katharine, having heard of Mary's illness, wrote to Chapuys requesting him to ask Henry to allow Mary to be brought to her. She would put her in her own bed and nurse her with her own hands. If it still pleased God to call Mary, at least Katharine would be satisfied that everything possible had been done and that the cause of death was natural. On receipt of the letter, Chapuys requested, and was granted, an audience with the king. He read the letter aloud. Henry, rather than responding as he usually did that he knew what was best for his daughter, replied that while he would do his very best to ensure Mary had proper treatment, he could not overlook the risk of her escaping abroad. In view of Charles's suggestion that Mary should marry the Duke of Angoulême, he could hardly ignore the rumours that the emperor was plotting an excape. Chapuys mendaciously denied that any such idea had ever been floated, nor any attempts made to do it in the last five years. Nevertheless, Henry responded that he would not let Mary go to Katharine. While he admitted that children owed some obedience to their mothers, it was nothing in comparison to what they owed their fathers, and Katharine had been encouraging Mary to defy him.

Could she perhaps have Lady Salisbury restored, asked Chapuys. Absolutely not, was Henry's response. Lady Salisbury was a fool, who knew nothing. Had Mary been under her care she would have died already, whereas Lady Shelton was experienced, even in female matters – one indication that Mary's trouble might be gynaecological, although that might have been a way of denying that her illness was caused by her circumstances. Chapuys argued no further and was pressed to stay to dine, with Richmond acting as host. In Chapuys's view, the hospitality shown him was merely to annoy the French.

The following day Chapuys discussed Mary's treatment with Cromwell, again trying to have Mary moved close enough to Kimbolton in Cambridgeshire, where Katharine was now lodged, for Katharine's physician to attend her, alongside Henry's. He also asked whether she could have some friendly faces around her. He thought there was no problem in leaving Lady Shelton in charge as, although he did not tell Cromwell this, he had had her warned that if Mary died under her care, there would be serious trouble, the result being that Lady Shelton was 'in terrible fear' every time the princess was poorly. Presumably, Chapuys had pointed out that she would be the scapegoat if anything went amiss. Chapuys reiterated that Mary's illness was caused by sorrow. Cromwell claimed he was always on the watch for opportunities to improve Mary's lot, and now that Chapuys had hinted that reconciliation with the emperor might be possible, he would continue seeking them. It seemed the French discussions were not going well. François would not come out firmly on Henry's side with the pope, and he was still considering marrying Princess Madeleine to James. Henry felt betrayed at every turn.

Mary sent a message to Chapuys, asking him to persuade Charles to write to Henry about placing Mary with her mother, or at least allowing her to leave Elizabeth's household. Apparently, Mary was frequently being told, presumably by Lady Shelton, that it would be better if she did die, as that would bring peace with the emperor, and absolve them all of the trouble of looking after her. Chapuys did not think Charles should make a direct request, lest it seem like interference.

Chapuys now told Charles that Mary might be able to escape if Charles sent a ship. But Charles had lost interest in the idea; he had too many balls in the air to be able to devote much time and energy to the safety of his aunt and cousin. His main aim was to detach Henry from François and to do this, he was willing to support the notion that the divorce sentence should be suspended until a General Council could be held, provided that in the meantime Katharine and Mary were well treated, Mary was not married off without Katharine's and his own consent, and Henry genuinely sought a

General Council. Charles had no idea of provoking Henry by allowing Mary to escape, or by plotting with Lord Sandys and Lord Darcy who had both hinted to Chapuys that they would support an invasion made with the aim of restoring the queen and princess.

Despite Charles being lukewarm about escape, Chapuys continued to turn over ideas for how it might be effected. He had heard Mary was to be moved from Greenwich, probably the easiest location from which an escape could have been arranged. Ever the optimist, he thought that even if she were to be moved to the Tower of London he would find a way for her to get out – all that was needed was for Charles to send the ships. He based his contention that Mary would be able to escape the Tower on the view that the constable, Sir William Kingston, was favourable to Mary.

Cromwell informed Chapuys that Mary was to be moved to a house some 18 miles from London, around 25–30 miles from Kimbolton. The most likely location is Hatfield or Hunsdon, although they are, in fact, nearer 45 miles from Kimbolton. Chapuys did not think this sufficient and again pressed for her to be close enough to share a doctor with her mother, and for her to have her own servants. Cromwell then mentioned that Henry was refusing François' overtures for war against the emperor and suggested all would run smoothly if Katharine, who was old and sickly, and Mary, who was young and sickly, died. Chapuys firmly negated this idea, pointing out that if the ladies died, people who had made little objection to their treatment so far might rise up, and, more threateningly, that the King of Scots might suddenly find himself courted by all and sundry. Cromwell laughed at the idea of James having any support, but ratcheted back from any hints about Mary being hurried out of the world, by affirming that he had as much love for the lady as Chapuys had. He again floated the idea of a match between Elizabeth and Philip, but seeing that Chapuys would not dignify the notion with discussion, let it drop.

There is a letter catalogued as addressed to Cromwell by Katharine and dating from September 1534, but the contents suggest it is more likely to date from spring 1535, and to have been sent to Chapuys. It was written in Spanish, which Katharine would not have used to Cromwell (all her letters to English people, including Henry and Mary, are in English) and addresses the recipient as her 'good friend'. The letter thanked him for persuading Henry to let Mary move to a house close by Katharine – not so that they could see each other, but so that Katharine could hear of her welfare and for ease of access for the physician.

> My good friend (*especial amigo*), you have laid me under great obligation
> by the trouble you have taken in speaking to the king my lord about the
> coming of my daughter to me. I hope God will reward you, as you know it

is out of my power to give you anything but my goodwill. As to the answer given you that the king is content to take her to some house near me, provided I do not see her, I beg you will give him my hearty thanks for the good he does to his daughter and mine, and for the peace of mind he has given me. You may assure him that if she were but a mile from me I would not see her, because time does not permit me to go visiting, and if I wished it as I have not the means. But you may tell his majesty it was my wish that he should send her where I am, as the comfort and cheerfulness she would have with me would be half her cure. I have found this by experience, being ill of the same sickness, and as my request was so reasonable and touched so greatly the honour and conscience of the king, I did not think it would be denied me. Do not forbear, I beseech you, to do what you can that it may be so. I have heard that he had some suspicion of her security – a thing so unreasonable that I cannot believe it entered into his heart, nor do I think he has so little confidence in me. If such a thing be assumed, I beg you to tell his majesty it is my fixed determination to die in this kingdom; and I offer my person as security that if such a thing be attempted he may do justice upon me as the most traitorous woman that ever was born.[7]

Katharine did not specifically undertake that Mary would not escape, only that she herself was determined to spend the rest of her life in England, and that justice could be meted out to her if Mary did leave. While Katharine would not put her soul at risk by an out and out lie, she had little trouble putting her body at risk by an equivocation. Of course, she may have meant the words at face value, believing Mary either would not be able to escape, or should not try.

In mid-March 1535, Mary had a relapse. She was still at Greenwich and for two days was so ill that the physicians feared she would not recover. Such a serious bout of sickness suggests that something other than gynaecological troubles was at work – although, of course, Mary may have had multiple health issues. Chapuys asked Cromwell to send someone to see her, and to ask Henry to do the same. Henry responded by going to Greenwich himself. He asked Lady Shelton and the other members of the household about Mary's sickness, but did not visit her or send a message of comfort. The physician, unasked, told the king Mary's illness was dangerous, at which Henry turned on the man, saying that his report was nothing but an excuse to plead for Mary to be reunited with her mother; this he would never allow as Katharine was so 'haughty in spirit' that she might raise an army on behalf of Mary and wage war as boldly as her mother, Queen Isabella, had done. Henry, completely furious, and lashing out, sent a message to Mary that she was the cause of mischief throughout Christendom, that he had no greater enemy than her, and that her conduct was encouraging conspiracies against him. Before leaving Greenwich the next day, he gave orders that Chapuys's servants were to be kept informed of Mary's health, but were not to be allowed to see her. The king in Henry was both furious and frustrated – Mary's refusal to accept her altered status was causing national and international problems, but the father in him could not just ignore her potentially fatal illness. Perhaps he had thought if she really were dying, he would see her but, understanding that she was not, took refuge in anger. Mary recovered, but Anne found someone to prophesy that while Katharine and Mary lived, she would not be able to conceive again.

This mixture of anger and fatherly feeling meant that Henry vacillated over Mary. He had sent two presents of money since Christmas, and when Elizabeth left Greenwich on 24 March for Hunsdon, Mary was permitted to remain for another week to recuperate, still supervised by Lady Shelton. When the time came for her to leave on 1 April, she was well enough to ride, but, as Chapuys had sent three servants to accompany her, this was not permitted, presumably lest she make a bolt for freedom. Instead, she travelled in a velvet litter with Lady Shelton, with around thirty horses in her procession.

Despite the earlier report that Mary would be moved to a place near Katharine, it is not clear this ever happened as Chapuys's next information was that rather than joining Elizabeth at Hunsdon, she was to go to some place around 12 miles from the Thames, but deeper into Kent, probably Eltham. Mary was still keen to try to escape and was sending Chapuys messages that he said almost reduced him to tears. She said she would walk out into the fields to see if arrangements could be made for her to appear to be abducted against her will, both to preserve her honour, and to irritate Henry less. Chapuys was confident Mary had the courage to carry it off, and that, other than her guards, no-one would try to impede her if she were surprised while out hunting. The reference to hunting is unexpected, again suggesting that Mary's bondage was not physically rigorous, however psychologically painful and damaging it may have been. Chapuys thought the matter was hazardous and left it to Charles to decide, who confirmed in April that he thought it should be attempted.

In mid-April, Cromwell visited Chapuys, and repeated that Mary was the only obstacle to agreement between Henry and Charles and, in her absence, all would be well. Chapuys responded that the girl should be with her mother and were she to die, it would be considered suspicious. Cromwell sniffed at the idea that Mary might fall ill again, but the very next day two of Chapuys's servants arrived in haste with the news that Mary was again sick. Terrified of being murdered, she pleaded for Chapuys to arrange an escape. Chapuys, thinking an escape too difficult, sent her calming messages, presumably reassuring her that Cromwell was very clear on what the result of a mysterious death would be. He asked Cromwell to direct Henry to send physicians and servants to her.

Chapuys suspected Cromwell of double-dealing because although the minister had always told the ambassador that he thought very highly of Mary, when Henry taxed Cromwell with having kept hidden some particularly virtuous behaviour of his daughter, Cromwell had told the king he had been lied to, then tried to persuade the person who had praised Mary to withdraw his remarks. If he did not, Cromwell would see to it that he lost both his goods and his life. The gentleman, whose name is unknown, refused. Perhaps he was one of the many men whom Cromwell ensured met a bad end over the following years.

By 23 April, Mary was better. Henry had sent his own physician, providing him with horses. It was a matter of honour, the king had told the doctor, to overcome his previous reluctance. This reluctance, according to Chapuys, was not from any lack of desire to serve Mary, but because Henry and Anne already thought the doctor too supportive of her. It was the doctor's opinion, Chapuys informed Charles, that Henry could be brought around to reinstate Mary either by illness, which would make him remorseful, or by an invasion by Charles. In such a case, Katharine and Mary would be sure to be safe, as they would be Henry's best hope of mediation.

At the end of the month, it was reported in Milan that Henry had visited Mary and spent a considerable amount of time with her, and 'made much of her', although the suggestion was that this was partly to annoy the French, as indicating a possible rapprochement with Charles. Chapuys does not mention such a visit, making it unlikely, but not impossible.

8

Sorrows

When sorrows come they come not in single spies but in battalions
Shakespeare

The first executions of those who had refused to swear the oaths of succession or supremacy took place in the early summer of 1535. Several monks of the London Charterhouse suffered an appalling death – dragged to Tyburn, hanged, drawn and quartered. More and Fisher were still in the Tower, awaiting their fates. Mary would have been able to draw her own conclusions as to the punishment of those who would not accept the oath. As well as More, whom Mary probably knew well from the early influence he had had on her education, a former chaplain of Katharine's, Dr Abel, and her own schoolmaster, Richard Fetherstone, were called on to take the oath. The men were given six weeks to contemplate their decision, but stoutly affirmed they would not sign. Chapuys reported that Anne (whom he referred to in this letter as the Concubine, although previously he had usually termed her 'the Lady') was urging Henry to proceed against his former wife and daughter as traitors. Anne told Henry that he should be grateful to her, as she had rescued him from sin, and given him the means of enriching himself at the expense of the Church. It is hard to imagine that Henry enjoyed hearing these words – he was not a man to feel grateful to others. Although Katharine had been obdurate beyond belief, she would not have spoken to him like that. Was he beginning to wish he had a more peaceable wife at his side? Not Katharine – he had absolutely convinced himself their marriage had been illegal – but perhaps another woman might be more suitable?

Overtures were made to Charles for peace in the face of rumours he was planning an invasion, and that, at the least, he would implement a trade embargo. A marriage between Elizabeth and Prince Philip would be the best solution, with an honourable marriage for Mary to a nominee of the emperor; she would receive a dowry as great as any queen or empress ever had. If Henry meant his offers, it was a strange turning of the wheel. Half his troubles had begun when Charles had jilted Mary, now he was offering Elizabeth to the next generation in the hope, yet again, that a grandson might become emperor, even if England had to be handed over in the process.

Mary, having been repeatedly told by Lady Shelton that the fate of the monks of Charterhouse would be her own if she did not conform, was still eagerly thinking of means of escape, but could not come up with a plan. Katharine's doctor sent Chapuys a letter, saying he had heard the oath would be put to Katharine, and that refusal would result in execution. In such an event, Katharine said, Chapuys was to leave the country immediately, effectively suspending diplomatic and trade relations with the Empire. As always, Charles took a more pragmatic view, instructing Chapuys in May that his main task was to keep Henry and François from allying against him. As for Mary, he had changed his mind about encouraging an escape – unless an almost foolproof plan could be invented, it should not be attempted.

Henry and his council gave instructions to the English ambassador in Spain, Sir John Wallop, in response to Charles's request for a General Council and the better treatment of his aunt and cousin. The gist of the instructions was that Henry was more than willing to renew his old friendship and alliance, which had been damaged because the emperor loved one woman (Katharine) more than his 'most loyal and perfect friend'. Henry would welcome a General Council to resolve matters of faith, provided it did not meet in any of the emperor's or the pope's lands. Further, he would not accept any discussion of the divorce case. So far as Henry was concerned, the majority opinion in his favour that he had received from the universities was the equivalent of a General Council, and Charles should tell Katharine to submit to their interpretation of the law of God. If she did, Henry would treat her honourably as his sister, and in accordance with her birth and parentage, as well as make similar provision for Mary. He would esteem them both as relatives of the emperor, as well as his own. If they had perhaps been treated with less respect in the sight of the world than was due to them, it was only because of their own obstinacy, encouraged by Charles.

Negotiations for a meeting between Henry and François at Calais continued, but Anglo-French relations were deteriorating. François could not care less about Henry's matrimonial matters – in fact, he was probably rather glad to see Katharine get her come-uppance – but he could not be seen to approve the butchery of the monks of the Charterhouse. Although his sister, the Queen of Navarre, was certainly an evangelical, if not an out-and-out Lutheran, the mood of France would not tolerate a break with Rome and several heretics had been burnt in Paris, with the king and queen in attendance.

It had been agreed between François and Rome that the sentence depriving Henry of his throne would not be executed until after the Calais meeting, in hopes of finding a compromise. The conference, originally planned for Henry and François in person, was attended by Norfolk, Rochford and FitzWilliam on the English side, and the admiral for the French. Norfolk's orders were to promote a marriage between Angoulême and Elizabeth. FitzWilliam reported the French were very off-hand, either because they felt England was now entirely dependent on France for protection against the papal sentence, or because they had come to a secret accommodation with Charles. FitzWilliam thought it better to play along until news came of whether the emperor could be brought around to renew the English alliance.

The talks broke up in early June, with nothing accomplished. The admiral would not say anything in favour of Henry's marriage to Anne or against the Church and, according to Chapuys, the French were not interested in Elizabeth. He reported they had sent a message to Mary that they still sought her hand for the dauphin. They might have taken Elizabeth for Angoulême as well, but Mary was the preferred option. Rochford reported to Anne, who was heard to speak 'a thousand shameful words' about François and the whole French nation.

Cromwell made some efforts to persuade a sceptical Chapuys to believe that François had reviewed Henry's matrimonial affairs and concluded that his marriage to Anne was valid, and he would do everything he could to promote it. Chapuys continued to indicate that a renewed alliance with Charles was possible, but only if Katharine and Mary were better treated, while Cromwell insisted they would be better treated if Charles accepted the divorce and entered an alliance.

In June, Pope Paul conferred a cardinalate on Fisher of Rochester. Whether this was meant as a compliment to one of Henry's most venerable bishops, or whether it was done to console Rochester in his bleak imprisonment, the upshot of this monumental lack of foresight was Henry vowing that he would send Fisher's head to Rome to be fitted for his cardinal's red hat, and hurrying the old man to the block. Too weak to make the journey to Tyburn, Fisher was executed on Tower Hill on 22 June 1535. He was urged to the last minute to accept the king's supremacy in return for a pardon but refused. Fisher had been the confessor and friend of Henry's grandmother, and was a man widely revered for his learning and his exemplary life as a priest, but Henry would not be mocked. Shortly after, More followed Rochester to the block. All Europe was shocked by their deaths. Pope Paul, who had previously expressed himself as willing to reconsider the sentence of excommunication and deprivation against Henry, now became determined to implement it.

Mary sent a message to Chapuys saying Henry and Anne were again on such good terms that unless Charles were to take real action by restraining trade, her position would never improve. As Lady Shelton took care to keep news of Henry and Anne quarrelling from Mary, she probably equally kept her informed when they were on good terms.

The French negotiations having fallen through, Cromwell repeated to Chapuys that if Katharine and Mary were dead, there would be no obstacle to friendship, as no one would then deny the validity of Henry's marriage to Anne; the only other cloud on the horizon would be James of Scotland, but he had neither money nor friends. Chapuys calmly replied that Henry's second marriage would be still be invalid and God might well provide James with friends in such a case. As for Cromwell's contention that there were no other heirs, Chapuys, earnest to make Cromwell realise that dispatching Katharine and Mary would not solve anything, said he could think of several.[1]

Relations with France were now so bad that war was discussed. Another emissary came to ask for Mary's hand, with instructions that if it were refused, François would no longer stand between Henry and the implementation of the papal sentence. Henry was particularly displeased to learn that Queen Eleonora was planning to meet with her sister, Mary of Hungary, to pursue a reconciliation between Charles and François. Katharine had also heard of this proposed meeting between her nieces, and wrote to Mary of Hungary that she hoped the regent would remind Charles of the desperate state in which things stood in England. Katharine also hoped Eleonora would urge François to act as Henry's friend by persuading him to return to the path of virtue. Katharine must have been corresponding secretly – certainly Mary was. She too, wrote to Mary of Hungary, thanking her cousin for the letters she had received, which 'enabled her to live in hope'. She herself was responding 'in haste and fear', perhaps hurriedly writing by candlelight, before slipping the letter to her accomplice for dispatch via Chapuys.

Another correspondent discussing Mary's affairs was James V, who wrote to Charles about his hopes for a General Council and the restoration of his aunt and her daughter. He thanked Charles for the suggestions for brides but, as Charles was on a very long voyage, and James needed to secure the succession, he had been obliged to agree terms with France. James, although only twenty-three, was a shrewd man – by playing Charles and François off against each other, he had secured the bride he always wanted, Princess Madeleine. Ordinarily, the emperor would not have concerned himself much with the king of Scots, but as a potential heir to the English throne, and possibly a rival to Mary, he needed to be kept sweet.

Chapuys's requests to visit Mary, which she had pressed him to make, were denied. Already suffering from a bad cold, the disappointment of not being able to meet what must have seemed like her only supporter, added to her misery. On 6 September, Chapuys wrote that he had asked Henry to send his physician to Mary, partly on account of the lingering cold, and also because she feared a return of her 'ordinary complaint, which she dreads, in the coming winter'.[2] A few days later, Chapuys confirmed that Mary had been visited by both Henry's and Katharine's physicians. She was well, but the doctors also feared a relapse. Apparently, Mary detested medicines – having heard of some of the favoured nostrums of Tudor doctors, one can hardly be surprised! Again, exercise and a return to her mother were recommended.

The Bishop of Troyes again asked Henry to fulfil the old treaty for the marriage of Mary and the dauphin, and requested that she be well treated, but to no avail – Henry could not permit the marriage. Once, Mary would have been an asset, married in either France or the Empire, but now, unless she accepted her illegitimacy, she would be a loose cannon and could not be allowed to leave England.

On 30 September, Cromwell wrote to Chapuys, assuring him of the delight Henry felt in Charles's recent military success in Tunis. As for Mary, Chapuys might be certain that everything was done for her benefit, as no-one could feel more anxious about her than her father. Any reports that her health was being neglected were quite untrue, and, in fact, as plague was rife in London, it would be too risky for Mary's health for Chapuys, living in London, to visit her as he had asked.

In October, the executorials – that is the papal orders for the execution of the sentence of excommunication and deprivation – were finally signed by the pope, but not published as a bull. Originally delayed in the hope that the summit at Calais would find a compromise, and because Charles did not wish to push Henry wholeheartedly into the arms of France now that Anglo-French relations had deteriorated, Paul wished to press ahead. The emperor's men in Rome were still trying to slow the matter down by asking to have the documents for examination before they were sealed, but it was clear they could not further delay the matter without it being obviously at Charles's command. For all Katharine and Mary's trust in him, and Chapuys's apparent belief that Charles was doing all he could for his aunt and cousin, the emperor was, if not condoning Henry's actions, at least enabling them. Tarbes, however, seemed convinced Charles would take action. According to his information, the English populace were murmuring against Henry, and particularly Anne, blaming the new queen for all the ills that had befallen the country, particularly the bad harvest. The people were sure that, despite Parliament's best efforts, Mary's rights as Henry's eldest daughter, born in wedlock, could not be overturned. When Mary had left Greenwich, a large crowd of women had gathered, calling out their support for her, and weeping at the wrong she had suffered. Some of the ringleaders were taken off to the Tower. The fear that Charles would impose a trade embargo was growing, and, according to Tarbes, many city merchants had told Chapuys that if Charles invaded, they would support him. Tarbes continued that, since his arrival in London, he had been informed the people of England, who had previously been reluctant to see Mary marry the dauphin as it would mean a foreign king, now thought it was the only way her rights could be maintained, short of war.

Tarbes and his colleagues paid a visit to Elizabeth. Mary was again housed with her half-sister. According to Tarbes, she had demanded to see the French envoys and had had to be physically restrained by Lady Shelton, only desisting on being informed that her father had expressly forbidden her to meet them, instantly showing her obedience. When Lady Shelton told her the dauphin was to marry the emperor's daughter, Mary had protested that such a union was impossible as the dauphin was betrothed to her. Such a tale could only have been invented to distress her. She had no hope but in the dauphin and was sure that eventually, God would be satisfied she had suffered enough; at that time the dauphin would demand the fulfilment of the marriage treaty, which Henry would not be able to reject as it had been made with both kings' consent. Chapuys gave quite a different account of the trip. He said the French had only visited Elizabeth because Anne had insisted. Far from Mary wishing to see the ambassadors and struggling over the matter with Lady Shelton, she had stayed quietly in her room, playing the virginals, both in obedience to Henry's orders, and because she was too modest to wish to flaunt herself in public.

Tarbes was certain that if the emperor urged François to pursue the marriage of Mary to the dauphin, this would avert war between the two. Tarbes, of course, was hoping Charles cared more about the situation in England and Mary's position, than about his rivalry with François, which was not the case – Mary and England were always peripheral to the emperor's thinking. Eventually, Tarbes returned to France; despite his hopes, his embassy had achieved nothing as Henry continued playing Charles and François against each other. Tarbes's apparent eagerness for the marriage with Mary tends to obviate the suggestion that he was the initiator of the idea that Henry and Katharine's marriage was invalid.

Katharine wrote to Pope Paul in October, mourning the deaths of More and Fisher, and saying she expected that both she and Mary would soon suffer a similar fate. She hoped he would have special consideration for Henry, Mary and the whole kingdom, and apply a remedy with all speed. Katharine's requests for help, although they are not specifically for military intervention, do not give a ready idea of what else she could have had in mind. Perhaps she still hoped that a sentence of deprivation would shock Henry back into line. She wrote in similar vein to Charles, saying that she expected martyrdom, although she could not pretend to the virtue of Rochester and More. As for Mary, she knew her to be in great danger, but could do nothing other than recommend her to God and Charles. She hoped he and the pope could find some remedy to prevent further suffering of innocents. She also asked him to show appropriate gratitude to Chapuys, who had done so much for her and Mary. The tone of these letters is, if not despondent, certainly resigned. Although no illness was mentioned, Katharine's health may have begun to decline.

Chapuys informed Charles that, despite Cromwell's fine words, there was little prospect of him being allowed to see Mary, and even less chance she would be able to live with her mother. Katharine was too great a supporter of the pope, and would encourage Mary in her disobedience. It is clear Mary's devotion to her mother was seen by Henry as the root cause of her obstinacy. Chapuys again encouraged Charles to implement a 'remedy'. Now would be the best time, while the populace was shocked at the brutality being meted out to the Carthusians and the expulsion of many of the religious orders from their houses – the Dissolution of the Monasteries had not yet begun, but the order of Observant Franciscans was suppressed in the autumn of 1534. If Charles did not act soon, despair would prevail and it would be too late.

* * *

Mary, too, was feeling grateful to Chapuys. She wrote to Chancellor Granvelle, praising his service to her and her mother and the parlous state of affairs in England, which could not properly be conveyed by letter. She was aware Charles was pre-occupied with Tunis but matters in England were quite as important, and he would attain just as much glory by righting affairs there. Despite Mary's pleas, Charles was reluctant to be goaded into war, certainly until he could see how the pope and France would react. The furthest he would go would be to decline to treat with Henry for as long as he lived with Anne, maintained the divorce and refused to recognise Mary as his heir. Nor was he so desirous of Mary's advancement that he wanted her to marry the dauphin – he was still pushing for a match with Angoulême, leaving the older brother free for his own daughter.

In Rome, debate continued over the publishing of the executorial bull. Charles distrusted François' assurances that if Rome moved against Henry, he and Charles could work together to enforce the sentence. Charles told the pope that François had been encouraging Henry all along, and he hoped by this ruse to provoke Charles into unilaterally declaring war. The only support France had given to papal authority and the validity of Katharine's marriage, was the demand at Calais for Mary's hand.

Lady Exeter sent word to Chapuys that Henry was determined to use the forthcoming session of Parliament to enforce his will. By making Parliament responsible for the legislation, the people would be inspired to defend themselves against any invasion by Charles. Henry was growing angrier by the day, reported Lady Exeter, who was so concerned about Henry's rhetoric that she visited Chapuys' house in disguise, to reiterate her warning. When talking of Mary, the king had said that soon she would not need any company, and that an example would be made of her to show that no one could disobey the law. As for himself, he would prove the truth of the prophesy that he would begin his reign as a lamb and end it as a lion. Although Henry's threats had moved some of his listeners to tears, the king had told them he would make the women submit, even if it cost his crown.

Lady Exeter attributed Henry's strength of purpose to Anne's influence – she was again pregnant and thought of nothing but the dispatch of her rivals. Anne had openly said of Mary: 'She is my death and I am hers, so I will take care that she shall not laugh at me after my death.' To placate her, Henry had promised that while he lived, Mary would not be permitted to marry and Chapuys was forbidden from sending his servant on the weekly visit to Mary.

On 13 December 1535 Cromwell let Chapuys know that Katharine was very ill. The ambassador was allowed to send a servant, while permission for a personal visit was considered. Before a decision was reached, Katharine's physician, Dr de La Sa, wrote that Katharine was not in any danger and had recovered enough to write to both Charles and Ortiz, repeating that she feared the outcome of the impending Parliament and begging them to implement some remedy before it was too late. Chapuys, therefore, need not be too importunate in his request for a licence to visit. Charles's response to the information about Henry's intention to use Parliament against Katharine and Mary was that he could not believe, despite Henry's threats, the women would be physically harmed. Chapuys was to prevent them from swearing the oath, if it could be done without immediate harm coming to them, lest it would dishearten others, and lay them open to punishment for previous disobedience, which they would seem to be acknowledging. However, if they were in danger of death, they must swear the oath and then affirm that it had been done under duress, with their protestation entered at Rome.

On 29 December de La Sa wrote that Katharine was dying. Chapuys asked Cromwell for urgent permission to visit, which the minister said would be forthcoming, but that Chapuys must meet Henry that day at Greenwich. The king and the ambassador talked at some length, with Henry pointing out he had been faithful to the emperor, despite many attempts to stir trouble between them, and wanting to know why Charles had not agreed to renew their alliance. He intimated that he thought Cromwell had gone too far in his overtures for reconciliation. Chapuys disagreed; all his advances had been met by Cromwell with a promise to take instructions, but no action. He asked Henry to state his terms plainly. Henry said he wanted the marriage of Elizabeth to Prince Philip. Chapuys admitted Cromwell had mentioned it, but timidly, 'like one offering a coin to an elephant', so he had not taken it seriously. The king added he wanted Charles to cease supporting Katharine and to have the papal sentence in Katharine's favour rescinded; since Katharine would soon be dead, Charles could have no further interest in matters in England. Chapuys rejected this, saying Katharine's death would make no difference and that the sentence in her favour was necessary.

Chapuys departed for Kimbolton. Henry sent Suffolk after him with the latest news – that Katharine was close to death, and would probably die before Chapuys arrived. The ambassador thought this an exaggeration but asked that Mary might be allowed to visit – a request which was refused. Chapuys was finally admitted to Katharine's presence for the first time in nearly five years. He explained the reasons for Charles's failure to at least attempt to remedy the wrongs done to her. The emperor had been too busy with other matters and, in fact, he assured her, the delay had been beneficial, as the French were now rejecting Henry's advances. Also, with the disgraceful treatment of Rochester, the pope himself would give a remedy, for which Katharine could not be blamed, as she might have been, had Charles intervened alone. Katharine professed herself convinced and when she expressed concern lest people had been drawn into heresy through her affairs, she was comforted by his assurance that heresy was necessary for good men to be proved. While it is hard to imagine Katharine believed Charles had done everything he could, she took solace from Chapuys's affirmation that she had been right to uphold her principles. Katharine was so cheered by the four days of Chapuys's visit that she began to laugh again, and felt herself to be out of danger. Chapuys left, so as not to abuse his licence.[3]

Katharine's optimism was misplaced, and she died two days later. There were rumours of poison, which Chapuys was inclined to believe, as her symptoms were violent stomach pains over a few weeks, which became noticeably worse after drinking some beer. Katharine had dictated her last wishes. As well as bequests to servants, she left Mary the furs from her gowns that were still in Henry's keeping and the collar of gold she had brought from Spain. She also asked for a small necklace containing what she believed to be a piece of the True Cross to be sent to her daughter. She wished to be buried in a convent of Observant Friars of the Franciscan order.

Henry greeted Katharine's death with an unseemly display of euphoria, dressing in yellow and carrying Elizabeth about as he rejoiced that England was now free from all threat of war from the emperor. He could now deal with François, who would do whatever Henry wished to keep England out of an alliance with Charles. The very day after Katharine's death, Henry sent a message to Gardiner, in France, that as Charles would now have no cause to quarrel with Henry, the ambassador should hold himself 'more aloof'. To add to the insensitivity, Wiltshire and Rochford were heard to say it was a pity that Mary had not died as well. We can only speculate about what Henry might have felt in his heart at the death of the woman he had known since he was ten years old and had once loved dearly, but the decade of unremitting struggle between them had probably drained away any remnants of affection.

Although Henry had refused to allow Mary a last visit, he was not completely heartless, and ordered that she be kept in ignorance of her mother's death until a suitable person could be sent to break the news – obviously, he was not so worried about her that he thought of doing it himself, or, if he did, he decided not to upset the pregnant Anne. Before any messenger could arrive from Henry, Mary had been told of her loss by Lady Shelton and had also received Chapuys's letter of condolence. Mary asked Henry, via Lady Shelton, as she was not permitted to write directly to her father, that Katharine's doctor and apothecary might visit her to tell her of her mother's last hours.

Even before Katharine's funeral, Mary thought more pressure would be put on her to swear the oath of succession. She wrote to Chapuys that she would try to continue her resistance and would prepare herself to die if necessary. Chapuys described her as 'showing great sense and incomparable patience and virtue to bear so becomingly the death of such a mother to whom she bore as much love as any daughter ever did to her mother, who was her chief refuge in her troubles'. He asked Charles to send his cousin a letter of comfort.

Chapuys enquired of Cromwell whether Katharine's choice of burial place would be honoured but was informed it would not be possible, as there were no such houses left. Nevertheless, Cromwell assured him, the chosen location of the Benedictine abbey at Peterborough was a fine and suitable resting place. As for the clothes and furs that Katharine had left, Henry would examine them to see if he wanted them before passing them on to Katharine's stated beneficiaries. At any rate, they would not be given to Mary until she had shown herself obedient. How could she dream of setting herself up in opposition to her father, or thinking herself wiser than he? As soon as she obeyed her father, she could have not only what Katharine had left her but anything else she wanted.

Chapuys responded that as all the pressure that had been put on Mary had only been to encourage Katharine to conform, now there was no hope of that, perhaps they would leave the grieving girl alone. More stress might well lead to illness and death. Cromwell repeated there was no excuse for Mary's disobedience, and her death would be no great loss – Henry had considered every contingency that might flow therefrom. As for Charles, *he* need not cry crocodile tears. The death of Katharine removed the only obstacle to a renewal of the alliance between him and Henry.

Consistent with Henry's contention that Katharine was his sister-in-law, orders were given for a dignified funeral, appropriate for the honour and respect due to the Dowager Princess of Wales. The chief mourner was Mary's cousin, Lady Eleanor Brandon, with eight other ladies in attendance.[4] Cromwell informed Chapuys that he could attend the funeral but Chapuys, taking the advice of Mary herself, and Mary of Hungary, declined, as Katharine was not to be buried as queen.

***

Chapuys was certain Mary would be asked to swear the oaths or, as he put it, Henry and Anne were determined to 'entangle the princess in their webs'. A last attempt was made by Anne to persuade Mary to accept her. Perhaps Anne was realising that with Katharine gone, her position, until she had a son, was less, rather than more, secure. If Anne could convince Mary to surrender, it would render Anne's marriage less of a stumbling block to alliance with France or the Empire. She sent a message via Lady Shelton that if Mary would be obedient, Anne would be a second mother to her, have her at court and not even expect her to carry her train. Lady Shelton pleaded with Mary to accept, but Mary merely replied that she would obey her father so far as she could in good conscience. There could be no compromise – if Mary could not be forced to accept that Elizabeth was the heir to the throne then, unless Mary were dead, Anne's daughter would be likely to lose any competition for the crown, and Anne could, very possibly, lose her life, if Henry died without leaving a son by her. Her treatment of Mary – the browbeating and bullying, the spiteful remarks and the separation of an adolescent girl from her mother, must be seen in the light of Anne's fight for her own and her child's chance of survival.

Mary, warned that Henry would send some of his councillors to her with orders to take the oath, asked Chapuys's advice. He told her to stay firm, keeping her modesty and dignity. The slightest hint of wavering would ensure their persistence. He thought it unlikely they would push her on the papal authority, but probable she would be asked to accept Anne as queen. With Katharine dead, it would be harder for Mary to resist. He then gave her some arguments to use: first, to avoid discussion and ask them to leave her to pray for her mother and herself; second, to say she was a poor, simple orphan without counsel or help, who could not possibly understand laws and canons; third, she should ask them to intervene with her father to take pity on her; fourth, she might say it was not the custom in England to swear fealty to queens consort. It had not been done for her mother, when she was reputed queen so, therefore, it would be strange to do it for Anne. If Anne were truly queen, nothing Mary did or said would make a difference. Finally, if pushed, she should declare that, as the sentence of the church had not only proclaimed the validity of Katharine's marriage, but denied that of Anne, she could not, in good conscience, accept it. He suggested she tell Lady Shelton there was no point in badgering her on the matter as she would not agree. She could also try asking Henry to wait until she was of full age.

Between this time and that (February of 1537) she might come to a different understanding, or be willing then to enter a religious house. Surely, it would be better to have the oath of an adult than a minor? Chapuys hastened to add that all these arguments were just suggestions. He would try to find a way to prevent her being asked to sign.

***

Following Katharine's death, perhaps to allay suspicions of poison, Henry had reinstated his permission for Chapuys to send a servant to see Mary once a week. One week Shelton denied the man access, saying that nobody could approach Mary without Henry's express licence. She would let him see Mary at a distance, but not speak to her. This concession, Shelton said, was made for Chapuys's sake. Probably some small presents that Mary had recommended Chapuys give to Lady Shelton had encouraged her to be helpful. Mary, overhearing the conversation (presumably through a window), called out that Shelton should let the man leave; she would not see anyone without her father's permission. As Mary had previously requested, she had been allowed to see Katharine's apothecary and physician, who had told her of her mother's last days, and given her Katharine's bequest of the necklace with the True Cross.

Chapuys urged Charles to have the sentence of deprivation against Henry enforced, for Mary's sake. Meanwhile Cromwell was continuing to put out feelers for a reconciliation with the emperor and suggested a papal legate might be allowed to come to England. To calm speculation that heresy was being encouraged, he issued orders to prevent controversial preaching against images, purgatory and the adoration of the saints. Henry himself was unimpressed by the bull of deprivation. He pointed out to the Scots ambassadors, who were passing through London from Paris and had offered to try to effect a reconciliation between Henry and Rome, that the Greek Church and much of northern Europe rejected papal authority, and that it had often been questioned – the pope would not wage a war to have his authority recognised and, with Katharine dead, there was no likelihood of further interference.

Fearing that unbearable pressure would be put on her to sign the oaths, Mary and Chapuys began to think seriously of an escape to Europe. Arrangements progressed far enough for a ship to be held in waiting. Mary was to slip out of the house, make her way to the Thames and be taken aboard. At the end of January, these plans were frustrated when she was moved to another house and Chapuys's servants were forbidden from being in the neighbourhood. This might have been a coincidence or, more likely, Cromwell had got wind of the plan.

Lady Shelton told Anne that Mary had refused her latest overtures. Anne replied in a letter:

Mrs. Shelton, my pleasure is that you do not further move the lady Mary to be towards the king's Grace otherwise than it pleases herself. What I have done has been more for charity than for anything the king or I care what road she takes, or whether she will change her purpose, for if I have a son, as I hope shortly, I know what will happen to her; and therefore, considering the Word of God, to do good to one's enemy, I wished to warn her before her hand, because I have daily experience that the king's wisdom is such as not to esteem her repentance of her rudeness and unnatural obstinacy when she has no choice. By the law of God and of the king, she ought clearly to acknowledge her error and evil conscience if her blind affection had not so blinded her eyes that she will see nothing but what pleases herself. Mrs. Shelton, I beg you not to think to do me any pleasure by turning her from any of her wilful courses, because she could not do me [good] or evil; and do your duty about her according to the king's command, as I am assured you do.[5]

Mary found the letter in the chapel, where Lady Shelton had either deliberately placed it for discovery, or accidentally left it. Lady Shelton, although she carried out instructions to put pressure on Mary, may have been attempting to help the girl by showing her what danger she stood in, if she refused to comply. But Mary would not bend. She copied the letter and returned the original. Meanwhile, she continued hinting to Lady Shelton, for relay to Anne and Henry, that, when she was of full age, she would perhaps become a nun. She could not do it immediately, as she did not wish it to be thought she had made such a decision lightly – and also because the recent reforms of the religious houses forbade entry under the age of twenty-one.

Lady Exeter told Chapuys that although Anne had rejoiced at Katharine's death, she was now crying over it, realising that her own position was suddenly far more vulnerable. Lady Exeter had heard (although not first hand) that Henry had complained to one of his courtiers that he had been seduced into the marriage with Anne by enchantment, which he knew because God did not permit him to have male heirs. Chapuys found the story difficult to believe but he ensured Lady Shelton received a hint of it so she might treat Mary better, considering that the tide might turn. He advised Mary to be as charming as possible to Lady Shelton so that the latter would not fear Mary being reinstated. Chapuys wrote these words on 29 January, the day of Katharine's funeral.

In this same letter, Chapuys mentioned that Henry had had a jousting accident on 24 January but, according to his information, had not sustained any great injury – probably spared, he thought, to suffer a worse end. Later, Dr Ortiz reported that Henry had been unconscious for two hours after his fall. But many of Ortiz's other reports are unreliable, so not much credence should be placed on this one. There is no other evidence that Henry was unconscious for that length of time – Wriothesley's Chronicle says 'he took no hurt'. On 10 February, Chapuys reported that Anne had had a miscarriage on the same day as Katharine's funeral. According to Chapuys's informant, the foetus was male, and about three-and-a-half months' gestation. Anne, Chapuys reported, blamed her uncle, Norfolk, whom she said had broken the news of Henry's jousting accident too brutally. Chapuys thought that this was nonsense – Anne had been told very gently. Other people suggested Anne was just unable to bear children and some thought fear of being treated as Katharine had been, had told on her health. She might well have had cause for trepidation as Henry had been courting Mistress Jane Seymour, one of Anne's maids-of-honour, and giving her rich presents. Lady Shelton had been very upset about Anne's loss and had avoided telling Mary about it – hoping that even when she heard of it, Mary would not hear that Henry was increasingly dissatisfied with Anne. Such knowledge of Lady Shelton's thoughts suggests that Chapuys's informant was very close to her.

Mary was receiving kinder treatment. When she relocated again, she was well attended and Henry sent her money to distribute in alms. Chapuys had heard from Cromwell that Henry intended to increase Mary's retinue. Here Chapuys made the famous remark that has been read as a description of Jane Seymour: 'I hope no scorpion lurks beneath the honey.' However, if the letter is taken in the round, it is obvious that Chapuys is not referring to Jane at all. He is worrying about whether more lenient treatment of Mary by Henry has a hidden catch.[6] Chapuys speculated on what Henry might do in regard to the oath now that Anne had miscarried. He thought a possible solution might be for Mary to refuse it, but suggest that she would reconsider if Henry had a male heir.

For a while, persecutions relating to the oaths had reduced but in early February, Dr Wilson, Dr Abel and Dr Fetherstone, who had been in prison for two years, were condemned to death. While the sentences were not immediately carried out, it may have been this news of the sentence against her old tutor that pushed Mary into seeking to escape. Chapuys, too, was worried Henry might turn his rage on his daughter. The number of guards about her appeared reduced and Mary thought it would be easy to drug her women, sneak past Lady Shelton's room and either climb over, or break, the garden gate. She was so keen on the idea that Chapuys thought she would 'put to sea in a sieve' if he advised it, but he was less sanguine. Mary's eagerness and her natural inclination to activity, rather than passivity, were causing her to underrate the difficulties involved. In fact, the very ease with which she thought it might be accomplished made him suspicious a trap was being laid. The house was at least 40 miles from Gravesend. Such a distance could not be covered without relays of horses, and she would also have to pass through several large villages. The best option might be to wait until after Easter, when Mary would return to the house she had just come from, which was some 15 miles closer to Gravesend – probably Eltham.

The waiting ship's Master was also nervous; vessels were being searched, so he would not be able to conceal soldiers.

It is very difficult to believe that Mary was so poorly guarded that Henry and Cromwell did not know exactly what was going on. Either Henry was half-hearted about keeping Mary confined, or his ministers were so uncertain about it, that they winked at Mary's constant smuggling out of messages and letters. On the other hand, perhaps their views of the courage and agency of a young woman were so limited that it just did not occur to them that Mary could be communicating secretly; but, more likely, it was a trap. Despite Mary's eagerness to escape, she would still prefer a full-scale invasion by Charles, as tending to save innumerable souls. If she left the country, Henry would double his defence measures. Mary's desire for an invasion can, of course, be seen as treason, although she would probably have defended herself by claiming the necessity of implementing the papal deprivation. Quite what she thought would happen if Charles did invade is never reported. Did she think Henry would remain king, but be forced back into papal obedience and be required to acknowledge her as his heir? Or was she envisaging being queen herself? Her grandmother, Isabella, had taken power at the point of a sword at a similar age. Perhaps she never thought beyond removing herself from an intolerable situation.

***

Again European politics affected Mary. In mid-February, François invaded the duchy of Savoy. Savoy, positioned as it was across the borders of modern France and Italy, was the gateway to the Italian peninsula. If the French held it, it would improve François' chances of re-taking Milan. Charles needed to take immediate steps to rectify the situation – exacerbated in his mind by the Duchess of Savoy being Empress Isabella's sister. Both Charles and François again wanted Henry's support and, with Katharine now dead, Charles was prepared to go to considerable lengths to get it. Invading England to maintain Mary's rights was certainly not on his agenda. Instead, he wanted to re-establish the alliance, if he could do so without prejudice to his cousin.

Cromwell, who seems always to have favoured the Imperial alliance (perhaps because it was important for trade) encouraged Henry to be receptive to any Imperial overtures. A secret meeting was arranged between Cromwell and Chapuys – or at least, Cromwell claimed it was to be secret. Cromwell repeated at length his conviction that Charles was a true friend to Henry, and it was owing to his goodwill that the papal fulminations had been delayed. Now that the only obstacle to friendship was gone, surely they could restore the old alliance? Chapuys complimented Cromwell on his prudence, confirmed Charles's goodwill towards England and asked plainly what the proposals might be. Cromwell said any overtures ought to come from Charles. As his previous proposals had related to Katharine, who was now dead, they were out of date, and should be renewed. Tired of the endless skirting around the issue, Chapuys asked how Henry would respond if Charles suggested first, that Henry submit to Rome, second, that Mary be declared legitimate, third that Henry enter a league against the Turks and fourth, that the two enter an offensive and defensive pact. Cromwell thought the pact would be no problem, Henry was only prevented from action against the Turks by distance, and would gladly contribute to a league against them. As for Mary, the time was probably now ripe for arranging matters to Charles's satisfaction. Submission to the pope was altogether a more difficult question, although there might be possibilities in that direction if Chapuys could obtain a definite set of proposals from Charles. Cromwell emphasised that Mary's situation might admit of improvement and he, personally, was committed to it.

Chapuys gave this information to Charles, adding that before Anne's miscarriage, Henry had hardly spoken to her for three months and when the miscarriage had occurred, all he had said was that he saw God did not intend to give him male children and he would speak to her when she was out of bed. Anne had protested the miscarriage was the result of her fears after his fall, and her grief when she saw he loved others. As she loved him more than Katharine had, she could not hide her pain. Apparently, Henry was touched by this, and was now spending time with Anne, leaving Jane at Greenwich. This may have inspired Anne's words to her ladies that they need not be upset about the miscarriage. She would soon be pregnant again and, as that child would be conceived and born after Katharine's death, his (for of course it would be a son) legitimacy could not be questioned.

Charles instructed Chapuys to suggest to Henry that matters between them might thaw if suitable provision were made for Mary. He would not go so far as a formal alliance while Henry was still 'so stubborn with his concubine (Anne)', but any discussion of terms would be bound to 'abate the insolence' of the French. He agreed Mary should feign an interest in becoming a nun. He did not write to her himself, lest the letter be intercepted, but wished Chapuys to tell her that he hoped to remedy her treatment whatever might happen.

Despite Cromwell saying Mary might soon be better treated, Henry sent a messenger to demand she relinquish the necklace with the True Cross. As this had been Katharine's last keepsake to her daughter, to demand it was downright petty. It was returned a few weeks later, having been judged to be of no monetary value.

Just as Charles wanted Henry's support over Savoy, so did François. Tarbes returned to England, to ask Henry for 500,000 crowns for François to prosecute the war, but the French king's failure to support the annulment came back to haunt him. Henry's response was frosty. Why should he help François, who had done nothing for him, against Charles, with whom Henry also had a treaty, and who had at least prevented the pope's issuing of the bull of deprivation? After Henry dismissed Tarbes, the bishop was approached by Norfolk, who said it was a pity that a treaty had not been concluded before Katharine's death – it would have been better if Mary had been married to Angoulême as Norfolk had advised. Nevertheless, Norfolk was sure Henry would help if Charles invaded French territory, even going in his own person. A couple of days later, Norfolk again said how well-disposed Henry was towards François, but the requested money could not be found, unless it were a reciprocal arrangement. Tarbes interpreted the whole negotiation as Henry wanting François to attack Charles, to keep the emperor from interfering in England. So long as England did not actually contribute to the French campaign, Charles could not consider himself provoked.

Charles gave detailed instructions to Chapuys on how to proceed to reinstate the Anglo-Imperial alliance. He was to try to persuade Henry to be reconciled to the Church through a private negotiation via Charles. Second, nothing was to be done to prejudice Mary's position. She must be declared legitimate and his heir or, if that were not possible, the matter should be held in abeyance during Henry's lifetime, with Mary to be honourably married. As for a husband for Mary, Chapuys was to suggest Dom Luis of Portugal, the brother of Empress Isabella, and Mary's cousin.[7] There were many advantages to a match with Dom Luis, Charles thought, including that the Portuguese were 'not quarrelsome'. Mary could leave England, and be delivered from fear of her life, while having a husband of suitable standing, and the possibility of maintaining her rights with his support. Further, if she had children, Henry might summon them back to England. Mary could later repudiate any agreement made under duress. As for Anne, Charles had now concluded it was better for Henry to remain with her than to find a new wife, as Anne's children, in his view, could never challenge Mary for the succession. He did not think that Mary could in good conscience do anything against her father during his lifetime, even if Katharine had been poisoned.

Charles added that if Anne did not agree to Mary being declared legitimate, or the matter suspended, she should yet be glad that either course would relieve her and her adherents of immediate danger. Chapuys should try to sound out Cromwell on Anne's views, and make the best terms with her that he could. Should Henry wish to marry again, Charles would support the match if it were honourable and, as neither Mary nor he could hinder it, he would turn it to advantage. Throughout the whole negotiation, Chapuys was to try to draw England away from France into a league with Charles. Whatever was in Charles's head, it was not the death of Anne, as he referred to the possibility of her having more children. The idea that Anne had to be dispatched to facilitate a reconciliation cannot be supported, as Charles was willing to find a way to accommodate her and, following his line of thinking about her children being unlikely to mount any successful challenge to Mary, in the event of Henry's death, might well have preferred her to remain in situ.

In late March, Chapuys held a dinner party. His guests included Lord Montagu, the Marquis of Dorset and the widowed Countess of Kildare. The talk was all of a quarrel between Anne and Cromwell, and rumours that Henry sought a new wife, probably Princess Madeleine, still not married to King James. Chapuys already knew Cromwell was in bad odour with Anne, who had told him she would like to see his head cut off. Chapuys had sympathised, wishing him a mistress who was more grateful for everything he had done for her and advising Cromwell to handle Anne more 'dexterously' than Cardinal Wolsey had done. Chapuys was so attached to both England and to Cromwell that he would be happy if Henry found a new wife, even if that did result in male heirs to Mary's detriment – not that he himself had any grudge against Anne, who, he said, had never done him any harm. Cromwell commented on the frailty of human affairs, especially of the court, and mentioned he had become aware of a few 'domestic' examples of late – a remark that, in retrospect, suggests he was already cooking up a scheme for Henry to be rid of Anne. As for Anne, Cromwell denied he had striven to bring her forward – he had only acted to smooth the way for Henry, who was set on her advancement. He was sure that Henry, although somewhat inclined to pay attention to other ladies, would be able to live chastely and honourably with Anne. This was said with such a lack of enthusiasm that Chapuys immediately inferred the exact opposite, although Cromwell had added there was no likelihood of Henry choosing a French wife.

Henry was still busy courting Jane Seymour and had sent her a present of money with a letter, which she had returned unopened, after reverently kissing the king's seal. She coyly sent back a message that, as a virtuous young woman, she could not accept a gift from the king, except, perhaps, on her marriage. This demurely submissive behaviour, whether genuine or feigned, was just the thing to please Henry after Anne's assertiveness and Katharine's royal dignity. According to Lady Exeter, Henry had been delighted, and decided he should only see Jane if she were chaperoned by her relatives.

Despite Charles's willingness to find a route to accepting Anne, Chapuys thought that if she could be removed from Henry's side, Mary would be pleased, even if a son ensued from a new match. She would be safer, and the spread of heresy, which he believed Anne was spearheading, would be reduced. Chapuys decided he would ask Mary's views on a new marriage for Henry, before deciding what, if anything, he should do or say.

***

On 14 April 1536, Henry's ambassador to Charles, Richard Pate, wrote an account of his audience with the emperor. Charles acknowledged how much he owed Henry and would gladly repay it, but he could not do so by declaring that Katharine had not been Henry's true wife. As for Mary, there was no possibility that she was illegitimate, and for Henry to acknowledge her legitimacy could not harm him. Charles could not believe that Henry, having previously treated her as 'well beseemed a natural father to make of his dear and well-beloved daughter' could treat her harshly. If a parent could be honoured by a child, he was sure that Henry would be as honoured by Mary as by any child who might be born to him. Furthermore, declaring Mary legitimate would improve relations within Christendom. Pate's meeting with Charles was followed by an audience with Granvelle, who intimated that if Henry would but reconcile himself to the pope, the emperor would find a way to have his marriage to Anne, or any other outcome Henry preferred, recognised. Pate, whose style is florid in the extreme, pleaded, apparently on his own behalf, for Mary's legitimation, referring to her as 'your dear, beautiful daughter' and asking that that 'redolent flower' be not suffered to 'wither away'.

On Easter Sunday 1536, Chapuys visited Cromwell to hear the answer to Charles's proposals. The matter of papal obedience Cromwell thought tricky, but if an alliance were re-established, who knew what Charles might not persuade Henry to do in time? As for Mary, Henry was just waiting for the right moment to show her more affection. Her legitimacy was a matter for the king's own honour, and thus ought not to be an express stipulation in a treaty. Cromwell thought he might be able to persuade Henry somewhat in this regard, but it would be much easier after a treaty was in place. With the possibility of reconciliation on the cards, Chapuys was invited to attend the court at Greenwich on Easter Tuesday. He was met by the council, including Lord Rochford, who was full of compliments about Chapuys's achievements. Chapuys generally avoided conversation with Rochford, who bored and irritated him by the incessant promotion of his Lutheran views.

Cromwell invited Chapuys to meet Anne and kiss her hand. The ambassador politely declined – he did not think that it would be advisable, although he would do so if the king commanded it. Cromwell consulted with Henry who seemed unconcerned. The king spoke for some time to Chapuys, politely holding his hat in his hand, after which Rochford conducted the ambassador to Mass. While he was there, Anne entered the chapel and turned to where the ambassador stood. Politeness demanded an exchange of bows. It seemed that the rest of the congregation thought more of it than Chapuys, who described the gesture as merely one of courtesy.

After dinner, Henry spoke to Chapuys again, but his mood had changed. Since Charles was the one making overtures, Henry wanted the proposals in writing; his relationship with the pope was none of Charles's business, nor was his treatment of Mary, to whom he would behave in accordance with how she obeyed him; he was not going to contribute to wars against the Turk until an agreement between he and Charles had been reached and finally, it was no good treating him like a child with carrot and stick. Chapuys, who during the day had taken the opportunity to make the acquaintance of Jane Seymour's brother Edward, withdrew, shaken by Henry's bad temper. Later he met Cromwell again, who seemed disheartened at the turn events had taken.

The following day, Cromwell told Chapuys the whole council had pleaded with Henry to take the opportunity to re-establish the Imperial alliance but the king had refused, unless it could be seen that Charles was asking him. Cromwell assured Chapuys that everything he had told him previously had been with Henry's authority, even when he seemed to be speaking for himself. He could give no reason for Henry's change of mind – it was not because Chapuys had provoked him; Henry had agreed the ambassador had spoken politely and gently. Cromwell could do no more than suppose that princes had 'spirits … which are hidden and unknown to all others'. If it were any consolation, the French ambassador had also been sent away with a flea in his ear. Chapuys was disappointed. He assured his master he had done his best, and suggested that if nothing could be done with Henry, the emperor should come to terms with François and have the papal bulls of deprivation promulgated with the additional proviso that Mary be recognised as heir to the kingdom and that no child of Henry born of Anne, or by another wife during Anne's lifetime, would be legitimate.

Although Chapuys had done no more than the minimum required by civility in bowing to Anne, and had declined to kiss her hand or speak to her, Mary, and some of her supporters, were not happy with him. Chapuys did not care about that – if he had thought Henry was truly willing to recreate the alliance with Charles he would have offered 'not two but a hundred candles to the she-devil'. As it happened, he was less inclined than ever to curry favour with Anne, knowing she was not in favour with Henry.

Henry's ambassadors in France and Spain were informed of the discussions about renewing the alliance with Charles. Henry was adamant that, as the injured party – he cited Charles's ingratitude when he had supported his candidacy as emperor and lent him money – so Charles must first apologise.

As to the legitimation of our daughter Mary, we answered that if she will submit to our grace without wrestling against the determination of our laws, we will acknowledge her and use her as our daughter, but we would not be directed or pressed herein, nor have any other order devised for her entertainment than should proceed from the inclination of our own heart, being moved by her humility and the gentle proceedings of such as pretend to be her friends.[8]

Part 3

'Mine own good daughter'

9

Submission

You will lose this wager.

Shakespeare

Chapuys was not the only one who had angered the king. Anne was disturbed to find her influence was no longer sufficient to gain the vacant Garter stall for her brother. Rochford was passed over in favour of Mary's friend, Sir Nicholas Carew, who was promoting Jane Seymour's cause. In the last weeks of April 1536, the knives were out for Anne. Exactly who was behind the plot has been debated at length. Either Henry told Cromwell to find a way to rid him of the woman who had once obsessed him but whom he had now come to hate, or Cromwell and others cooked up a scheme to defame Anne, which Henry, for the sake of his pride, could not overlook. As shown earlier, the suggestion that Anne had to be removed to effect any reconciliation with the emperor is misplaced.

It is certain that members of the court knew something serious was afoot. Carew, Geoffrey Pole and others of the king's chamber, who were long-term friends and supporters of Mary, wrote to her on 25 April that she should be of good cheer; matters would soon improve as Henry was sick and tired of Anne.[1] This news, which must have been the best that Mary had heard in many a long day, may have made her ready to act immediately to seek a reconciliation with her father after the shocking events that soon unfolded. Could Mary have been aware of what was being planned? The court was full of networks of friends and relatives with competing loyalties. One of the women questioned about Anne, her sister-in-law, Jane Rochford, who has been damned for 500 years for giving evidence against Anne and Rochford, appears to have been a friend of Mary's, judging from the frequency with which she later attended the princess. Jane Rochford's reputation may have been blackened unfairly – there is no actual information about what she said, even if it appears to have been injurious. One of the few women for whom Mary later made a direct request to be her lady-in-waiting was Margery Baynton, whose brother, Sir Edward, was Anne's chamberlain; so Mary may well have been kept informed of any gossip about Anne. But it hardly seems likely that she would have envisaged Anne being accused of treason. We know that Mary contemplated a divorce, which she told Chapuys she would favour, even though another marriage by her father might result in a son. Chapuys told Charles that Mary wanted Anne set aside, not for revenge for the wrong done herself or her mother, but for the sake of her father's conscience; she herself had forgiven any actions against her. This may be true, Mary showed herself later to be of a forgiving nature, but should probably be taken with a pinch of salt in the circumstances of 1536.

Promotion of a divorce between Henry and Anne was unnecessary labour. On 1 May, Anne was taken from Greenwich to the Tower on suspicion of adultery with a musician, Mark Smeaton. Henry Norris, one of Henry's closest companions was also arrested, as was Rochford. On the day of Anne's arrest, the Duke of Richmond went to bid Henry goodnight, and Henry began to weep, saying that Richmond and his sister should be grateful to God they had escaped the hands of that 'accursed whore' and her plans to poison them. This anger against Anne, and the fact that the executioner from Calais was sent for before Anne had been tried, make it clear that there was never any possibility Anne would escape death.

Mary's reaction to the news that Anne had been arrested and imprisoned on charges of adultery can only be surmised, as there is no record. It is probable, initially at least, that she believed the charges; after all, she would have considered Anne to be committing adultery from the beginning with her father, and there was always a strong presumption of guilt when someone was arrested – the idea of 'innocent until proven guilty' was not a feature of sixteenth century criminal proceedings. Shocked whispers would have echoed round the court, with few people likely to suggest that the arrests were unfounded.

Charles responded to Henry's Easter outburst to Chapuys in a conciliatory tone, agreeing that Henry did not need his help with the pope, but that he was well-disposed to help if he could, and would perhaps have more influence than others. As to Mary, he was sure Henry would act as a good father ought, especially in consideration of her virtues. It was only his close relationship to her that led him to urge Henry to treat her with fatherly regard. Surely it was not unreasonable for kin to intercede for children? If an alliance were made, he would consider Henry to be 'another father' to his own children and would not object to him speaking up for them.

Charles described Henry to Chapuys as 'of an amorous complexion and always desiring to have a male child' so he was quick to come up with an alternative wife for the king, whom he assumed would have Anne put to death. Rather than let the prize slip to France, he offered the Infanta Maria of Portugal, daughter of Queen Eleonora, and the empress's half-sister, although the Treaty of Madrid bound her to the dauphin. The young lady would have a dowry of 400,000 ducats. Dom Luis should also be offered again for Mary. Both those marriages would be very satisfactory for overcoming any past hostilities.

On 14 May, Cromwell wrote to Gardiner and Wallop in France that not only had Anne not been kept busy enough with adultery and inces, but that she and the others had been involved in a plot against the king's life – an idea even more far-fetched than the mass adultery, but necessary as Henry was now affirming that he had never been truly married to Anne. If they had not been married, it would be hard to justify a death penalty for adultery – some more egregious offence must be claimed.

Chapuys was sure the king would marry Jane Seymour. His account of her is not especially flattering. She was over twenty-five, very pale, and not of great wit, although she might have 'a good understanding'. Chapuys insinuated that Jane, having lived in the English court for some time, could not possibly be a virgin, but that would not be a problem for Henry, as when he was tired of her, he would be able to find witnesses against her. He had heard Jane was somewhat 'proud and haughty', but she was to be welcomed as she bore a great deal of love and reverence towards Mary.[2] Chapuys believed everyone was delighted with Anne's downfall, and anticipated the restoration of Mary, but Henry, although he had recently sent her £20, was not showing himself in any hurry to mend fences with his daughter. When the possibility of her restoration had been spoken of by his council, he had 'shown himself obstinate'. He had even quarrelled with Jane when she had suggested that Mary be restored, calling her a fool for not seeking the advancement of their future children. Jane's response had been that the restoration of Mary would promote Henry's tranquillity and that of the whole realm, as it was the only thing that would satisfy Charles. But Henry could not back down first – he would never admit error in any disagreement. He would be conciliatory if the other person admitted to wrong doing, but not otherwise. Chapuys planned to encourage the lords about to attend Parliament to push Mary's restoration forward. He thought Elizabeth would be disinherited, and Parliament asked to beg Henry to remarry. He reported what was known of the trials of Anne, Rochford and the others. While he clearly did not care about Anne's fate, the tone of his letters is contemptuous and it is obvious he thought the trials rigged.

Anne's marriage was declared invalid on 17 May 1536. There is no certainty as to the grounds, but Chapuys believed it was related to Henry's prior relationship with Mary Boleyn. As both parties had known of the impediment, the good faith exception to illegitimacy would not apply to Elizabeth. The same day, Sir Henry Norris, Sir William Brereton (whose brother had recommended in 1526 that he curry favour with Mary) Sir Francis Weston and Mark Smeaton were arrested, as was Anne's brother. Anne was able to see the executions from her window, and two days later, she, too, was beheaded. Anne had sworn, both before and after taking the sacrament, that she had never been unfaithful to the king.

Before Anne had been tried, let alone judged, a number of court ladies and gentlemen had hurried to wait on Mary, lending credence to Mary's belief that her ill-treatment had been Anne's doing. Shelton had permitted them to visit but Chapuys warned Mary not to retain any members to her household without Henry's express permission. He was quite sure Mary would not be restored to the succession without acknowledging the dissolution of her parents' marriage and denying the pope's authority. Chapuys did not think that Mary would wish to accept either proposition, although he would encourage her to go as far as her conscience permitted. He urged Charles to send a new envoy to conclude an alliance before Parliament met, as that would be advantageous for Mary.

***

A few days after Anne's execution, Mary had a visitor, Lady Kingston, the wife of Sir William Kingston, Constable of the Tower. Lady Kingston had attended Katharine for many years, including at the Field of Cloth of Gold, and knew Mary well. As the constable's wife, she had waited on Anne during her imprisonment – to Anne's dismay, as she felt herself surrounded by women 'who had never loved [her]'. Lady Kingston had two errands. The first was a personal one, a message from Anne who had expressed remorse for her treatment of Mary and for having conspired her death – by which she had probably meant in the general sense of wanting Mary executed for failure to swear the oaths, rather than admitting any poison plot. Faced with death, Anne, like a good Christian, might well have thought over her life, wished she had done some things differently, and tried to put right any wrongs she could.[3] Lady Kingston's second errand was to deliver a draft letter to Mary for her to copy and sign, in which she was to beg forgiveness of her father in suitably humble terms. Cromwell told Chapuys that Henry himself had suggested Lady Kingston be sent so Mary could solicit his forgiveness, although later information is not consistent with this claim and it is perhaps more likely that Cromwell instigated it. Cromwell urged Chapuys to persuade Mary to write the said letter, which he would be willing to have translated into Latin for Chapuys to check that it was honourable for Mary to write. Chapuys replied that he would not encourage Mary to sign any letters that denied her rights, or the honour of herself or Katharine, or that conflicted with her conscience. He was horrified when he read the draft, which he thought did all those things, as well as trying to trap Mary into naming Chapuys as her secret supporter.

Cromwell assured Chapuys that an alliance between Henry and Charles would be far easier to arrange now that Anne was dead, and boasted he had 'discovered and followed up' Anne's misdeeds. The good news, Cromwell continued, was that Henry, knowing how the people were disposed towards Mary, had determined to have her declared his heir at the next Parliament. Chapuys did not believe for a minute that Mary would be reinstated until she wrote the letter of repentance. He was also aware that, whatever Cromwell might say, other privy councillors were certain Henry would not relent over Mary. The Earl of Sussex had said that, since both Mary and Richmond were illegitimate, the son should be preferred, which Henry had chosen neither to confirm nor deny. Chapuys also knew Henry was fuming because, having again suggested a match with Angoulême, he had been informed the French required such a marriage to be predicated on Mary being declared legitimate. The king had lost his temper, and raged against Mary's obstinacy and ill will to such an extent that Chapuys thought he had little love for her.

At their next meeting, Chapuys asked Cromwell whether Henry intended to marry Princess Madeleine. Cromwell responded that he would not marry out of the kingdom – because a foreign princess who misconducted herself could not be punished as Anne had been! Chapuys said, drily, that properly brought up princesses would be unlikely to commit adultery. He raised the prospect of Dom Luis again. Cromwell asked more particulars about the prince and, most importantly, how many brothers he had. There was no prospect, Chapuys said, of him inheriting the throne of Portugal, but he was of sufficiently good estate to maintain a wife of Mary's station, and was a better prospect than the Duke of Suffolk or the Earl of Angus, who had married Henry's sisters, had been.

Mary wrote to Cromwell on 26 May. Even if this were in response to Lady Kingston's visit, the speed with which Mary sought reconciliation with Henry demonstrates her genuine belief that it had been Anne keeping her father from her. According to Chapuys, her letter in no way resembled the draft Cromwell had drawn up. Mary apologised for her bad handwriting, saying she had written very little for over two years and was only able to do so now, because Lady Kingston had given her means. Since we know she had communicated regularly with Chapuys, she was either lying, or her messages to him were verbal. We also know she had sent letters to Mary of Hungary and Gattinara, but that might fall within the 'occasional' exception. Mary said nothing about the draft letter, either because she thought it so unsuitable, or because Lady Kingston had not broached the matter. She assured Cromwell she would have written to him before to be a suitor for her to the king but knew that no one would dare speak for her while 'that woman' was alive. Now, she begged Cromwell to ask Henry for permission to write to him.

Three days later, Cromwell told Chapuys that the matter of Mary was at the forefront of Henry's and his own mind. He suggested Chapuys redraft the letter of submission into something that Mary could sign, and persuade her to do so. As an inducement, Cromwell, exaggerating, said Henry and the whole council would agree to Mary being appointed as the king's heir, and her marriage to Dom Luis, once she had been restored. Henry would not be interested in marrying the Infanta Maria of Portugal; he was going to marry Jane Seymour, as Chapuys had predicted. Chapuys asked whether it was true that the French request for Mary for the dauphin had been countered with the offer of Angoulême instead. Cromwell had to admit it, but then said it was merely one of the artifices of princes – he himself would cut off his arm before acting in such an 'extravagant and dishonest' fashion.

Henry responded graciously to Mary's request that she might write to him, and sent her his fatherly blessing. That very day, he was presenting her with a new stepmother as he married Jane Seymour in the Queen's Closet at Whitehall. Mary immediately sent a letter to Cromwell, thanking him for his efforts so far, and assuring him she would be as obedient to the king as Cromwell could 'reasonably require'. She hoped to come into her father's presence – it was what she desired 'above all worldly things'. She would write no more, because of the 'rheum' in the head from which she was suffering.

Whatever inclination Henry might have been feeling towards forgiving Mary for her obstinacy, it was completely destroyed by the delivery of Reginald Pole's opinion on the papal supremacy and the divorce in the very week that Mary was sending her letters. In a long and complex paper, which Henry, hopeful of his cousin's support, had asked him to write, Pole, once beloved of the king, likened his royal cousin to Nero and Domitian, accusing him of 'tearing to pieces' the true defenders of religion, and being worse than the Turks. Not only that but he had robbed his people, made a sport of the nobility and torn like a wild beast those who had been the most honourable in the kingdom. Faced with that extraordinary tirade, Henry was incandescent and immediately determined that he would not put up with any more disobedience from his daughter or anyone else. He certainly could not allow it to be thought that his actions of the last ten years had been the result of infatuation with Anne, and that he would now change his mind.

Unaware of Pole's monumental lack of tact or consideration for his relatives remaining in Henry's power, on 1 June Mary penned a submissive letter to her father. It is possible this was based on Cromwell's letter, as the tone is extremely humble. She asked Henry's forgiveness for any offences she had committed against him and assured him that 'next to God', she would 'submit to all things to [his] goodness and pleasure'. She asked him to consider that she was 'but a woman and [his] child' and had committed her soul to God, and her body to be 'ordered in this world as it shall stand to [his] pleasure'. She continued by expressing her delight at the news of his marriage to Jane, obviously hoping that her acceptance of this marriage would be sufficient payment for her refusal to acknowledge his union with Anne. She hoped to be able to 'wait upon the queen and do her Grace such service as shall please her to command'. To make it even clearer that she accepted his new marriage, she hoped that God would shortly send him a prince, which happy event would be more welcome to her than any 'creature living'. If Mary hoped that this general submission would be enough, she was to be rudely disappointed.

Cromwell informed Chapuys that Henry and Jane were delighted with the 'wise and prudent' letters that Mary had written to her father. Henry was also, said Cromwell – almost certainly lying – talking of recognising her as his heir until such time as Jane had a child. She would not, however, have the title of 'Princess', which implied the legal status of heir. Chapuys thought this might be a good starting point. Once Henry was used to the idea of Mary as his heir, once he remembered all of her excellent attributes, and once he realised that he and Jane would not have children (which Chapuys thought probable) it would be easier to put the arrangement on a formal footing. In the meantime, Henry was certainly not going to allow Mary to marry the dauphin, nor yet Angoulême, who was too young for her. The two men concluded that a treaty between Henry and Charles was quite the best thing that could possibly happen, and that the French were not to be trusted.

Chapuys attended court on 6 June. Henry was pleased to see him and suitably grateful to hear Charles was delighted that he had escaped the conspiracy against him that Anne was alleged to have constructed. He requested Chapuys to wait upon his new queen. Chapuys kissed Queen Jane's hand, remarking that although Anne had taken the motto '*The Most Happy*', he hoped it would be more applicable to her. The emperor was delighted that his old ally had such a good and virtuous wife, especially as he had once been served by Jane's brother, Edward. Not the least of Jane's happiness, Chapuys remarked, was that, without the trouble of giving birth, she had a daughter from whom she would receive more joy and consolation that she could from any child of her own. While Jane was well-disposed toward Mary, one can hardly suppose that she took this idea very seriously. Nevertheless, she told Chapuys she would favour Mary's interests and strive for peace. This idea of Jane as peacemaker was repeated by Henry, who came to relieve her of her first ambassadorial interview. The new queen would promote peace, he said, not just from her own gentle nature, but because she would not wish to be parted from Henry if he had to go to war – a hint that Henry was planning to do just that, as he was satisfied that François was justified in his invasion of Savoy. If Charles invaded France in retaliation, Henry would see him as the aggressor and would be obliged to support François. Besides, Henry added, Charles had failed to support Henry in conquering France back in 1525, after the Battle of Pavia. How could he be sure that any new alliance would not end the same way – in disappointment and betrayal?

More soothing words were expended by Chapuys, who was then dismissed to talk to Edward Seymour, now Lord Beauchamp, while Henry discussed the Imperial propositions with his council. Chapuys emphasised to Beauchamp the advantage to his sister, himself, the country, and all of Christendom of restoring Mary to her rights. In subsequent conversation with Cromwell, Chapuys presumed that Henry had not been more positive about aid for Charles in Savoy because, in his role of arbiter between François and Charles, he needed to blame both for bad conduct. Cromwell, sincerely or not, complimented his grasp of Henry's character – and assured him that he thought Mary would be restored by the following Saturday. Already Chapuys's words had affected Jane, who had spoken warmly in Mary's favour.

Suffolk also hoped for a reconciliation with Charles and wanted to lead a troop of Englishmen into his service. Norfolk favoured France now, either to keep the treaties, or because his pension from Charles had not been paid, but Richmond agreed to do what he could to promote peace. The young man was now part of his father's circle of advisors – what he thought about Mary's possible restoration is an intriguing mystery. Many of his household were later aligned to the Reformed faith, so he may have believed Mary to be as illegitimate as himself, and therefore, as the male, he ought to be preferred. There is absolutely no information about any personal relationship he and Mary might have had, other than that she called him 'brother'.

As Mary had not talked to Henry since late 1532, she probably had not grasped that his actions in dismissing papal authority, although mixed with his desire to marry Anne, now had far more complex motivations. Having received no reply to her letter of 1 June, on the 7th, she wrote again to Cromwell, saying she longed to hear that her father of his 'princely goodness and fatherly pity' had 'withdrawn his displeasure'. She sent with it a 'token' for her father, and hoped he would send one in response. The following day, she made a further attempt to soften Henry's heart directly. She wrote that although she understood that he had withdrawn his 'dreadful displeasure, long conceived against [her]' her 'joy [would] never be full' until he had written to her or sent her a token. It seems Cromwell sent a reply to this missive, as the next link in the chain of correspondence is a letter from Mary to him, enclosing one for her father. From the letter addressed to Cromwell, it is clear he had told her that she had not humbled herself enough. She wrote that she had followed his 'advice and counsel', for which she thanked him and confirmed that she would continue to do so in all things concerning her duty to the king – adding 'God and my conscience not offended'. She then asked not to be importuned to go further in her submission than she had already done in the enclosed letter for Henry. 'I desire you, for Christ's passion, to find means that I be not moved to any further entry in this matter than I have done; for I assure you I have done the utmost my conscience will suffer me.'[4] Indeed, the whole letter to Henry engenders a feeling of queasiness as Mary described herself as 'most humbly prostrate before your noble feet, your most obedient subject and humble child, that hath not only repented her offences hitherto' and so forth.

Cromwell (or Henry) was still not satisfied, and wrote a letter that called forth a response from Mary that she could tell he was unhappy with her exception to total obedience, by reference to her conscience. She had not meant, she assured him, that she thought Henry would require her to do something that would offend God, only that '[she had] always used both in writing and speaking to except God in all things'. Nevertheless, she appreciated his efforts and would copy out the even more abject letter that he had drafted for her. She enclosed it, unsealed, as her head and her teeth were so painful that she had hardly slept for two or three days and could not endure to write a further copy. She thanked Cromwell again for his efforts, saying she had no one but him from whom she could ask advice. The letter she copied for her father noted that she was 'enforced to cry to his merciful ears, and, prostrate at his feet, implore him to put apart his displeasure. His grace has never been wanting to those who repented, and who did not offend by malice but by youth, frailty, and ignorance' and that she had no hope but in Henry's 'blessed nature'.

Mary's protestations of obedience were not enough. Around 9 June, Henry sent a delegation to her, led by Norfolk, with the Earl of Sussex, the Bishop of Chichester, and others, to deliver his orders. Their instructions began with a rehearsal of Mary's wilfulness and obstinacy in rejecting the king's laws. This was an example of ill-conduct bound to be displeasing to God as well as the king. She had written three times to Henry, declaring her repentance, but not agreeing to accept Henry's laws. Any private individual would have suffered from the full rigour of the law, but Henry's 'gracious and divine nature', his 'clemency and pity', his 'merciful inclination and princely heart' meant he was always ready to 'take pity and compassion on all offenders repentantly crying'. In the case of his daughter, since she was 'frail, inconstant and easy to be persuaded', he would be glad to remit some part of his displeasure. They were to put several questions to her to test the truth of her repentance. First, did she acknowledge Henry as her sovereign lord, and would she not only obey all the laws and statutes of the realm, but also set them forth, and maintain them, in accordance with her duty?

Second, would she accept Henry as Supreme Head, under Christ, of the Church in England and utterly reject the Bishop of Rome's pretended authority? Third, would she acknowledge that the marriage between her parents was invalid? As neither Henry, nor any of his councillors could conceive that a young woman could be so firm in her opinions and impervious to pressure, without having been encouraged and supported by others, she was to tell them who had been behind her disobedience. They were also to find out why Mary had suddenly thought it was a good time to approach her father – negating Cromwell's statement to Chapuys that it had been Henry's idea to send Lady Kingston to her. The council might have supposed that the disposal of Anne had led Mary to believe her father might have a change of heart. In a spirit of reasonableness, if Mary were to say she needed to think over what was put to her, they could give her three or four days to contemplate her answers, if they believed that she honestly required the time. But after that, she must answer in writing.

Mary still refused to co-operate and so, having been unable to argue her into submission, the men took to bullying her. They told her she was so unnatural a daughter they could scarcely believe her to be Henry's and that, if they could, they would beat her and bang her head against the wall until it was as soft as a baked apple. Lady Shelton was told to keep her under lock and key and have someone watch over her at all times. Nevertheless, Mary got word to Chapuys to send her advice. He recommended she resist until the point where she felt her life might truly be endangered, but then submit herself to the king. Because she would be doing it under duress, it would not count against her, since God cared more about the intention than the deed. If swearing would bring her back into the succession, and perhaps able to redress matters in future, she should do so. If Mary took this reassurance to heart, it may explain her later determination to return England to papal obedience. Only success in that endeavour could excuse her acceptance of Henry's supremacy over the English church. Mary was gambling her hope of salvation against the possibility of later being in a position of power that would enable her to rescue all of the imperilled (as she saw it) souls in England.

Henry, furious at Mary's response to the commissioners, still could not believe she was replying unprompted. Various women were questioned, and one of her servants was kept at Cromwell's house for two days. At this point, according to Chapuys, Henry consulted the judges about proceeding against Mary in accordance with the law. They advised giving her warning that, if she did not conform, steps would be taken, and this is probably what prompted a final broadside from Cromwell, who was now afraid his support of her had endangered his own head.

I have received your letters, whereby it appeareth you be in great discomfort, and do desire that I should find the means to speak with you.

Your discomfort can be no greater than mine, who upon your letters have spoken so much of your repentance for your wilful obstinacy against the king, and of your humble submission to obey his pleasure and laws in all things without exception or qualification. Knowing how diversely and contrarily you have proceeded at the late being of his Majesty's Council with you, I am ashamed of what I have said and afraid of what I have done. What the sequel shall be God knows. With your folly you undo yourself, and I say to you, as I have said elsewhere heretofore, it were a pity you should not be an example in punishment, if you will make yourself an example in the contempt of God, your natural father and his laws by your only fantasie, contrary to the judgments and determinations of all men that ye must confess do know and love God as well as you. To be plain with you, I think you the most obstinate woman that ever was, and I dare not open my lips to name you unless I have such a ground thereto that it may appear you were mistaken, or at least that you repent your ingratitude and are ready to do your duty. I have therefore sent you a book of articles to subscribe, on receiving which from you again with a letter declaring that you think in your heart as you have subscribed with your hand, I will venture to speak for your reconciliation. If you do not leave all sinister counsels, which have brought you to the point of undoing, I take leave of you for ever, and desire you to write me no more, for I will never think you other than the most ungrate, unnatural, and most obstinate person living, both to God and your most dear and benign father.[5]

This was the moment of truth for Mary – should she sign, dishonouring her beloved mother and herself and endangering her immortal soul, but live to fight another day, or should she stand firm, and risk trial and execution? Would her father go to that length? It was a gamble too far for Mary. She copied Cromwell's draft of a letter of toe-curlingly abject submission. She signed the articles she had been given, although apparently without reading them – acknowledging Henry as her sovereign, and agreeing to uphold and maintain his laws; acknowledging the king as 'Supreme Head under Christ' of the Church in England, disavowing the Bishop of Rome's authority; and finally acknowledging her parents' marriage as incestuous and unlawful. The council re-appeared and Mary made a further humble submission to her father, after which they addressed her on their knees, and apologised for their former harsh language – probably with the excuse they had but sought to shock her into her senses. She wrote again to Henry:

Most humbly lying at your feet, my most dear and benign father and sovereign, I have this day perceived your gracious clemency and merciful pity to have overcome my most unkind and unnatural proceedings towards you and your most just and virtuous laws. I cannot express my joy or make any return for your goodness, but my poor heart which I send unto your Highness to remain in your hand, to be for ever used, directed, and framed, whiles God shall suffer life to remain in it, at your only pleasure. I beg you to receive it as all I have to offer. I will never vary from that confession and submission I made to your Highness in the presence of the Council. I pray God preserve you and the queen and send you issue. 26th June, Hunsdon.[6]

Throughout the rest of Henry's reign, Mary never said or did a thing publicly to suggest she had not been sincere in her submission – an impressive feat of acting, as we know that as soon as she could, she asked Chapuys to send to Rome to request the absolution she had been led by him to believe would be forthcoming.

Mary was initially sunk in depression at having finally been defeated. She had betrayed her mother's memory, and her own beliefs. Chapuys tried to comfort her with the thought that the pope would praise her decision, presumably as tending to the greater good. This, with the confirmation that he gave her of Charles's approval, cheered her. Her friends, too, were relieved and Chapuys reported receiving many congratulations on her submission.

Mary's supporters at court may well have breathed a sigh of relief. Before she had signed the articles, at least two of Henry's gentlemen of the Privy Chamber had been examined by the council. Both Sir Anthony Browne and Sir Francis Bryan had been asked a series of searching questions about whether they though Mary should be Henry's heir, and what they might do if Henry died, while Elizabeth was still legally his heir? They had responded that they wanted Mary to submit to Henry's laws, but that if she did, they would think her a very suitable heir, until Queen Jane bore a child. While the law named Elizabeth as heir, they would, of course, obey it.

Having given Mary's supporters a final scare, Henry, delighted with her submission, granted her permission to choose her own household. She wrote to Cromwell, again thanking him for his advice, and for having saved her from being 'almost drowned in folly'. Cromwell had obviously asked her for her opinion on Elizabeth. She referred to the little girl as 'princess', saying she thought she currently ought to use the title, for she was 'loath to offend'. She would, in future, always call Elizabeth 'sister', as she had offered before. As for the servants she would like, she named Susan, daughter of Clarencieux Herald, and Margery Baynton. She also requested Mary Browne, who had served her in the Marches. In a trick question, Cromwell asked Mary's opinion of purgatory, relics and pilgrimages. Mary was quite astute enough not to fall into the trap and said she could have no opinion until her father had spoken on the matters. She begged again to be admitted to the king's presence.

With impressive speed, Mary was granted a new suite of servants, numbering forty-two in all, while Elizabeth had thirty-two. The difference in the number of attendants probably reflected their ages rather than Henry wishing to give the impression that Mary was legitimate, whereas Elizabeth was not, although once both had been pronounced illegitimate, Mary was treated as of higher status until the end of Henry's reign. This was probably a combination of her being the elder and of the royal rank of her mother.

Mary's request for Susan Clarencieux and Margery Baynton was granted, and Frances Aylmer who had served her for many years returned, as did her chaplain, Richard Baldwin, Randall Dodd, her gentleman usher, and her laundress, Beatrice ap Rice. Frances Baynam, Lady Kingston's daughter-in-law was also appointed. There was a Keeper of the Greyhounds and several grooms, suggesting she would soon be able to return to hunting and taking physical exercise, and also a tumbler, named Lucretia. This final touch suggests a direct intervention from Henry, who had once sent jugglers to Mary in the Marches.

The Bishop of Faenza, the papal nuncio in Paris, reported on 26 June, rather getting ahead of events, that the forthcoming Parliament would declare Mary legitimate. He thought both Norfolk and Cromwell were in favour of such a move, and that Henry was 'much softened' towards Mary, while she was universally loved. In fact, he had been told that when Lady Salisbury went to court, a crowd of up to 5,000 people went to meet her, on hearing that Mary would be with her. An astonished Henry had asked the meaning of the crowds and learning that they were there in hopes of seeing Mary, had assured them they would see her soon. It may be this very popularity that prevented Henry from declaring Mary legitimate, lest it undermine the position of Jane's children.

Charles praised Chapuys's conduct of affairs, particularly his visit to Jane and his efforts to interest her in Mary. He wrote that the French were going from bad to worse, and he was not interested in Henry's arbitration, only in a declaration of support. He continued with the information that François was now attacking the Low Countries as well as Savoy, and rebuffing Charles's latest offer for comprise. This consisted of an offer of an Imperial bride for the Duke of Angoulême, with the couple to be invested with the Duchy of Milan. François had rejected the idea – he would prefer the duchy to be granted to his second son, the Duke of Orléans. There could be no benefit to Charles in this, since Orléans was already married, so no agreement could be reached. As for Mary, Charles still wished to pursue the match with Dom Luis, ideally with Mary declared legitimate, or at least in the succession after Jane's children. If Henry could not be moved on the point, Chapuys was to find out what dowry she would receive and, in return, Charles would do what he could financially, to 'content' the couple and Henry. Meanwhile, the

English, aware that Milan might be available for Angoulême, were hinting to François that, in those circumstances, a marriage between Angoulême and Mary might be acceptable.

On 1 July, Mary sent Cromwell a letter of thanks for his labours in effecting a reconciliation. Surprisingly, she did not take up the offer obviously made either by letter or messenger for new clothes. She told him she had written to her father saying she required no more clothes than her father's favour. She was, however, very pleased with the present of a horse as she did not previously have one, and looked forward to riding for her health.

Henry may have been relieved and pleased that Mary had at last submitted, but he was not in a pleasant frame of mind. He was, in fact, so furious that one of the gentlemen of the Privy Chamber sent for five of Chapuys's musicians to play soothing music to him each morning. Given the hints at Anne Boleyn's trial that Henry suffered from impotence, perhaps he was enraged by difficulties in the bedroom. Chapuys was certainly under the impression that Jane would be unlikely to have children. He was therefore sanguine that Mary would be well treated and named as heir in default of children by Jane. On 5 July, Cromwell wrote to Gardiner in France, declining to give him all of the salacious details of the trial of Anne, saying the confessions were too shocking to have been given in evidence. In reality, the shocking fact was the lack of confessions. He added that 'Lady' Mary was a most obedient child, while the former princess, Elizabeth, had been declared illegitimate by Parliament.

The reconciliation between Mary and Henry was now so far advanced that Jane wrote to her step-daughter. There is no copy of Jane's letter, but Mary responded with thanks, and a request that the queen 'with such acceleration as shall stand with [her] pleasure' would remember Mary's 'desire to attain the king's presence'.

Cromwell divulged to Chapuys that Henry and Jane were going to meet Mary secretly and assured the ambassador that after seeing Mary's 'beauty, goodness and virtue', the king would be more inclined to listen to Charles's requests for Henry to attack François, to divert him from Savoy. So far, Henry had maintained that François had acted within his rights.

The first meeting between Mary and her father since 1532 took place at Hackney. She rode there on the night of 6 July, and the next afternoon, Henry and Jane arrived. They were very kind to Mary; Jane gave her a diamond, and Henry gave her 1,000 crowns in cash, and told her she could have as much money as she wanted. She was served at table with great ceremony, and before leaving on the evening of the 7th, Henry told her Cromwell would let her know about her household. She was to return to Hunsdon while the king undertook a visit to Dover and the coast but, after that, she would be recalled to court, to live with him and Jane. From a subsequent conversation, Chapuys discovered it had not all been sweetness and light in the meeting and that within the 'honey, there had been a dram of gall' – only to be expected after years of frustration. This may have prompted another letter from Mary to Henry, dated 8 July in which she again, prostrate[ed]' herself and 'humbly with the very bottom of [her] stomach' begged,

> as I am now in such merciful sort recovered, being more than almost lost with mine own folly, that your Majesty may as well accept me justly your bounden slave by redemption as your most humble faithful and obedient child and subject by the course of nature planted in this your most noble realm.

We can only hope that Mary had her tongue firmly in her cheek as she wrote this.

* * *

Despite the hopes of Mary, Chapuys and others, the Parliament of 1536 was not asked to recognise Mary as legitimate, nor to return her to the succession, either before, or after, any children Jane might have. Instead, it specifically ruled that both she and Elizabeth were illegitimate and declared Henry's heirs to be Jane's children, and, if she should have none, whomever Henry might nominate. Thus, in the Act of 1536, Parliament did what the ecclesiastical courts could not – declare illegitimate a child who had been born in good faith. Under common law, if neither Mary nor Elizabeth were legitimate, then Henry's heir was James V of Scotland. If the view that a statute of Edward III precluded foreign nationals from becoming king were correct, then Henry's heir was Lady Margaret Douglas. But Lady Margaret, too, was in disgrace, it having emerged that she had betrothed herself to Lord Thomas Howard, half-brother to the Duke of Norfolk. She had been dispatched to the Tower to consider her sins.

Chapuys seemed sanguine that Henry's choice of heir would fall on Mary, if Jane had no children. He was still in favour of a match with Dom Luis, but Cromwell was nudging for James of Scotland, declaring that if he succeeded in making peace with Scotland, and reconciling Mary to Henry, he would die happy.

On 21 July, Mary sent a letter to her father, enquiring about Henry's and Jane's health. She hoped she was not being too importunate in requesting frequent news of them. In a line which shows generosity of spirit, she praised 'my sister, Elizabeth' as a 'child toward (forward and clever for her age)' in whom she thought Henry would 'rejoice in time coming'. Considering the pain that Mary and her mother had been put to for the sake of Elizabeth's birth, it shows real kindness in Mary that she did not blame the little girl, and even tried to promote her to their father's attention at a very delicate time in her own reconciliation. Cromwell kept her messenger, Dodd, at Richmond until Henry's return so that he might take fresh news, but sent one of his own messengers in the meantime, in case she was worried by Dodd's non-appearance. Mary thanked him for this kindness. She also wrote to Thomas Wriothesley, Cromwell's colleague, expressing gratitude for his kindness both to Dodd, and also to Anthony Roke, an old servant of Katharine's who had frequently been employed to deliver messages during Mary's childhood. More personally, she was grateful to Wriothesley for organising the recruitment of her cook. She thought the man had been found much sooner thanks to his efforts.

No mention had been made of Richmond in the Act of Succession – if Henry had had any idea of including him it would have been wasted effort, as the young man died on 23 July 1536, aged only seventeen. On hearing the news, Chapuys rather coldly wrote that his death was a good thing for Mary, to whom Henry was becoming more affectionate each day. Cromwell had ordered a ring to be made with a picture of Mary on one side, and of Henry and Jane on the other, with a Latin inscription. When Henry saw it, he was so taken with it that he decided to give it to Mary himself. The length of the inscription makes it difficult to believe it was a finger ring; a bracelet seems more likely. The gist of the motto was that obedience brought peace of mind, tranquillity and constancy, and that the example of obedience of Christ to His Father should be followed.[7]

Perhaps the ordering of this gift for Mary was one of the factors behind a rumour that Henry intended to marry Mary to none other than Cromwell himself, to keep her in England, lest a marriage abroad result in her going back on her affirmation of the oath, and invading at the head of an army. Chapuys did not think Henry would entertain such an idea, or that Cromwell would be willing to be embroiled in such a potentially explosive situation. Cromwell had already been rewarded with the office of Lord Privy Seal, taken from Wiltshire, and a barony, which signs of Henry's gratitude Chapuys believed him thoroughly to deserve.

Charles and François were heading for open war. While Henry had given orders that French ships in the Channel should not be assisted, he was still cool towards Charles's desire for an offensive alliance, and warned Chapuys that if Charles attacked France, it should not be in such a way as would compel him to assist François.

In early August, Chapuys visited Henry. He was armed with the information from Mary that the king, while outwardly not leaning towards Charles, was annoyed about François' provocation of the emperor; nevertheless, he was determined to remain neutral as neither protagonist would do anything for him. We do not know where Mary gleaned her information – she was not yet back at court. A possible route is via one of her friends in the Privy Chamber – Browne, Bryan or Carew, who may have shared information with their relatives in Mary's and Elizabeth's households. Henry was also communicating with Mary directly; he was obviously still suspicious of her true feelings, as he asked her if she had been obstinate in yielding to him for hope of help from Charles, and reminded her that the emperor could do nothing for her during Henry's lifetime. He also wanted to know if either Charles or Chapuys had written to her. We can only suppose that Mary spent a good deal of time with her confessor, admitting to lying – if she had told Henry that she had been in pretty constant communication with Chapuys throughout the period of her disgrace, the fur would have flown.

Amusingly, Henry told Mary he wished her to confirm that she had truly consented to his will from her heart, because he hated 'dissemblers'. When his council urged him to dissemble to ambassadors, he refused. He hoped she would be his daughter in this. Indeed she would – the evidence suggests that she could 'dissemble' while affecting an air of candour, quite as well as Henry! Henry was clearly eager to believe Mary's protestations. She was increasingly well served and, although a full household had not been arranged, she had plenty of company, even Elizabeth's followers paying her court. As to the title of 'princess', Chapuys was comfortable that it was not given in England while there was hope of a male heir and Cromwell continued to reassure him that it would be granted in due course. Chapuys appeared quite overcome with Mary's 'beauty, grace and prudence' and thought that, once she was at court, with her 'good sense' and Cromwell's support, everything would fall in her lap.

> Even Secretary Cromwell has congratulated her in his letters, and thank God she now triumphs, and it is to be hoped that the dangers are laid with which she has been surrounded to make her a paragon of virtue, goodness, honour and prudence: I say nothing of beauty and grace, for it is incredible. May God raise her soon to the Crown for the benefit of his Majesty [the emperor] and all of Chrisetendom![8]

Chapuys warned Mary there might be a scheme for her to be married to someone unsuitable (perhaps thinking of the story of Cromwell) to which she responded, as he had no doubt hoped, that she would not marry without Charles's advice, and then only if it would promote the peace of Christendom. She herself had no desire to marry. This was, of course, the coy attitude that a young lady was supposed to take toward matrimony.

Mary had signed the documents of submission to Henry in the belief that the pope would absolve her of an oath made under duress, but it transpired that matters were not so simple. Cifuentes, Charles's envoy in Rome, was appalled to discover Chapuys had encouraged Mary to submit to Henry's demands. He had received her request for papal absolution, but he thought that unless she renounced her oath in front of two witnesses, it could not be given. As it would be dangerous for her request to be known, Cifuentes had not asked the pope, but was referring the matter to Charles. When Chapuys heard this, he was annoyed – he replied that Cifuentes was quite wrong to think Mary should have held out and if the pope had not given her absolution, he ought to.

Requests for places in Mary's household came in. Sir John Russell asked for a position as chamberer for the wife of his servant; Mary was willing, if Cromwell agreed. When Richmond's household was broken up after his death, some of his servants were put forward for Mary. On 16 August Sir John Shelton wrote to Cromwell for money for the household of the two sisters; he thought £4,000 per annum would not be too much to maintain them.

On 12 August, Cromwell was still stringing Chapuys along, saying Henry was despairing of having more children and feeling his age. Mary was bound to be named his successor soon, which would be plenty of time to think of a marriage with Dom Luis, although, of course, the French were again offering the dauphin's hand, or, when he was rejected outright, Angoulême's. Later that month, Mary wrote to Cromwell, saying she had not heard from Henry, so was sending her servant to ask news of him and Jane; she hoped she was not annoying Henry with her 'rude letters'. She thanked Cromwell for another horse and saddle for she found 'great ease' in riding.

Chapuys told Charles that Mary had been prayed for in a church near his lodgings, the implication being the congregation now thought of her, once again, as the heir to the throne. Nothing more is heard of this. It seems likely that orders would have been given for such practices to cease. He was full of praise for Mary and hope for her future, as well as observing how much she loved Charles and Isabella. She was 'endowed with such wisdom, beauty, uprightness and other virtues that no one can help praising her'. All these high-flown compliments suggest that he had been allowed to see Mary, although he does not specifically say so. A few days later, Cromwell was still assuring him that Mary would be named as Henry's heir, and then married to Dom Luis.

Objectively, if Henry had allowed the marriage with Dom Luis to go ahead, it would probably have made most sense all round. Portugal was an ally from which England had nothing to fear, Luis had no obvious prospect of becoming king of Portugal and, as a younger son, he probably would not have had sufficient money or backing to mount a challenge to any sons Henry might have. Dom Luis was somewhat older than Mary (ten years) but still in the prime of life, and would have been more acceptable to the populace as king in her right than a Frenchman would have been, and he and Mary could have provided a male successor. The genetic disadvantage of his being Mary's first cousin would not have factored into Tudor thinking. This close relationship would have required a dispensation from the pope, which, of course, Henry would not have asked for, but presumably he would not have objected to Dom Luis obtaining for his own satisfaction. Henry was probably waiting to see if Jane would fall pregnant before making any commitment.

Charles took all the information about Mary fairly coolly. He thought a match with Dom Luis would be excellent and was glad she was back in favour, but he would not write to her lest Henry be annoyed. He doubted Cromwell's sincerity in promoting either Mary's marriage to Dom Luis or her restoration to the succession, and was far more interested in finding out whether Henry would support him and Ferdinand against the Turks.

Henry, meanwhile, was telling the French that Mary would be legitimated after a marriage with Angoulême. She could then succeed in default of other issue. But first, François should share his thoughts on jointure and dower, and about where Angoulême should live. Henry would want him to live in England, until Jane produced children, so that if Angoulême succeeded to the throne as Mary's husband, he would understand the laws and customs of the people and be more acceptable to the English as a king. There was no reason not to send Angoulême immediately, they were both of age to consummate the union, Angoulême having passed his fourteenth birthday the previous February. If François were to send an embassy (it was only polite for them to seek a bride, rather than for Mary to seek a husband), Henry would consider the matter. He and Mary were now reconciled and, considering her 'qualities and parentage', he would treat her so generously that regardless of whether she inherited or not, she would be able to live as a king's daughter.

On 2 October, Mary wrote to Henry, asking after his health and promising faithful obedience. By now she had moved to Hertford Castle, the previous arrangement for her to return to court after Jane's coronation having been postponed as the ceremony had been delayed – probably for fear of plague.[9] Chapuys was disappointed – the delay in Mary's return to the centre of affairs would not benefit either her, or his hopes for a warmer alliance between Henry and the emperor.

Henry was still resisting being drawn into the Franco-Imperial conflict. Despite what he may have told Mary, his sympathies seem to have been with François, but not to the extent of a break with Charles. He was obviously still nervous about Mary's sincerity, as he sent her a draft of a letter he wanted her to write to her cousin, in which she was to explain that, through better instruction and the help of the Holy Spirit, she had 'freely and willingly, without duress', assented to the Parliamentary statutes that proclaimed her parents' marriage invalid and Henry Head of the Church. She was to request Charles to refrain from hindering these decisions, either in a General Council or elsewhere. Then came the veiled warning – if Charles did act against these declarations, it might cause Henry, who currently treated his daughter so kindly, to treat her less well. Mary informed Chapuys so that he could forewarn Charles about the letters. She also suggested that Charles should reply, with an appearance of being angry with her. Chapuys, however, was not sure that would be the right tack but reminded Mary to sign a declaration that she was writing the letters under duress. Where Mary kept these secret papers is a mystery – her mother's recommendation to keep her keys herself was no doubt followed, but unless she kept them on her person, it must have been difficult to ensure total secrecy, especially as she was not always in the same residence.

***

During the previous summer and autumn, that of 1535, the great visitation of the monasteries had taken place. There were two elements – the *Valor Ecclesiasticus* enquired into the wealth of the monasteries, and a parallel investigation into how well, or badly, the monks conducted themselves. Unsurprisingly, corruption was discovered in some houses, but in many others, there were reports of monks and nuns obediently living to the Rule. Nevertheless, monasticism as a movement had had its day. The sixteenth century was a time of growth, of looking out, of change; the concept of an inward spirituality was no longer admired or revered and those who practised it were out of their time – at least so far the Evangelicals were concerned. In February 1536, the Suppression of Religious Houses Act closed all monasteries under £200 annual value. The inmates could either leave religion, or join larger houses. The closed houses became the property of the Crown and were either retained for Crown income, or given as grants to favoured courtiers in what became the largest redistribution of land since the Norman Conquest.

The other enormous religious change unleashed in the summer of 1536 was the promulgation of the Act of Ten Articles. Although the Articles now appear to be a conservative definition of faith, at the time they were considered radical – in particular, only three sacraments were mentioned, and Masses for the dead were considered superfluous. As mediaeval Christianity has been described as 'the cult of the living in the service of the dead' and a whole industry of Masses, chantries, prayers and bequests had grown up around the idea that souls could be released from purgatory through intercession, this was a radical blow at grassroots religion.[10] There had been little real resistance in Parliament to the Acts of Supremacy, or Suppression, but beyond London and the south-east, feelings were very different and when it was rumoured that the gold and silver ornaments of parish churches, paid for by the faithful, would be confiscated by the king, there was widespread distress. On 2 October 1536 near Louth, in Lincolnshire, rebellion broke out. Although this first wave of revolt was suppressed, it rapidly spread into Yorkshire, and became known as the Pilgrimage of Grace, from the badge of the Five Wounds of Christ that the insurgents wore. The rebels had a multitude of fears and objectives, which have been interpreted differently by generations of historians. The Pilgrimage of Grace has been seen as mass movement to restore the authority of the pope and save the monasteries. But it was more complex than that. It was a struggle between the conservative North, and a rapidly changing South; between the old agriculture of arable and common land, and the new methods of sheep-running and enclosures; between a rigidly hierarchical concept of society and a more fluid, meritocratic one; between the old faith of saints, pilgrimages, relics and the Mass, and the new faith in the Word alone. Perhaps most of all it was a struggle between the centralising, all-powerful Tudor monarchy and the last remnants of feudalism.

From Mary's perspective, the most relevant of the Pilgrims' demands was that she be acknowledged as heir, and married to Reginald Pole. Henry commanded her to write to both the pope and and Mary of Hungary, emphasising that she agreed that her mother's marriage had been invalid, and she hoped the pope would not meddle. She was to ask Mary of Hungary to inform Charles that she was quite content, and did not wish him to intervene either, particularly with the idea of supporting the match with Luis. The letters were written, but again, Mary secretly told Chapuys to inform Mary of Hungary and the pope that they were not reflective of her true feelings. Henry may have demanded the letters because of the wider political situation, or it may be he knew his daughter well enough to know that her heart was not in her protestations. Yet Mary was probably genuinely torn – while she did not accept for a minute her parents' divorce, or Henry's Supremacy, her upbringing had taught her that to be a dutiful, obedient and loving daughter was her duty, next only to her duty to God. For these fundamental duties to be in conflict must have been hard to bear.

As the Pilgrimage of Grace became more serious, Chapuys sent his nephew to Mary of Hungary to persuade her that now was the time to lead an invasion against the 'Schismatic', Henry, in revenge for his intrigues with the French against Charles, his treatment of her aunt, and the 'innumerable iniquities' heaped on the 'patient Princess', but there was no concerted effort from Europe to support the rebels.

In the face of the rebellion, Henry moved to Windsor, and sent for both Mary and Elizabeth to join him, probably for a combination of their safety and to prevent a potential monarch being in the hands of rebels. Chapuys, unaware of the rebels' demands in regard to Mary, thought the visit reflected Henry's regret at not having spent more time with 'such a daughter whose virtues people cannot stop praising'. Mary was treated with honour, next in rank after the king and queen and had the privilege of handing them the napkin, before being seated opposite Jane. Elizabeth was too young to dine with them but Henry played with her and was very affectionate towards her.

Although Mary's restoration was one of the aims of the rebels, there is no evidence that Henry suspected her of any direct involvement, and he must have discussed the insurrection with her, as she told Chapuys that Henry had estimated the cost of it at £200,000. In fact, the only member of the king's household openly to show sympathy for the rebels was the queen. Jane had begged Henry on bended knee to restore the abbeys but had been brusquely told not to interfere in politics, and to remember what had happened to her meddling predecessor. As Jane still was not pregnant, she was probably already feeling insecure – so stern a warning discouraged her from further intervention. By the late autumn of 1536, the rebellion had been crushed – mainly because its naïve leader, Robert Aske, had persuaded the Pilgrims to trust Henry's word that he would consider their grievances and would convene a Parliament in York. With the reduction in the threat, Mary returned to Hunsdon.

* * *

In late 1536, Mary was again being half-offered as a bride to three different spouses. François had at last agreed to a match between Princess Madeleine and James V. To prevent it, Henry hinted to the Scots that Mary might be available for her cousin and also made overtures to France. The dauphin François had recently died, to be replaced as heir by Henri, formerly Duke of Orléans, already married to Catherine de' Medici. The third son, previously Duke of Angoulême, was now Duke of Orléans. Gardiner and Wallop were instructed to continue giving the French encouragement about a marriage between Mary and the new Duke of Orléans without seeming over-eager. But the usual game of offer and counter-offer ensued. Henry would not give a firm answer on a match between Mary and Orléans, until the French communicated their 'desire and earnest suit'. He did not think his daughter of so little value that she should not be asked for correctly. Nor would he confirm her legitimacy. He hinted that she would be legitimated, and restored to the succession following any children he had by Jane or any subsequent wives, regardless of gender, but that he would not affirm this until after a marriage with Orléans, whereas the French wanted the matter resolved before the nuptials took place.

At the same time, Cromwell sent for Chapuys to say that all that was needed was an official embassy and request for Mary's hand for the match with Luis to be agreed. Henry spoke to Mary of the possibility often, saying he thought he would not now have sons, and perhaps a son-in-law might be as good. Cromwell and Norfolk were encouraging Charles to believe in the prospect with assurances that Mary would be recognised as heir in default of more children, and have a commensurate income. Luis ought to be satisfied with this, as James would have been happy to take her on those terms.

On 8 December, Mary wrote to Cromwell. She was short of cash and, although embarrassed, had to ask Henry for more, even though he had sent her £40 each quarter. She found Hunsdon a particularly costly house to keep and it was now the expensive Christmas quarter. The upshot was that she was ordered to take up residence permanently with her father and Jane, with her household being discharged immediately (other than her personal attendants). She was to meet them at Richmond, and proceed to Greenwich, where Elizabeth was to join them.

Mary addressed a letter from Richmond to Cromwell on 14 December. As she could not conveniently 'thank him with [her] mouth' for his daily goodness, she wrote to advise him of her good will, considering that it was all she had to repay his 'perfect friendship', of which she desired the continuance, 'which, besides the purchasing of my tedious suits, wherewith I do ever molest you, shall be my great comfort'.[10]

10

Return to Favour

... she is well-treated as the king's daughter.

Chapuys, Imperial Ambassador

Mary had not spent any time with her father, unshadowed by the annulment suit, since the spring of 1527, when she had been eleven years old, the pretty little girl whom he proudly shown off for her musical skill and her flaxen hair. The last protracted period they had spent together had been in the summer of 1531, when he was still treating her as his legitimate daughter, but was about to embark on a campaign of severity towards her mother that Mary had become embroiled in. Now she was twenty, and had been openly flouting him, as he saw it, for years. He had at last broken down her resistance, but how would their relationship develop, now she was an adult? Mary is the only person that Henry ever seems to have forgiven for openly defying him. Others who were pardoned for some disobedience, were all eventually condemned – retribution often came years later, but it always came. Henry wanted to forgive Mary; she was his daughter, and, in his way, he loved her, but he also needed to maintain total control at all times – both to support his kingship, and satisfy his own domineering nature. From the time of their reconciliation, it is apparent he wanted to believe her protestations of loyalty, but that his suspicious nature – or perhaps his knowledge of her character – sometimes made him question it.

For Mary, their relationship was fundamentally altered. The father whom she had been taught to revere, next to God, had treated her mother appallingly – while she could, and did, slide most of the blame for that onto Anne Boleyn, nothing could take away the truth that it was Henry's decision to force her into submission after Anne's death. Now, having broken, she had to reconcile this tyrant with the father she had loved.

The presence of Jane Seymour probably made the transition from king and disobedient subject back to affectionate father and loving daughter easier. Jane had been Katharine's maid-of-honour, and she and Mary seem to have genuinely liked each other. While Jane is not admired by twenty-first century people as Katharine and Anne are, in her own time, no-one spoke ill of her, and records refer to her as kind. This would have been a welcome character trait to both Henry and Mary, after the upheaval of the previous ten years. Jane wanted to avoid the mistakes that her predecessor had made – making enemies at court and being over-familiar with the gentlemen of the Privy Chamber. While the possibility that Anne was guilty of adultery is vanishingly small, her failure to observe a regal distance enabled the charges to at least seem plausible. Jane could safely be friends with her step-daughter, and that would also help Henry politically in his campaign to show Charles that Mary had accepted her demotion.

On 22 December 1536, Mary was present at the ceremony at which Ralph Warren, the newly elected Lord Mayor of London, was knighted in the Great Hall at Westminster. Afterwards, Henry, Jane and Mary rode in procession, behind the mayor, from Westminster to London. The city streets had been gravelled from Temple Bar to Southwark and hangings of arras were suspended from the buildings. At Fleet Street, they were greeted by priors of the four orders of friars (Franciscan, Dominican, Augustine, Carmelite), dressed in gold copes, with candles and censers to waft incense over the royal family. They continued to the west door of St Paul's, to be greeted by the Bishop of London, the Abbot of Warham, and the Abbot of the Crutched Friars, Tower Hill. The cathedral choir was assembled to sprinkle more incense. From the north door (abutting Cheapside), the streets were lined with two priests from every parish church in London, robed in their copes, and holding crosses and candlesticks. Also lining the streets were the representatives of the Guilds, dressed in their liveries, with their hoods draped over their shoulders. The weather was exceptionally cold that year, and the court was able to cross the Thames to Greenwich, by riding over the thick ice.

* * *

Now that she was back in favour, Mary had money in her pocket, and for the next several years we can discover a good deal about her tastes and habits from the meticulous account books. She had no landed income of her own, but Henry gave her a quarterly allowance of £40 and he and his queens sent her additional presents of cash, while her servants' wages were paid by him. To give generous presents and cash tips to her friends, courtiers and servants was expected of a lady of royal blood but Mary's accounts also suggest that, like Henry, she was personally open-handed, as well as responding to the social conventions. Her grandfather and her half-sister both had reputations for parsimony, but such a charge was never levelled at Mary. She was careful, though, to review and sign her accounts personally and took particular note of items of jewellery, adding notes about how she had received them, and to whom she had given them. She also sometimes noted the reason for particular presents, as in her addition to the line recording payment for a painting for Lady Carew's daughter, recording that the girl was her goddaughter at the bishopping.

Mary's expenses fell into several categories. First, and most numerous, were the tips ranging from pennies to pounds, given to the servants of courtiers and friends bringing her gifts. The gifts themselves were often small delicacies, particularly fruit, of which Mary was clearly fond – cherries, pears, oranges and strawberries feature regularly in the accounts. Presents of the latter were received from Lady Page and Lady Kingston in summer 1537 and from Lady St John in 1543.[1] Artichokes were another favourite food. Cakes, too, were brought by local women from near the palaces where Mary resided from time to time. The lady mayoress, Mrs Warren, sent bonnets and frontlets – possibly for Mary herself or perhaps for her to give as presents. The most frequent time for gift-giving was New Year, and the tips for delivery of items can run into several pages. Next, there are the gifts that Mary gave to her numerous godchildren at their christening or bishopping. These were the children of courtiers, but often the offspring of parishioners around Hunsdon, Hatfield and Eltham. One godchild, Mary ap Rice, probably the daughter of Beatrice and David ap Rice who both had places in Mary's household, received many gifts. There were frequent presents for marriages too – such as for the marriage of Mr Finche and a kirtle for the new Mrs Finche for her wedding day, and to various servants in the palaces. A third category was alms or charities. Mary dispensed small sums as she travelled and to villagers around her various dwellings. She seems to have particularly favoured Welsh people, perhaps her way to still feel herself Princess of Wales without drawing attention to herself. One of her regular donations was to prisons. In the sixteenth century, prisoners were obliged to pay for their keep, which could put an intolerable burden on families. She also gave money to friaries and monasteries, before their suppression, and poorhouses after. Another area of expenditure was clothes. Mary spent enormous sums on fabulous fabrics. The concept of understated good-taste did not exist. Ostentatious display was an important indicator of power and the higher your social standing, the more sumptuous your clothes.[2] Mary bought dozens of yards of cloth of gold and silver, velvet, tinsel, damask and satin in white, silver, yellow, purple, crimson, carnation and black. She received presents of cloth and jewellery from her father, who also loved finery. There was the cost of making up the clothes, furring them, decorating them – £7 7s was paid for 'pipes and pearls' – altering, refashioning and mending them. Even housing the clothes had a cost; at Greenwich in February 1537, Mary was obliged to rent a room in the town for her robes, at a cost of 10s per month.

Finally, there were Mary's amusements. Here, too, we can see shared tastes with Henry. Most important was music. She regularly tipped choristers and minstrels, as well as continuing to perform herself. There are references to her regals (a type of organ) being sent for and very frequent payments for mending her virginals – it may be that moving them necessitated regular tuning. She took music lessons each month. Mr Paston, who received 7s for each lesson, taught the virginals, while her lute master, at 5s a time, was Philip van Wylder, a Flemish lutenist, who was a member of Henry's Privy Chamber and one of the court's chief musicians. Mary gave him a wedding present too. There were outdoor pastimes. Mary had her own kennel of greyhounds and paid their keeper, Christopher Bradley, regular sums of 3s 4d, in addition to the nearly 5s per month for the dogs' 'meat'. The first dog was acquired in August 1537 for 7s 6d, shortly after the reconciliation with Henry, suggesting Mary was eager to be out and about. The kennel cost a further 7d. The greyhounds were used for coursing and there was a payment to the Keepers of Waltham Forest in the summer of 1538 for coursing there. Henry was also at Waltham in late May or June, and they may have hunted there together. The greyhounds sometimes caused problems: Mr William Allen of Richmond had to be compensated when the dogs killed two of his sheep. Greyhounds were outdoor animals, but Mary was also given indoor pets – spaniels, other small dogs and even a parrot from Lady Derby. What Mary made of the exotic creature, and what, if anything, it could say, are sadly unrecorded. Lady Derby's servant received a tip of 2s. Archery was another sport that Mary partook in, with Henry and the rest of the court, and she bought bows, arrows and a quiver at various times. There are numerous entries for tips to gardeners and for presents of flowers, both real and artificial. This was another taste shared with Henry, who took a personal interest in his gardens – the ordering of new apple trees for Hampton Court was one of his last acts. Other frequent payments are for Jane the Fool – her board, her clothes and the keeper of her horse are all mentioned at various times.

There has been considerable discussion of the 'factions' in the Tudor court and the presents Mary gave and received give an insight into the circles in which she moved. Surprisingly, perhaps, Mary was on present-giving terms with a wide cast of courtiers. A comparison of Mary's tactics in appointing women once she was queen, with the practice of her sister Elizabeth, identifies that Mary had a very inclusive household, and although her attendants were required to conform to her religious policies, many were friends and relatives of those who did not. Elizabeth's immediate circle was drawn largely from her Howard relatives.[3] This practice of being on good terms with all, and above faction, was practised by Mary from the first time she had any autonomy and is demonstrated in the list of people with whom she exchanged presents, to whose children she stood as godmother, and whose parties she attended. A case in point is that of Lady Shelton. We might suppose that, with Anne dead, Mary would, at the very least, never have wanted anything to do with Lady Shelton again, but this is not borne out by the facts. The servants of Lady Shelton, and those of her daughters Mary and Elizabeth, received tips for bringing presents. Elizabeth (Bess) Shelton and her sister-in-law, Amy, received cash presents, with the latter also receiving a brooch, and Lady Shelton was given embroidered cushions. Presents Mary received over the years include 'sweet waters and (per)fumes' as well as a gold salt from Cromwell and a clock from Lady Rochford, who received black velvet in return. Her father, Lord Morley, was a great admirer of Mary's, praising her 1527 translation of the letter of Thomas Aquinas. He sent her books each year. The Bishop of Exeter, once head of her council, sent gifts and so did both her former lady mistresses, Lady Calthorpe and Lady Salisbury. On the other side of what later became a political and religious divide, but on good terms with Mary, was Anne Stanhope, the second wife of Lord Beauchamp, shortly to be to Earl of Hertford. Mary was godmother to their daughter, Jane, giving 20s to the child's nurse at the christening in February 1537. There are frequent references to visits to and from the Hertfords, Mary attended a dinner party at their house, tipping the musicians, and she also later sent a joint letter to Lady Hertford, with Queen Katherine Parr. Mary stood as godmother in February 1537 to one of the children of Lady Dudley, the wife of Sir John Dudley who, as Duke of Northumberland, would attempt to block Mary from the throne. Another surprising name in Mary's list of visitors, fellow gamblers and present givers or recipients, is Katherine, Duchess of Suffolk. Katherine, Baroness Willoughby in her own right, was the daughter of Maria de Salinas, Katharine of Aragon's oldest friend, and Katherine had married the Duke of Suffolk within weeks of the death of Mary's aunt, the French Queen. Duchess Katherine, although only fourteen at the time of her marriage, soon made her presence felt at court. She was later a noted Reformer, going into exile in Mary's own reign, but all the evidence suggests that they were on good terms during Henry's reign.

Last, but by no means least, was the money Mary spent on gambling. The quantity of cash she spent on cards, bowls and wagers suggests a serious habit. Gambling was not condemned in the sixteenth century with the moral fervour of later times. It was a widespread pastime at all levels of society, and Henry himself bet extremely heavily, although for much higher stakes than Mary could afford. She regularly took several pounds of cash into her purse for cards, and frequently borrowed money from her friends to gamble more –

30*s* from Lady Carew on one occasion, and 22*s* 6*d* from the Countess of Sussex on another. She did not just gamble for money – she lost her breakfast once, wagered on a game of bowls. Mary, far from being the timid, indecisive figure of many biographies, with no interests beyond her prayers, showed her true nature in her pastimes. She was vigorous and sociable – hunting, dancing, enjoying the entertainment provided by her tumbler and her fool. She dressed magnificently, tipped generously and wagered extravagantly.

***

On 7 February 1538 Charles pressed João III of Portugal about Dom Luis's possible marriage to Mary. Charles rehearsed the dismal behaviour of Henry to their aunt Katharine, and his evil dealings with the Church, but felt that the alliance was so important that they would have to overlook this delinquent behaviour. The stumbling block was Henry's unwillingness to settle the succession on Mary before the daughters of his current, or any subsequent, wife. While they could all understand a preference for a male heir, Mary should surely come before other females. However, if that could not be agreed, Charles was willing for the matter not to be mentioned, as he was fairly confident that Henry would have no more children – he was not to know that Jane was in the first few weeks of pregnancy. Further, even if more children were born, Charles thought it probable Henry would die before they were adults.

It was highly unlikely that any future offspring of Henry's would have the powerful relatives that Mary did. If he and João could gain control of Mary and her dote, matters would sort themselves out. There was some urgency on the emperor's part, as the French were again pushing a match with Orléans, and there was even the possibility that Mary would be given an English husband, who must necessarily be of inferior rank. Charles proposed sending a special envoy, who would also have letters from Portugal and summed up the man they would have to deal with: 'Although the king is obstinate in the things which he undertakes, those which he promises and assents to he observes entirely.'[4] This would explain Henry's real anger when other rulers entered treaties and broke them. If the matter progressed, Luis would need to live in England, and might be asked to swear, with Mary, to Henry's statutes. If absolutely necessary, Charles would encourage him to swear with prior reservations.

While these discussions were going on around her, Mary took part in the usual court entertainments, including the ritual of drawing valentines. She drew Cromwell, who sent Thomas Wriothesley to her with a gift of £15. That month, she also tipped a workman for making a new window in her chamber. The accounts do not state which house she was in, although it was probably Greenwich, but we can infer that she expected to stay in the same apartments every time she visited it, and that the room was sufficiently hers for her to have asked Henry to have a new window installed. According to Chapuys in a despatch to Rome,

> These last days the king had his daughter fetched from the North to his Court, where she remains, with satisfactory indications that she will be well-treated. Thus she would seem to have arrived in port, although not to what she is entitled, as she has not the title of princess or heir, notwithstanding that she is well-treated as the king's daughter. The whole kingdom not only loves her, as one would desire, but seems almost to overvalue and to adore her, desiring her every good, because they know her rights, and because they loved the queen, her mother, and because of the great virtues which it has pleased God to give to her Highness, so that she is a veritable paragon to the world.[5]

On 17 February 1537 Henry wrote to Gardiner. Since the French continually 'harped upon that string' of legitimation of Mary before a marriage, Henry declined to discuss the matter further. He was willing enough for the alliance, if it were to be on his terms. Gardiner was to indicate that he, personally, would welcome a match, but say that he feared that the French had trifled over it so long that it would not happen.

Henry had already explained to the French ambassador, de Pommeraie, that he could not legitimate Mary without her then being in line for the succession above any daughters of Jane's or subsequent wives. This could not be right as the daughters of subsequent wives would be legitimate from birth. The French counter-argument was that if legitimate children were to be preferred, that would rank all of Henry's legitimate relatives above Mary. Henry replied that although it was the law that legitimate claims were preferred, it was perfectly acceptable for all those with some claim to defer their claim to another as, at that time, everyone with some title to succeed to Henry's crown had agreed by way of the Parliamentary Act to allow him to choose between them. The French argued that, in that case, as Mary's title would only be by Parliament, not by common law, any son Henry had might interpose a different successor between himself and Mary and Orléans. While Henry acknowledged the logic of the argument, he thought the French should not believe the English Parliament would be so inconstant as to disinherit Mary without cause, even if Henry's son desired it – which was also unlikely, as Mary would be his sister, and although illegitimate, of noble parentage on both sides. This was ironic in view of the fact that Mary's brother did indeed try to disinherit her. While Mary was no longer to be referred to as 'princess', let alone as Princess of Wales, her old position had not been entirely forgotten. On 1 March 1537, the feast day of St David, the patron saint of Wales, the Yeomen of the King's Guard presented her with a leek, the country's symbol.

***

Sir Thomas Wyatt replaced Pate as ambassador to Charles. His orders were to deliver letters and compliments, and say he hoped for a renewal of the old amity between the countries, which had been damaged by Charles trying to have a sentence passed in Rome on the matrimonial affairs of the king that properly belonged in the local jurisdiction. If Charles complained that Mary was considered illegitimate, even though born in good faith, the response was to be that 'good faith' could not be alleged when a fundamental law of God had been breached, and that repetition of the point would aggravate Henry. Wyatt was to take Charles the letter that Mary had written, agreeing that she was illegitimate. As for a marriage with Dom Luis, again, matters could be arranged so that Mary would succeed after Henry's legitimate children.

Charles sent an official embassy to London, under Don Diego de Mendoza. Regardless of the difficulties that Henry might raise, the envoys were to persist in promoting the match, unless they thought that Henry was stringing them along to improve terms with France. As to what Mary and Luis might be given by João to live on, that was to be fudged, with the words that 'such a gracious king' would do everything to Henry's satisfaction and the emperor would stand surety for the Portuguese – given Charles's poor record in repaying his debts, this could hardly have been reassuring. Excessive demands from Henry were to be discouraged by telling him that for a king of his wealth and power, a good and obedient son should be enough. Henry need only compare the ancient friendship with Portugal and the enmity with France, to know the match would be the best possible for all parties. There were letters of compliment and credence for Jane as well – a politeness that Anne had never received. Two letters were prepared for Mary, one to be handed over publicly, and the other to be conveyed to her in secret. Both encouraged her to favour the match – presumably the secret one gave advice on what she and Luis were to do if presented with the oath of supremacy. Charles went so far as to suggest that, if Henry were determined to arrange a French marriage, steps were to be taken to abduct Mary, although that would be difficult, dangerous and provoke open war, which François would capitalise on. Whether Mary would have agreed to leave the country now that she and Henry were reconciled is moot – there is no evidence that she was suggesting such a course. The ambassadors also had letters for Parliament and various individuals – there were different letters to be used depending on circumstances. If Henry were disposed to the match, they praised him, but if not, they were to be used to try to rekindle rebellion, although only if there were a real prospect of success – Charles thought popular movements tended to fade quickly, especially in England.

* * *

The Pilgrimage of Grace had been defeated, but in early February 1537, further rebellion had broken out in Cumberland under Sir Francis Bigod and, although Aske and the other leaders of the Pilgrimage disowned it, Henry took the opportunity to blame them all. The Cumberland rising was easily crushed and the reprisals were vicious – designed to be 'a spectacle of the end of such abominable treasons and a mean to reduce that country to a perfect quietness'.[6] On 11 April, Robert Aske was examined in the Tower. He deposed that among the chief grievances of the rebels were the suppression of the monasteries, the supremacy of Henry over spiritual matters, the statute allowing Henry to dispose of the Crown by will, the illegitimacy of Mary, and the new law that words alone could constitute treason. Aske and his fellows thought the statute declaring Mary illegitimate wrong on several counts. First, Mary's mother came of 'the greatest blood in Christendom', and from a country long allied to England; second, the annulment pronounced by Archbishop Cranmer was invalid, pending the appeal to a General Council, and they also had some doubt as to whether Cranmer's consecration was lawful. Mary should only be considered illegitimate if the whole Church agreed 'for she is marvellously beloved by all the people'. If the marriage was finally declared valid, but Mary already ruled illegitimate, it would seem that the statute had been aimed at her personally, contravening the belief that public laws should not unfairly target individuals. Further, Mary should be declared legitimate, lest the emperor declare war, or ban trade with Flanders, which would wreck the economy. So far as allowing the king to dispose of the crown at will, this was particularly irksome – what if the monarch willed the crown away from the natural heir? This could lead to civil war. It was necessary either for this statute to be qualified so the people would know the heir-apparent, or that the crown should go by next of blood, as before. It was also the law that no one born out of the realm could claim inheritance within it – what would then happen if the king nominated an 'alien', presumably meaning the King of Scots? All of Aske's arguments, and even the pardon he had received from the king, were useless, and he was condemned to death.

Easter that year fell on 21 April, and Mary and the court observed it at Greenwich. Mary took the sacrament on Maundy Thursday and gave various offerings both at the altar and as alms. Unlike the practice of later times, the elite, even royalty, were involved far more closely in the day-to-day life of their servants, even the lowest ranks. Mary gave tips to the king's cooks, the pastry department, the scullery and to the gardeners for bringing her fresh flowers and herbs as well as to 'poor men' who helped carry her possessions between Westminster and Greenwich.

Despite the seemingly amicable relationship she had now re-established with Henry, it was an anxious time for Mary. Among those who were to be executed following the Pilgrimage was her old chamberlain, Lord Hussey. He wrote to the king, seeking pardon for all his wrongdoing, except treason, which he swore he had not committed. Even though Hussey had argued with Lady Salisbury over the relinquishing of Mary's jewels in 1531, and taken part in both Anne Boleyn's coronation, and Elizabeth's baptism, Mary must surely have felt a pang of grief at his death, and deep sympathy for his widow, Anne, who had once been imprisoned for calling her 'princess'. However, there are no records of Mary deviating from her usual course of activity – playing cards, hunting with greyhounds and taking music lessons. She also acquired another godchild, from Lord William Howard, probably his daughter Mary, and laid out money for hunting bows.

During May, Mendoza had an audience with Mary when the court was probably at Westminster. After the usual compliments, she assured him she was very much in favour of friendship between her father and her cousin, and would support it as long as it existed. On being questioned whether the letters she had written to the emperor and Mary of Hungary admitting herself to be a bastard were really written by her, she affirmed they were, and that she had written what she thought to be the truth. He departed after complimenting her on her wisdom.

In late June, the Bishop of Tarbes, still ambassador in England, took Henry some letters intercepted en route to the emperor from his envoys in Rome. The letters gave information on Charles's intentions with regard to the marriage between Mary and Luis. Tarbes reported that, from Henry's expression, he was unhappy with the content but brushed the matter away with the words that the men were so far away, they could not know his intentions. Tarbes's response was that they certainly knew Charles's intentions. It was obvious, said Tarbes, that the emperor wanted to inveigle money from Henry and João for his own benefit, drawing Henry into an expensive burden and separating him from François, but Henry should be too wise to fall for it. Besides, 'many people' (i.e. the King of France) would object to Milan being in the hands of the brother of the King of Portugal. Henry replied that as Mary had been offered for Orléans, and not accepted, while Luis would take her on any terms Henry liked, he had done France no wrong. Nevertheless, he had not concluded terms as yet and would not do so until the emperor divested himself of allies Henry did not like, meaning the pope. In fact, said the unblushing Henry, the Spanish were already considering throwing off papal authority, and had asked for copies of papers proving the invalidity of his marriage to Katharine. Henry then assured Tarbes that, while neither of their councils was so well disposed to the other as the kings were to each other, he loved François like a brother.

Tarbes gave the French government details of what he understood the Imperial offer for the marriage to Luis to be: Mary was to have her mother's dote of 300,000 ducats, to be delivered when Milan, or alternatively, Florence, at Henry's nomination, was in Luis's hands and Mary's dower assigned from the duchy; nothing was to be said about Mary's rights of inheritance, and Luis would be free to take her abroad. Henry was not in agreement with these propositions. He did not want Mary to leave the country until he had another heir, and nor was he happy that her dower should be secured on lands so far away – he would prefer it to be paid out of Flanders. Finally, Henry would insist that Charles, João and their Estates General swear that the marriage of Katharine and Henry was invalid and that the pope had no jurisdiction in England. Since Henry could not force them to throw off papal authority, this was the best he could do to undermine the pontiff.

François, unconcerned, assured Tarbes that the only reason the marriage with Orléans had not gone forward was because Mary was not declared legitimate. If Luis would take her without that, he would be happy for them. He was sure Henry would not agree to anything prejudicial to François or his children.

* * *

During Jane's pregnancy, she had a craving for quails, which Henry's cooks struggled to keep pace with. Mary arranged for a present of the delicacy to be given to the queen. But despite her improved life, and the exercise of riding, hunting and archery that she could now indulge in, Mary was again sick that June. Her doctor was still Dr de La Sa, Katharine's old physician. Mary paid the barge expenses of 7s 7d for him and his apothecary to attend her at Greenwich. She recovered enough to attend a party at Mr Page's house, to which she travelled by barge. The entertainment was provided by the king's own sackbut players to whom Mary gave 20s. By July, the court had moved to Hampton Court, where Mary tipped the queen's gardener 5s 4d. A few days later, she was at Guildford Castle, where she paid for a new door to her room. More food and fruit were brought to her, and she also purchased cucumbers for herself and the queen.

Henry was now thinking differently about allowing Mary to marry. There was little likelihood he would make any decisions about Mary until the outcome of Jane's pregnancy was known. If Jane had a living son, Mary would not be allowed to be a threat to him as the wife of a foreign prince who might be able to furnish her with an army. What Henry's attitude might have been to a daughter by Jane is unknowable – and also what Mary might have thought about it. Henry's stated position for the rest of his life was that any legitimate daughter would come before Mary in the succession, but she herself might well have challenged that, had the occasion arisen.

Mary was still at court, now at Windsor, where she was obliged to pay rent for kennels for her greyhounds at a cost of 8*d* and additional board for Beatrice ap Rice's son, lodged in the town. She enjoyed walking in the palace grounds and gave a payment to the gardener's wife. The court then moved to Hampton Court for Jane's confinement.

On 10 October, Wyatt was instructed to tell Charles, pretending it to be his own opinion, that he was sorry he had seen so little of the affection towards Henry he had expected. As Charles had declined, from family affection, to treat Henry as he deserved over the divorce, now that the cause of trouble was removed, the old warmth should be renewed. If Charles asked why the marriage with Dom Luis had not progressed, Wyatt was to reply that Mendoza had not had sufficient powers and that Henry was surprised he had been sent with so little authority. This missive came with a covering note from Cromwell, asking why Wyatt had not yet delivered Mary's letters to the emperor. It is not clear what Cromwell is referring to – her earlier letter, denying her legitimacy had certainly been sent, as Mendoza had asked her about it – perhaps she had been obliged to write again on the same topic. Wyatt was accompanied by Sir John Dudley, to whom Mary gave 40*s* to buy 'certain stuff' for her in Spain. At the same time, Lord William Howard, going on a mission to France, received £12 to buy 'stuff'. The word stuff tends to mean fabric, so perhaps Mary wanted something elaborate for a new gown.

On Friday, 12 October, the eve of St Edward's day, Jane delivered a son. The country rejoiced. Bonfires flamed, church bells rang out and the cannon at the Tower were fired. Messengers bearing gifts were sent out to all the great cities of the realm. King Henry had a male heir at last. The christening took place the following Monday in the palace chapel. The Earl of Wiltshire, father of the late Queen Anne, carried the taper, with his granddaughter, the Lady Elizabeth, holding the chrism. As Elizabeth was only just past her fourth birthday, she was carried by the queen's brother, Beauchamp. Lady Exeter carried the baby, as her mother-in-law had once carried Mary, and as she had carried Elizabeth. She was supported by her husband and the Duke of Suffolk. The canopy over the prince was held by Sir Edward Neville, Sir John Wallop, Richard Long, Thomas Seymour, Henry Knyvett and Mr Ratcliffe. The lady mistress, Lady Bryan, came next, with the nurse and midwife on hand.

After the prince walked Mary, who was to be godmother. Her kirtle was of cloth of silver, for which she had paid the large sum of £10 to Mr Peacock for fabric and making up. Her train was borne by Lady Kingston, and she was followed by all the other ladies of honour, according to rank. The ministering bishop, the Duke of Norfolk and the Archbishop of Canterbury were godfathers at the baptism, and Suffolk for the confirmation. After the ceremony, Mary and Elizabeth were served spices, wafers and wine, with Lord Hastings bearing the cup to Mary, and Lord De La Warr to Elizabeth. Mary's christening gift was a cup of gold, carried by the Earl of Essex. On leaving the chapel, Mary took Elizabeth by the hand (Beauchamp now being loaded down with Suffolk's gift of two great pots and flagons of silver and gilt). Mary's train was still carried by Lady Kingston, while that of Elizabeth was taken by Lady Troy of Herbert. But Henry's rejoicing was cut short. On 23 October, Norfolk wrote to Cromwell, urging him to come to comfort 'our good master, for as for our mistress, there is no likelihood of her life'. The queen died the next day from puerperal fever or septicaemia, plunging the whole court into mourning.

On Wednesday, 30 October, the Great Chamber, the gallery and the chapel at Hampton Court were draped in black. A hearse was prepared in the chapel with the arms of Henry, Jane, Edward, York, Normandy, Guienne, Ireland and Cornwall on it. The Bishop of Carlisle, Jane's almoner, assisted by the Bishop of Chichester, the Dean of the Chapel and the sub-dean, went to Jane's chamber and sprinkled the corpse with holy water while the *De Profundis* was intoned. Torches were lit and the procession formed up – a cross, followed by priests, then gentlemen, esquires, pursuivants, heralds, then noblemen, Garter King of Arms, the Earl of Rutland, Jane's chamberlain, and the Duke of Norfolk as high marshal. The corpse was brought out, followed by Lady Exeter, who was acting in Mary's place as Chief Mourner, Mary being too upset to perform her office. After Lady Exeter came two earls, then eight ladies as mourners. The procession passed the whole household, double ranked, lining the corridors, with unlit candles. Once the corpse reached the chapel, Lancaster Herald gave the cry 'Of your charity, pray for the soul … '. The dirge was sung, and the company departed. Each night, for twelve days, a watch was kept, being replaced by ladies during the day. At 9 o'clock each morning Mary entered the chapel and Mass was offered. The daily Masses continued until Monday, 12 November, when the funeral procession formed. Archbishop Cranmer walked in procession with Chapuys, while Cromwell walked with the French ambassador, Castillon. Mary, now in control of her emotions, followed as Chief Mourner, on a horse draped in black velvet and attended by Lord Clifford (husband of her cousin, Lady Eleanor Brandon). Then came her other cousin, Lady Dorset, the countesses of Rutland, Oxford, Sussex, Bath and Southampton, and Lady Margaret Howard.

Following the first carriage of ladies were four more. The other ladies of the court had left at 5am to ride to Windsor. The procession made its way via Colnbrook and Eton to Windsor where the company dismounted to enter the chapel, Mary's train being borne by Jane, Lady Rochford. A solemn watch was kept that night, and services held the next day. On 14 November, the offering of palls was made – Mary was led to the altar by the dukes of Norfolk and Suffolk and offered seven, with Lady Dorset offering four. As Mary sincerely mourned the stepmother to whom she had become attached, did the solemn obsequies give her the chance to mourn her own mother, imagining an elision between the two queens? Or did it just make it harder for her, to think that her mother had been treated with less ceremony than this daughter of a knight?

To add to Mary's misery, she had toothache – not for the first time. Henry sent Nicholas Sympson (presumably one of his own surgeons) to extract the offending tooth at a cost of 45s.

***

An inventory was taken of Jane's jewels, and many of them were given to ladies of the court, including Mary and Elizabeth. Among Mary's selection were seven different 'pairs of beads' (rosaries) of various precious materials, such as agate, gold and pearls.

Queen Jane was hardly cold in her grave before the emperor was proposing a new alliance. Henry was reported on 3 November by Sir John Wallop to be as 'merry as a widower might be' and the idea of reconciling their differences through a marriage with the king himself appealed to Charles. Again on offer was João's half-sister, Maria of Portugal. There was also Christina of Denmark, Dowager Duchess of Milan. Christina was said to be tall and of 'competent' beauty, mainly speaking French, but also Italian and High German. Henry's envoy to the Low Countries, Hutton, reported that the duchess resembled Mary Shelton, perhaps to tempt Henry, who was reputed to have had an affair with Mistress Shelton. In his next letter, Hutton named several other possible brides, including the daughter of the Duke of Cleves, but 'there is no great praise either of her personage or her beauty'.

On 30 December, the French ambassador, Castillon, wrote that Henry, who had been depressed at the thought of an alliance between François and Charles, had been cheered when the emperor promised that nothing would be agreed without Henry's being informed. Henry, now feeling himself to be courted by both sides, immediately became hard to please. François should assure him that nothing would be agreed about a General Council without his input. Henry was eager to marry Marie of Guise, widow of the Duke of Longueville, whom Wallop had praised. Henry waved away the information that she was promised to James of Scotland (who had been widowed within a few months of his marriage to Madeleine) saying that he could do more for François than James could. François' own daughters were too young, and he would not dream of taking Marie of Vendôme, whom James had rejected. Despite this preference for Marie of Guise, Henry instructed Wyatt to suggest to the emperor 'as if of himself', that Henry might honour Christina with marriage.

Mary and the rest of the court, including the baby prince, spent Christmas of 1537 at Richmond. She paid the astonishing sum of 40s 4d each for 100 pearls, probably for decorating clothes, amounting to over £267. Again, numerous tips were given to the servants bringing their masters' or mistresses' presents. She herself selected a cap for the prince's New Year gift. Other gifts Mary gave included a cushion embroidered in gold for Wriothesley, and a trinket box worked with silver thread for Elizabeth. The payment to embroiderers suggests that, unlike her mother, Mary was not especially handy with the needle. Doublets of satin were purchased for her serving men, and of cloth for the clerk of the kitchen and Dr Owen, the prince's physician. There was a bonnet and frontlet for Lady Bryan, and gifts for the prince's nurse and Lady Troy of Herbert, Elizabeth's lady-in-waiting.

During 1538, the endless negotiations for Mary's marriage with either a French or an Imperial candidate continued. There were several strands to Henry's thinking. He did not want to offend either François or Charles to the point of no return. He also wanted to have the position of mediator between them – if mediation were carried out by the pope, then François and Charles might combine against him. He was worried, too, about the prospect of a General Council. Although he said he would welcome one to discuss matters of faith, he would not countenance discussion of the old annulment suit, and nor would he be satisfied with a General Council that took place on either Imperial soil or in the papal States. He continued to hope that he would persuade François to abandon papal authority, although he knew it would be fruitless to suggest such a course to Charles. So Mary was offered first to one, then to the other. Ideally, she and her husband would be vested with Milan, but Charles was as reluctant to commit himself to handing over the duchy, as Henry was to handing over Mary. Henry had more bargaining power than he had previously had – there was the possibility of marriages for Elizabeth and Edward, and, with Jane dead, he himself was now available. Discussions waxed and waned, but nothing was agreed.

At the end of February, Chapuys and his colleagues were invited to Hampton Court. They were given lodgings for a visit of several days. They went 3 or 4 miles to another house where Edward and 'Madame Isabelle', as Chapuys referred to Elizabeth, were lodged, probably Hanworth, and the following day to Richmond, Mary having returned there after a short sojourn with her siblings. She entertained them with excellent performances on both lute and spinet.[7]

As an unmarried woman, Mary could not live at court unchaperoned. She moved frequently between Richmond and Hanworth, making day trips to Hampton Court to see Henry from time to time. Lady Margaret Douglas had been released from the Tower of London after her ill-advised romance with Lord Thomas Howard, then confined to Syon Abbey, but was allowed to return to court around the time of Jane's death. As she, too, was unmarried, she was probably residing with Mary and making regular visits to court. Although still in mourning for Jane, Mary bought herself 6 yards of cloth of silver. A sample had been brought to her by Abraham of London, and it had obviously met with her approval. She also purchased nearly 13 yards of mulberry coloured damask and three ells of taffeta of the same shade. The usual tips were given to Edward's minstrels and Mary paid for venison to celebrate the wedding of the royal tailor, John Scutt – with the quantity of clothes Mary ordered from him, he could well afford to marry!

* * *

In spring of 1538 the surrenders of monasteries continued, and many of the relics that had been venerated for generations were exposed as fakes and destroyed – the Rood of Boxley was one example: it was a crucifixion, the eyes and lips appearing to move. It had been taken to Henry at Westminster and the workings shown to him. He ordered that it be displayed in the market square at Maidstone, and the trick exposed to all viewers. It had also been ordered that the Bible be available in English in every parish. There is no record of Mary's opinion on these matters. During her own reign, a new English version of the Bible was planned, suggesting she supported the principle of it, and there is no evidence that she herself had any particular interest in relics or miraculous cures. Mary's thoroughly humanist education had probably made her sceptical of such things, while she maintained a deep devotion to the core element of her faith, the Mass, and cherished the monastic ideal.

Just before Easter, which fell in March that year, Mary sent a message to her father, wanting to know whether she might leave off mourning, which she had been wearing since Jane's death. Henry himself had stopped wearing black in early February. He replied that 'she might wear what colour she would'. This could be interpreted either as Henry wanting Mary to be happy and dress as she pleased, or alternatively, that he did not care. Lady Kingston sent a second request via Wriothesley, for permission for Mary to wear her white taffeta gown, edged with velvet which 'used to be to the king's liking'. Mary wanted to wear white for the joyous occasion of Easter Day. From this we may conclude that Mary did not feel she could write directly to Henry on a trivial topic, that she would be spending Easter with him, that Henry was extremely conscious of details, and that Mary feared to irritate him.[8] That same month, Mary stood as godmother to the Countess of Sussex' daughter, with Lady Kingston attending as her deputy. Henry was godfather, with Sir John Dudley and Cromwell. Queen Jane's sister, Elizabeth Seymour, now Cromwell's daughter-in-law, asked Mary to be godmother to her son, Henry.

In late April, Castillon reported that Henry had been very ill for nearly two weeks. An ulcer in his leg had closed, leaving him unable to speak and black in the face, as the poison turned inward. Castillon was not sure whether Henry's death would be rejoiced in or not – he had heard there would be a party for the prince, and one for Lady Mary, implying that male inheritance was not always considered the best, presumably in this case because of the relative ages of the parties. Edward was only eighteen months old, while Mary was twenty-two. There were also some who doubted Edward's legitimacy, as the marriage of his parents had taken place without papal sanction and Jane had not been crowned. Perhaps ambitious lords also saw an opportunity for one of their sons to marry Mary and be king.

On 20 May, Chapuys wrote that following a visit by Henry to Mary (probably on 5th when he dined with her at Richmond) Mary seemed less trusting of the emperor. Perhaps Henry had shown her that he was dragging his feet over the Dom Luis marriage, and not offering her a very fair dower – Henry had complained that for a quarter of the sum he was offering in dote, Mary could obtain a 'better living' being married in England.

In late May, a former Observant Friar of the Franciscan Order, John Forrest, was burnt for heresy. He had upheld the supremacy of the pope and traditional teaching on purgatory and penance. Watching the burning was the majority of Henry's council, including Norfolk, Suffolk, Sussex and Hertford, as well as the mayor and alderman and a crowd of thousands. The burning of Forrest must have agonised Mary – he had sworn the oath of supremacy, but later declared that it was only his 'outer man' that had done so. In his heart, he had not accepted it. This was exactly the position she was in. If she were probed or questioned, what would she say? Her sleep may have been further disturbed when she received a letter, probably from Cromwell, telling her that Henry was concerned that she had been lodging 'strangers' at Richmond – usually taken to mean foreigners. She thanked her correspondent for his 'wise and friendly counsel' and promised that she would never willingly offend the king. She thought that her hospitality had been reported 'to the worst' but she would never do it again and would take his advice to 'eschew things whereby [she] might seem to give any other occasion than should be expedient' for her. She asked him to continue to advise her.[9] The visit referred to may have been that of Chapuys, although it seems unlikely he would have gone to her without royal permission. Perhaps to take her mind off the state of her inward turmoil, or to show herself unaffected by Forrest's death, Mary was buying clothes freely – black damask, yellow damask, purple taffeta and sarcenet all found their way into her wardrobe. She also made several visits to Edward, riding to Hanworth and returning downstream to Richmond by barge. Her frequent payments to his minstrels suggest that music was a regular part of her visits. During May, she gave a tip to the Earl of Hertford's minstrels, and she lost 26s 4d to the Duchess of Suffolk at cards.

Henry and his council continued to prevaricate with Castillon and Tarbes for Mary's marriage with Orléans, and with Chapuys and Mendoza over her marriage with Dom Luis. Castillon was informed the only way the marriage would be considered would be if François were to give up his planned meeting with the Bishop of Rome and Charles. The ambassadors refused – François could not now abandon the meeting without giving offence. Henry turned to the Imperialists, but finances could not be agreed. He then reverted to Castillon: if Mary and Orléans married, Henry would contribute to any war that François was exposed to as a result. Castillon was convinced the marriage was a possibility, or if not that match, then another French husband for Mary might possible. Henry was willing to consider the Marquis du Pont (son of the Duke of Lorraine) or the Duke of Vendôme.[10] Henry was also interested in a French marriage for himself, preferably to the widowed Marie of Guise. The Imperialists made another offer of Christina and Luis. Although Charles was now being offered a million crowns for the duchy of Milan for Orléans, with a daughter of Ferdinand as bride, nevertheless, he would give it to Luis and Mary for an increased dowry. In return, Mary would renounce all rights to the throne, both for herself and her children. It is hard to know why Henry refused this offer. His daughter would be a Princess of Portugal, Duchess of Milan, and pose no threat to his son. Did he want her to stay at home? Did he fear that Edward might not live, or that Mary might repudiate any oath? Whatever his reasons, Henry was distinctly cool in his response. Currently he was at peace with everyone, so getting involved in an offensive as well as defensive pact with Charles would embroil him in wars, and finally, if Charles gave Milan to Luis and Mary without François' agreement, Henry might be seen as promoting war.

In June, Mary joined Henry in London, probably at Whitehall. Her visit may have been related to another prospective marriage – this time with the new Duke of Julich-Cleves-Berg, Wilhelm, who had also been recognised as Duke of Guelders, to Charles's intense annoyance. She once again enjoyed listening to the king's sackbut players, and Henry gave her some goldsmith's work – jewellery, or dress ornamentation. A warrant was issued for clothes for her and for four of her attendants. Paget wrote that the bruit in France was that Lady Mary's illness during May and early June was hampering the match with Luis. There are no details of what ailed her, although she seems to have had blood let, but the death of Forrest, and the continuing religious turmoil in London may have brought on another bout of stress-related illness. The shrine of Our Lady of Walsingham, which both her parents had visited on pilgrimage, was cast down and the jewels and other offerings brought to Henry, before the statue was burnt at Chelsea. This was followed by the removal of the cross on the north door of St Paul's and, by the end of the summer, all icons in places of pilgrimage throughout England and Wales were destroyed. For Mary, even if she were not especially interested in relics, and for many others, this wholesale destruction must have been deeply disturbing. The removal of the relics was followed up by the banning of most of the candles in churches – only those in the rood-loft, and before the sacrament and the sepulchre remained. Finally, the great shrine of Thomas Becket at Canterbury was destroyed, the saint's bones burnt and the jewels and gold appropriated by Henry. As he slipped the great ruby from the shrine onto his finger, did Henry remember offering at the altar sixteen years before, with the emperor by his side?

While Chapuys thought Henry was inclined to agree a match with Cleves for Mary, Castillon became convinced that Henry truly wanted an alliance with France. So much for Henry's claim that he never dissembled! In July, the king urged on Castillon the desirability of another meeting with François. The important thing, in Castillon's view, was for the French to provide a queen for Henry. François had been too slack in the matter.

On 16 July, the emperor and François met and, in an elaborate show of courtesy, swore a truce and eternal brotherhood – although they loathed each other so much that they would not enter the same room, and negotiations were carried out by the pope scurrying to and fro. News of this Treaty of Nice chilled Henry's attitude to Castillon, especially as François had refused to allow a selection of ladies to be sent to Calais for Henry to choose one. Unlike any other royal personage, Henry was certain that he ought not to marry a woman he had not seen and personally liked. He had told the emperor that he wished to see Christina before committing himself. It was, of course, deeply offensive for the ladies to be paraded about, and then shamed by being rejected. In order to placate him, Castillon recommended a meeting with the Queen of Navarre, who could legitimately be accompanied by the ladies.

Charles gave Mary of Hungary a commission on 20 July to conclude the treaty for Mary and Dom Luis's marriage, and that of Henry with Christina of Denmark. Less than two weeks later Constable Montmorency of France wrote to Castillon that François and Charles were now such good friends that there was no possibility the emperor would countenance either match. François wished to be on good terms but not at the price Henry was asking. François again insisted his kinswomen were not horses to be trotted out at the fair for approval by Henry. Henry waved aside Montmorency's views. He was confident of the emperor's friendship and assured Castillon that the marriage of Mary, at least, would take place.

In August 1538, Mary received instructions, via Cromwell, to meet Charles's ambassadors when they came to visit Prince Edward. Chapuys and

Mendoza would talk to her of marriage and she was to tell them that she was disappointed in the emperor's apparent dissimulation over the matter of her marriage to Luis. It affected her personally, and more might have been expected of him. Being a woman, she was to continue, she could not help bringing the matter up, although she herself was in no hurry to marry, but would only be obeying her loving father's commands. She was to inform them that her understanding was that even merchants' daughters had a quarter of the revenues of their husband's lands settled on them in cash, but she was only being offered an income of 20,000 ducats, and no knowledge of the source of the income. She was then to inform Cromwell exactly what had passed. Mary sent a copy of the letter to Chapuys so that the ambassadors might prepare themselves.

The visit duly took place. Mary told the ambassadors exactly what Cromwell had instructed and then repeated their answers back to him. They had argued that the delay had all been on Henry's side, which annoyed Cromwell. After visiting the prince, whom they described as the 'prettiest child in the world', they met Mary again. She informed them that she trusted the emperor as though he were both father and mother to her, and was sure it was not he who was stalling the marriage, despite Henry's words. On being asked if she would attempt a secret escape, she was not sure. If matters deteriorated, she would, but her father might treat her better, in which case, she would remain. How she communicated this to them is unclear. She certainly would not have been alone with the ambassadors. It seems unlikely she would have spoken frankly in front of her ladies – spies were everywhere, and information could be extracted even from the most reluctant. She must have either slipped them a letter, or perhaps spoken in Latin or Spanish – languages her ladies probably did not speak, although many of them would have been reasonably conversant with French. Mary was taking considerable risks in keeping the emperor's ambassadors informed of secret matters. While England and the Empire were not at war, Mary's actions might well have left her open to charges of treason. We can assume that she feared her father; the treatment he had meted out to those he had once loved – Katharine, Anne, Wolsey, More – and the vengeance he wreaked on Fisher, Aske, Hussey and others, can have left her in no doubt as to his ruthlessness. Had her actions been discovered she might well have found herself in the Tower. Contrary to characterisations of Mary as timid, her actions suggest she had a high tolerance of risk and this duplicity makes it clear that she was prepared to scheme for her own ends. In 1538 there were two goals she might have been pursuing – recognition as Henry's heir, after Edward, or marriage to enable her to escape the complexities of life in England, perhaps with a view to an invasion of England later to assert her rights. In fact, we can see from correspondence that Mary was not privy to, that her trust in Charles was, if not entirely misplaced, certainly greater than he merited. While her plight was one of the factors he took into account in his diplomacy, it was by no means the issue at the forefront of his mind. Other possibilities might be that Henry and Cromwell knew Mary passed on information and deliberately planted it, or that Mary was working with her father and only appearing to pass on secret information. She was deceiving somebody – but who?

Castillon had quarrelled with Henry. Having told the king that the idea of parading the ladies about for his approval was completely unacceptable, he added that the next thing Henry would ask would be try them out and keep the one he liked best. Henry grew angry at this and told Castillon that France need not be so sure of the emperor, who was still proposing Milan for Mary and Luis. Castillon responded that Henry would only have Milan by defeating both France and the Empire, and that it was not the time for boasting. François approved of Castillon's firmness and told Henry that none of the French brides Henry was interested in were at his disposal. Henry got over his anger with Castillon, on the surface at least, and continued to give the impression of wanting an alliance with France, by sharing information on the latest discussions over Christina and Luis.

Mendoza returned to Flanders, refused a last interview by Henry. He did have a conversation with Cromwell, during which Cromwell castigated him for telling Mary the delays in her marriage were caused by Henry, although he admitted that the English had not been as forthcoming as they might have been. Cromwell was sure that now Henry would pursue the match. Before he left, Mendoza reported that although Mary had been well at the time of their visit, she was once again in poor health, and also she was dissatisfied as she was being kept strictly and her state had again been reduced. Perhaps Henry and Cromwell had become suspicious of her dealings with the Imperial ambassadors.

At the end of September, Thomas Wriothesley was sent as ambassador to Mary of Hungary. Both sides frequently touched on the old alliances between their houses, which had been obscured by 'clouds and mists', for so Queen Katharine was euphemistically referred to. These inconvenient weather patterns had now gone 'clean away', but despite more tedious negotiation, nothing was achieved.

II

Stepmothers

I love my daughter well, but myself and my honour more.

Henry VIII

New dangers appeared on Mary's horizon in October 1538. Geoffrey Pole, Lady Salisbury's son, had been sent to the Tower, under suspicion for his correspondence with his brother, Cardinal Pole, whom Henry saw as his chief enemy. Their older brother, Lord Montagu, a man with a very credible claim to the throne, was also questioned about his letters to the cardinal. Montagu appeared to have accepted Henry's annulment, had brought troops to support the king during the Pilgrimage of Grace and acted as the loving cousin he had always been. But he had never really recovered from the execution of Buckingham. Cromwell suspected that Montagu, with his brothers, and the king's cousin, the Marquis of Exeter, would all have been glad to see Henry deposed and replaced with Mary, who would have married either Exeter's son (although he was only a child) or, more probably, Cardinal Pole who, despite his cardinalate, had not taken vows as a priest.

The examinations of Montagu's friends and servants show a man increasingly concerned about the direction public affairs were taking, and who was particularly concerned that the Statute of Treasons (making imagining or speaking of the king's death a crime) was too severe. Montagu's recorded remarks are difficult to interpret as treason – they are critical of the 'knaves' with whom Henry surrounded himself, by which we may infer Cromwell, and less than complimentary about the king's person ('full of flesh and unwieldy') and character.[1] Montagu, Geoffrey Pole and Exeter (with whom Cromwell had quarrelled violently) were dispatched to the Tower, and Montagu's mother Lady Salisbury to house arrest with the Earl of Southampton at Cowdray Castle. One of the go-betweens in the conspiracy, if such it was, was Elizabeth Darrell. Elizabeth had been a maid-of-honour to Katharine of Aragon, but from around 1537 became the mistress of Sir Thomas Wyatt. She was thus in a position to share what Wyatt might have heard at the Imperial court. She was also close enough to Mary to have received several gifts of money from her. Wyatt was a friend of Cromwell's so information could have been travelling in that direction, too. Certainly, Wyatt was not accused of any involvement, despite being on the fringes of the Montagu-Exeter circle.

With Mary's name on the alleged conspirators' lips, it was possible she would be suspected of involvement and her servants may have been questioned, but there is no record of it. Instead, the marriage with Luis was still being pressed, with the further stipulation that the couple should live in England until they had a child. Cromwell wrote to Wyatt of the 'horrible treasons' of which Montagu and Exeter had been guilty. He also told the French ambassador that Exeter meant to usurp the kingdom and marry Mary to his son. Letters had been found in the coffers of the Marchioness of Exeter from Katharine and Mary. Cromwell told Chapuys that the Exeters had 'suborned' Mary, turning her from her duty to her father, filling her head with 'fancies' and encouraging her to resist signing the oath of supremacy.

Mary spent Christmas 1538 at Blackfriars, once again ill with her 'old sickness'. On New Year's Day she was so faint that she was obliged to go to bed, although the next day she was somewhat better. Lady Kingston, in attendance, wrote to Wriothesley, asking that Henry might send Dr Butts to her as he had ministered to her previously when she had suffered similarly. Despite illness, propriety had to be observed and gifts distributed. Mary's New Year gift to Edward was a coat of embroidered crimson satin, decked with gold and pearls, with tinsel sleeves.[2]

If Mary's illness were stress-related, a relapse would hardly be surprising – reaction to the executions of her cousins, Montagu and Exeter, and the house-arrest of Lady Salisbury may well have been a contributing factor. In January, old servants of Katharine's were also questioned and admitted carrying letters between the late princess dowager and her daughter. One admitted he had taken letters from Sir Nicholas Carew in 1536. Nervous, he had asked Carew about the contents, and been assured that they were letters urging Mary to accept Henry's will and that Secretary Cromwell would be glad if Mary submitted. The man then confirmed that he had, at Mary's request, copied her letters to Henry and Cromwell, and sent them to Chapuys. He named various other people who had carried letters or messages between Katharine, Mary and others.

No action was taken against Mary for sharing her correspondence with the king with the Imperial ambassador but Carew was arrested and sent to the Tower, after discovery of a letter of his in Lady Exeter's coffer. Chapuys was told that some of his own letters were in the self-same coffer, which puzzled him, as the only people he had written to were Katharine and Mary, who would both have burnt anything incriminating. He sent Mary at least a dozen innocuous letters for her to produce if required. Carew, in hopes of saving his life, testified that Exeter (who was already dead and beyond help) had looked 'melancholy' at the news of the birth of Edward. Chapuys believed that such treasonable facial expressions could only have arisen from Exeter's attachment to Mary, in whose service the marquis had told Chapuys he would willingly shed his blood. Similarly, Chapuys thought that Carew, too, was devoted to Mary, and that any incriminating letters might relate to her. He was certain that Henry intended to leave her with as few friends as possible. Other than the loss to Mary, Chapuys was unconcerned about Carew, whom he thought favoured a French alliance.

Following the execution of his brother Montagu, Pole denounced Henry publicly in a long letter to Charles and named Cromwell as the spawn of the devil. Henry heard that Pole proposed coming to England, and asked Charles to detain him, as Pole had a 'viper's' nature, and plotted not only the overthrow of Henry, but harm to all of the king's children. Henry was taking the line that Mary was just as much a victim as he was of any conspiracy that might have existed.

Wyatt reported from Spain that Henry could easily have Christina. As for Milan, although the emperor would like to give it to Luis and Mary, that would provoke the French. Since Milan would be a drain on Henry's finances, with its only benefit being that discussing it created tension between Charles and François and irritated the pope, Wyatt recommended Henry cease pursuing it, especially as Wyatt was sure that Orléans would never get it either. If the matter of Milan were dropped, Henry would find that the financial matters resolved themselves. Wyatt was very much in favour of Luis having an estate in England, as it would cost Henry little, and the money would be spent in the country, rather than being sent abroad. Similarly, Luis's income from Portugal would benefit England. Henry would also be able to have his family around him and Mary's children, should they eventually inherit, would be English born. The negotiations for both marriages rumbled on without ever reaching a conclusion.

On 12 January 1539, Henry's worst fears were realised when Charles and François made a treaty at Toledo not to league with England, particularly in the matter of marriages for either Henry or Mary. English policy must now be to seek an alternative defensive strategy against the joint might of Charles and François. There was talk of joining a league with the dukes of Saxony and Cleves and the King of Denmark, with Mary to be married to the Duke of Cleves, who was disputing with Charles over the duchy of Guelders. Chapuys's opinion was that Henry would never marry Mary out of the realm, and that he was just muddying the waters around a match for Duchess Christina with either Lorraine or Cleves. The ambassador thought he would shortly find out the truth, as Henry was planning on visiting Prince Edward and would see Mary at the same time. This suggests that Henry spoke freely to Mary, probably in the knowledge that she passed on information to Chapuys. Henry might have seen this as a way to float ideas to Charles to gauge reaction, before committing himself officially.

Cromwell sent instructions to his servant, Christopher Mount, to sound Cleves in regard to a marriage for Mary with the duke. While Henry would listen to offers, he would not open negotiations, and he would not send a picture of Mary – she was of too high a rank for her picture to be sent abroad, even if she were only his illegitimate daughter. In any event, the Duke of Saxony's own envoy, Burgatus, had seen Mary and could testify to her 'beauty, learning and virtues'. At the same time, the Duke of Cleves might like to offer his oldest sister for Henry.

For Easter 1539, Henry, at Greenwich, paid for 7 yards of purple velvet for his own palm, and as much crimson velvet for the palms of his 'dearest children, Prince Edward, Lady Mary and Lady Elizabeth', who may all have been with him, since Cromwell was able to write to Wyatt that they were all 'merry', a report borne out by Lady Lisle who had visited the siblings. She wrote to her husband that she thought Edward the prettiest child she had ever seen and Mary sent her 'heartiest wishes' to her Uncle Arthur. Henry also authorised payment of £275 2s 7d for Mary's clothes.

Negotiations with Cleves intensified. Henry sent ambassadors, headed by Dr Wootton, to enquire of Duke Wilhelm about suitable brides for himself, adding that, if the duke mentioned Mary, he was to be invited to send ambassadors to England to discuss a match. Charles, nervous at the thought of an alliance between England and Cleves, offered Duchess Christina to Duke Wilhelm, although others thought the duke would still look for Mary as a wife, unless the delegation of Germans who arrived in England on 28 April, successfully negotiated a match for Mary to the Duke of Saxony's son.

On 11 May, 1539, the Empress Isabella, Mary's cousin, died. Her passing was marked in England with a solemn ceremony at St Paul's. Charles sincerely mourned his wife, but the old story of him marrying Mary was quickly talked of, first in Spain, then in Rome. The idea terrified the pope, who immediately gave orders to Cardinal Farnese, his nuncio in France, to persuade Charles to take a French wife instead. Charles rejected the idea – he was too old to want to marry Princess Marguerite of France – with a son and two daughters already, his thoughts must be of them.

Later in May, Parliament passed Acts of Attainder against Lady Salisbury, Lady Exeter, Sir Adrian Fortescue, Sir Thomas Dingley and others.

The charge was a treasonable plot to marry Mary to Cardinal Pole, and to rejoin the English church to Rome. The evidence was a coat of arms, found in Lady Salisbury's house. On one side were the lions of England, surrounded by pansies, signifying Pole, and marigolds for Mary. From the pansies and marigolds, a tree sprouted, with a branch from which was suspended a purple coat, taken to mean Christ's coat. On the reverse were the symbols of the Passion of Christ, the banner used by the Pilgrimage of Grace. For this outrageous crime, all were dispatched to the Tower under sentence of death. Again, there is no indication that Mary was involved or investigated, although, of course, Lady Salisbury and Lady Exeter had been very close to her.

In June 1539, the Act of Six Articles was passed. This was more conservative than the 1536 Act of Ten Articles that it superseded and the German reformer, Melancthon, who believed that the Act would endanger many Reformers, thought its tone might have been adopted as part of a negotiation for marriage between Mary and Charles. But while Henry may have been promoting a more conservative definition of faith, that did not mean he wanted reconciliation with Rome. Lest anyone think he was weakening in his determination to be recognised as Supreme Head of the Church in England, on 17 June a water pageant was held on the Thames, in which, after a good deal of shooting of ordinance and grappling, the barges containing the pope and his cardinals were defeated, with the unlucky performers getting a ducking. No-one was drowned, as the actors had been chosen from men who could swim, and the king's own barge was 'hovering', ready to rescue them. The ladies and gentlemen of the court looked on but there is no information on Mary's presence.

In early September, the commission to finalise a match between Henry and Anne of Cleves departed, Henry having been reassured that a previous negotiation for Anne with the son of the Duke of Lorraine was not binding. The proxy marriage took place in October and Anne set out shortly afterwards for her new country. Henry was excited at the thought of his new bride – her portrait by Holbein had whetted his appetite and he was looking forward to a happy fourth marriage. Preparations began for Anne's reception. Mary was to lead the ladies, who included Elizabeth; Lady Dorset; Mary, Dowager Duchess of Richmond; Lady Margaret Douglas and others. After the marriage, Anne's permanent staff was to be led by Lady Margaret Douglas and among the newly-appointed maids-of-honour, was Katheryn Howard, niece of the Duke of Norfolk.

Mary's favourite abbey of Syon surrendered to the king on 25 November. It had been founded by Henry V, enhanced by Henry VII, and she had frequently visited it. No breath of scandal had ever been raised about the conduct of its inmates, but that could not save it from bowing to pressure. Although after the Pilgrimage of Grace there were no more forcible suppressions, one by one, the abbots and abbesses caved in and surrendered their houses. The closure of Syon grieved Mary. Although she could say and do nothing at the time, it was one of the houses she refounded when she became queen and to which she left substantial sums in her will.

In late December, Mary had a new suitor: Philip, Count Palatine and Duke of Bavaria. He visited on Henry's express invitation, fortunately missing the storms that kept Anne of Cleves captive in Calais for a fortnight. Henry sent Wriothesley to Mary, now at Hertford Castle, on 17 December, with a letter and his 'hearty commendations'. He wanted her opinion on the proposed match. Mary responded that she would prefer to remain unmarried, nevertheless, remembering both her natural duty to her father and her own promises, she would be obedient to his will. Wriothesley was equally impressed by her dutiful response, and by the gravity of the six-year-old Elizabeth, whom he compared with a forty-year-old for 'manner'. Mary wrote her response to Henry, and also sent a second letter to Cromwell, thanking him for his advice and assuring him that Henry would ever find her his obedient and humble servant. She apologised for dictating the letter, but writing to her father had tired her hand.

Cromwell and Duke Philip rode to meet Mary at Enfield three days before Christmas. There is no record of what Mary made of Philip, but we can infer that she did not make any objections. Henry obviously felt that this was consent enough and a marriage treaty was drawn up. Mary, declared incapable of inheriting the crown of England, was to be married to Philip with a dowry of 40,000 golden florins, worth 3s 4d each, and an annual pension of 12,000 florins payable by Henry. The dowry was to be paid half down, and half within the year. Philip was to bear the cost of taking Mary to Bavaria, by a route to be agreed with Henry, and to pay an allowance to his new wife of 10,000 florins a year. Henry and Philip agreed to a defensive pact, and Philip confirmed that the 'usurped' authority of the Bishop of Rome had been removed in England. There were several drafts, some omitting the passage relating to Mary's disqualification from inheritance. If she were to be widowed, she could return to England with her jewellery and personal effects, still in possession of the 10,000 florins per year from Bavaria, but could not remarry without Henry's permission. The new French envoy in London, Marillac, thought the purpose was to give her to a relatively powerless prince to minimise any risk of her husband claiming the throne, to Edward's detriment.

Mary probably spent Christmas at Baynard's Castle in London. She went to the abbey at Westminster and, while she walked in the gardens, Philip again visited her. He kissed her in greeting, which the French ambassador thought a sure sign that the marriage would go ahead within the following two or three weeks. The couple conversed in Latin and German through an interpreter. Philip declared he wished to go through with the match, while Mary agreed she would do as her father required. It was perhaps at this time that Philip gave Mary the gift of a diamond cross, set with four pearls with a large hanging pearl. Later, she was obliged to surrender it to Chancellor Audley, at Henry's command.

The year 1540 opened with the usual present giving. Mary gave Edward a gold brooch with the image of St John, set with a ruby – a very traditional gift, combining monetary and spiritual value. Lady Elizabeth sewed him a garment. Mary also purchased numerous items of gilt and silver, bracelets of gold and yards of yellow satin and damask as well as frontlets and bonnets for presents. The usual tips were given to the grooms of the various household departments and to the servants who delivered gifts from her friends and courtiers. Mr Gates, who brought Henry's gift, received 40s. The chaplains of Elizabeth and Margaret Douglas received 10s and 7s 6d respectively. Mary's most expensive purchase was 6¾ yards of cloth of gold, totalling £37 10s 6d, probably for her own use. An annual income of £20 was enough to keep a gentleman and his family in a modest way, so spending this much on a gown was a spectacular indulgence.

Henry did not preside over the usual New Year festivities. Impatient to meet his new bride, he had set out for Rochester, where he walked into her room unannounced, disguised as a merchant. Anne, unimpressed by the stranger's manners or appearance, greeted him coldly and then ignored him. Henry was furious – she was supposed to have been overcome with love at first sight. This awkward meeting soured their relationship from the start. No matter how gracious and willing to be pleased Anne was after the formal introduction, Henry could never get over the knowledge that she had shown no interest in him as a man. Despite Henry's failure to take to Anne, he could not offend the German princes by sending her back – the wedding had to proceed. The queen's household was formed, and she was assigned the jointure lands of the late Queen Jane, and others of the 'late Katharine, sometime dowager, then called queen'. A grand procession formed up on 5 January at Greenwich to meet her on Blackheath. Marillac described her as looking 'about thirty, tall, thin and of medium beauty'. He commented that she and her ladies were dressed in German fashion, which 'some thought strange'. He added that while she did not seem so young or beautiful as reported, she was very assured in countenance and carriage. He thought that she might well have wit and vivacity, rather than beauty. Her attendants were even less beautiful, but their German clothes were so awful, he could hardly tell. Marillac made a few more snide remarks about the ceremonies, then added that he had heard that Philip of Bavaria was to be admitted to the Garter the following day, making his marriage with Mary seem more likely, although there had been no announcement.

On 17 January 1540 news came to the Duke of Bavaria, the Chancellor of Saxony and the other German gentlemen with Anne, that the emperor was preparing for war against them. They decided to leave England immediately, before their safe-conducts, granted the previous autumn, expired. Philip waited a few more days before departing with a present of around 5,000 crowns. Marillac still thought he would return to complete a marriage with Mary.

So long as Charles and François were in league, Henry needed to make the best of his marriage to Anne, and also to placate James V. Ralph Sadleir was sent to Scotland to encourage James to remain on good terms with his uncle – for what could France or the Empire give him but 'fair words'? Despite the fact that Philip of Bavaria had left without any resolution having been taken on his marriage to Mary, the French and Imperial ambassadors in England conferred over the implications of the union. Chapuys had been instructed that a marriage between Mary and Philip must be tolerated, provided Mary was not obliged to do anything prejudicial to her religion, and he was to give her a form of protestation to swear – presumably against any clause that excluded her from the succession. Nevertheless, Charles did not believe the rumours that Philip had received the Garter could be true. As a Knight of the Golden Fleece, he could not accept the honour without Charles's permission. Nor did Charles think it at all likely that Henry would allow Mary to marry a foreign prince.

On 7 February, Cardinal Farnese wrote to Pope Paul from France that the Queen of France had heard that while the new Queen of England was 'old and ugly,' she was also 'worthy and Catholic'.[3] Henry, disliking her clothes, had made her dress in French fashions, which no doubt the French believed enormously improved Anne's attractiveness. Henry was still hoping to drive a wedge between Charles and François. To that end, he sent Norfolk to France. During a private audience, the French king assured Norfolk of his love for Henry and Norfolk denied the story that Mary was already married to Philip of Bavaria. Norfolk deduced that, unless François had Milan, his pact with Charles would fail, and also that the emperor was determined to wrest Guelders from Wilhelm of Cleves. Norfolk then had an audience with Marguerite of Angoulême, widowed Queen of Navarre, whom he thought the wisest woman he ever met. Whatever agreement her brother François had come to with Charles, Marguerite hated the emperor for depriving her husband, Henri II of Navarre, of half his kingdom. Marguerite was sure the emperor could not hold Milan, that he and François would soon fall out, and Charles would not be able to take Guelders. She also thought Charles would seek to marry Mary himself, to which Norfolk replied that Henry would be unlikely to allow it. Norfolk emerged from his conversation with Marguerite, believing François had nothing but good will toward Henry. Either he was naïve or Marguerite was very convincing. It was finally agreed that the Duke of Cleves would retain Guelders and marry Ferdinand's daughter, Archduchess Maria, while Charles kept the title.[4] Cleves and the emperor were thus back on good terms, rendering the alliance with England less important.

With a queen in residence, Mary could join the court and in early 1540, she is listed as having a 'double lodging' in the Inner Court at Hampton Court, near those of Edward, Lady Margaret Douglas and Cromwell. As always, gambling on cards was the pastime of choice. Mary gave 20s to Elizabeth to play with, and herself lost a frontlet to Margaret Douglas in a bet. It is easy to see how Queen Anne, who had not been taught any of these pastimes, had difficulty fitting in. Nevertheless, it was anticipated that Anne would be crowned at Whitsun and that Philip of Bavaria would return to continue his courtship of Mary.

May Day was again celebrated with a joust at Westminster, proclaimed throughout Europe to gather participants. The Challengers were led by Sir John Dudley, and the late Queen Jane's brother, Sir Thomas Seymour, while the Defenders were headed by Lord William Howard, Cromwell's son Gregory, and Lord Clinton (married to Henry's former mistress, Bessie Blount). The whole court was there, probably including Mary. The fun lasted for five days. Later in May, Mary was at Tittenhanger, perhaps ill again as Christopher the surgeon came from London to let her blood. This did not prevent more fabrics being ordered for clothes – yellow satin, white satin and black velvet. Elizabeth was still with her sister, and again received money to play with.

The use of patronage to support friends and servants was a key part of the role of a great lady; using influence to gain favours or employment for your family or clients was the normal way of conducting business. In return, they supported you. Mary exercised her patronage in a letter of April 1540, to Cromwell. She called him her 'sheet anchor', and thanked him, as always, for his conduct of her business. She asked for favour for Mistress Coke, an old servant of Katharine's, in a dispute with New College, Oxford, over the farm of Rysbrydge. Mary did not think that the College Warden had treated either Mrs Coke or Cromwell 'gently' in the matter.

Mary might have relied on Cromwell to guide her but soon she would have to look for allies elsewhere. On 10 June, Cromwell, Lord Privy Seal and Earl of Essex, was accused of treason. The matter was soon all over Europe, with the old rumour that Cromwell had intended to marry Mary and set himself up as king. At first glance such an allegation seems utterly preposterous. But while it is impossible to believe that Cromwell would have attempted to overthrow Henry, it is not beyond the realms of possibility that, having arranged the marriage of his son, Geoffrey, to Queen Jane's sister, Cromwell might have envisaged a future after Henry's death as Mary's consort. From Mary's letters to Cromwell, and the presents exchanged between them, we can infer that they were personally on good terms – Mary never sought to undermine or circumvent his power with Henry. It is impossible to know whether, secretly, she hated him as the author of the destruction of papal authority, and the Dissolution of the Monasteries, or whether she was sincerely grateful to him for effecting the reconciliation with Henry. Nevertheless, even if she had personally liked him, she would never have countenanced marrying a man so far below her in rank. It would have been 'disparagement', a concept of loss of honour that was taken so seriously that it was illegal for guardians to make disparaging matches for their female wards.

On 30 June 1540 in a desperate bid to return to favour, Cromwell detailed all the conversations he had had with Henry about Anne of Cleves, and Henry's concerns that the marriage was not valid. In passing, he noted that, at Lent, Henry and Anne had discussed Mary (although what they said was not repeated) and Henry had found that Anne was 'waxing stubborn and willful'. From Cromwell's evidence, it emerged that Henry had been unable to consummate the marriage – a problem he attributed to his body's instinctive knowledge that Anne's pre-contract with the son of the Duke of Lorraine was an impediment to her marriage with Henry. Anne, although not as thrilled to have her marriage annulled as she has been portrayed, acquiesced. With far less powerful relatives than those of Katharine of Aragon, she had little choice. She accepted the position of the 'king's sister', and a handsome settlement, which, disappointingly for Mary who often stayed there, included Richmond.

The French were delighted at Cromwell's fall – as much for the fun of laughing at Henry as for the dispatch of a man who was believed to favour the Lutherans. They thought Henry well rid of such a 'ribald' as plotted to marry the Lady Mary and that this ambition was the cause of Cromwell muddying every marriage proposal made for her. On 28 July 1540, Cromwell was executed. Although he had been degraded from all his offices, Henry permitted him to be beheaded, rather than hanged, drawn and quartered, the usual method of execution for non-nobles. He had the dubious privilege of sharing his hour of execution with Walter, Lord Hungerford, condemned for magic, sodomy and the rape of his own daughter.

A few days after Cromwell's death, Mary once again had cause to grieve – and to fear. Three men who had been imprisoned since 1536 were dragged from the Tower and executed by hanging, drawing and quartering: Dr Wilson, Henry's confessor; Dr Abell, Katharine's chaplain, and her own old tutor, Dr Fetherstone. At the same time, three Evangelicals were burnt for heresy.

Losing no time following the dismissal of Anne of Cleves, Henry married Norfolk's niece, Katheryn Howard. Marillac reported that she was said to be 'of great beauty' and rumoured to be already pregnant. On 3 October, instructions were sent to Richard Pate, back on embassy in Spain, to discuss with Van Dyke, one of Charles's ministers, how Pate would gladly forward a marriage between Charles and Mary – since it had only previously been prevented by de Chièvres and the late Cardinal (Wolsey). While Van Dyke told Pate he was not a member of the emperor's inner circle, he believed that the emperor's closest advisors thought a marriage with Mary would be extremely suitable, on account of her parentage and personal virtues, and the fact that the emperor loved her like a daughter (an interesting logic!). But Van Dyke did not think it would happen as he had heard that Henry, out of 'small love to his own flesh' intended to marry her to some 'low born person in England', probably another manifestation of the rumours about Cromwell.

***

Mary found it difficult to accept her new stepmother. Katheryn, who was at least five years, and possibly as much as seven years, younger than Mary, felt her stepdaughter did not treat her with sufficient respect. When Mary heard that two of her maids were to be dismissed, she thought that Katheryn had instigated it to punish her. She quickly mended her manners and found means to conciliate the queen, who was a good-natured woman and soon forgave Mary her transgressions. But whatever grovelling Mary had done to Katheryn, it did not result in her being recalled to court. For New Year, she sent presents to both king and queen, at which Chapuys reported that Henry was pleased, and sent magnificent presents in return. Nevertheless, at least one of her maids was removed, and died shortly thereafter. Chapuys, reporting Mary's distress at the woman's death, rather exaggeratedly attributed her demise to grief at being parted from her mistress.

At the end of February 1541, François was still pushing Marillac to find out if Mary was going to marry Charles. Marillac responded that he could find no indication of any current discussions. There were a number of reasons why Marillac thought it would not happen, including Henry's fear that Edward would be ousted on the grounds of being born after England left papal authority, of a woman never crowned. Clearly, the emperor could not marry an illegitimate woman, so the Parliamentary Act would have to be undone and Katharine's marriage recognised, effectively returning England to Rome. Marillac does not seem to have considered that an Act could have been passed rendering Mary legitimate as born in good faith. As Henry appeared to be hoping for issue from his fifth marriage, which had somewhat rejuvenated him, it seems unlikely he would have wished to legitimate Mary at this juncture. Philip of Bavaria's agent had arrived in mid-April, but had not received a firm answer about the marriage going forward, only sufficient encouragement for it to seem likely that he would visit again.

In early May 1541 Mary asked Henry and Katheryn to visit the prince. No reason was specified but Katheryn was certainly eager to do so. Henry, perhaps pleased with Mary's affection for her brother, gave her permission to return to permanent residence at court, Katheryn being either actually agreeable, or deeming it politic to seem so. On 28 May, Mary suffered another blow to her emotions. Lady Salisbury was taken from her cell and executed, protesting that she did not know what her crime had been – there had been no trial, and no opportunity for her to protest against the Act of Attainder. Exactly what triggered Henry's wrath at this point, when earlier in the year he had paid for new clothes for Lady Salisbury, is uncertain, but he seems to have got wind of another conspiracy, about which there are no details, other than that an abbot and two other men were hanged, drawn and quartered. Lady Salisbury herself was butchered by an amateur headsman. Her last speech was a prayer for the king, queen, prince and Mary. There is no direct evidence of Mary's reaction but unless she were completely heartless, which is not the impression to be gained from her letters or general demeanour, she grieved deeply for the woman who had been her 'second mother' and who had loved and cherished her since her childhood.

Marillac assured François that there was no possibility of Mary marrying Charles. Chapuys had not been near the court for six months – in fact, a martyr to gout, he had barely stirred from his bed. Even when Chapuys had come to court, Marillac reported that Mary had refused to see him. He entered her chamber, but she walked out of another door, protesting she would not incur her father's wrath by speaking to him, as had previously happened. It is tempting to think was a ploy – the whole of Mary and Chapuys's relationship suggests that she liked and trusted him – unless the death of Lady Salisbury had so cowed Mary that she determined to avoid any action that could be interpreted unfavourably.

***

Among the promises the government had been constrained to make to the insurgents during the Pilgrimage of Grace, had been one to hold a Parliament in the North, and to crown the then queen, Jane, at York. Although neither of these events had occurred, Henry decided, in 1541, to make a progress north, with his new queen and the vast majority of the court, including Mary and the French and Imperial ambassadors. The route they followed took them via Peterborough, Stamford, Gainsborough, Lincoln, Hull and

Pontefract to York. Marillac recorded that, as the king passed, there were no special ceremonies, but that the streets would be cleaned and decorated, and the town inhabitants would ride through in their ordinary clothes, followed by the nobles, riding in twos, then the king, on a huge horse, with Queen Katheryn, the Lady Mary and other ladies of the court following, and sixty or eighty archers behind.

By early August, the court had arrived at Suffolk's castle at Grimsthorpe in Lincolnshire. While there, Marillac had a long conversation with Norfolk about whom the Duke of Orléans should marry. Would one of Henry's daughters be a possibility? As for Elizabeth, replied Norfolk, that was quite impossible; she was only seven, and the reputation of her mother made it unsuitable. Besides, Parliament had declared her illegitimate. Further, as she was Norfolk's great-niece, he could not be seen to forward the idea. Mary was far more appropriate. But, the French Ambassador innocently asked, surely Mary was promised to Charles? No, not at all – Henry would never give her to the emperor. As for her being illegitimate, Norfolk could tell Marillac, in confidence, that king and council were resolved to give her a place in the succession after legitimate sons. So, if Henry were willing to consider giving her succession rights, why go into the whole question of legitimacy?

A couple of days later, after Norfolk had told Henry of the overtures, the two men spoke again. Henry was very eager to reconnect with François, provided the French king made the first move. The rapprochement between François and Charles had been badly damaged by the assassination of François' ambassadors to the Ottoman Court. Although France's relationship with the Ottomans was deeply controversial in Europe, the murders were considered an outrage. François described them as 'dirty and dishonourable'. Certain that Charles was behind them, he turned to Henry and could think of no better way to promote amity than through marriage. Marillac was empowered to make enquiries as to Mary's availability, and what would be offered with her. François would like her dowry to consist of the extinguishing of the French pensions paid to England, and he also wanted the inclusion of Scotland in the treaty. Since part of Henry's plan in travelling to York had been to meet James V, his inclusion seemed a fairly straightforward matter.

The dauphin, despite having been married for more than seven years to Catherine de' Medici, had no children. François, therefore, thought it likely the succession would devolve on Orléans or his children and instructed Marillac to report back on Mary's physical attributes. In particular, he was to enquire whether the 'melancholy and ennui' she had suffered from for so long precluded her from bearing children. He was also to find out about any medicines she took.[5]

On 18 September Henry, Katheryn and Mary entered York. Marillac was still talking to Norfolk, who was growing nervous and wanted the discussions to involve the whole council. The duke pressed for detailed terms, but the ambassador would respond only with generalities. Norfolk talked it over with Henry, who sent the message that once the finances had been settled, he would talk about Mary's status. Norfolk himself thought there would be no difficulty about her being considered legitimate, but, as for the succession, Edward was likely to live, and any future children Henry might have would come before Mary, although she would come ahead of Elizabeth. As ever, the whole discussion deteriorated into a wrangle about who would show his hand first. Henry would not discuss anything with Marillac until the ambassador had authorisation from François under the Great Seal of France, but François would not send that until he knew on what terms Henry would negotiate. Marillac thought there were three areas of difficulty – the worry the English had of a foreign king; that the English wanted to know all of the French offers before saying how Mary would be ranked; and that while the English would not expect a French prince to marry a bastard, how Mary could be declared legitimate? It was out of the question that Henry would recognise his marriage to Katharine, so there was the possibility either that Henry would declare her legitimate 'of his grace', or that the French could just assume she was the eldest legitimate daughter, as the pope recognised Katharine's marriage.

Mary continued her patronage of Mrs Coke. The council with Henry during the progress wrote to Lord Chancellor Audley, still in London, at Mary's request, asking him to stay Mrs Coke's legal matter until their return. The note was signed by Wriothesley, among others. To exercise patronage at this level shows Mary had every confidence that her father's ministers would accede to her wishes. Far from being in the political wilderness, she was at the centre of affairs. The negotiations with France continued. James V's ambassador wrote home that François was intending to send suitably prestigious envoys to England to conclude the matter and the French king advised James to do the same, so all three could conclude a treaty. François had received Marillac's report on Mary. It is quoted in full as it is the most detailed pen-portrait of Mary as a young woman.

Sire, I have taken pains not only to see her and consider her stature and proportions, but also to inform myself, via a woman who has served in her chamber since her infancy and has remained in her place. She is married to one of your subjects who is well-known to, and loved by your ambassadors. She [the informant] saw the time of her [Mary's] 'ennui' (perhaps best translated as troubles), which she suffered because of her afflictions, and [knows] other characteristics, from which one hopes she [Mary] may bear children. To begin with what everyone can see, the said Lady Mary is of medium stature, bigger boned than is consistent with lightness and grace, however she is well-enough made. Her face, particularly her mouth, is like her father's, as is her laugh and her voice, although she has a more masculine voice for a woman, than he has for a man. As for her chin, that recedes somewhat, as did the queen, her mother's, which I have seen in the portraits of the said deceased lady. Her skin is smooth and fresh, and she does not look more than eighteen or twenty, although she is twenty-four. Her beauty is moderate, and one could say she is one of the beauties of this court. (Marillac obviously did not think much of English women's looks). As for her walk and bearing, one can assume that she is not delicate. Above everything, she likes early morning exercise and when the weather is good she enjoys walking two or three miles in the park and one seldom sees her sitting down when indoors.

As for her intelligence, I believe, Sire, that she speaks French very well, and you may assure yourself that she writes it perfectly, as I have seen the letters she wrote to the Imperial Ambassador during the time of her troubles. She understands Latin excellently and delights in reading good books and *humaines lettres* (the types of open letters sent by scholars such as Erasmus or More). During the time she was being harassed, she used to wake in the middle of the night and read them. She also enjoys musical instruments, playing, amongst others, the virginals particularly well. And with all this knowledge, Sire, everyone who talks to her affirms that with all the sweetness and benignity that one sees in her, there is also great prudence in everything she says and does and that she is very reserved.

The said chamber woman also described how, at the beginning of the repudiation of the queen, her mother, to be truthful, she fell ill with depression and after being visited and comforted by her father, she soon convalesced and since then has not been ill in any similar way. As for her doctor, Sire, both he and her apothecary are Spanish, so I could not talk to them without arousing suspicion. As for the other apothecary, who is my neighbour, he told me that he had never prescribed anything for her other than light things, such as casses, conserves, and similar drugs, which she takes more often at her father's command, than because she needs them. Moreover, the chamber woman told me that she did not know of any impediment to her bearing children. On the contrary, she perceives all the characteristics required in a lady for her to have children as soon as she is married. I have tried Sire, to obtain a portrait of the lady, and to avoid suspicion, have asked the king for one of the queen and all his children, but there is no painter who would dare to do one without the express permission of the king ... [6].

Marillac's secretary was secretly in the pay of Chapuys and showed him a copy of the ambassador's instructions. This led Chapuys to reassure Mary of Hungary that a marriage with Orléans would not take place. François' demands that the marriage should settle all Henry's claims for a pension would never be agreed and nor would Mary be given a place in the succession above any subsequent legitimate children Henry might have. The French council was also concerned that aggrandising Orléans would be dangerous for the dauphin. François would not want his younger son to be king of England, for fear of war between his sons, who did not get on, and nor would Henry want such a potentially powerful son-in-law as, in Chapuys's biased view, the hatred many felt for Henry might be transferred to Edward, allowing Mary and Orléans to take the throne. Chapuys also learned, rather more straightforwardly over dinner, that Marillac was waiting for Norfolk to return to court to continue negotiations.

In early November 1541 scandal rocked the English court. It was being said that Queen Katheryn had been betrothed to Francis Dereham, one of her gentleman ushers, prior to her marriage with Henry. As if that were not bad enough, shortly after, Marillac wrote that she had been shown to have been 'familiar' with seven or eight men before her marriage. He said that it was now suspected she had continued her 'incontinent' living after her marriage to Henry. The poor girl was in such distress that it had been necessary to prevent her having access to anything by which she might bring on her own death, although Marillac was of the opinion that if adultery were to be proved, she would soon die anyway. Norfolk had spoken to Marillac 'with tears in his eyes' of the distress of Henry who had loved Katheryn so much. Norfolk then informed Marillac that he had been mistaken to think Katheryn had had any lover previous to her marriage other than Dereham, but that she had been meeting in secret with Thomas Culpepper, a gentleman of the Privy Chamber, and so many 'signs and tokens' had passed between them that he thought they must have committed adultery. The king was so grieved that he thought he would never marry again. Katheryn was dispatched to Syon with a greatly reduced household. Her half-sister, Isabel, Lady Baynton, was permitted to stay with her, and the whole household remained in the control of Isabel's husband, Sir Edward Baynton.

Unlike the women of Katheryn's household, Mary was not questioned about her stepmother. Instead, she, with a 'convenient number' of Queen Katheryn's servants, was escorted by Sir John Dudley to Hertford Castle to stay with the prince, who had been ill, while Lady Margaret Douglas was to go with Mary Richmond to the latter's home at Kenninghall. Lady Margaret was again in disgrace herself, for a flirtation with Queen Katheryn's brother. Katheryn's jewels were inventoried, and it was noted that while the court had been at Pomfret, she had given Mary 'a pomander of gold wherein is a clock enamelled with divers colours, garnished with xii small rubies', although she had kept the bejewelled chain of gold that had hung from it.

There was never any possibility that Katheryn would survive. Henry might have meant what he said about never marrying again while overcome with shock and grief at Katheryn's perceived betrayal of him, but it would have been impossible for him to do so unless it could be shown that Katheryn's relationship with Dereham constituted a marriage, which she firmly denied. Even in such a case, it would be debatable whether Henry would be free, so Katheryn had to die. She was executed on 13 February. Mary may not have found Katheryn particularly personally congenial, but she is likely to have been shocked and upset that the young woman who had liked her enough to give her a gold pomander, was to be beheaded. Given the apparent strength of Henry's affection for Katheryn, Mary probably redoubled her efforts to show her obedience to him; if even his petted wife could be cast aside so violently, no-one was safe. There was, too, the execution of Jane, Lady Rochford, condemned with Katheryn, to grieve her. Mary and Jane had been friendly for many years.

In early January 1542, the marriage negotiations with Orléans were no further forward. Chapuys opined that the French only wanted it so the pension could be written off, while Henry saw it as a means to get back some of the arrears. Marillac too, began to think matters were not going well. On 17 January, he suggested to François that the negotiations be pursued with rather more sincerity, as although Henry would prefer a match with Orléans for no cash outlay, rather than putting his hand in his purse for a marriage with Charles, the English might assume that they were only sought when the emperor was riding high. If François did not want to pursue the marriage, Marillac asked to be replaced with someone who could credibly claim ignorance of the negotiations, as he could not now withdraw without losing face. In response, François sent powers to Marillac to treat of the marriage between Orléans and the 'eldest, legitimate, daughter' of Henry. He was insistent that James of Scotland should be present at any meeting between himself and Henry. Nothing would frighten the pope more than an alliance between France, Scotland and England.

In France, Paget, who had replaced Lord William Howard as ambassador, waited on Marguerite of Angoulême, still promoting fellowship with Henry, reminiscing about previous suggestions that she might have married either Henry's father, or Henry himself. She and Henry were alike 'for neither of us loveth the pope', whom she thought would be glad to see the end of both of them. Marguerite informed Paget that Orléans loved Mary as much as his deceased brother, the first dauphin, had done, who had once said he would give his hand to have her. All of François' Council, and his mistress, Mme d'Étampes, wanted alliance with England, although Queen Eleonora wanted

Orléans for her daughter. Paget was non-committal, saying that God worked 'all things for the best' after which he was dismayed to be treated to an hour long sermon from the queen.

In response to Marillac's official commission, the Duke of Norfolk, the Lord Privy Seal, the Bishops of Durham and Winchester and Sir Thomas Wriothesley, opened negotiations. The first obstacle they found was the insufficiency of the French commission, which spoke only of a marriage, not of a general 'amity' and also referred to Mary as 'legitimate'. They could not accept such a commission without perhaps incurring charges of treason. The word 'legitimate' would have to go, as it was presupposing the outcome of negotiations. Marillac could not change the commission, without orders, but they might as well know that if Henry would not consider Mary legitimate, nothing could come of the matter. On hearing that, the English deputies requested further instructions from the king. Henry would go so far as to say that if the commission omitted the offending word, and included general powers to conclude 'amity', he would give Mary as successor to the crown after all legitimate male and female heirs to be born to him. If Henry had been willing to put her above other legitimate daughters, he would already have found a more impressive match than Orléans – presumably meaning the emperor. Frankly, the English added, even as heir only after legitimate issue, she was of higher rank than the dauphin's wife had been. Very likely, responded Marillac, but Orléans would be better marrying a gentleman's legitimate daughter, than a king's bastard.

Throughout the negotiation, Paget was kept informed of proceedings so he could discuss them with François, Marguerite or the Admiral of France, in such a way as to throw failure of progress onto the French. François protested to Paget how much he loved Henry and wished for alliance, but surely his friend could not want him to marry his son to a bastard? There was more to-ing and fro-ing, about Mary's status and the dowry versus the pension arrears. François said he had offers from the emperor and the pope, but would not listen to them until Henry had denied him. Eventually, François decided that money mattered more than the place of Mary in the English succession – he perhaps thought it unlikely Henry would have more children. He gave Marillac consent to negotiate with Mary coming after legitimate children, provided the arrears were wiped out forever. Mary would also be assigned a large dower for life, and she and Orléans would hold the appanage of Milan in survivorship, heritable by their heirs male. The flaw in the plan was, of course, that Milan was firmly in the grip of the emperor, and Henry would need to provide military assistance for its capture. Meanwhile, the faction in France that favoured the Imperial connection was promoting the marriage of their Princess Marguerite with Charles, and Orléans with the Infanta Maria. In an effort to promote Franco-Imperial warmth, Mary of Hungary sent her brother-in-law, François, two wild boars, for which he expressed gratitude to Queen Eleonora, saying that he would not have had them but for her.

Marillac outlined the latest French offers. Henry, asking Marillac to take his response 'in good part' responded that even when François and Charles had been so close 'as to seem one' he would not have accepted such a derisory offer. François seemed to be seeking financial gain, rather than amity. To be fair to Henry, his current offer of a dote of 200,000 crowns for a younger son was very reasonable. To Marillac's response that accepting the French terms would enhance his daughter's status, and there was a good chance that Mary's children would inherit the French throne, Henry responded that he loved his daughter well, but he loved himself and his honour more. Perhaps one occasion when Henry truly knew himself! As she was a king's daughter, and Orléans a king's son, they were equal. The possibility that he might, if the marriage came off, arrange it so that only one boy stood between Mary and the throne should add to her value.[7] Besides, the dauphin was married and might have children yet, and in any event, he wanted a duke for a son-in-law, not the king of France. This was certainly true – Henry had never wanted Mary to take a kingdom with her to a foreign sovereign. It had been just about bearable in the 1520s, when she might have been empress, but having gone through so much to preserve his kingdom from the threat of foreign domination, he would not go back now.

Mary was severely ill during March and April of 1542. Henry put his own physicians at her service but in early April she still suffering with 'palpitations of the heart' and was considered in danger of her life. On 22 April Chapuys wrote to Mary of Hungary that the princess's health was still giving cause for grave concern. The heart palpitations might suggest a chest infection or even perhaps post-traumatic stress disorder – which may sound far-fetched, but her symptoms are consistent with it, and it is a syndrome that can afflict people after repeated trauma, as well as after one-off events. The stress of her submission, and the executions of so many of Mary's friends and supporters can hardly be characterised as anything less than trauma.[8] Marillac was also aware of her illness. He reported that she had had a fever since Easter, and sometimes lay 'as one dead'.[9] Towards the end of the month, her health began to improve and by 4 May, she was sufficiently recovered to write to Chapuys, thanking him for the letters he had sent during her illness.

Charles wrote to Chapuys, asking him to promote an offensive alliance against France. He did not think that François had ever been serious about the Mary–Orléans marriage, only wanted it to escape his debts, and perhaps usurp the English throne. Nothing must be said by Chapuys that might injure Mary, such as discussing her legitimacy, and efforts must be redoubled to obtain Henry's aid against the Turk.

On 5 May, Southampton, Gardiner and Wriothesley put forward Henry's final offer to France. Mary, although a prospective heiress, and only marrying a second son, would be offered the same dote as her aunt Mary had taken to Louis XII, or as she would have taken to the dauphin François, provided she received a corresponding dower. The pensions were to be dealt with separately. The idea that his pension should be settled on the couple was an outrage – effectively, Henry would be providing both dote and dower. If François really had any intention of letting the marriage go forward, he should accept this reasonable offer. Assuming Henry was genuine, it was an excellent offer. Long and tedious discussions about the debts, the life pension, and the personal pension continued, but nothing was resolved. Marillac wrote to François that the English were being completely unreasonable, and going back on early promises regarding acquittance of the arrears. Negotiations once again were at an impasse.

Chapuys thought Henry was well-disposed towards yet another invasion of France. He noted that the French, in all their negotiations, had been careful not to deny the pension or refuse outright to pay it, lest that push Henry straight into Charles's arms. He asked Mary of Hungary to provide him with firm instructions, although, given that Henry, once enthused, would throw himself into something, they should agree principles and confirm details later. He advised Mary of Hungary not to refer to Henry in her handwritten letters as '*bel oncle*', as that only reminded Henry of the whole annulment nightmare. Even if the marriage had been legitimate, the relationship had ceased on Katharine's death. Nor should she refer to Mary as 'princess of England', as Henry had a son and heir. Mary of Hungary agreed that both she and the emperor would be accommodating in these small points.

Mary was frustrated. She was twenty-six years old – ten years past the age at which she might have expected to be married. According to Marillac, she told one of her ladies (probably the same one who was reporting information to Chapuys, as she was married to a Frenchman) that it was 'folly' to think a marriage would ever be arranged for her, either at home or abroad, so long as her father lived. If one were arranged, it would most likely be to France, as the government would prefer to write off the debt, rather than actually hand over a dowry elsewhere. But she was sure there would be nothing but fine words and while Henry lived, she would be only Lady Mary, the most '*malheureuse*' lady in Christendom. *Malhereuse* can be translated as either 'unfortunate' or 'unhappy'. Either might reflect Mary's feelings.[10] Marillac was sure now that Mary would not be allowed to leave England, recounting that Henry had once told him that he could consider Henry as 'demented' if he ever gave Mary to Charles. He thought a more likely outcome was the marriage of Mary to one of the sons of Ferdinand, with the couple being granted the duchy of Bedford and the earldom of Richmond, and settling in England. Henry did not want a great man for his son-in-law, or one with foreign resources. On the other hand, this too, might just be window-dressing.

Regardless of the state of marital negotiations, Henry and Mary were on the best of terms in the autumn of 1542. He dined with her and Elizabeth on 17 September, gave her some fine jewellery, and, according to Chapuys, was very 'flattering' towards her. Chapuys thought an increase in Mary's happiness was caused by the news that Mary of Hungary had repelled the French who had crossed into her territory, but that might have been wishful thinking on his part.

Conflict had broken out again in Navarre and the truce between England and Scotland was breaking down. James would not visit England until his queen was delivered of her current pregnancy and then would only go as far as York. Henry would not accept those terms and intended to march against his northern neighbour, not even desisting when James's mother, Henry's sister, Margaret, died in October.

Towards the end of December, Chapuys reported that Henry, who had been depressed since the execution of Katheryn Howard, had been marvellously perked up by victories against the Scots. His army had won a victory at Solway Moss, and James V had died shortly after, leaving a week-old baby girl, Mary, as his heir. Henry welcomed this as the opportunity he had always dreamed of to dominate Scotland. A marriage between the little Queen of Scots and Prince Edward was suggested and Henry was to pursue this idea vigorously for the rest of his reign.

Friendship

... most noble and most beloved lady ...

Queen Katherine Parr to Mary

While Christmas cheer had not been anticipated for 1542, because of Henry's depression, he brightened up and gave orders for Mary and a great suite of ladies to come to Hampton Court for the feast. Workman were labouring night and day on her apartments at the palace to refurbish them.[1] Chapuys thought Henry so cheerful that remarriage might be on his mind, although he had not heard any gossip on the subject. On 21 December 1542, Mary entered London and rode through the city, greeted in 'triumphal manner', on her way to Hampton Court. Most of the gentlemen of the court rode out to receive her, and her father met her as she entered the park. Pleased to see her, Henry spent some time talking 'graciously' to her.

For New Year, he gave her presents of jewellery and plate, including two large rubies. For previous years, Mary's accounts only show that gifts were given and received, but for New Year 1543, there are copious details, which make it apparent that Mary was worth courting. Starting with gifts from those closest to her, her father gave her two long girdles of goldsmith's work, with pomanders; a rosary of lapis lazuli with a heart at the end; another rosary of garnets and gold; a mirror, in a gold frame set with diamonds and rubies; two large rubies, plate and three pictures, framed in gold. Prince Edward's gift to Mary, presumably selected by Lady Bryan, was a gold tablet, and a silver and gilt standing cup. Elizabeth gave her a chain and a pair of gold and silk hose, while Margaret Douglas presented a gown in Venetian style of carnation satin. Her other cousin, Frances, Lady Dorset, sent a smock and handkerchiefs, while Frances's stepmother, Katherine, Duchess of Suffolk, sent a gold salt, a pair of embroidered sleeves and 'embroidered pullers out' for an Italian-style gown. Lady Baynton, hopefully somewhat over the grief of her sister, Queen Katheryn's, death, presented white damask. Other gifts Mary received included artificial flowers, a silver and gilt pepper box and a combcase worked with pearls. Sleeves were popular gifts; Lady Calthorpe sent two pairs, one of gold with lace, and the other of worked silver, while Lady Lisle sent another embroidered pair. Lady Shelton sent two cushions. Mrs Brayes gave a desk – a lockable, portable box which opened to create a writing-slope. Most valuable of all was the gift from the Earl of Hertford and his wife – a diamond ring and another pair of sleeves. A more exotic present, from 'three Venetians', was a looking-glass. Then as now, handkerchiefs were the last resort for the unimaginative – 'my young lady of Norfolk', probably the Countess of Surrey, sent half a dozen, as did Mrs Chamberlayne and Lady Russell. Perhaps more welcome was the £40 sent by the old Bishop of Exeter. Lord Morley, a scholar (although not, according to modern historians, a particularly able one) and an admirer of Mary's scholarly prowess, gave her a book. He sent books each year, including a manuscript of a commentary by Richard Rolle, a fourteenth century mystic, on the Psalter, accompanied with a letter apologising for sending her an old book, but thinking that her 'high and excellent wit' would appreciate the content, rather than the cover. Another of his gifts was a translation of Erasmus' *Paean Virgini Matri dicendus*.[2]

Mary herself, as well as the cash given to servants delivering presents, spent £70 on gold and plate for gifts and another 70s on a gold brooch for Margaret Douglas. She also had a book edged with gold to give to Edward, who, aged five, was probably learning to read. Mary does not show much evidence of interest in needlework. Marillac's report that she seldom sat down when indoors suggest a nature too restless for close work. Nevertheless, like all women of the time, she did some and in January 1543, she paid 5s to one of Lady Derby's servants for drawing a design for her. The usual New Year's tips were given to the various household departments, with the musicians especially mentioned – luters, sackbut-players, recorder-players, the Welsh minstrels and the harpist. The king's juggler received 20d. Even in January, Mary received presents of fruit, and also paid for oranges, which must have been shipped from Spain.

Mary kept abreast of events, either by talking to her father, or keeping her ear to the ground and networking with her wide circle of friends. She informed Chapuys on 1 January that she did not think that discussions with France were well enough advanced to disrupt any agreement with the emperor. She later added that Henry had told the French he did not seek a quarrel with them but, if François started to interfere in Scotland, one could be found. She thought she was again being offered to Orléans, as it was being said the French were less picky than the Imperialists and would take her as a bastard.

The court left Hampton Court and progressed to Syon and then Whitehall, Mary perhaps riding the gelding delivered by the servant of Henry's Master of the Horse, Sir Anthony Browne. Her ladies were conveyed on horses provided by Katherine Suffolk.

Mary was now in high favour with Henry, and during the early months of 1543, new lodgings were completed for her at Whitehall. They were situated to the south of the main palace complex, at the end of the long river gallery that extended from the privy steps, where the court could enter the barges that were the principal means of transport between the palaces along the Thames. The construction benefited from the most up-to-date architecture and comprised a courtyard house, with the windows overlooking the river. The first-floor windows were a series of oriels, cantilevered over the supporting buttresses, with further windows in the flat surfaces between.[3] Mary took a personal interest in the construction, and tipped the workmen 3s 4d as the building was completed in February 1543. The construction of the lodgings was hardly the work of a few weeks so we can be certain that Henry's affection for Mary, and perhaps loneliness following the execution of Katheryn Howard, led him to seek his daughter's companionship. Henry was visiting Mary two or three times a day in late February and treating her generously and affectionately. Chapuys took this to be intended, at least in part, as a compliment to Charles. Others have interpreted it as a dawning interest in one of Mary's friends, Katherine Parr, Lady Latimer. It is not clear whether Lady Latimer, whose mother, Maud Parr, had been one of Katharine of Aragon's ladies, had an official position in Mary's household or was just visiting. Her sister, Anne Herbert, had been one of Jane Seymour's ladies and was now with Mary, so that might have been the original motivation for visiting. An entry in Mr Scutt's book for 16 February, shows an order for £8 9s 5d headed 'My Lady Latymer', paid by the royal treasury. The clothes included gowns in the French, Italian and Venetian styles, as well as Venetian sleeves and French hoods. There were also items of cotton and linen, and tippets. Halfway down, is the note 'for your daughter'. This has given rise to speculation that Lady Latimer either had an official post in Mary's household, and was ordering clothes on her behalf, or that some of the clothes might have been for herself, a gift from Henry. There is no record of payment of wages to Lady Latimer and on the date of the bill she was still married. Generally married women only held posts in the royal households if their husbands did, which was not the case here. Katherine might have made the list for Mary as a friend but is unlikely that in such a case Katherine or Scutt would have written 'for your daughter', as a reference to Mary. First, Henry would not have seen the bill personally so 'your daughter' would not make sense and second, both Henry and Mary would have been referred to more formally as 'His Majesty' and 'the Lady Mary's Grace'. A more plausible explanation is that Henry was giving Lady Latimer a gift, and that she was ordering the clothes for herself and her stepdaughter, Margaret Neville. Gifts from the king to courtiers, even of clothes, were not unusual, but the scale of this one suggests a particular interest in Lady Latimer.

Easter that year fell in March, and Mary was still with the court, taking the sacrament on Maundy Thursday as was her custom. In April, she again had blood let, but perhaps it was intended as a prophylactic, as her women did the same. If she were ill, the ordering of a new gold girdle and pomander may have cheered her up as may have the gift of a spaniel from one of the yeomen of the chamber.

Paget took his leave of François, who was extremely cross that the ambassador was departing without a replacement having arrived – something which might smack of warlike intent. Paget assured him that he had been promised recall within a year as he suffered from sciatica and an 'infirmity not meet to be named' which made riding difficult. Perhaps haemorrhoids – a hazard of the high protein diet of the time! Nevertheless, the Dean of York was to be sent in his stead. François calmed a little, but said he knew the emperor wanted to marry Mary so that Henry would have to turn on François, whereas if she married Orléans, Henry would both receive money and remain friends with the emperor.

Henry was busy with Scotland – he was treating not only for the marriage of Edward with Queen Mary, but also for a marriage between Elizabeth and Governor Arran's son. Although neither of these marriages eventuated, the speed with which a marriage treaty for Edward and Mary of Scotland was agreed shows that, where the parties were willing, an accommodation could soon be reached. This leads inevitably to the conclusion that neither side ever truly intended that Mary would marry Orléans or the emperor.

Towards the end of May, an old suitor of Mary's reappeared in London – Philip of Bavaria. He assured Henry's council that the Lutheran princes had agreed that if the Elector of Saxony died, he himself would accede to that position. There is no record of whether he saw Mary again, but it is unlikely, as the council seemed unimpressed by his offers, and sent him away with a present of 2,000 crowns.

Again in June, there were repeated payments by Mary for strawberries – she obviously loved them. She was staying in Beddington, probably at Carew Manor, which had been forfeited to the Crown on the execution of Sir Nicholas. That month, she lost a wager to one of her doctors, and paid out £10 – an enormous sum, but, frustratingly, there is no record of the subject of the bet. During the month, she went to Greenwich and visited Edward at Havering. She sent for the doctor again, not, this time for herself, but for her laundress, Beatrice ap Rice. Jane the Fool, too, was sick that summer, and had her treatment paid for by Mary.

In late June, Katherine Parr, widowed since March, and her sister Anne, Lady Herbert, were still with Mary. Elizabeth was also with her half-sister. By now, Katherine's presence was definitely related to Henry's interest in her, although she herself preferred Thomas Seymour, brother of the late Queen Jane. But a king's request is a command, and Katherine had little option but to accept Henry's offer of marriage. Mary was present on 12 July in the Queen's Closet at Hampton Court as her father went through his sixth wedding ceremony. Elizabeth; Lady Margaret Douglas; Katherine, Duchess of Suffolk; Anne, Countess of Hertford; Jane, Lady Dudley, and Lady Herbert were also there.

If her father had to marry at all, it is likely that Mary was pleased by the choice of her friend, rather than an unknown foreign bride with whom she might have had nothing in common. She may also have reflected that since Katherine had been twice married, with no children, it was unlikely that any children would be born from her marriage to Henry, to displace Mary. With a queen in situ, Mary could permanently reside with the court as she had done from December 1536 until the death of Jane, and again during the period of Anne of Cleves's queenship and part of that of Katheryn Howard. Once Katherine was elevated to royalty, who could be a better companion than Mary, who was already her friend? This was borne out in a letter by Chapuys of 13 August in which he commented that Henry continued in his good treatment of Mary, and that he kept her with the queen who showed her 'all affection'. Elizabeth was housed with Edward. At ten, she was too young to be always at court.

It has often been said that Katherine reconciled Henry to Mary. While Katherine undoubtedly fostered good relations within her new family, we have seen that Mary and her father had largely enjoyed a good relationship since her submission to his authority in 1536 and Mary already took part in court life. Similarly, the ladies who surrounded Katherine as queen – Lady Hertford, Lady Suffolk, Lady Lisle and others – were already on terms of friendship with Mary. It is more likely that the princess introduced them to her new stepmother, who had spent most of her life away from court. This is not to detract from the happiness that Katherine's presence in the royal family brought to Henry and all his children.

In early September, Mary again fell very ill, this time with what Chapuys described as a 'colic'. Nevertheless, he thought her best medicine had been good news of the emperor's success in Guelders. Charles followed up his military success by sending an envoy to Henry in December 1543 to treat of an invasion of France. Don Ferdinand de Gonzaga had instructions to pay the emperor's respects to Queen Katherine and to Mary, and thank Katherine for her attentions to his cousin. He was also to try to visit the prince and enquire as to the boy's health – no doubt from the kindest of motives.

In late 1543, Parliament agreed what was to become the Act of Succession of 1544. This reflected the negotiating position Henry had taken with regard to Mary since 1536. She was named as successor after Edward, should he have no children; and any further legitimate children Henry might have, whether male or female. By establishing the matter in Parliament, it closed off any opportunity for further argument by prospective suitors. Similarly, if Mary died childless, Elizabeth was to succeed. Neither Mary nor Elizabeth was to be regarded as legitimate, but their position in the succession could only be undone by an Act of Parliament, and it was on this Act that Mary later based her claim to the throne. Katherine has long been credited with Mary's return to a fixed place in the succession, but the whole course of the discussions for potential marriages, and Mary's presence at court during his previous marriages do not support this. While Katherine undoubtedly bore Mary goodwill and affection, Mary's place in the Act was not her doing.

Mary spent Christmas and New Year of 1543 to 1544 with her father and Katherine at Hampton Court. The usual extravagant presents were exchanged. Mary had expended considerable thought, as well as cash, on her gifts. For her father, increasingly immobile, she had ordered a chair, covered with panels of embroidery. Katherine received a jewel and an embroidered cushion, and Edward had a clock. On New Year's Day, Mary stood as godmother to one of the children of Sir Thomas Wriothesley.

The court was back at Whitehall in February, and received the Duke of Najera. He waited on the king, who gave him a half-hour audience before going to the queen's chamber, where Katherine, Mary, Lady Margaret Douglas and other ladies were waiting. The company danced for several hours, the queen first, with her brother, the Earl of Essex, and then Mary and Lady Margaret with various other gentlemen. Presents were given to the duke from the queen, after which he kissed her hand, and then attempted to kiss Mary's. Mary offered her lips instead – this was a great honour, as although the duke was a grandee of Spain, he had only the most distant blood relationship with her. His secretary described Mary:

> The Princess Mary has a pleasing countenance and appearance. It is said of her that she is endowed with very great goodness and discretion, and among other praises I have heard of her is this, that she knows how to conceal her acquirements; and certainly this is no small proof of prudence ... This Princess is so much beloved throughout the kingdom, that she is almost adored. The dress she wore was a petticoat of cloth-of-gold, and gown of violet-coloured, three-piled velvet, with a headdress of many rich stones.[4]

In April 1544, Chapuys wrote to Prince Philip, Charles's son, passing on the congratulations of the king, queen and princess, on his marriage the previous

November to his cousin, Maria Manuela of Portugal. Eager to maintain familial relations, Philip and his wife requested news of Henry and Mary, and from time to time asked Chapuys to visit Mary on their behalf. Philip's sister, Infanta Maria of Spain, sent Mary a present of Spanish gloves, having heard that her cousin was fond of them.

War between the emperor and Henry on the one side, and the French on the other, was imminent. In hopes of averting it, François sent a large and valuable ring to Boulogne, to be given to either Henry's wife or daughter, but to no avail as Henry planned a grand assault.

The closeness of Mary and Katherine is evident in a joint letter to Anne, Countess of Hertford. Lady Hertford had been one of Katharine of Aragon's ladies, was sister-in-law to Queen Jane, and Mary was godmother to Lady Hertford's daughter. The letter was begun by Mary, then finished by Katherine. Mary apologised for not writing in her own hand, saying she had again been ill. She continued that she had passed on the countess's letters to Katherine, who had received them well. The context suggests Lady Hertford had been concerned that she would not see her husband before Henry left for the campaign he intended to prosecute in France. Katherine chided Lady Hertford slightly for not trusting that she would keep her promise. Katherine and Lady Hertford later quarrelled bitterly – this letter may hint that they were never very close.

Fortunately, Mary was well enough by the end of June to take part in the festivities surrounding the marriage of Lady Margaret Douglas to the Earl of Lennox on 29 June 1544. The prince and Elizabeth were also in attendance. Five courses were served, of numerous dishes each, followed by a 'void' – a collection of sweetmeats and wine consumed after leaving the table. Mary's gifts to her cousin included a 'balas' (a type of ruby) with a diamond and three small pearls suspended from it.

***

In early July 1544, Henry landed at Calais, ready to invade France, having left Katherine behind as regent, as thirty-one years before, he had left Mary's mother. By the end of the month, to enable him to concentrate on the English threat, François was suggesting peace with Charles, with the Infanta Juana, whom he would take 'in her smock', if necessary, to be married to Orléans with the grant of Milan. Charles was initially reluctant but, eventually, Queen Eleonora patched up a peace between her husband and her brother, affirmed in the Treaty of Crèpy. England and France continued at war. Henry wrote to Katherine from the siege of Boulogne, which he was conducting himself, sending his blessings to all his children, and to Margaret Lennox. Once the town was captured, Henry returned to England, leaving it heavily guarded.

In the period 1544–1545, a number of portraits of the royal family were painted. One, that of Mary by Master John, may date from November 1544, as there is a payment of £5 possibly relating to it in her accounts – a larger sum than she would have given as a tip, if the painting were commissioned by her father. In the painting, Mary is sumptuously dressed in a gown of orange figured brocade, with her red velvet sleeves drawn back to show exquisitely stitched lawn undersleeves, embroidered with gold and black thread. On her head is a hood in the fashionable French style, placed far enough back for her blonde hair to show. The slight kinks in the hair suggest a natural curl, firmly suppressed for the sake of elegance. Her eyes, which are gazing over the viewer's left shoulder, are blue under finely arched, fair brows. Her round face, small mouth and receding chin are consistent with Marillac's description of 1541.

Master John lacked the skill of his contemporary, the great Hans Holbein – there is little psychological depth to the portrait, so while it is a thing of beauty, both for the richness of the clothes, and also for the glowing ultramarine background, it does not give any insight into Mary's character – only her status. Behind her, gold lettering reads 'Anno Domini 1544. Ladi Mari, daughter to the most vertuous Prince, Kinge Henri the Eight. The age of XXVIII yeres'. Another painting from the period is the huge mural, now at Hampton Court, which was perhaps intended to reflect the new Act of Succession. In the centre, under the cloth of estate, sits Henry, with Jane Seymour, rather than Katherine Parr, painted as his queen. He has his arm on the shoulders of the prince. Mary and Elizabeth are to the right and left, respectively, both excluded from the cloth of estate, Mary a little taller than her eleven-year-old half-sister. There are also paintings of Prince Edward, Queen Katherine and Lady Elizabeth from around this time.

On 27 December 1544, Chapuys went to court with his new colleague, Van der Delft. They were summoned for audience on the morning of Sunday 28th. They waited for Henry as he passed to his oratory for Mass, and handed him their latest missives from Charles. Having spoken to Henry, they went to the queen's oratory, where they thanked Katherine for her kindness to Mary. Mary herself was there, and was 'humbly thankful' for the emperor's enquiries after her wellbeing. Chapuys and Van der Delft returned to Henry who they thought was showing a marked decline since his return from Boulogne, signalled first by him omitting to ask after the emperor's health. Henry then repeated very loudly that the French had been thoroughly trounced at land and sea. Unfortunately, he and the emperor were now at odds as to how to conduct the peace and he and Chapuys quarrelled vigorously. Eventually, the king said there was no point in continuing their 'wrangling' and the envoys could discuss the matter with his Council the following day. Chapuys, in his report to Charles suggested Henry was confused as to the timings of various events, but we should bear in mind that he had to justify himself to his master for quarrelling with a foreign monarch. Not unreasonably, Henry was offended that, having entered a war with Charles against France, the emperor had once again made peace with François before Henry's aims had been satisfied, and was failing to support him in the maintenance of Boulogne.

Henry therefore looked for other allies and, as in 1539, turned to the German princes. Christopher Mount, Henry's envoy to the princes there, had met with the Landgrave of Hesse. They talked of a general league and it was suggested that Mary should marry Prince Adolphus of Denmark, Duke of Holstein (a duchy in Denmark). This would combine England, the German princes and Denmark into a firm alliance against pope, France and Spain. While he was there, Mount saw the letters that were being sent by the pope to call the prelates to the Council of Trent, scheduled to begin on 25 May. This was causing concern in the Lutheran states of the Empire as Charles's concessions to them were to lapse on the convening of a General Council.

In late January 1545 Mr Bucler, Katherine's secretary, and Christopher Mount, were again sent to Germany. They were to go to Maurice, Elector of Saxony, who had sent word to Henry that he was prepared to support him against France. Maurice was seconded in this by his father, the Landgrave of Hesse. Bucler and Mount were to pay the usual compliments, then refer to the previous failed efforts to agree a religious settlement, which, if now handled more carefully, would be bound to succeed as they had a common enemy in the Bishop of Rome. If the matter of Philip of Bavaria's suit for Mary came up, the English were to say that Duke Philip had been unable to meet Henry's conditions, so the matter had dropped. He would not be considered again, but Henry would lend an ear to any other matrimonial suggestions for her. They had a letter also for the landgrave, answering his suggestion regarding a marriage with the Duke of Holstein. Henry had two daughters, they were to explain, both well-educated and suitable to be married to a prince 'of the highest honour'. They both had a place in the succession, and so honourable offers needed to be made by Denmark, on the principle that Henry always adhered to, of the gentleman seeking the lady. The terms required for Mary were higher than those for Elizabeth, so it was inadvisable for the duke to fix on Mary unless he could meet them.

At the end of March, Henry sent word to François, that they should combine against Charles, who was seeking to ruin them both. If the French king agreed, he would marry Mary to Orléans, and they would be likely to take the crown as Edward was weak. But François was not interested. He wanted the return of Boulogne, and began to raise a force to invade England. In the meantime, he sent aid to the Scots, who were close to collapse in the face of English aggression, led by the Earl of Hertford.

Chapuys was finally recalled as ambassador. During his long service in England, his health had markedly deteriorated. He requested audience to take his leave and a time of 10am on 9 May 1545 was appointed. He arrived an hour early and waylaid Katherine and Mary in the garden. Katherine declared her desire to remain on good terms with the emperor, and sent her compliments to Mary of Hungary, then tactfully withdrew to allow Mary and Chapuys to talk. And so Mary said goodbye to a man who had been first her mother's champion, and then her own, for sixteen weary years. Chapuys never forgot his first duty was to the emperor, whose interests were not always consistent with Mary's, although she may not have realised it. But so far as possible, he influenced his master, and the successive regents of the Netherlands, to consider Mary in their negotiations. By keeping Mary's plight in the early 1530s at the forefront of Charles's mind, he probably made her lot better in England than it might otherwise have been. Personally, Chapuys's dispatches give the impression that he liked Mary, and admired her intelligence, her courage and her resourcefulness. His successor Van der Delft inspired no confidence in Mary at all.

* * *

Writing messages and notes of affection in friends' Books of Hours was common practice among both men and women. There are two example of this practice by Mary, in the period prior to being stripped of her title. The first is in the Book of Hours of the Virgin where her 1527 translation of the prayer of Thomas Aquinas is inscribed. The recipient is unknown, but the message reads:

> I have read that nobody liveth but he [...] but he that followeth virtue and by reckoning you to be one of them, I pray you remember me in your devotions. Mary, Princess.

The second, rather longer note, is in another breviary and sounds like the words of a more mature writer. The content suggests it may date from the period just before she was stripped of her household and title – it may even have been a parting message to one of the ladies who was dismissed in December 1533.

> Create you such riches as when the ship is broken away, swim away with the Master (Christ). For diverse chances take away the goods of fortune, but the goods of the soul, which be only the true goods, neither fire nor water can take away. If you take labour and pain to do a virtuous thing, the labour goes away and the virtue remains. If through pleasure you do any

vicious thing, the pleasure goes and the vice remains. Good madam, for my sake, remember this. Your loving mistress, Mary, Princess.[5]

Mary's warm affection for Katherine is shown in a similar handwritten message in Katherine's prayer book. This book, preserved at Elton Hall, near Peterborough, consists of *Psalms or Prayers Taken out of Holy Scripture*, published by Thomas Bertelet in 1544, and a copy of Cranmer's *Litany*, bound together later. Mary's inscription is in the latter, and reads,

Madam, I shall desire Your Grace to accept this rude hand and unworthy, whose heart and service unfeignedly you shall be sure of, during my life continually. Your most humble daughter and servant, Mary.[6]

The presence of Mary's loving and respectful message in Cranmer's *Litany* suggests that the stereotype of Mary as wedded to the ancient forms of Catholicism, with no flexibility in her approach, may not give a true picture of her feelings. The *Litany*, published in 1544, was the first authorised service in English. It could not be called a Protestant service – Cranmer's biographer, MacCulloch identifies clearly that it was largely a translation of the old Sarum rite, but it was a move away from conservative Catholicism, to a more evangelical stance.[7] So long as the changes to religion did not undermine the Mass, Mary seemed able to accept her father's religious innovations. Henry's religion, while still fundamentally Catholic, had come a long way from the mediaeval construct of his childhood. It had been influenced by the reformers, although the king still resisted any overt Lutheranism. Most of all, it reflected the Erasmian world of the 1520s, where Mary, too, seemed comfortable but, by the early 1540s, Henry's view was more conservative than it had been ten years before. *The King's Book,* promulgated in 1543, was Henry's own exposition of faith, that he thought suitable not just for his own subjects, but also for the Scots, whom he urged to accept it.

In 1545, Nicholas Udall, a graduate of Winchester and Corpus Christi, Oxford, put forward his project for the translation from Latin to English of Erasmus' *Paraphrases on the New Testament* to Katherine, whose interest in religious evangelicalism was increasing. She took up the project enthusiastically and involved Mary in it. The Paraphrases were retellings of the Bible, rather than translations, intended to help the educated, Latin-speaking lay readers of the time, who had an increasing hunger for spiritual guidance, to understand their faith. Erasmus began the *Paraphrases* in the decade after 1517. Not originally intended as a complete work, he undertook each part piecemeal, first the Epistles, then, at the urging of the cardinal of Sion, the Gospel of Matthew. The Gospel of John was requested by the Archbishop of Mainz and dedicated to Archduke Ferdinand. Erasmus observed he had struggled with John, because it is the only one of the Gospels that attempts to explain the divine as well as the human nature of Christ. He followed up with Luke, Mark and Acts by 1524. After their initial publication in 1524, Erasmus made a number of changes and alterations and two new versions were published in 1534 and 1535. Henry had a copy, which he read closely – there is one of the manicules (little pointing fingers) that he used to emphasise passages, indicating Erasmus' confirmation that Christ was really present in the bread and wine of the Mass.

Just as Erasmus had wanted to make the Gospel more accessible to the educated, so Katherine wanted to make it available to lay people who spoke only English. Each paraphrase was to be translated by a different individual. Mary, the only woman among the translators, was requested to undertake that of John. We can infer from this that Mary's skill in Latin was considered of a sufficiently high standard to undertake such a complex and significant work. There are no records in her accounts of her continuing to take Latin lessons as an adult, so either she studied by herself, or her grounding had been so thorough that she could take it up again after more than ten years. The other translators were Udall, who took Luke, which he had completed by September 1545, and Thomas Keys, who translated Mark. The translator of Matthew and Acts is unknown.

Mary was unable to complete her section, owing to illness. Udall wrote that only when she had 'with overpainful study of labour and writing, cast her weak body in a grievous and long sickness' had she given the work to be 'made complete' by another.[8] It has been suggested that Katherine asked Mary to do the translation as a way of encouraging her down the road of reform, and that Mary took refuge in illness as a way of avoiding it. However, we know that Mary had no objection to the Bible in English in principle (a new edition was planned before her death), and later, when queen, she took possession of Katherine Parr's own copy of the Bible in English and French. Erasmus had been one of the great influences on her own education – these very Paraphrases had been on Vives' reading list, and much admired by her mother. Other evidence that she was frequently ill, and that her ailment affected her ability to write are too prevalent not to accept her inability to complete the work as genuine. It was finished by Francis Malet, chaplain first to Katherine, then to Mary herself. That they shared a chaplain suggests Mary and Katherine's views on religion had not diversified markedly by this point. Malet himself was no reformer – he was later imprisoned during the reign of Edward VI for refusing to use the new, English service rather than continue the Mass as laid down in Henry's reign. How much Mary did and how much Malet finished can never be identified, but Katherine's letter to her of 1545 (or possibly 1547 when the Paraphrases were finally published) suggest Mary did the vast majority of it. This is the view elegantly explained by Aysha Pollnitz in her essay *Religion and Translation at the Court of Henry VIII: Princess Mary, Katherine Parr and the Paraphrases of Erasmus.*[9] Pollnitz mentions some inaccuracies in Mary's work, inferring it had been but lightly edited by Malet or Udall, while also identifying the very broad range of knowledge and understanding that Mary brought to her task.

That Katherine saw Mary as the substantive translator of John is obvious from a letter to her, in which the queen wrote:

> I pray you signify ... whether you wish it to go out most happily into the light under your name. To which work really in my opinion you will be seen to do an injury if you refuse the book to be transmitted to posterity on the authority of your name: for the most accurate translation of which you have undertaken so many labours for the highest good of the commonwealth: and more than these (as is well enough known) you would have undertaken, if the health of your body had permitted. Since none does not know the amount of sweat that you have laboriously put into this work, I do not see why you should reject the praise that all confer on you deservedly.[10, 11]

The state of semi-warfare with France rumbled on, with a marriage between Mary and Orléans, or Edward and Princess Marguerite being considered as a means of peace, but with no real enthusiasm.

Henry and Katherine were at Portsmouth in late July and August, reviewing naval preparations to fend off the expected attack from France. It was then that Henry's great flag-ship, the *Mary Rose*, sank in full view of the court, which probably included Mary, unless she was ill at this juncture. The court travelled back to London via Petworth and Guildford.

In September 1545, another death changed the deck of Mary's potential marital alliances. The Duke of Orléans died, having foolishly entered a house whose inhabitants had died of an infectious disease. Did she regret his passing, as another hope of matrimony, children and a place in Europe was lost, or did she thank God that she would not have to marry a Frenchman, younger than herself, and travel to a distant land? The Duke of Vendôme was put forward as an alternative, but again, nothing came of the discussions.

By September, Henry was so infirm that arrangements were made for many documents to be signed by stamp. Among them that month were a benefice for Richard Baldwin, who had been Mary's chaplain since her household had been formed for her role in the Marches in 1525. The benefice had been granted at the joint suit of Mary and Katherine. There was also a warrant for Mary's clothes.

On 15 October 1545 Henry sent Gardiner to Flanders to discuss peace. He had a commission to treat for a marriage between Mary and Charles, Edward and Maria of Spain and Elizabeth and Philip of Spain (whose young wife, Maria Manuela of Portugal had died having borne a son, Carlos).

In Flanders, Gardiner discussed the emperor with Chapuys, who was part of the peace discussions. Chapuys informed him that the emperor was 'lustier' than previously, probably meaning in good health, rather than that Charles was becoming excessively amorous. Although perhaps Chapuys's second statement that he had made 'the emperor's mouth to water' at the prospect of marrying Mary, supports the other meaning! On hearing this, Henry instructed Gardiner, that, if the idea of Mary made Charles's mouth water, the match should be pushed forward, although Henry's preferred match was one for Edward. Elizabeth's marriage to Philip was to be promoted to prevent Philip marrying Princess Marguerite. Charles was not enthusiastic about any of the proposals – while he would like to marry his daughter to Edward, he had promised her to Portugal. Perhaps one of Ferdinand's daughters might be suitable – they were 'as goodly babes as ever seen' and of suitable age. He would treat such a marriage as if it were one of his own daughters. As for Philip, he was so upset at the loss of Maria Manuela that he could not be prevailed upon to marry yet, and the emperor himself would not consider remarriage, even to Mary. Henry was happy enough with the thought of a marriage for Edward with one of the archduchesses, and Gardiner was permitted to talk terms in more detail. He was rather suspicious about Philip's reluctance, since he knew there had been discussions about a marriage with Princess Marguerite of France.

While Gardiner had one set of instructions, Paget and Tunstall of Durham had a competing set for negotiation with François, who had hinted he would not treat further for marriages with the emperor, intended to resolve the problems of Savoy and Milan. If that were the case, and François agreed to cede Boulogne, Ardres (a dog hole, in Henry's opinion) and the rest of Guisnes, then Henry might come to terms and similarly cease negotiations for marriages with the Imperial family.

Mary stood as godmother, with Katherine, Duchess of Suffolk, to one of John Dudley, Lord Lisle's, numerous children in late November. The ceremony took place at Suffolk House, and Mary was attended by two of Queen Katherine's maids-of-honour. The godfather was the Imperial envoy, Van der Delft. During the proceedings, Van der Delft and Mary talked, in several languages, in which he noted that she was proficient. She told him her constant prayer was for 'good friendship' between her father and the emperor. Probably true, as well as polite.

On 30 November, Gardiner had to send a sensitive letter to Henry, to be delivered into the king's own hands. In it, he revealed the cause of the emperor's reluctance to treat of marriages with either Mary or Elizabeth. As to the first, the emperor had heard that Henry would not go through with the matter, as he would distrust what Charles might do in England if he were Mary's husband, and as for Elizabeth, her 'qualitas' was insufficient – from which we might infer that he would not marry his son and heir to a bastard. Nevertheless, the match for Edward and one of the nine archduchesses seemed to have all round favour.

During 1546 the first evidence of the warm relationship between Mary and her half-brother, Edward, who was now eight, appears. In mid-January, she received a touching letter from him. He apologised for not writing more frequently, saying he hoped that she did not think he had forgotten her. Affection for her and his (step)mother, Katherine, held the 'chief place in his heart'. He hoped to see her soon. The original was in Latin but this and Edward's other letters to Mary are so much less stilted and complex than those to his father or Queen Katherine that it suggests he actually composed them himself. Mary had spent more time with Edward than any other adult of his family.

In February, Van der Delft reported that when an ambassador from Poland had been received and honoured with a knighthood and a golden collar, Katherine had teased Mary that he had come to negotiate for her hand.[12] In the same letter, Van der Delft passed on a rumour that Henry was seeking to replace Katherine, with the recently widowed Katherine Suffolk. While Delft reported that Henry had shown no alteration in his treatment of her, unsurprisingly, Katherine was said to be annoyed by the rumour.

Charles made an offer for Edward, but Henry considered it so paltry that, offended, he revived negotiations for a marriage for Mary with Philip of Bavaria, who arrived incognito in London at the end of March. Henry wrote to Philip's uncle, the Elector of Saxony that Philip had reminded him of 'the old familiar acquaintance between the ... Elector and us, with the ancient noble family of the Palatines'. This, with Philip's own 'noble qualities' encouraged Henry to seek a 'special amity' between the elector and his confederates, including the Landgrave of Hesse. This would be of great benefit to Christendom. Further, since Mary was now 'made legitimate and heritable to the crown of this realm' ... and she was 'of such reputation in the world thereby, and other the good qualities of her person ... as both the emperor for himself and the French king for his son have much desire to have her and have made great means for the same' they would be honoured to have her. The elector would have to agree with Henry over religion, but, in the king's mind, that should be straightforward as the elector would find Henry's doctrine 'conformable to Holy Spirit'. Since Philip had no lands, no dower would be expected, and the implication was that Mary would have no dote other than her chance of the crown. Nevertheless, Van der Delft and his colleague, Scepperus, thought an alliance with the elector unlikely, as Henry's council was disinclined to provoke Charles.

Despite again being indisposed, Mary received Duke Philip and talked to him for over an hour. He was a Lutheran, and his comment that he had never heard Mass until coming to England made him an unpopular choice with the clergy, and part of the council, although we might suppose that the reform-minded councillors, such as Hertford, and perhaps Queen Katherine who was leaning more and more towards the Reformed faith, were rather pleased with the idea of a Lutheran match. Henry presumably thought that this difficulty would be resolved if Hesse accepted his interpretation of the faith – it is highly unlikely he would have allowed Mary to worship as a Lutheran – and nor would she have done so.[13]

By 11 May, Duke Philip was back home. He wrote to Henry that he had passed on the king's, queen's and Princess Mary's salutations to the elector and electress. He was disappointed matters had not proceeded further and wanted to know what more he could do to bring about the marriage. In the meantime, as agreed, he was mustering troops. It seemed the elector was less inclined to come to terms than Philip. While he was very much in favour of the marriage, the other negotiating points were more difficult. He was not part of the confederation of Lutheran princes, but he was firm in his adherence to the Confession of Augsburg and would not discuss religion further.

Mary received another very sweet letter from her brother in May. In it, he again apologised for not writing very often, and went on to say that he loved her just as much as if he wrote to her frequently. Although he did not wear his best clothes very often, he loved them most, so, although he rarely wrote to her, he loved her best. He added he had heard she had been sick, and was glad she was now better. A letter a few days later to Katherine shows he was as concerned about Mary's soul as about her health. In it, he wrote in elderly tones that probably made both Katherine and Mary laugh out loud, that the queen should discourage Mary from 'attending to foreign dances and merriments, which do not become a most Christian Princess'.

There was a further affectionate epistle from Edward at the end of May. First, he said that her failure to reply to his letter of 8 May was of less concern to him than his sorrow in hearing that she had been too ill to write. He repeated his love for her, and told her not to write unless her health permitted. He then hoped that God would give her the wisdom of Esther, before sending his regards to three of the queen's ladies – Elizabeth, Lady Tyrwhitt; Anne, Lady Herbert, and Maud, Lady Lane. all of whom were of distinctly evangelical temperament.

In May warrants were sent to the Great Wardrobe for clothes for Mary and Elizabeth for Whitsuntide, and for a saddle for Mary. That same month, Mary was listed as customarily part of the queen's household as Elizabeth now was, with their cousins Margaret Lennox, Frances Dorset and Eleanor Clifford.

As Henry's health declined, his ministers were jockeying for position. It was obvious he would not survive until Edward reached his majority, and there would have to be a regency. The two factions have been described as the conservatives, including Gardiner, Norfolk and Norfolk's son, Surrey, with Wriothesley, Cromwell's old colleague, and the reformers, led by Henry's brother-in-law, Hertford, allied with Lord Lisle, Cranmer and Sir William Paget. While the groupings largely reflected religious leanings, this was not a hard and fast division. Surrey was a religious reformer, as was his sister, Mary, Dowager Duchess of Richmond. Throughout the summer and autumn of 1546, the two sides strove for dominance, and Katherine Parr, whose religious beliefs were becoming more radical, was caught in the cross-fire. The conservatives had latched onto Katherine's reforming zeal, and her possible connection with the martyr, Anne Askew. Askew, amongst the most outspoken of the Reformers, had been racked by two of Henry's own councillors – Wriothesley and Rich – before being burnt for heresy. They mounted a campaign to undermine the queen. According to the account in Foxe's *Acts and Monuments*, Katherine's increasingly evangelical stance, and her tendency to pontificate on religion to a husband who believed he had all the answers, was beginning to irritate Henry. He therefore gave permission for Katherine to be arrested. Katherine, getting wind of what was afoot, immediately broke into hysterical weeping, which only ceased when Henry sent to find out what was wrong, and the two were reconciled with Katherine urging her wifely submission. The following day, those who came to arrest her were given short shrift by the king. In her *Katherine the Queen: The Remarkable Life of Katherine Parr*, Dr Linda Porter examines the incident in detail in its wider context.

There is no information about Mary's reaction to the potential loss of yet another stepmother – and a woman she was deeply attached to. Her feelings may have been torn between her affection for Katherine, and her conservative religious sympathies. Mental turmoil may have contributed to the bout of illness she suffered shortly after the incident, in August 1546. She was again too ill to write with her own hand and dictated a reply to the Duke of Albuquerque who had asked her to intervene in a dispute. The letter was signed from Westminster, with the words 'Mary, daughter of England'. This was a clever way to avoid putting any titles in, and was a formula that Anne of Cleves had used to avoid similar difficulties.[14]

Henry may have been angry with Katherine, but Mary still basked in his favour. At the end of July, she received generous gifts of jewellery from him, including two brooches set with the history of Abraham in rubies, diamonds and pearls, and three 'biliments' set with pearls, rubies and diamonds. He also gave her over two hundred loose pearls of assorted sizes.[15]

At the beginning of September, Philip of Bavaria visited yet again, in hopes, according to the French, of either chiselling money out of Henry, or being granted his daughter. While Henry gave a generous gift, and a pension of 3,000 crowns, he would not agree the marriage. As autumn wore on, the king's health declined. He knew he would not live to see Edward grow up, and he could not risk giving Mary any support that might encourage her to try to usurp her half-brother – although there is no evidence that Henry thought Mary had any such ideas and she obviously loved her little brother dearly, and he her. Edward wrote again to Mary on 26th September. In a rather more flowery epistle than he usually sent her, he told her not only that he loved her, but that he would love her even if she were not his sister, because of her 'eminent virtue'. Since virtue is the 'lodestone of love', he must necessarily think of her often, and then write to her, which he hoped she would take kindly. He hoped God would be her shield against all evils.

In November, Mary received another pleasing letter. It was from Maria of Portugal, twenty-six-year-old daughter of her cousin, Queen Eleonora of France. The Infanta wrote that the fame of Mary's virtue and learning made Maria eager to establish a literary correspondence between them. She would write whenever a messenger could be found, and hoped that Mary would respond. Maria was later noted as a great patron of arts. Unusually, she never married.[16]

Mary was popular that month – another letter came from Edward, residing at Hatfield, although this time in response to one of hers. He thanked her for her letter, which showed her 'inexpressible love' and in which she had hoped for his honour and that he would grow and prosper in all 'pietate', which might mean piety, dutifulness or filial love. Presumably, Mary was encouraging her brother in all three!

During his last few months of life, Henry ordered a large consignment of crossbow equipment for hunting. Two dozen arrows were allocated to Mary at Henry's own command, and he also gave her a grey gelding, purchased for £5, suggesting that hunting was a pastime they enjoyed together. In mid-November, Charles's envoy at François' court wrote that Henry's death was now anticipated. The French looked forward to it as an opportunity to take back Boulogne, seeming to believe they would be pitted against Mary, rather than Edward, anticipating dissension in England over who should succeed. Nevertheless, the ordinary life of the court went on. In November, there were warrants for pay for Mary and Elizabeth's gentlewomen and for 'necessaries' for Mary herself as well as warrants for their clothes and those of their women for Christmas. The king's physician provided 'lectuaries' and boxes of 'lozenges' to Mary and to Katherine as well as some rather horrible-sounding medicines, including numerous enemas – perhaps another hint that Mary had digestive problems.

There were few festivities that Christmas. Henry had retired to Whitehall, leaving Katherine and Mary at Greenwich. Mary never saw her father again. The usual New Year gifts were exchanged. Katherine sent portraits of Henry and herself to Edward, and Mary dispatched something that he described in his thank-you letter as 'of great beauty'. Although he expected to see her soon, he still wanted to write to her as he could not but love someone 'ardently' by whom he felt himself so beloved.

On 10 January 1547 the resident French envoys wrote to François that Henry had rallied. His ulcerated legs had been so bad they had had to be cauterised, but although he was now somewhat better, they thought him unlikely to last much longer. Neither Katherine nor Mary had been permitted to see him and, so far as he could tell, they would not be allowed to. He did not speculate on the reasons why not, but we can infer from the rapid takeover of the government after Henry's death by Hertford and his allies, that they were already positioning themselves to take power immediately, lest Mary strive to put herself forward, as queen or perhaps regent. Katherine certainly expected a role – she had been nominated as regent in Henry's will of 1544, should he be killed in France.

On 28 January, early in the morning, Henry died. Initially, the news was kept secret as Hertford swiftly manoeuvred to become Lord Protector, negating the terms of Henry's will, which had provided for a council of equals, and perhaps also to make sure that power was firmly in his hands, if Mary had had any idea of challenging the succession. Before he could have heard of the death of the king, Chapuys wrote to Mary of Hungary that he was convinced the Earl of Hertford and the Admiral, Lord Lisle, meant to take over the government. The only counter-weight to them was Norfolk, and that was the reason for the duke being in the Tower and the execution the previous autumn of his son, Surrey. According to Chapuys, Hertford and Lisle were following in the footsteps of Cromwell, by introducing heresy to unite the realm against the emperor, whereas previously the English had loved him. Since Charles had not intervened in Mary's favour, when he could have done, after the discarding of Katharine of Aragon, it was too late now. Hertford and the admiral were the only members of the government with any ability, and if Henry were to die soon, the affairs of the Empire would be more damaged than if he had died twenty years before. All of which proved to be true, allowing for Chapuys's perspective that deviation from the Catholic Church was to be deplored.

In accordance with custom, Mary did not attend her father's funeral, and there is no information as to who broke the news of his death to her or when or what her immediate reactions were. She probably felt a mixture of grief, relief and trepidation for the future. Perhaps she was simply stunned. Her father had loomed larger than life; his word had been law and he had both loved and bullied her, given her lavish gifts, but destroyed her friends. He had once seemed to acknowledge that she would be his heir, but then snatched the prospect away. He had tantalised her with glimpses of a life free of his tyranny as a prince's wife in a foreign land, and then rejected every possibility before it came to fruition. So fearful was he that she would challenge his male heir that he could not let her out of his sight.

Perhaps Henry's last words to the daughter he had loved in his own strange way, are those inscribed in Katherine Parr's prayer book:

Mine own good daughter, I pray you remember me most heartily when you in your prayers do pray for grace to be attained assuredly to your loving father. Henry R'.[17]

Epilogue

Henry had remade his will. There has been much discussion as to its validity – were elements of it forged, or added later? Henry, whatever his differences with the pope, was born and died a Catholic. He committed his soul to God and requested the prayers of the Blessed Virgin and all the company of heaven. He wanted prayers said for him after his death and for Masses to be said at an altar near his tomb in St George's Chapel, Windsor, in perpetuity. The crown was devolved to Prince Edward, and his heirs and then to any children Henry might yet have by Katherine Parr or any subsequent wife. In default of such, Mary was to inherit, on the condition that she could only marry with the consent of a majority of the surviving Privy Councillors named in his will for Prince Edward. Failing heirs of Mary, Elizabeth was to inherit under similar conditions. If either sister married without such consent, she would lose her rights. If Henry had no grandchildren, the throne was to pass to the heirs of his nieces, the Lady Frances, then the Lady Eleanor. Following them, the succession should pass to his 'right heirs'. Mary and Elizabeth were both left £10,000 or more, as thought fit by the council, for appropriate marriages, and £3,000 per annum for maintenance. The low level of dowry that Henry left for his daughters was probably another sign that he did not wish either of them to attract powerful spouses. £10,000 equated to about 40,000 crowns, and, as we have seen, this was the least dote that Henry had offered with Mary during his lifetime – to Philip of Bavaria. All other matches suggested a dote of at least 400,000 crowns.

Soon, the Privy Council changed the terms of the will, giving control to Hertford, now Duke of Somerset. The provisions relating to Mary and Elizabeth were changed too. Instead of receiving a cash income, Mary was given a huge grant of lands – these included the mighty stronghold of Framlingham Castle, Suffolk. As she rode out of London to begin a new life as one of the richest magnates in the country, Mary may not have realised that the possession of land would enable her to challenge her brother's later attempt to oust her from the succession – the very thing that Henry feared would happen if Mary had too much freedom. Although the challenge was not to Edward himself, but to a usurper, Jane Grey, Henry had perhaps seen in his daughter the courage, the determination, the pride and the will to maintain her rights that her mother and grandmother had displayed. Had he appreciated and nurtured those qualities in her as a young woman, instead of following his blind obsession to have a son, the whole course of English history might have been different.

Appendix A: European States

England

Torn by weak government and civil war for half a century, the country and Crown made a remarkable recovery during Henry VII's reign. By the time of his death in 1509, he had amassed, if not the reputed vast fortune, enough to make the Crown comfortably solvent. He avoided war, and preferred to build up strength through alliances, with Spain, the Low Countries, Scotland, and even France. The population of the country was growing, and beginning to climb back to the levels seen before the Black Death. Trade in wool was creating a new middle class, and government was becoming more professional and secular. When Henry VIII inherited the throne, he hankered for military glory, harking back to the days of Henry V. He pursued an aggressive policy against France in his early days, which had the corollary of creating confrontation with Scotland, of which Henry claimed to be overlord.

Scotland

Scotland, far smaller in population and wealth than England, had long been allied with France. Having suffered repeated minorities during the fifteenth century, it entered a more prosperous and well-governed period under James IV. This came to an abrupt end when James was dragged into the Anglo-French conflict and killed at Flodden, leaving a baby son, and a nobility divided between pro-English and pro-French factions. When James V reached maturity, matters improved but he died suddenly, at the age of thirty, leaving a week-old daughter as his heir. The faction fighting, now extended by religious differences, broke out again.

Rulers during Mary's life

1513–1542 James V – effective rulers included his mother Queen Margaret, the Duke of Albany and the Earl of Angus.

1542–1568 Mary, Queen of Scots, Mary's first cousin once removed – effective rulers the Earl of Arran, and the queen mother, Marie of Guise.

Spain

Spain had been formed by the union of Castile and Aragon on the marriage of Mary's grandparents, Ferdinand II of Aragon and Isabella I of Castile in 1469. They expanded their territories to incorporate the last Moorish kingdom in the Iberian peninsula by 1492, when Mary's mother, Katharine, was seven years old.

In that same year, Isabella's funding of the Italian explorer Columbus bore fruit when he discovered the American continent, which over the succeeding 150 years funded an enormous growth in Spanish power. Despite these fascinating new discoveries to the west, Ferdinand's ambitions remained largely European. He was a talented soldier and general, although he had a reputation for lying and double-crossing his allies. His mission was threefold: to recover Roussillon, a province on the Franco-Aragonese border; to take control of Navarre, to which he had a dubious claim of inheritance, and to maintain Aragonese dominance in Naples. In 1516, a month before Mary's birth, Ferdinand died. His daughter, Mary's aunt Juana, had been Queen of Castile since 1504, but her fragile mental state[1] led to her son, Charles, Duke of Burgundy, being proclaimed as her co-ruler in both Aragon and Castile. Despite being only sixteen at the time of his accession, he ruled for them both, with the title King of Spain coming to be used more widely than King of Castile or Aragon. For simplicity, Spain is generally used in these pages.

Rulers during Mary's life

1504–1555 Juana, Queen of Castile and Aragon, widowed Duchess of Burgundy – excluded from all power and influence. Mary's aunt.

1516–1556 Charles, King of Spain, Duke of Burgundy, Holy Roman Emperor – Mary's first cousin.

1556–1598 Philip II – Mary's first cousin once removed (twice over). Later Mary's husband.

Navarre

The ancient kingdom straddled the Pyrenees. Blanche I of Navarre married Juan II of Aragon in 1420. On her death, her widower refused to hand over power to their son, Charles. Juan remarried, and by his second marriage had

Ferdinand II of Aragon. When Charles died, in suspicious circumstances, the rightful heir was his sister Blanche, but she was held captive by her father and died in custody. She was succeeded by her sister, Eleanor, married to Gaston de Foix. Eleanor did not challenge her father for supremacy, but ruled as 'governor'. She was sworn as queen on Juan II's death, but died herself within two weeks. Her half-brother, Ferdinand II of Aragon, was determined to annexe the country by ousting Eleanor's granddaughter, Catherine. This led to the first rupture in the relationship between Mary's parents. In 1512, when Henry was in alliance with Ferdinand to invade France, Ferdinand diverted all his attention to Navarre, capturing Upper Navarre (south of the Pyrenees). Henry's men were left destitute of food and water, and were obliged to return home dishevelled and half-starving. Navarre was split in 1515, between Upper Navarre, incorporated as a separate kingdom under the Spanish crown, and Lower Navarre, under King Jean and Queen Catherine.

Rulers during Mary's life

Upper Navarre

1516–1556 Charles, King of Spain, Duke of Burgundy, Holy Roman Emperor – Mary's first cousin

1556–1598 Philip II of Spain.

Lower Navarre

1515–1517 Catherine I of Navarre and her husband Jean II d'Albret

1517–1555 Henri II of Navarre

1555–1572 Jeanne III of Navarre

Low Countries/Netherlands/Burgundy

The Low Countries were an agglomeration of smaller dukedoms and counties – Burgundy, Flanders, Hainault, Guelders, Charolais, etc. One of the first regions in Europe to engage in international trade, it was wealthy and influential. The court of Burgundy during the fifteenth century was seen as the arbiter of culture and fashion, a status that by the time of Mary's birth was shifting to France. Burgundy was England's most valuable trading partner; England exported wool in vast quantities for the Burgundian cloth trade. Any hiatus in this trade had extremely damaging effects on the economies of both countries. Within the Low Countries was the once-independent Duchy of Guelders. France's support of Guelders in its efforts to escape Imperial control was a continuing thorn in the side, first of Maximilian, then of Charles.

In 1477, the Burgundian lands were split between Mary, Duchess of Burgundy, and France, which refused to recognise a woman's right of inheritance and took back those territories, held from the French crown.

Following the untimely death of Duchess Mary in 1483, her remaining territories were ruled by her husband, the Holy Roman Emperor Maximilian, and then her son, Philip the Handsome, who was married to Juana of Castile. On Philip's death, leaving a young son, the abovementioned Charles, the regency was taken over by Philip's sister, Marguerite, Archduchess of Austria. Marguerite, who had been briefly married to the son of Ferdinand and Isabella, and was thus sister-in-law to Katharine of Aragon, was one of the most important European figures in the first third of the sixteenth century. Charles spent a good deal of his time passing between the Low Countries and Spain, usually by ship to avoid having to travel through France, a country with which he was almost constantly at war, in word, if not in deed, over their territorial rivalries.

On the death of Archduchess Marguerite, the regency was taken over by Mary, Dowager Queen of Hungary and Bohemia, Charles's sister and Mary's cousin.

Rulers during Mary's life

1506–1556 Charles, Duke of Burgundy, King of Spain, Holy Roman Emperor

1506–1530 Regent – Marguerite of Austria, Dowager Duchess of Savoy – only distantly related by blood. Aunt by marriage through deceased Prince Juan of Spain. Aunt of Mary's maternal cousins.

1530–1558 Regent – Mary of Hungary, Archduchess of Austria, Dowager Queen of Hungary and Bohemia – Mary's first cousin.

France

France was the richest, most powerful, populous and centralised state in Europe. It had incorporated the independent Duchy of Brittany by forcing its duchess, Anne of Brittany, to marry, first, Charles VIII, then Louis XII. On her death in 1514, rather than allowing her territory to pass out of the French crown's hands, her heir, her daughter Claude, was married to the king's own heir, François of Angoulême.

France's kings, Charles VIII, Louis XII and François I, sought to dominate Italy. They had a claim, which they prosecuted vigorously, to the Duchy of Milan. In 1515, François led his troops to a huge victory over the Imperial troops at the Battle of Marignano, one of the major battles of the Italian Wars. The war for Milan dominated the period up until 1525, when Charles's victory at the Battle of Pavia gave him precarious control. The diplomacy of the next twenty years often centred on who should be installed as Duke of Milan – a French or a Spanish ally.

For England, France was still the old enemy. Henry VIII, essentially mediaeval in his outlook, never gave up his dream of reconquering France – emulating in his mind, if not in his achievements, Henry V, who had forced the French to recognise him as heir to their throne.

Rulers during Mary's lifetime
1516–1547 François I – only very distantly related to Mary
1547–1559 Henri II – only very distantly related to Mary, but father-in-law of her paternal first cousin, Mary, Queen of Scots.

The Holy Roman Empire

The Holy Roman Empire was a loose federation of states in modern-day Germany, eastern France, the Netherlands, Switzerland and Austria. The title King of the Romans was granted by election and, once the king had been crowned, he became emperor (strictly, the coronation needed to be performed by the pope to translate the title.) Maximilian of Hapsburg became emperor in 1508. Maximilian was perennially short of money, while having enormous ambition to control Europe and, particularly, to extend his control south of the Alps. His influence over his grandson, Charles, Duke of Burgundy and King of Spain, was strong. Maximilian centred much of his strategy around marital alliances – his son and daughter, Philip and Marguerite, were respectively married to Juana and Juan, the Infantes of Spain; his second grandson, Ferdinand, and his granddaughter, Mary, were betrothed young to Mary and Louis, the children of the king of Bohemia and Hungary. As a second wife for himself, Maximilian chose Bona Sforza, daughter of the Duke of Milan. Charles became emperor in 1519, after a hotly contested competition with François I, and some half-hearted efforts by the English to secure the title for Henry VIII.

Rulers during Mary's lifetime
1493–1519 Maximilian I, Holy Roman Emperor. Only very distantly related to Mary
1519–1556 Charles V, Holy Roman Emperor. Also King of Spain and Duke of Burgundy. Mary's maternal first cousin.
1556–1564 Ferdinand I, Holy Roman Emperor. Also King of Hungary and Bohemia. Mary's maternal first cousin.

Italy

To speak of Italy as a country in the sixteenth century is anachronistic. The Italian peninsula was made up of a number of independent states, as well as the kingdom of Naples, under the control of the crown of Aragon. The republic of Venice was the single richest state, trading with the East as it had for centuries. The central belt formed the temporal lands of the papacy. There were also the duchies of Ferrara and Mantua, the republic of Florence and various other smaller territories. Much of the scandal that surrounded the papacy in the late fifteenth and early sixteenth centuries was created by successive popes' determination to increase their temporal power, and that of their relatives.

The war for control of the peninsula lasted from 1494 to 1559. Milan was the main fighting ground, after Naples had been successfully captured by Ferdinand of Aragon in 1504. Milan, once a republic, had been instituted as a duchy within the Holy Roman Empire in 1395, with Gian Galeazzo Visconti as duke. By 1450, it was in the hands of the Sforzas but, as it had passed through an illegitimate line, it was claimed by Louis XII, based on his descent from the Visconti. Louis won control in 1499, but was ousted by Maximilian. The tables were turned by François I, who carried off the prize, following a decisive victory at Marignano in 1515.

The support by the pope – now of the French, and now of the Empire – tipped the balance from time to time, as did the changing role of Venice. By and large, Venice was pro-French, as it preferred a variety of neighbours on its doorstep, rather than complete encirclement by the Empire. Venice was also suspected of being on too-good terms with the Ottomans, to the detriment of their Christian duty.

Savoy

Savoy was a duchy straddling modern France and Italy. François I's mother, Louise, was the daughter of Philip II, Duke of Savoy. Her brother, Philibert II, who inherited in 1504, married Marguerite of Austria (Maximilan's daughter). The French wished to annex it to maintain their hold over Milan. Philibert and Marguerite had no children, so he was succeeded by his half-brother, Charles III. In an effort to gain protection, Charles III married Beatriz of Portugal, whose sister, Isabella, was married to the Emperor, Charles V. In 1536, France invaded Savoy, and the ensuing struggle for control between France and the Empire continued until the 1559 Treaty of Cateau-Cambrèsis restored the Duchy to Charles and Beatriz' son, Emanuel Philibert.

Rulers during Mary's lifetime
1504–1553 Charles III of Savoy
1553–1580 Emmanuel Philibert of Savoy

Portugal

When Mary was born, Portugal was ruled by Manuel I, who had been married consecutively to her aunts Isabella and Maria of Aragon. Widowed for the second time, Manuel then married the sister of Charles and Ferdinand, Mary's cousin Eleonora. Manuel and Maria's son, João III, married Charles's sister, Catherine of Austria, while their older daughter, Isabella of Portugal, married her cousin, Charles V, and their younger daughter, Beatriz, married the Duke of Savoy. The second brother, Dom Luis, was a suitor for Mary's hand. João and Catherine's daughter, Maria Manuela, married the son of Charles V and Isabella, Philip. Not surprisingly, with all of this cousin inter-marriage, Maria Manuela and Philip's son, Don Carlos, was decidedly peculiar.

Rulers during Mary's lifetime
1516–1521 Manuel I
1521–1557 João III. Mary's maternal first cousin.
1557–1580 Enrique

Hungary & Bohemia

Hungary was in the front line of the war against the encroaching Ottoman Turks. It was an elective monarchy, and at Mary's birth was in the hands of Vladislaus II, who also ruled Bohemia. Vladislaus died in 1516, leaving a greatly weakened state to his son, Louis, betrothed to Maximilian's granddaughter, Mary, Archduchess of Austria. As Louis was only ten, central power declined and the country became vulnerable to attack from Suleiman the Magnificent. Louis was eventually killed at the battle of Mohács in 1526. Rival factions voted for his sister Anne's husband, Ferdinand, Archduke of Austria, (brother of the Emperor Charles V) and for John Zapolya. Ferdinand and Anne fought a non-stop rearguard action against the Turks but, despite fine words, they received little help from most of their European neighbours and in 1541, Buda was captured by the Turks, dividing Hungary into three.

Rulers during Mary's lifetime
1516 Vladislaus II
1516–1526 Louis II
1526–1563 Archduke Ferdinand, in dispute with John Zapolya, Voivode of
    Transylvania
1526–1540 John Zapolya
1540–1571 John Sigismund Zapolya

Ottoman Empire

Following the fall of Constantinople in 1453, the Ottoman Turks were on the march. Much of the diplomacy of Mary's childhood related to treaties made in hopes of uniting Christendom to fight the Turks and, although the idea of crusading is hard for us to understand, there were many European Christians who sincerely believed that resistance to Turks was not just a political, but a religious, duty. Unfortunately for the zealous, the rulers not directly affected by the Turks continued to put their own interests first, and François went so far as to enter an alliance with Suleiman the Magnificent.

The Ottoman Empire extended into Africa. Algiers, on the north coast, had been fortified, in parts, by Spain after 1510, but it was captured by the Barbarossa brothers in 1516, and held by them until it became part of Suleiman's territory in 1524. It became a hotbed of piracy and attacks on European shipping. Charles V, determined both to expel the Ottomans and reduce piracy, had some success in Tunis in 1536, before mounting a major campaign in 1541, partially in hopes of balancing the loss of Buda. The campaign was not successful. The expansive Ottoman Empire remained a menace throughout Mary's life.

Rulers during Mary's lifetime
1516–1520 Selim I
1520–1566 Suleiman the Magnificent

Appendix B: Who's Who?

Anne of Cleves, Queen of England 1515–1557: Sister of Duke Wilhelm of Cleves, she married Henry VIII in January 1540. The marriage was annulled but she remained in England, on good terms with Henry and Mary.

Arborio, Mercurin de, Marquis-Cardinal of Gattinara 1465–1530: Served Marguerite of Austria, then Charles V as his Grand Chancellor from 1521.

Blount, Elizabeth or Bessie *c.* **1498–***c.* **1540:** One of Katharine's maids-of-honour, she had an affair with Henry that culminated in the birth of a son, Henry Fitzroy.

Blount, Sir William, 4th Baron Mountjoy *c.* **1478–1534:** Katharine of Aragon's Lord Chamberlain and Governor of Tournai at the time of Mary's birth. Mountjoy introduced Erasmus to Henry VIII when the latter was ten years old. Sir William married four times. Among his wives was one of Katharine's Spanish ladies-in-waiting, Inez de Venegas.

Boleyn, Anne, Queen of England *c.* **1501–1536:** After serving at the courts of Flanders and France she returned to England. She was Henry's second wife, executed for treason.

Boleyn, Anne, Lady Shelton, see Shelton, Anne

Boleyn, George, Viscount Rochford *c.* **1503–1536:** Anne Boleyn's brother, he was devoted to her and a strong evangelical. He was executed with her, charged with incest and treason.

Boleyn, Jane, Lady Rochford d. 1541: Alleged to have been the source of the evidence against her husband, George, she was lady-in-waiting to Anne Boleyn, Jane Seymour, Anne of Cleves and Katheryn Howard. She was executed immediately after Katheryn Howard, for having aided and abetted Katheryn's alleged adultery.

Boleyn, Sir Thomas, Viscount Rochford, Earl of Wiltshire and Ormond *c.* 1477–1539: Thomas Boleyn was a talented diplomat and part of Henry's council from early in the reign. Married to Lady Elizabeth Howard, his daughter, Anne, was Henry's second wife. Boleyn was an early supporter of religious reform.

Brandon, Charles, Duke of Suffolk 1484–1545: Henry VIII's closest personal friend, he was a talented jouster. In a risky move that could have cost him his head, he married Henry's sister, Mary the French queen, in 1514.

Bryan, Lady Margaret *c.* 1468–*c.* 1551: Lady Mistress to all of Henry's children. Her mother, Elizabeth Tilney, had been Countess of Surrey by a second marriage, and gave Margaret some seven siblings whose marriages connected Lady Bryan to almost all of the leading people at Henry's court. Among her half-siblings were the 3rd Duke of Norfolk, and Lady Elizabeth Boleyn (née Howard), mother of Anne Boleyn.

Butts, Dr William *c.* 1486–1545; Mary's physician in the Marches, he later joined the king's household but frequently treated Mary and was deeply sympathetic to her, although he was a friend of Cranmer, and a committed Reformer.

Calthorpe, Sir Philip: Mary's chamberlain from 1521.

Calthorpe, Jane, Lady: Lady Governess to Mary from 1521 to 1525, and remained in her household in Wales.

Campeggio, Cardinal Lorenzo 1474–1539: In 1518, he came to London as the legate of Leo X. Campeggio was granted the bishopric of Salisbury. A canon lawyer, he later sat with Wolsey to hear Henry VIII's annulment suit.

Carew, Sir Nicholas *c.* 1496–1539: A gentlemen of Henry's Privy Chamber and a close friend of the king for many years. He supported Jane Seymour, and was one of Mary's contacts in the circle around her father, communicating with her during Anne Boleyn's period as queen. Executed as part of the Exeter Conspiracy.

Castillon, see Perreau, Louis de,

Chabot, Philippe de, Sieur de Brion *c.* **1492–1543:** A friend of François I, he succeeded de Bonnivet as Admiral of France in 1525. He negotiated on Mary's marriage in 1527, and again in 1535.

Chapuys, Eustace *c.* **1490–1556:** A lawyer from Annecy in the Duchy of Savoy, he served as Charles's permanent ambassador in England 1529–1544. Katharine's most diligent champion, he was equally loyal to Mary and kept up secret contact with her during throughout his time in England. He retired to the Netherlands, but continued to take part in diplomacy with England.

Charles, Duke of Angoulême, Duke of Orléans 1522–1545: Third son of François I and Claude de Valois, he was considered as a husband for Elizabeth, and then for Mary.

Charles, Duke of Bourbon 1490–1527: Constable of France and Governor of Milan, after the French victory at Marignano in 1515. He lost favour with François I who confiscated territory from him, driving Bourbon into alliance with Charles V. Bourbon's failure (or inability) to pay his troops led to the Sack of Rome in 1527, in which he was killed.

Chièvres, Guillaume de Croy, Seigneur de 1458–1521: Tutor of Charles V during his youth in Burgundy. He manoeuvred to reduce the influence of Marguerite of Austria over her nephew, and was considered pro-French.

Cifuentes, See Fernando de Silva y Álvarez de Toledo

Claude, Queen of France 1499–1524: Salic law prevented her from inheriting the French throne, although she did inherit her mother's duchy of Brittany. She was married at fifteen to her father's heir, François and became Queen of France. She bore eight children in ten years, and was obliged to tolerate not only her husband's infidelity, but also a domineering mother-in-law. She died, exhausted, at the age of twenty-five.

Clerk, Dr John, Dean of Windsor, Bishop of Bath and Wells d. 1541. A protégé of Wolsey, he undertook numerous diplomatic missions in the 1520s and 1530s. Appointed as one of Katharine's counsel for the annulment, he supported Henry's position throughout.

Clement VII, Pope, (Giulio de' Medici) 1478–1534: Elected as Pope in 1523. He was Henry's preferred choice among the cardinals and it was to

Clement that Henry directed his request for an annulment of his marriage to Katharine. Clement's niece, Catherine, married Henri, Duke of Orléans and was subsequently Queen of France.

Courtenay, Henry, Marquis of Exeter: 1496–1539. First cousin of Henry VIII and his close friend in the first half of the king's reign. Executed in 1538.

Cranmer, Thomas, Archbishop of Canterbury 1489–1556: He put forward the idea of asking the universities their opinion on the legality of Henry and Katharine's marriage. He annulled Henry's first two marriages, and moved the Church along Reformed lines. He was burnt for heresy in Mary's reign.

Cromwell, Thomas, 1st Earl of Essex, c. 1485–1541: After the fall of Wolsey, Cromwell became Henry's right-hand man. An evangelical in religion, he presided over the Dissolution of the Monasteries and engineered (presumably with the king's sanction) the fall of Anne Boleyn. He facilitated Mary's reconciliation with her father but was executed in 1541.

Douglas, Lady Margaret, Countess of Lennox 1515–1578: Daughter of Margaret, Queen of Scots, she was Mary's cousin and friend.

Dudley, Sir John, Viscount Lisle, later Duke of Northumberland c. 1504–1553: He held a variety of military roles under Henry. He later attempted to block Mary from the throne.

Eleonora of Austria, Queen of Portugal, Queen of France 1498–1558: Brought up in Flanders by her aunt, Archduchess Marguerite, she married Manuel of Portugal, in 1518. Widowed in 1521, she married François I as part of the settlement following the Battle of Pavia.

Ferdinand, Archduke of Austria, King of Hungary and Bohemia 1503–1564: Brought up in Spain by his grandfather, Ferdinand of Aragon, he married Anne of Hungary and Bohemia, and became King of Hungary after the death of her brother, Louis. He acted as Charles's representative in the Empire, and was elected King of the Romans. He spent most of his life fending off the Ottomans in Eastern Europe.

Fisher, John, Bishop of Rochester c. 1469–1535: Renowned for his pious life and scholarship, he was a member of Henry VIII's council, although the king did not favour him. Appointed as counsel to Katharine during the annulment suit, although she did not feel he was of much use. He was executed for refusing to accept Henry as head of the Church in England.

Fitzroy, Henry, Duke of Richmond and Somerset 1519–1536: Mary's half-brother, he was a possible alternative heir to the throne, but although Henry gave him important titles and offices, he was never formally put forward as heir. He married the Duke of Norfolk's daughter, but died young.

FitzWilliam, Sir William, Earl of Southampton *c*. 1490–1542: Lord Privy Seal, Lord Chancellor. FitzWilliam was brought up with Henry VIII from an early age, and remained his friend for life. He was a member of the Privy Council and Lord Privy Seal, following Cromwell's demise.

Foix, Odet de, Vicomte de Lautrec, Marshal of France, 1485–1528: Served François as Marshal of France, and regent in Milan. Led the troops of the League of Cognac that sought to free Clement VII from Imperial control

François I, King of France 1494–1547: King of France from 1514, he was by turns an ally and an enemy of Henry VIII. The implacable opponent of Charles V, he was disliked and distrusted by Mary's mother. He was the father of Mary's first betrothed, and at one time planned to marry her himself.

François, Dauphin of France, Duke of Brittany 1518–1536: Mary's first betrothed, he was held as a hostage in Spain for five years, and never fully recovered his health. He died in August 1536.

Gardiner, Stephen, Bishop of Winchester: One of Henry's chief ministers, a rival for power with Thomas Cromwell. He was seen in the 1540s as leading the conservative faction at court. In Mary's own reign, he became Lord Chancellor.

Gattinara, Cardinal: See Arborio, Mercurino

Gouffier, Guillaume de, Seigneur de Bonnivet, Admiral of France. *c*. 1488–1525. Admiral of France from 1515. He played an important role in the French attack on Navarre in 1521 and led the French Army in Milan that ended in the Battle of Pavia, in which he was killed. French Ambassador for Treaty of London in 1518.

Granvelle, Chancellor: See Nicolas de Perrenot

Grey, Thomas, 2nd Marquis of Dorset 1477–1530: The grandson of Mary's great-grandmother, Elizabeth Woodville, Dorset was a great favourite with his first cousin, Henry VIII, despite his military failure in 1512. He was an early patron of Thomas Wolsey.

Henri, Duke of Orléans, dauphin. Later Henri II: 1519–1559: Considered a possible husband for Mary in the treaty of 1525, he married Catherine de' Medici, niece of Pope Clement VII in 1532.

Henri II of Navarre 1503–1555: Son of Catherine I of Navarre, he married Marguerite of Angoulême, and had his brother-in-law's support for his attempts to reconquer Upper Navarre.

Henry VIII 1492–1547: Mary's father. Henry was the second son of Henry VII and Elizabeth of York. His increasingly desperate search for a male heir led him to break with the pope as leader of the Catholic Church.

Howard, Agnes, Duchess of Norfolk 1477–1545. The second wife of Thomas Howard, 2nd Duke of Norfolk, she bore at least eight children and was stepmother to another eight. Despite being Mary's godmother, she was a firm supporter of her step-granddaughter, Anne Boleyn.

Howard, Katheryn, Queen of England *c.* 1521–1542: Granddaughter of 2nd Duke of Norfolk, she became Henry's fifth wife. Executed on charges of adultery.

Howard, Thomas, 2nd Duke of Norfolk 1443–1524: A talented general, at the age of seventy, he led the English troops in their overwhelming victory at Flodden over James IV of Scotland. Married twice, he sired at least 22 children, of whom 16 lived to play their parts on the English political stage.

Howard, Thomas, Earl of Surrey, later 3rd Duke of Norfolk 1473–1554: Henry's chief military commander, after the death of his father, and one of Henry's most prominent councillors. His first wife was Mary's great-aunt, Anne of York. After her death, without surviving children, he married Elizabeth, daughter of the Duke of Buckingham.

Hussey, Anne, Lady Hussey 1490–1545: Wife of Mary's chamberlain, she was one of Mary's ladies and was imprisoned for several weeks for calling Mary 'princess'.

Hussey, John, Baron Hussey 1466–1537: Lord Chamberlain to Mary following her return from Wales, he accepted Anne Boleyn as queen, but was executed following the Pilgrimage of Grace.

Isabella of Portugal, Holy Roman Empress 1503–1539: Daughter of Manuel of Portugal and Maria of Aragon, she was Mary's maternal first cousin.

She married Charles V in 1526. They were devoted to each other, and she acted as his regent in Spain.

James V, King of Scots 1512–1542: Son of Mary's aunt Margaret, Queen of Scots, and James IV, he became king at eighteen months old when his father was killed at the Battle of Flodden. James himself was deeply hostile towards his uncle, as English policy sought relentlessly to undermine Scotland's independence.

Katharine of Aragon 1485–1536. Mary's mother. The youngest daughter of Ferdinand II of Aragon and Isabella I of Castile, Katharine was briefly married to Arthur, the eldest son of Henry VII, and then to Henry VIII. She and Henry had no sons, and the changing political climate in Europe rendered the alliance with Spain that she represented less valuable. Henry wanted their marriage annulled, but Katharine fought to maintian it to her dying day.

Kingston, Mary, Lady Kingston (née Scrope) d. 1548. One of Katharine's ladies, she was married first to Sir Edward Jerningham, by whom she had two children, one of whom was later Mary's Privy Councillor. She became the third wife of Sir William Kingston, Constable of the Tower.

Lannoy, Charles de *c.* 1487–1527: Viceroy of Naples for Charles V, he was also the leader of Charles's troops in Italy, although on poor terms with Bourbon. He commanded the victorious Imperial troops at the Battle of Pavia in 1525.

Lautrec, Sieur de, Marshal of France, See Foix, Odet de.

Leo X, Pope (Giovanni de' Medici) 1475–1521: Leo's primary motivations were the promotion of the temporal power of the papacy, and the enhancement of Medici power in Florence. Faced with the challenge of Luther, he reacted strongly, but not by reforming the abuses of the Church. He was eager, or claimed to be, to unite Europe against the Turkish threat.

Louise of Savoy, Duchess of Angoulême, 1476–1531: Daughter of Duke Philip II of Savoy, Louise was married aged eleven to twenty-eight-year-old Charles, Duke of Angoulême. They had two children, François and Marguerite, before she was widowed. When François became King of France, she remained one of his closest advisers. She negotiated for François' ransom after the Battle of Pavia, and agreed the Ladies' Peace with her sister-in-law, Marguerite of Austria.

Manuel, King of Portugal 1489–1521. Himself first cousin twice removed of Mary, he married successively, her aunts, Isabella and Maria of Aragon, and her cousin, Eleanora of Austria. His son by Maria, Dom Luis, was a suitor for Mary.

Margaret, Dowager Queen of Scots 1489–1541: Married to James IV under the terms of the Treaty of Perpetual Peace, she was widowed when James was killed at Flodden. Named as Governor to their infant son, James V, she forfeited the role when she married Archibald Douglas, Earl of Angus. Her third marriage was to Henry Stewart, Lord Methven. She generally pursued a pro-English policy in Scotland.

Marguerite of Angoulême, Duchess of Alençon, Queen of Navarre 1492–1549: The sister of François I, she was also his confidante and counsellor. She married Charles, Duke of Alençon, but had no children. Her second marriage was to Henri III of Navarre, by whom she had a daughter, Jeanne III of Navarre. Marguerite was a poet and author, and a support of the evangelical movement, although she never formally left the Catholic Church.

Marguerite, Archduchess of Austria, Dowager Duchess of Savoy 1480–1530. Daughter of Emperor Maximilian and Mary of Burgundy, Marguerite was jilted by Charles VIII of France. Aged seventeen, she married Juan, heir to Ferdinand and Isabella. Juan died and Marguerite miscarried their child. She returned to the Low Countries, and married Philibert II, Duke of Savoy in 1501. Widowed again, she refused further marriages, and acted as regent in the Netherlands. She was a powerful presence in Europe until her death in 1530, shortly after negotiating the Ladies' Peace, with her sister-in-law, Louise of Savoy.

Marillac, Charles de, *c.* 1510–1560: French Ambassador to England from 1538. Wrote a detailed description of Mary.

Mary, the French queen, Duchess of Suffolk 1496–1533: Married Louis XII of France. Widowed after three months, she secretly married Charles Brandon, Duke of Suffolk. She played a part in important court ceremonies, but largely retired from view in the late 1520s – either from ill-health or as a protest against Anne Boleyn. Her rights to dower as Dowager Queen of France were the subject of much discussion in Anglo-French negotiations.

Maximilian, Holy Roman Emperor 1459–1519: Maximilian, despite his prestigious title, was perennially short of money. He spent his life manoeuvring to limit French power in Milan, and in the Netherlands, which he ruled first in right of his wife, Mary of Burgundy, then his son Philip, and finally his grandson, Charles. He was notorious for his flagrant disregard of treaties.

More, Sir Thomas *c* 1475–1535. One of Henry's councillors and involved in numerous diplomatic missions. A friend of many European humanists, he was an early supporter of education for women. As Lord Chancellor following Wolsey, he gained a reputation both for strict justice, and zealous pursuit of heretics. His refusal to accept Henry's reformation legislation resulted in his execution.

Mountjoy, See Blount, Sir William

Ortiz, Dr: Katharine's Proctor in Rome. His reports to Charles and the Empress Isabella contain every rumour and piece of gossip he heard – much of it uncorroborated.

Parker, Henry, 10th Baron Morley *c.* 1480–*c* 1556: Lord Morley was the half-first cousin of Henry VII. He was a translator, and a great admirer of Mary's intellectual attainments. His daughter, Jane, married George Boleyn.

Perrenot, Nicolas de, Cardinal Granvelle: 1486–1550: A Burgundian lawyer and diplomat, he advised Charles from an early age, and was one of his leading councillors. A correspondent of Chapuys's.

Philip of Bavaria, also known as Duke of Palatinate-Neuberg 1503–1548: Philip's territory was in a part of Lower Bavaria, and he shared it with his brother, Otto-Henry in a complicated agreement following the War of the Landshut Succession. Mary's suitor during the 1530s and 1540s.

Perreau, Louis de, Sieur de Castillon: French Ambassador to England.

Pole, Henry, Baron Montagu 1492–1539: Son of the Countess of Salisbury, Montagu was close to Henry during the first half of the king's reign. He supported Henry during the annulment, but fell under suspicion because of the activities of his brother, Reginald. Executed in the wake of the Exeter Conspiracy.

Pole, Geoffrey c. 1504–1558: Son of the Countess of Salisbury, it was his loose talk that led to his brother, Lord Montagu, and his cousin, the Marquis of Exeter, being suspected of treason and executed.

Pole, Lady Margaret, Countess of Salisbury 1473–1541: The cousin of Mary's grandmother, Elizabeth of York, Margaret had been married to one of Henry VII's closest supporters to counteract any potential for making a claim to be the legitimate Yorkist heir. Margaret was Katharine of Aragon's closest English friend, and both godmother and Lady Governess to Mary. She held the Earldom of Salisbury in her own right, and was an influential landowner. She was executed in 1541.

Pole, Cardinal Reginald *c.* **1500–1558**. Son of the Countess of Salisbury. After vacillating over the annulment, Pole wrote a virulent attack on Henry's stance. During the Pilgrimage of Grace, it was suggested by the rebels that Mary and Reginald should marry to unite the Tudors once more with the House of York. Under Mary, he was England's last Catholic Archbishop of Canterbury.

Sampson, Dr Richard, Dean of Windsor and Bishop of Chichester d 1554: Sampson was frequently sent on diplomatic missions by Henry VIII, but also was greatly favoured for his musical gifts. He was one of Henry's chief negotiators during the annulment proceedings.

Scutt, John: Tailor to all of Henry VIII's wives, he was also responsible for many of Mary's clothes.

Seymour, Edward, Viscount Beauchamp, Earl of Hertford *c.* **1500–1552**: Oldest brother of Jane Seymour, he was an accomplished military commander, and served Henry diligently in the War of the Rough Wooing with Scotland. He and his wife, Anne Stanhope, were friends of Mary's despite both being Reformers in religion.

Seymour, Jane, Queen of England d. 1537: Probably a maid-of-honour to Katharine of Aragon, she then fulfilled the same role with Anne Boleyn. Henry began courting her in late 1535. She promoted reconciliation between Mary and her father.

Shelton, Anne née Boleyn, Lady Shelton 1475–1555: Anne Boleyn's paternal aunt, she was appointed as Lady Governess to Mary in Elizabeth's household, while her husband, Sir John was Chamberlain. Her daughter-in-law, Margaret Parker, was one of Mary's attendants.

Stafford, Edward, 3rd Duke of Buckingham 1478–1521: The highest ranking noble in England, Buckingham was descended from Edward III and had a realistic claim to be the senior representative of the House of Lancaster. He was also Henry's first cousin once removed, being the son of Katherine Woodville. He was executed for treason in 1521.

Stewart, John, Duke of Albany 1484–1536: Albany was first cousin to James IV and as heir to the Scots throne, was invited by the Lords to act as Governor during the minority of James V. A thankless task in general, and made more difficult by the rival claim to the regency of the Dowager Queen, Margaret. Albany remained a close ally of François I.

Tunstall, Cuthbert, Master of the Rolls, Lord Privy Seal, Bishop of London, Bishop of Durham 1474–1559: Reckoned to be the most learned man in England, he wrote an influential mathematics primer, was a member of humanist circles, and one of Henry VIII's longest-serving councillors. He was appointed as one of Katharine of Aragon's counsel during the annulment. He accepted the break with Rome, but remained conservative in religion.

Vesey, John, Bishop of Exeter c.1462–1554: A protégé of Wolsey's, he became Bishop of Exeter in 1519. He served as Lord President of the Council of the Marches while Mary was its head.

Vives, Juan Luis 1493–1540: A native of Valencia, he had various roles at the court of Archduchess Marguerite in the Low Countries. He studied at the University of Paris, then took a Professorship at the University of Leuven. In England, he was Reader in Greek, Latin and Rhetoric at Wolsey's Cardinal College, Oxford. He was the first scholar to write a treatise promoting State assistance for the poor – *De Subventione Pauperum Sive de Humanis Necessitatibus*. He advised on Mary's education. His support for his patron, Katharine of Aragon, during the annulment proceedings led to house arrest and a permanent departure to Bruges.

Warham, William, Archbishop of Canterbury c. 1450–1532: As a member of Henry's Council, Warham promoted the more cautious, less militaristic policies of Henry VII. He was appointed as one of Katharine's counsel during the annulment, but was not of much help to her. He put up mild resistance to Henry's first claims to be head of the Church, but died before being put to the final test.

Wilhelm, Duke of Cleves-Julich-Berg 1516–1592: A suitor for Mary during the 1530s, his sister, Anne, was Henry VIII's fourth wife. While not a Lutheran, he and Charles were in conflict over the Duchy of Guelders.

Wriothesley, Sir Thomas, Earl of Southampton, Lord Chancellor 1505–1550: A member of Wolsey's household, he became a close associate of Cromwell's although he remained conservative in religion. Notorious for racking the Reformer, Anne Askew, with his own hands. On excellent terms with Mary.

Wolsey, Thomas c. 1475–1530: Cardinal and Archbishop of York and Lord Chancellor, he was Henry's most powerful minister from 1515 until his fall in 1529. Mary's godfather.

Notes and References

Abbreviations

Letters and Papers, Foreign and Domestic, Henry VIII, Volume 1–28, ed. J S Brewer (London, 1864). Abbreviated to 'L & P' with page references from British History Online version.

Four Years at the Court of Henry VIII, Selection of Dispatches written by the Venetian Ambassador Sebastian Giustinian, Volumes 1 & 2 (trans. R Brown) (London, 1854) Abbreviated to 'Giustinian'.

The Union of the Two Illustrious Families of Lancaster and York, Edward Hall (London, 1809) Abbreviated to 'Hall's Chronicle'.

Letters of Royal and Illustrious Ladies of Great Britain Vols 1–3, M. A. E. Wood. Great Marlborough Street, London: Henry Colburn 1846) Abbreviated to Wood.

T. Livii Foro-Juliensis vita Henrici Quinti, regis Angliæ. Accedit Sylloge Epistolarum a variis Angliæ Principibus scriptarum. E codicibus descripsit ediditque T. Hearnius, etc. MS. notes. 1st ed. Oxonii. Frulovisiis T., Hearne, T. and Henry, (1716). Abbreviated to Hearne's Sylloge.

Calendar of State Papers Henry VIII Vols 1 & 2. Abbreviated to CSP.

Calendar of State Papers, Spain Volumes 1–8, 1st ed. 1866. Ed. G A Bergenroth. British History Online. Abbreviated to CSPS.

Calendar of State Papers Relating To English Affairs in the Archives of Venice, Volumes 2–5 ed. Rawdon Brown (London, 1867) British History Online. Abbreviated to CSPV.

Calendar of State Papers, Milan 1385–1618 Abbreviated to CSPM.

A Chronicle of England during the reigns of the Tudors. Charles Wriothesley. Camden Society 1875. Abbreviated to Wriothesley's Chronicle.

I Diarii di Martino Sanuto 1483–1533 Abbreviated to Sanuto.

Inventaire Analytique des Archives des Affaires Étrangères (Angletterre 1537–1542). 1st ed. Paris: Félix Alcan. Kaulek, J. (1885). Abbreviated to Kaulek.

1 A Bride for the Dauphin

1. Giustinian. 21 Feb 1516.
2. Another possible male heir was born two weeks after Mary, to the French queen. Tactfully, he was named Henry and was christened on 11 March 1516, with the king acting as godfather. He and the brother born after him both died young.
3. Born Elizabeth Jerningham, she is mentioned as a married woman in her father's will of 1473, meaning she cannot have been born after 1461. A theory has been floated that she was once the mistress of Henry VIII – an idea so far-fetched as not to be worth refuting.
4. Eleanor was closely connected to the royal family – her mother, Edith St John was Lady Margaret Beaufort's half-sister, and her brother, Richard Pole, had been married to Lady Salisbury.
5. Giustinian. Volume 2 p161 & p311
6. Giustinian. Volume 2 p232.
7. Signatories to marriage treaty with the dauphin 1518: Wolsey; Warham, Archbishop of Canterbury; the Dukes of Buckingham, Norfolk and Suffolk; the Marquis of Dorset; the Bishop of Durham; the Earls of Surrey, Shrewsbury and Worcester; the Bishops of Ely and Coventry & Lichfield; Lord Mountjoy; Lord Docwra, Grand Master of the Knights Hospitaller in England; Sir Edward Poynings; Sir Henry Marney; Sir John Pecche; Sir Henry Guilford; Sir Thomas Boleyn; Cuthbert Tunstall, Master of the Rolls; and others including Sir Thomas More, Sir Thomas Lovell and Sir Davy Owen. Hall's Chronicle p. 595
8. Giustinian. Volume 2 p. 232.
9. When Isabella of Castile had taken the throne she had beaten off a rival claimant – Juana, known as La Beltraneja. This Juana was the daughter of Juana of Portugal, wife of Isabella of Castile's half brother, Enrique IV of Castile, but was probably not his daughter, and, owing to the complicated circumstances of Enrique and Juana's marriage, probably not legitimate if she were his. La Beltraneja had been forced into a convent in Portugal, after Isabella won the war, and cordial relations between the two countries maintained through the marriages of Isabella's daughters, and then her granddaughter to Manuel of Portugal. With Manuel's death, the Castilian Cortes were concerned that Charles's rights to the throne would be challenged by La Beltraneja.
10. L & P, Volume 3, 1519–1523, pp. 15–33
11. Channel 4's Time Team investigated Beaulieu, finding the remains of Mary's nursery apartments. https://www.youtube.com/watch?v=fZPfrviK2qI

12. L & P, Volume 3, 1519–1523 pp. 172–183 Boleyn to Wolsey

13. Katharine and Marguerite were sisters-in-law. Back in 1497, Marguerite had been briefly married to Katharine's brother the Infante Juan and had lived at the Spanish court. Sadly, Juan had died young. Katharine must have been intrigued at the thought of seeing Marguerite again after 25 years.

14. L & P, Volume 3, 1519–1523, pp. 249–264. De La Sauch to Chièvres

15. L & P, Volume 3, 1519–1523, pp. 265–274.

16. Lady Margaret Herbert was born Lady Margaret Courtenay, daughter of Katherine of York. She did not die young, choking on a fish-bone, as is sometimes reported, but married Henry Somerset, son of the Earl of Worcester.

17. L & P, Volume 3, 1519–1523, pp. 320–331

2 Empress in Training

1. D. Erasmus and F. Nichols, *Epistles of Erasmus, from his earliest letters to his fifty-first year, arr. in order of time*, 1st ed. New York: Russell & Russell, 1962. Letter to Bombasius

2. Valerie Schutte in her fascinating book *Mary I and the Art of Book Dedications* discusses the political nuances of Giles Duwes' dedication.

3. E. García Hernán, *Vives y Moro*, 1st ed. Madrid: Cátedra, 2016.

4. Sanuto pp. 589; Funeral oration cited in Madden.

5. References to virginals, harpsichords and spinets were used fairly interchangeably by non-technical observers. They were all keyboard instruments, although there were variations in the mechanisms of how the strings were struck. The harpsichord was the largest, and most complex to play. Virginals were more portable and it is probably the portable keyboard instrument that is frequently referred to in Mary's accounts. It is likely that Mary could play all three as well as the regals – a type of organ.

6. A transcript may be found in Alexandra Barratt, *Women Writing in the Middle Ages: An Annotated Anthology*. The prayor of Saynt Thomas of Aquyne, translatyd oute of Latyn unto Englyshe by the moste exselent Prynses [erased] Mary, doughter to the moste hygh and myghty Prynce and Prynces kyng Henry the viij. and Quene Kateryne hys wyfe [erased], in the yere of our Lorde God m'.ccccc.xxvij. and the xj yere of here age. It is also in Madden.

7. An indulgence was the remittance of the worldly penance that had been proscribed for a sin that had been confessed, truly repented and absolved. Unfortunately, the requirement for true repentance and the fact that only the worldly punishment was remitted was sometimes lost in translation, and it began to be believed that sins could be absolved for money – a dangerous idea, and extremely disturbing for those who could not afford to buy indulgences.

8. John Stewart, Duke of Albany, from a cadet branch of the royal house of Stewart, was a close friend of François. Invited by the Scots Lords to replace

Henry VIII's sister, Margaret, as Governor of the Realm, and guardian of the young King James, his presence in Scotland was taken by Henry as a personal affront and an act of aggression by France

9. It was open to anyone who had had a provisional marriage contracted in his or her name in childhood to refuse it on reaching maturity. In fact, Henry had done just this in 1505, when he rejected the betrothal with Katharine of Aragon, arranged in 1503. He would later use this as part of his annulment campaign.

10. One of the earliest recorded quarrels between Henry and Katharine had occurred in 1510 when Buckingham, hearing a rumour that his sister, Anne, Lady Hastings, was having an affair with one of Henry's Gentlemen of the Bedchamber, Sir William Compton, insisted on Anne being banished to a convent. Henry was furious, and it has been speculated that, in fact, Compton was just a cover, and that it was the king himself having an affair with Lady Hastings. Buckingham felt the king's wrath, as did his sister Elizabeth, Lady FitzWalter, who was banished from court for telling her brother about Anne's misdemeanours. This caused Katharine, who was attached to Lady FitzWalter, to be 'vexed' with Henry. Lady Margaret Beaufort was Buckingham's great-aunt-by-marriage and he had been her ward. Buckingham was also first cousin to Elizabeth of York, on the Woodville side.

11. A recognisance was an agreement to pay a certain sum to the king if they defaulted in any way. Bergavenny's bond was for £10,000 – clearly not a sum ever intended to be paid, but he was required to promise not to go to Kent or Sussex, nor to approach the king without licence. He also had to find sureties, or surrender to the king and face imprisonment. It was the requirement for sureties that rendered recognisances such a clever method of control. To stand as a surety was to take a significant risk, and encouraged nobles to keep each other on the straight and narrow – an unsuccessful attempt at rebellion would result in the sureties losing their money.

12. CSPS Supplement to Vols 1 & 2 pp. 59–78 Lachaulx to Charles.

13. CSPS Vol. 2 1509–1525 June 1522 pp. 426–434

14. ibid.

3 Princess of Wales

1. CSPS, Volume 3 Part 1, 1525–1526

2. CSPV Vol. 3 1520 1526 pp. 393–397 Contarini to the Council of Ten.

3. Quoted in *The First Governess of the Netherlands*, Eleanor Tremayne.

4. CSPS Volume 3 Part 1, 1525–1526 pp. 62–88

5. MS. Cott. Galb., B. viii., f. 135 Quoted in Madden.

6. L&P Volume 4, 1524–1530 pp. 570–583

7. L&P Volume 4, 1524–1530 pp. 538–556

8. L&P Volume 4, 1524–1530 pp. 610–626

9. L&P Volume 4, 1524–1530 pp. 626–633

10. L&P Volume 4, 1524–1530 pp. cx–clxxv

11. Vesp. C. III. 176. B. M Quoted in *Madden*.

12. Calendar of State Papers, Spain, Volume 3 Part 1, 1525–1526, pp. 274–290

13. Adrian of Utrecht died in September 1523, and was succeeded by Giuliano de Medici as Clement VII. There were some rather half-hearted attempts to promote Wolsey, but his election was never pursued with the money and promises that would have been required. Clement had been Henry's preferred choice among the other cardinals.

14. L&P Volume 4, 1524 – 1530 pp.665-673

15. Calendar of State Papers, Spain, Volume 3 Part 1, 1525-1526, pp. 274 - 290

16. From I Diarii di Marino Sanuto, Vol. xxxix, quoted in J Stone: *The History of Mary I, Queen of England.*

17. Cited in J. McIntosh, *From Heads of Household to Heads of State: The Pre-accession Households of Mary & Elizabeth Tudor 1516–1558.*

18. Cott. App. (No. 38.) XXIX. 51. B. M

19. Lord Morley was half-first cousin to Henry VII.

20. D. Loades, *Mary Tudor*, Stroud, Gloucestershire: Amberley Publishing, 2016.

21. Transcript in *Letters of the queens of England.*

22. Thanks are extended to the owners of Tickenhill for kindly allowing me to see their beautiful house.

23. The letter is calendared in L & P as 3 May 1528, but that cannot be right, as the household had been broken up by then. It cannot be 3 May 1527, as Mary was at Greenwich, entertaining the French ambassadors, leaving only 1526 for this letter.

24. There are two letters from the Bishop of Exeter, calendared to August and September 1526, but they must pertain to the previous year. The first refers to travelling from Woburn to Reading on Assumption Day (15 August), but since Mary was definitely in Worcester on Assumption Day 1526, it must relate to her initial departure, which also makes sense as Exeter is concerned that a physician had not yet been appointed. It has been suggested that the same letter, praising the hospitality of My Lady of Lincoln must mean my Lord of Lincoln – i.e. the Bishop, John Langland, who was Henry's confessor. However, there was a Lady Lincoln – the widow of John de la Pole, killed at the Battle of Stoke. She was alive in 1526. The letter of 1 September is dated from Thornbury and is referenced in Wood. We know from a letter of 3rd September 1526 that Mary was at Langley, Oxon on 1 September 1526. (*See* 7.)

25. The letter, in Latin, is in Hearne's Sylloge, noted as addressed to Cardinal Pole. The original is no longer extant. There is a translation in Wood, where Wood correctly identifies that it must have been written to Wolsey, as it addresses him as godfather, as well as from the content.

26. L & P Vol. 4 pp.1081–1093 Ralph Brereton to William Brereton

4 Queen, Dauphine or Duchess?

1. L & P Vol. 4 pp. 930–943 Lee to Wolsey
2. L & P Vol. 4 pp. 1152–1166 Clerk to Wolsey
3. L & P Vol. 4 pp. 1653–1672 Undated expenses from the accounts of Lord Bergavenny refer to a visit by Lady Bergavenny to Richmond on 13 March, before the arrival of the French ambassadors at Greenwich. It fits the other dates to put it at this time.
4. Vit. B. IX. 64. B. M. – Quoted in L & P
5. L & P Vol. 4 pp.1333–1352 – Ambassadors to François.
6. L & P Vol. 4 pp.1333–1352 – Clerk to Wolsey
7. L & P Vol. 4 pp. 1352–1361 – Lee to Wolsey
8. CSPM 1385–1618 pp. 474-517

5 The King's Secret Matter

1. Henry read the Latin Vulgate Bible – this translation is Tyndale's from 1526. Tyndale was burnt in the Low Countries for heresy but was opposed to the annulment.
2. L & P Vol. 4 pp. 1431–1446 – Wolsey to Henry
3. L & P Vol. 4 pp. 1490–1507 – Charles to Mendoza
4. L & P Vol. 4 pp. 1514–1524 – Knight to Wolsey
5. As no names are mentioned, it cannot be ascertained whether Anne's offending pre-contract was with James Butler, Earl of Ormond, with whom her family had tried to arrange a marriage, or with Henry Percy, now Earl of Northumberland, with whom Anne had once been in love.
6. L & P Vol. 4 pp. 1672–1689 – Du Bellay to François
7. L & P Vol. 4 pp. 1807–1824 – The Princess's Council to Wolsey
8. Isabel of Austria, Queen of Denmark, had lost her throne when Christian was deposed, and Mary of Hungary's husband, Louis, had been killed at the Battle of Mohacs.
9. L & P Vol. 4 pp. 2523 2531 – Du Bellay to François I
10. CSPM pp. 517–533
11. L & P Vol. 5 pp. 130–140 – Chapuys to Charles
12. CSPM pp. 533–538
13. The More was a palace on the scale of Hampton Court, or larger, owned by Wolsey as Abbot of St Albans. Channel 4's Time Team excavated it, and the film is available on YouTube.
14. CSPS Vol. 4(ii) pp. 335–351 – Ortiz to Empress Isabella.
15. Although much is made of Anne possibly having been in the household of Marguerite of Angoulême, Queen of Navarre, and being influenced by Marguerite's evangelicalism, Ives shows that Marguerite did not develop her own thinking in this direction until after Anne's time in France. Marguerite

had no hesitation in supporting a fellow-queen. Queen Eleonora was, of course, Katharine's niece and Henry did not want to meet her. In fairness, Ives suggests that François may have declined for the ladies as he did not want to irritate Charles.

16. Sanuto Vol. LVII p. 160
17. Chapuys's account is in L & P Vol. 5 pp. 670–681 – Chapuys to Charles. The Venetian report is from Sanuto Vol. LVII p. 439.

6 The Bastard's Servant

1. CSPS Vol. 4(ii) pp. 628–646 Chapuys to Charles V.
2. L & P Vol. 6 pp. 466–477. A full transcript is also in A. Crawford, *Letters of the queens of England, 1100–1547*
3. For the text of Jerome's Epistles see http://www.newadvent.org/fathers/3001. htm
4. Pole was the greatnephew of Edward IV and Richard III. He was also related paternally to Henry VIII, his grandmother, Edith St John, was half-sister to Lady Margaret Beaufort, although Edith had no royal blood.
5. L & P Vol. 7 pp. 61–68 Katharine of Aragon to Charles
6. Some books note that Mary was in the charge of Anne's aunt, Alice Boleyn, Lady Clere, but all the documents which mention the lady's name say it was Anne's other aunt, Anne Boleyn, Lady Shelton. The sometimes contradictory attitudes of the lady support the idea that both aunts were in the household at Hatfield, but I can only find evidence for Lady Shelton's presence.
7. Calendar of State Papers, Spain, Vol. 5(i) pp. 53–70 Chapuys to Charles
8. *Henry VIII's Use of His Spiritual and Temporal Jurisdictions in His Great Causes of Matrimony, Legitimacy, and Succession,* Mortimer Levine, *The Historical Journal,* Vol. 10, No. 1 (1967), pp. 3-10
9. L & P Vol. 7 pp. 156–177 Chapuys to Charles
10. Calendar of State Papers, Milan 1385–1618 pp. 565–574

7 Resistance

1. L & P Vol. 7 pp. 259–270 – Chapuys to Charles
2. L & P Vol. 7 pp. 305–310 *Ita ut universa et singula in hac scriptura habentur, dicimus, narramus, asserimus, asseveramus ac pretestamur de meia nostra scientia ac matura deliberatione, teste meo manuali signo et sigilio meo.*
3. L & P Vol. 7 pp. 401–407
4. L & P Vol. 7 pp. 493–502 Chapuys to Charles
5. L & P Vol. 7 pp. 576–582 Chapuys to Charles

6. L & P Vol. 8 pp. 53–75 – Gontier to Chabot

7. Full transcript in Wood, Vol. II.

8 Sorrows

1. Charles and his siblings had a claim, via their paternal grandparents who were both descended from Philippa of Lancaster, daughter of John of Gaunt. The Empress Isabella and her siblings were also descended from Katherine of Lancaster, another of John of Gaunt's daughters. There were, of course, English claimants, too.

2. L & P Vol. 9 pp. 96–114

3. In his *Six Wives of Henry VIII*, Dr Starkey takes the line that Katharine's marriage to Arthur was consummated. I disagree – while Katharine can be detected in equivocations about the truth, it is hard to imagine that she would have sworn a lie on the sacrament. The idea that she was not sure in 1502 whether the marriage was consummated is vaguely plausible (although sixteenth century women were not the shrinking violets of the nineteenth century) but any such ignorance could not have continued for 30 years.

4. Some authors have the chief mourner as Lady Frances Brandon, but the report refers to the Duke of Suffolk's daughter. Lady Frances was married in 1533, and would have been referred to as the wife of the Marquis of Dorset.

5. L & P Vol. 10 pp. 108–126

6. L & P Vol. 10 pp. 98–108 'It is rumoured that the king, as Cromwell sent to inform me immediately after the queen's death, means to increase her train and exalt her position. I hope it may be so, and that no scorpion lurks under the honey.'

7. L & P Vol. 10 pp. 217–240 Charles to Chapuys

8. L & P Vol. 10 pp. 287–310

9 Submission

1. CSPS Vol. 5(ii) pp. 104–118 Chapuys to Charles

2. L & P Vol. 10 pp. 287–310 Chapuys to Chancellor Granvelle

3. Chapuys reported a couple of weeks after Anne's death that she had sought Mary's forgiveness, presumably hearing it directly from Mary. The visit of Lady Kingston is the logical occasion for this to have occurred.

4. The whole correspondence is in Hearne's Sylloge pp. 123 ff.

5. Hearne's Sylloge p. 137 The letter there is presented in full. R.B. Merriman's *Life and Letters of Cromwell* transcribes it from 6 M Otto C. x. 273. But there are so many illegible words it is impossible to tell whether Hearne's version is accurate.

6. Hearne's Sylloge p 142.
7. L & P Vol. 11 pp. 54–73 *Obedientia unitatem parit, Unitas animi quietem et constantiam; Constans vero animi quies thesaurus inestimabilis. Respexit humilitatem Qui in Filio nobis reliquit Perfectum humilitatis exemplar. Factus est obediens Patri, Et ipsa etiam natura parentibus Et patrie obediendum docuit.*
8. L & P Vol. 11 pp. 90–107 Chapuys to Charles
9. The idea that Jane was not crowned because Henry was reluctant to spend the money on a queen who had shown no sign of pregnancy is not necessarily borne out by later concerns that Edward's claim was weaker because he was born of an uncrowned wife, suggesting that the ceremony of crowning was important.
10. A. N. Galpern, *The Legacy of Late Medieval Religion in Sixteenth-Century Champagne*, in C. Trinkaus and H. O. Oberman (eds.), The Pursuit of Holiness in Late Medieval and Renaissance Religion (Leiden, 1974), p. 149.
11. Hearne's Sylloge p 133.

10 Return to Favour

1. Lord and Lady St John appear to have had very fruitful gardens, sending regular presents of strawberries and pippins.
2. This changed somewhat with the puritanical ideas of the early 1550s, which pitted soberly dressed reformers against gaudy Catholics – hence the incident of Lady Jane Grey and the brocade dress. But during this period of Mary's life, display was important.
3. There is a fascinating essay on the topic in Hunt, A. and Whitelock, A. (2010). *Tudor Queenship; The Reigns of Mary and Elizabeth (Queenship and Power).* 1st ed. New York: Palgrave Macmillan.
4. L & P Vol. 12 pp. 154–198 Instructions to Mendoza
5. CSPM pp. 580–587
6. L & P Vol. 12 pp. 144–154 Privy council to Norfolk
7. Ferdinand's son was less closely related to Mary than Luis, who was her first cousin, whereas the archduke was a generation removed.
8. CSPS Vol. V ii No. 214
9. Wood Vol. 1. Letter VIII
10. These gentlemen later married Christina of Denmark and Queen Jeanne III of Navarre, respectively.

11 Stepmothers

1. L & P Vol. 13 pp. 11–22
2. Quoted in Borman – *The Private Lives of the Tudors* 2016

3. Anne's mother was reputed as a particularly devout woman, and her father, although he had thrown off papal authority, had not accepted Lutheran doctrines.

4. Duke Wilhelm and Archduchess Maria are the ancestors of most of the crowned heads of Europe today, including HM Queen Elizabeth II.

5. Kaulek, 17 September 1541. Translated in L & P, but with slight updates to the passage about Mary's physical appearance.

6. ibid. 12 October 1541

7. L & P Vol. 17 pp. 115–126. The Council to Paget in France.

8. The Royal College of Psychiatrists gives the following as symptoms of PTSD: muscle aches and pains, diarrhoea, irregular heartbeats, headaches, and depression, all of which Mary suffered from according to the records. It can occur after a single incident, or after repeated traumatic occurrences, and is particularly likely to happen where the sufferer is in regular contact with the perpetrator of a traumatic event.

9. Kaulek 22 April 1542

10. ibid. 3 June 1542

12 Friendship

1. CSPS Vol. 6(ii) pp. 183–192 Chapuys to Mary of Hungary

2. Madden

3. For architectural details, see S. Thurley and A. Cook, *Whitehall Palace*, 1st ed. New Haven: Yale University Press, 1999 and S. Thurley, *Houses of Power*, 1st ed. London: Bantam Press, 2017.

4. *Narrative of the visit of the Duke of Najera: Archaeologia, or Miscellaneous Tracts relating to Antiquity Vol. 23 London 1831* – Society of Antiquaries.

5. Hearne Sylloge p. 226

6. Transcribed in *Katherine Parr: Complete Works and Correspondence*. University of Chicago Press. Mueller, J. (2014).

7. D. MacCulloch, *Thomas Cranmer: a life*, 1st ed. New Haven: Yale University Press, 1997.

8. Udall's dedication is quoted in full in *Katherine Parr: Complete Works and Correspondence*. University of Chicago Press. Mueller, J. (2014)

9. *Mary Tudor: Old and New Perspectives*. 1st ed. Basingstoke: Palgrave Macmillan. Doran, S. and Freeman, T. (2011).

10. Letter quoted in full in *Katherine Parr: Complete Works and Correspondence*. University of Chicago Press. Mueller, J. (2014). Mueller prefers the date of 1545, but I would strongly suggest that it dates from 1547, for the following reasons: first: Katherine says that she had thought of visiting Mary – as queen, Mary would have come to her; second, the queen refers to a gift of money *from* Mary – it is unlikely that the princess would have given money to Katherine

while she was queen; third, it is dated 20 September, from Hanworth, which was one of Katherine's dower properties – she is unlikely to have lived there during Henry's life-time, and the court was at Windsor in September 1545, Katherine signed a letter from there on 25th – although it would not be impossible for her to have been at Hanworth on 20th and then Windsor by 25th.

11. The English Paraphrases became part of the authorised service in Edward's reign, and were later banned under Mary – presumably because of their association with the more radical Protestantism of her brother, rather than the slightly reformed Catholicism of Henry's reign.

12. CSPS Vol. VIII 204.

13. ibid 243

14. ibid 304.

15. Madden

16. Hearne's Sylloge p 158

17. *Katherine Parr: Complete Works and Correspondence.* University of Chicago Press. Mueller, J. (2014).

Bibliography

Ackroyd, P. (1998). *The Life of Thomas More*. London: Chatto & Windus.

Baldwin Smith, L. and Cambridge University Press on behalf of The North American Conference on British Studies (1962). The Last Will and Testament of Henry VIII: A Question of Perspective. *Journal of British Studies*, [online] Vol. 2, Number 1, pp 14–27. Available at: http://www.jstor.org/stable/175305.

Barratt, R. and Barratt, A. (2010). *Women's Writing in Middle English: An Annotated Anthology*. United Kingdom: Longman Pub. Group.

Birrell, T. (1987). *English Monarchs and their Books*. 1st ed. London: British library.

Borman, T. (2016). *The Private Lives of the Tudors*. 1st ed. Hodder & Stoughton.

Brigden, S. (2012). *Thomas Wyatt*. 1st ed. London: Faber & Faber.

Brown, R. and Giustinian, S. (1854). *Four Years at the Court of Henry VIII*. Cornhill, London: Smith, Elder & Co.

Byrne, M. (1981). *The Lisle letters Edited by M. St. Clare Byrne Vols 1–6*. 1st ed. Chicago, Ill., the University of Chicago Press.

Cappelli, A. (2016). *Cronologia, Cronografia e Calendario Perpetuo*. 7th ed. Milan: Hoepli.

Carley, J. and Starkey, D. (2005). *The Books of King Henry VIII and his Wives*. 1st ed. London: British Library.

Crawford, A. (1994). *Letters of the Queens of England, 1100–1547*. 1st ed. Stroud, Gloucestershire: Alan Sutton.

de Lisle, L. (2013). *Tudor: The Family Story*. United Kingdom: Chatto & Windus.

Devereux, E. (n.d.). *The Publication of the English Paraphrases of Erasmus*. [online] https://www.escholar.manchester.ac.uk.

Doran, S. and Freeman, T. (2011). *Mary Tudor: Old and New Perspectives.* 1st ed. Basingstoke: Palgrave Macmillan.

Dormer, J. (1616). *The Life of Jane Dormer, Duchess of Feria.*

Dumitrescu, T. (2007). *The Early Tudor Court and International Musical Relations.* Aldershot: Ashgate Publishing.

Duncan, S. and Schutte, V. (2016). *The Birth of a Queen.* 1st ed. Palgrave MacMillan.

Edwards, J. (2011). *Mary I: England's Catholic Queen.* New Haven: Yale University Press.

Ellis, H. (1824). *Original letters, illustrative of English history: including numerous royal letters: from autographs in the British Museum, the State Paper Office, and one or two other collections.* 1st ed. New York: Printed for Harding, Triphook, & Lepard.

Erasmus, D. and Nichols, F. (1962). *Epistles of Erasmus, from his earliest letters to his fifty-first year, arr. in order of time.* 1st ed. New York: Russell & Russell.

Fantazzi, C. and Vives, J. (2000). *The Education of a Christian Woman: A sixteenth-century manual.* United States: University of Chicago Press.

Fegan, E. and More, W. (1913). *Journal of Prior William More 1472–c. 1559.* Worcester Historical Society.

Freeman, T., Doran, S. and Perspectives, N. (2011). *Mary Tudor: Old and New Perspectives (Hardback).* ed. Basingstoke: Palgrave MacMillan, United Kingdom.

Froude, J. and Thomas, W. (1861). *The Pilgrim.* London: Parker, Son and Bourne.

Frulovisiis, T., Hearne, T. and Henry (1716). *T. Livii Foro-Juliensis vita Henrici Quinti, regis Angliæ. Accedit Sylloge Epistolarum a variis Angliæ Principibus scriptarum. E codicibus descripsit ediditque T. Hearnius, etc. MS. notes.* 1st ed. Oxonii.

García Hernán, E. (2016). *Vives y Moro.* 1st ed. Madrid: Cátedra.

Giustinian, S. and Brown, R. (1854). *Four Years at the Court of Henry VIII.* 1st ed. London: Smith, Elder & Co.

Grimestone, E. (1608). *A Generall Historie of the Netherlands.* London: Islip & Elder.

Hamilton, W. and Wriothesley, C. (1877). *A chronicle of England during the reigns of the Tudors, from AD 1485 to 1559.* 1st ed. [Place of publication not identified]: Printed for the Camden Society [by J. B. Nichols and Sons].

Hardy, W. (1895). *The Handwriting of the kings and Queens of England.* 1st ed. London: The Religious Tract Society.

Hayward, M. (2004). *The 1542 Inventory of Whitehall.* 1st ed. London: Illuminata Publishers for the Society of Antiquaries of London.

Hayward, M. (2012). *The Great Wardrobe Accounts of Henry VII and Henry VIII*. United Kingdom: London Record Society.

Hernan, E. (2016). *Vives y Moro*. Editiones Catedra.

Hunt, A. and Whitelock, A. (2010). *Tudor Queenship; The Reigns of Mary and Elizabeth (Queenship and Power)*. 1st ed. New York: Palgrave Macmillan.

Ives, E. (2009). *The Life and Death of Anne Boleyn*. 1st ed. Malden, MA: Blackwell Pub.

Johnson, J. (1835). *The Life of Thomas Linacre, Doctor in Medicine to Henry VIII etc*. London: Edward Lumley.

Johnson, J. and Graves, R. (1835). *The life of Thomas Linacre, Doctor in medicine, physician to King Henry VIII, the tutor and friend of Sir Thomas More, and the founder of the Royal College of Physicians: With memoirs of his contemporaries, and of the rise and progress of learning, ... from the ninth to the sixteenth century inclusive*. 1st ed. London: Edward Lumley.

Kaulek, J. (1885). *Inventaire Analytique des Archives des Affaires Étrangères (Angletterre 1537–1542)*. 1st ed. Paris: Félix Alcan.

Kleineke, H. (2015). The Medicines of Katherine, Duchess of Norfolk, 1463–71. *Medical History*, 4(59), pp.511–1524.

Le Glay, M. (1848). *Negotiations Diplomatique entre La France et L'Autriche*. Paris: Imprimerie Royale.

Levine, M. (1967). Henry VIII's use of his spiritual and temporal jurisdictions in his great causes of matrimony, legitimacy, and succession. *The Historical Journal*, [online] 10(1), pp.3–10. Available at: http://www.jstor.org/stable/2638058 [Accessed 24 Sep. 2016].

Lipscomb, S. (2009). *The Year that Changed Henry VIII*. 1st ed. Oxford: Lion Publishing plc.

Lipscomb, S. (2015). *The King is Dead*. United Kingdom: Head of Zeus.

Loades, D. (2016). *Mary Tudor*. 1st ed. Stroud, Gloucestershire: Amberley Publishing.

MacCulloch, D. (1997). *Thomas Cranmer: A Life*. 1st ed. New Haven: Yale University Press.

Mackay, L. (2014). *Inside the Tudor Court*. 1st ed. Stroud: Amberley Publishing.

Madden, F. (1831). *Privy Purse Expenses of the princess Mary*. London: William Pickering.

Mallett, M. and Shaw, C. (2012). *The Italian Wars, 1494–1559*. 1st ed. Routledge.

McIntosh, J. (2007). *From Heads of Household to Heads of State: The Preaccession Households of Mary & Elizabeth Tudor 1516–1558*. Project Gutenburg.

Merriman, R. (1968). *Life and Letters of Thomas Cromwell: Volume I: Life, Letters to 1535*. United Kingdom: Oxford University Press.

Mueller, J. (2014). *Katherine Parr: Complete Works and Correspondence.* University of Chicago Press.

Muller, J. (2014). *The Letters of Stephen Gardiner.* Cambridge, United Kingdom: Cambridge University Press.

Newadvent.org. (2017). *CHURCH FATHERS: Letters of St. Jerome.* [online] Available at: http://www.newadvent.org/fathers/3001.htm [Accessed 26 Mar. 2017].

Parr, K. and Mueller, J. (2014). *Katherine Parr: Complete works and correspondence.* 1st ed. Chicago. Ill. [u.a.]: Univ. of Chicago Press.

Pierce, H. (2009). *Margaret Pole, Countess of Salisbury: 1473–1541: Loyalty, Lineage and Leadership.* Cardiff: University of Wales Press.

Pocock, N. (1870). *Records of the Reformation: The Divorce 1527–1533.* Oxford: Clarendon Press.

Porter, L. (2009). *Mary Tudor: The First Queen.* London: Piatkus Books.

Porter, L. (2010). *Katherine the Queen: The Remarkable Life of Katherine Parr.* 1st ed. London: Macmillan.

Rabil, A. (1979). Erasmus' Paraphrase of the Gospel of John. *Church History*, 48(02), p.142.

Rymer's Feodera. (n.d.).

Sanuto, M. (1859). *I diarii di Marino Sanuto: (MCCCCXCVI-MDXXXIII) dall' autografo Marciano ital. cl. VII codd. CDXIX-CDLXXVII.* 1st ed. Venice: F Visentine.

Sanuto, M. (n.d.). *I diarii di Martino Sanuto.* 1st ed. Venice: Fratelli Vientine, p.Vol. LIV pp. 589.

Scalingi, P. (1978). The Scepter or the Distaff: The Question of Female Sovereignty, 1516?1607. *The Historian*, 41(1), pp.59-75.

Scarisbrick, J. (2012). *Henry VIII.* 1st ed. New Haven: Yale University Press.

Schutte, V. (2015). *Mary I and the Art of Book Dedications: Royal Women, Power, and Persuasion: 2015.* United Kingdom: Palgrave Macmillan.

Sidney, H. and Collins, A. (1746). *Letters and memorials of state in the reigns of Queen Mary, Queen Elizabeth, King James, King Charles the First, part of the reign of King Charles the Second, and Oliver's usurpation.* 1st ed. London: Printed for T. Osborne.

Skeel, C. (1904). *The Council in the Marches of Wales.*

Slysz, G. (2015). *Mary Tudor, England's First Queen Regnant: Truth is the Daughter of Time.* 1st ed. Gracewing Publishing

St Clare Byrne, M. (1936). *The Letters of King Henry VIII.* 1st ed. London: Cassell and Company.

Starkey, D. (2004). *Six Wives: The Queens of Henry VIII.* 1st ed. London: Vintage.

Thurley, S. (2010). *The Royal Palaces of Tudor England.* United States: Yale University Press.

Thurley, S. (2017). *Houses of Power*. 1st ed. London: Bantam Press.

Thurley, S. and Cook, A. (1999). *Whitehall Palace*. 1st ed. New Haven: Yale University Press.

Tremayne, Eleanor E. (1908). *The First Governess of the Netherlands*. 1st ed. London: Methuen & Co.

Tremlett, G. (2011). *Catherine of Aragon: Henry's Spanish Queen*. United Kingdom: Faber & Faber.

Trinkaus, C. and Oberman, H. (1974). *The Pursuit of Holiness in Late Medieval and Renaissance Religion*. 1st ed. Leiden: Brill.

Whitelock, A. (2009). *Mary Tudor: England's First queen*. ed. London: Bloomsbury Publishing PLC.

Whitelock, A. and MacCulloch, D. (2007). 'Princess Mary's Household and the Succession Crisis, July 1553.' *The Historical Journal*, 50(02), p.265.

Wood, M. (1846). *Letters of Royal and Illustrious Ladies of Great Britain*. Great Marlborough Street, London: Henry Colburn.

List of Illustrations

15. Great Hall at Hartlebury Castle, another of Mary's homes during 1525–1528. (© Melita Thomas)

16. Ludlow Castle, official seat of the Council for Wales and the Marches. (© Melita Thomas)

17. Tewkesbury Cathedral, another abbey visited by Mary. (© Melita Thomas)

18. Book of Hours, with Mary's translation of a prayer by Thomas Aquinas, and a personal message to a friend in her own handwriting. (© British Library Board MS 17012 f. 192b)

19. James V of Scotland, there were negotiations for a marriage between Mary and her cousin. (© Amberley Archive

20. Anne Boleyn, by an unknown artist. (© Ripon Cathedral)

21. Farnham Palace, Mary came here for a 'change of air' in 1531. (© Melita Thomas)

22. Otford Palace, the palace of the Archbishops of Canterbury. Mary lived there during 1532– 1533. (© Melita Thomas)

23. Guildford Castle, where Mary had apartments. (© Melita Thomas)

24. Hatfield House, the Great Hall. Mary was sent here after Elizabeth's birth, as the junior member of the household. (© Melita Thomas)

25. Holbein portrait of John Fisher, Bishop of Rochester, executed in 1535 for refusing to accept Henry as Supreme Head of the Church in England. Mary feared she would suffer the same fate. (Wikimedia Commons)

26. Tomb of Katharine of Aragon, in Peterborough Cathedral. (© Melita Thomas)

27. Thomas Cromwell, Henry's chief minister; he helped bring about the reconciliation between Henry and Mary in 1536. (© Alamy Stock Photo)

28. Jane Seymour, third wife of Henry VIII, she and Mary were friends. Mary was chief mourner at Jane's funeral. (© Ripon Cathedral)

29. Dom Luis of Portugal, Mary's cousin, and a potential husband during the 1530s and 1540s. (Creative Commons)

30. A drawing, perhaps of Mary, by Hans Holbein, from the late 1530s. (© Elizabeth Norton/Amberley Archives)

31. Grimesthorpe Castle, Lincolnshire, the home of the Duke and Duchess of Suffolk. The court visited en route to York. (© Melita Thomas)

32. Wilhelm, Duke of Cleves, a brother of Anne of Cleves; he was a suitor for Mary in the 1530s. (Creative Commons)

33. The Whitehall Portrait, painted in 1544, showing the Henry, the late Jane Seymour, Edward, Mary and Elizabeth. The background figures are probably Will Somers and Jane the Fool, Henry and Mary's jesters. (© Alamy Stock Photo)

34. Henry in later life, represented in the Great Gate at Trinity College, Cambridge. (© Elizabeth Norton/Amberley Archives)

35. Mary Tudor on a lead plaquette. (Courtesy the Metropolitan Museum of Art)

Index